**Red Tape**

**Stanford Studies on Central and Eastern Europe**

*Edited by Norman Naimark and Larry Wolff*

# Red Tape

*Radio and Politics in Czechoslovakia, 1945–1969*

**Rosamund Johnston**

Stanford University Press
Stanford, California

Stanford University Press
Stanford, California

© 2024 by Rosamund Therese Johnston. All rights reserved.

No part of this book may be reproduced or transmitted in any form or by any means, electronic or mechanical, including photocopying and recording, or in any information storage or retrieval system, without the prior written permission of Stanford University Press.

Printed in the United States of America on acid-free, archival-quality paper

Library of Congress Cataloging-in-Publication Data
Names: Johnston, Rosamund, author.
Title: Red tape : radio and politics in Czechoslovakia, 1945–1969 / Rosamund Johnston.
Other titles: Stanford studies on Central and Eastern Europe.
Description: Stanford, California : Stanford University Press, 2024. | Series: Stanford studies on Central and Eastern Europe | Includes bibliographical references and index.
Identifiers: LCCN 2023044023 (print) | LCCN 2023044024 (ebook) | ISBN 9781503635166 (cloth) | ISBN 9781503638693 (paperback) | ISBN 9781503638709 (ebook)
Subjects: LCSH: Československý rozhlas—History. | Radio broadcasting—Political aspects—Czechoslovakia—History. | Radio journalism—Czechoslovakia—History. | Radio audiences—Czechoslovakia—History. | Communism and mass media—Czechoslovakia—History.
Classification: LCC HE8699.C95 J64 2024 (print) | LCC HE8699.C95 (ebook) | DDC 384.5409437—dc23/eng/20231108
LC record available at https://lccn.loc.gov/2023044023
LC ebook record available at https://lccn.loc.gov/2023044024

Cover design: Jason Anscomb
Cover photograph: Anna Suchánková and Oldřich Nový edit a radio program in 1965. Photograph courtesy of Czech Radio

*To Marie Leslie Davenport*

# Contents

| | | |
|---|---|---|
| *List of Figures* | | ix |
| *Acknowledgments* | | xi |
| *List of Abbreviations* | | xv |
| | | |
| | Introduction | 1 |
| **1** | The Radio Revolution | 21 |
| **2** | "The Brain Becomes a Phonograph Playing a Disc over Which It Has No Control" *Show Trials and Stalinist Radio* | 51 |
| **3** | When Travelogues Became News *The Africa Reporting of František Foit, Jiří Hanzelka, and Miroslav Zikmund, 1947–1952* | 87 |
| **4** | De-Stalinization Disturbs Listening | 117 |
| **5** | Listening in on the Neighbors *The Reception of German and Austrian Radio in Cold War Czechoslovakia* | 145 |
| **6** | Spring in the Air? *Czechoslovak Radio's Foreign Correspondents, 1958–1968* | 168 |
| **7** | All Together Now? *Czechoslovak Radio during the Prague Spring and Warsaw Pact Invasion in 1968* | 197 |
| | Conclusion: From Socialist Media to Social Media | 228 |
| | | |
| | *Notes* | 233 |
| | *Bibliography* | 287 |
| | *Index* | 301 |

# List of Figures

1 Illustration from Jan Antonin Baťa, *Budujme stát pro 40 000 000 lidí* (*Let's Build a State for 40 Million People*) ... 31

2 Radio with the "paper tag" that Charles Heller mentioned ... 36

3 Still from Jiří Brdečka and Jiří Trnka's film *Springman and the SS* (1946) ... 39

4 The image of a BBC listener in *Springman and the SS* ... 39

5 Journalists' conditions in Nuremberg ... 47

6 Article from *L'Alger Républicain* about František "François" Foit's second African tour ... 88

7 Foit's sketches of how he and Jiří Baum customized their car ... 95

8 Still from the film *Africa, Part I* ... 96

9 Still from *Africa, Part I* ... 96

10 Still from *Africa, Part I* ... 96

11 Poster for *Africa, Part I* ... 102

12 Cartoon of Pavel Tigrid from 1953 ... 135

13 Journalists questioning Bruno Folta at his press conference ... 136

14 Journalists questioning Bruno Folta at his press conference ... 136

15 Caricature of Ferdinand Peroutka from *Rudé Právo* ... 153

16 Map displaying the reach of Radio Free Europe jamming 159
in Czechoslovakia, September 1952

17 *Autofahrer Unterwegs* film poster from 1961 162

18 Věra Šťovíčková at work in Guinea, circa 1958 172

19 Hungarian-language poster for Czechoslovak Airline's 174
Prague-Bamako service from 1961

20 Promotional shot from *Songs with a Telephone* 214

21 Script from *Songs with a Telephone*, 1968 217

22 Two flag-wielding Czechoslovak citizens outside 222
the Czechoslovak Radio headquarters in Prague

# Acknowledgments

**THIS BOOK HAS DISPELLED** any illusion I might have had that writing is a solitary task. What follows is recognition of a tiny fraction of the people who have helped this manuscript along the way.

Firstly, I thank my colleagues at the Research Center for the History of Transformations (RECET) in Vienna for their help with every step from book proposal to image rights. In particular, Rasa Navickaitė, Jannis Panagiotidis, Philipp Ther, and Dean Vuletic provided invaluable feedback on chapters of this manuscript, and Anna Calori read the whole thing. At the University of Vienna, I also benefited from Eva Spišiaková's enthusiasm for this project and feedback, and the time to think about socialist radio afforded by a REWIRE postdoctoral fellowship.

This book began at New York University (NYU). Its writing was greatly enhanced by the expertise of Michael Beckerman, Melissa Feinberg, Monica Kim, Mary Nolan, Alice Lovejoy, and Larry Wolff. I am especially grateful to Mary Nolan and Melissa Feinberg, who read multiple drafts of the chapters I struggled with most (both before and after my defense), providing constructive criticism and encouragement in equal measure. I also thank my supervisor Larry Wolff for his mentorship, in particular when preparing this work for publication. Also from the NYU days, I thank Joanna Curtis, Gaurav Garg, Paul Kreitman, Timo McGregor, Joshua Sooter, and Gillian and Kevin Sheehan, whose smart ideas and feedback continue to shape this text many years later.

What follows has been improved enormously by the peer reviewers through whose hands it has passed. I thank them in their anonymity. Their feedback has, in each instance, been transmitted to me by editors who have themselves made extremely helpful suggestions on how to enhance this text. They were Monica Black, Muriel Blaive, Hana Bortlová Vondráková, Margo Irvin, Alice Lovejoy, and Mari Pajala, and each of their names belongs firmly in this list of those who have my gratitude. An edited version of chapter 5 of this text appeared in *Central European History* and is reproduced here with that publication's permission.

Support to draft this manuscript has been offered by the Leibniz Center for Contemporary History (ZZF) in Potsdam, New York University in Prague, the Department of Communication and Media at Lund University, the Masaryk Institute and Library of the Czech Academy of Sciences, and the Collegium Carolinum in Munich. At each of these institutions, I found not only the time and space to write, but generous and stimulating interlocutors. In particular, in that capacity, I thank Sune Bechmann Pedersen, Anna Bischof, Frank Bösch, Christiane Brenner, Marie Cronqvist, Thea Favaloro, Juliane Fürst, Christoph Hilgert, Ulrike Lunow, and Mária Škripeňová.

At Czech Radio, I am grateful to Ivana Zuranová for introducing me to authors' papers, scripts, and sounds that I would not otherwise have found, and for making archival research a pleasure. I would also like to thank Eva Ješutová, Tomáš Dufka, Martina Bílá, and Jarmila Lakosilová at Czech Radio for the reading materials, introductions to journalists active in the 1950s and 1960s, and cakes. At the Muzeum Jihovýchodní Moravy in Zlín, Magdalena Preiningerová shared her encyclopedic knowledge of Jiří Hanzelka and Miroslav Zikmund's life and work with me, as well as guiding me through the pair's archive.

I thank my in-laws, Miroslav Horalík and Marta Horalíková, for sharing stories that breathed life into the hypotheses I explored here (and for leaving no stone unturned when seeking copyright holders with whom to negotiate image rights!). Tomáš, you have been there while this manuscript has spread its wings, which I don't believe to be coincidental. Thank you. And Edwin, your early years have added so very much to the process of writing this book. I am very lucky to have been able to share them with you.

This work was begun in the memory of Granny Davenport and Grampadad, about a time when they were young and about which they got me enthused. It was improved by my dad, Thomas George Johnston, through his proofreading, and has connected us over these past years in a way that makes me glad. It is dedicated above all to Marie Leslie Davenport, however, who has taught me more than any academic degree possibly could. For that, *and* all the patient hours spent with this scrawl, I hope you find yourself on every page, and I hope that the end result makes you proud.

# List of Abbreviations

**BBC**—British Broadcasting Corporation

**CBS**—Columbia Broadcasting System, a US commercial broadcaster

**CIA**—United States Central Intelligence Agency

**ČTK**—Československá tisková agentura, the Czechoslovak Press Agency

**HSTD**—Hlavní správa tiskového dohledu, the Main Press Observation Office (the censor's office)

**ORF**—Österreichischer Rundfunk, Austrian public media

**RFE**—Radio Free Europe

**RIAS**—Rundfunk im amerikanischen Sektor

**RTVS**—Rozhlas a televízia Slovenska

**RWR**—Rot-Weiß-Rot, Red-White-Red, a radio station in the American zone of Austria

**SPN**—Státní pedagogické nakladatelství

**SS**—Schutzstaffel, a Nazi paramilitary organization

**StB**—Státní bezpečnost, State Security (the Czechoslovak secret police)

**ÚSTR**—Ústav pro stadium totalitních režimů, Institute for the Study of Totalitarian Regimes

**VoA**—Voice of America

**Red Tape**

# Introduction

THE FIRST DAY OF a new job can be scary. When reporter Jana Peterková stepped into her role at Czechoslovak Radio in 1967, she recalls feeling nervous, "because lots of known writers worked there, and I had the impression that I was not up to their standard."[1]

When I began researching this project nearly a decade ago, I probably assumed that the people who would make novice reporter Peterková feel the most nervous in a socialist news organization would be the powerful-but-distant radio management, or perhaps the not-at-all distant police censors prowling the radio headquarters. But Peterková suggested that, for her, the radio amounted to "known writers" and that her nerves were caused by admiration for, rather than fear of, this institution.

This book, like Peterková, focuses on reporters as the defining group shaping state media during state socialism. It sets out to explain why she, alongside thousands and thousands of others who listened to and wrote in to state radio in Czechoslovakia, might have articulated their relationship with Communist-controlled media in terms of admiration. One might argue that the situation Peterková describes in Czechoslovakia in the late 1960s is quite exceptional and completely incomparable to how radio staff and listeners would describe the more restrictive Stalinist years. I would not be one of them. By taking a longer-term view here, I highlight important continuities and institutional inertia, as well as incremental shifts in the political environment in Czechoslovakia during radio's second "golden age," between 1945 and 1969. In examining how reporters went about their jobs and were praised for so doing by radio listeners throughout this period, I ultimately show how a nondemocratic society established, stabilized, and reproduced itself.

An editor-in-chief or media boss is often understood to hold immense power over what a media organization publishes and, resultantly, over what the people who use that media think. But, even at the most restrictive of moments, journalists in socialist Czechoslovakia did so much more than merely following orders passed down from Communist higher-ups. It is precisely in the work that they did that we can understand the mechanics by which a socialist society actually functioned, which is to say through the creative efforts of entire cohorts of invested elites and those with whom they entered into uneven dialogue, rather than through the unilateral command of a detached handful of rulers.

The subjects of this book are threefold: as well as examining the role played by reporters, I focus on the influence held over radio by politicians (though less here than in traditional histories of early socialist Czechoslovakia) and listeners. Taking the view from the newsroom out, I show how each of these constituencies came and went from the forefront of radio staff's, concerns. Despite holding a great deal of power over reporters' ability to work in the first place, I show that there were indeed moments when intervention-prone Communist politicians were *not* at the forefront of radio staff's concerns. By taking reception seriously, I shed new light, moreover, on radio listeners (encompassing practically the entire population) as themselves important historical actors in a socialist state.

Czechoslovak journalists such as Peterková worked as dutiful servants of the state, even as they sometimes resisted that very state system. From the first days after the Second World War, the Communist Party was the ultimate arbiter of journalists' right to work where they did, with the social prestige, income, and benefits that accompanied this. Their work came to be censored by employees of the Ministry of the Interior and critiqued, first by staff at the Communist-controlled Ministry of Information and then by members of the Communist Party's Ideological Commission. The knowledge of all of these checks and balances shaped the way that reporters penned even the most innocuous game show questions. But these journalists also used the structures in which they worked to disseminate knowledge, information, and models of speech for Communist ministers and audiences alike in the nascent Party state. They cocreated the rhetorical environment in which Czechoslovak ministers and citizens could safely affirm their commitment to socialism after Stalin's death, and in which they could later formulate the political reforms and potential of the Prague Spring. At times, these reporters went as far as petitioning Communist functionaries to acknowledge their unique social insight and expertise and to formulate legislation based on their suggestions. None of the reporters profiled here were straightforwardly and specifically mouthpieces for the party bureaucracy. And if they were indispensable in the construction and maintenance of socialism in Czechoslovakia, then they also show how constructive criticism of socialism in Czechoslovakia could emerge from inside the regime's very own institutions.

At the dawn of this era, journalists worked according to a professional creed of communicating and contextualizing the aims of those in power. Their sense of purpose shifted gradually, with reporters seeking increasingly to transmit messages from citizens to the authorities. Journalists became ever-noisier intermediaries in the news that they relayed, leaving an increasingly legible fingerprint on the reports that they authored. They emphasized their years of journalistic experience and travel as justification for making their own opinions heard. Just as politicians removed formal political oversight (in the form of censorship) from the newsroom during the Prague Spring, a number of radio journalists in fact decided to make the leap into professional politics.

Listeners' opinions of radio changed over time too—a shift captured in the mail they sent to reporters. In an increasingly affluent society, letter writers sought fewer material tokens from the radio personalities that they addressed and described with increasing frequency what those stars meant personally to them. Fans' tendency towards personal disclosure was prompted by the changed rhetorical environment that radio helped bring about following Stalin's death. The way that reporters handled the mail they received from listeners over these decades also transformed. Upon receipt of listener mail, socialist journalists had traditionally exercised their influence behind the scenes. But by 1968, reporters incorporated listeners' views into the fabric of their reports—often seizing upon correspondence with which they did not agree and entering into debates with its authors.

By following how the relationships between officials, journalists, and "ordinary" listeners shifted in Czechoslovakia, as well as assessing how the porosity between social strata changed, *Red Tape* uncovers the autonomy of journalists and listeners in a socialist state—as well as its limits. The journalists focused on here belonged to what Muriel Blaive describes as "a specific generation, that of young postwar communist intellectuals [that] supported Stalinism, were disappointed by the end of the 1950s, felt guilty about their previous commitment, and so participated in the Prague Spring movement."[2] Whether driven by "guilt," disappointment, or other motivations, these reporters—as a highly politically minded cohort that stood outside the central decision-making structures of the Communist Party (though the majority were party members)—are indicative of the political work that people engaged in outside of the official structures of the party in socialist Czechoslovakia. As such, they begin to show us how the Communist Party and ideology took root and blossomed in Czechoslovakia during the postwar years, when party membership swelled to more than one million people, making it the biggest political party that Czechoslovakia has ever recorded.[3]

## Approaching Czechoslovak Airspace Transnationally

It is a truism that radio "is no respecter of boundaries," as its early theorists Gordon Allport and Hadley Cantril had proclaimed in the 1930s.[4] This held true across the sturdiest of iron curtains well into the Cold War too. Located at the westernmost edge of the Eastern Bloc, Czechoslovakia's ether was hotly contested from the beginning of this era (as it had been during the Second World War and interwar periods). Reporters and citizens devised ways to use this to their advantage.

*Red Tape* stresses the transnational nature of radio broadcasting and listening in postwar Czechoslovakia to make two particular claims. Firstly, by tracing the work of Czechoslovak foreign reporters from the first postwar years until the late 1960s, I foreground official attempts to foster international linkages during the Stalinist years and beyond, in particular with countries in what we would today term the Global South. This both challenges the idea of a "closed" East propounded during that moment by politicians East and West, and traces an important prehistory to studies on socialist globalization which tend to take Khrushchev's consolidation of power in the Soviet Union around 1956 as a starting point.[5] By examining in depth the careers of radio reporters Jiří Hanzelka, Miroslav Zikmund, and Věra Šťovíčková in particular, I show indeed how reporters could go as far as inflecting foreign policy in a state which had, according to some onlookers, no independent foreign policy of its own as a Soviet "satellite."[6]

My second claim is for the continued importance of the German-speaking world for radio listeners in Czechoslovakia deep into the Cold War, and with it for the enduring relevance of a mental map of Central Europe (reflecting the names of cities clustered on the radio dial). Czechoslovakia's neighboring states of Austria and the two Germanies—its citizens' historic points of comparison—housed the foreign stations of most note in Czechoslovakia between 1945 and 1969: Radio Vienna routinely pulled in more Czech and Slovak listeners than the Communist government's sworn nemesis, the American-sponsored station Radio Free Europe (RFE). A study of radio significantly alters, therefore, our image of the nature of the Cold War in Czechoslovakia (if the Cold War has commonly been defined as a bipolar competition between two blocs led by the Soviet Union and the United States).

A bipolar confrontational attitude did shape official discussions of radio broadcasting and technology. It affected which stations were singled out for frequency jamming and which were spared the tones of "Stalin's bagpipes." But it did not mark the way that listeners approached radio entirely. An altogether recognizable mix of longing for connection, peer pressure, self-improvement, habit, curiosity, a desire to vent personal grievances, and material aspiration inflected Czechoslovak citizens' foreign radio listening preferences—and these should not simply be reduced to "resistance to communism," as some analysts from the period and several recent works of popular history have claimed.[7]

While Czechoslovak Radio's history and significance have been, in particular in the Czech-language literature, narrated in nationalistic terms, the scale and resonances of cross-border, multilingual media usage in Eastern Europe following the Second World War is reconstructed here.[8] Such usage has largely been overlooked as historians have taken state-led drives to homogenize the region ethnically as a starting point to explore citizens' behaviors. Most media histories pertaining to this time and place have, moreover, assumed that listeners sought, and followed most closely, foreign stations broadcasting from across the Iron Curtain in their mother tongues. But listeners' behaviors were conditioned by earlier habits of cultural consumption, the multiple languages that were not simply forgotten as the geopolitical situation changed, and older infrastructural links reworked using new technologies like FM receivers, personal telephones, and transistor radios.

Czechoslovakia never became an ethnically homogenous state, no matter how much some of its nationalist activist citizens may have wished, and continued throughout socialism to comprise speakers of multiple mother tongues. Some of these, such as Ukrainian and Hungarian, were recognized and granted programming on state broadcaster Czechoslovak Radio, while others, such as German and Romani, were, for long years, less well acknowledged. A bilingual dialogue between the state's two most widely spoken, mutually comprehensible languages, Czech and Slovak, meanwhile, shaped the fabric of flagship statewide station Czechoslovakia I's daily programming.

The RTVS (Rozhlas a televízia Slovenska) sound archive in Bratislava, Slovakia, provided invaluable resources for the research of this book. *Red Tape*, however, draws overwhelmingly from Czech archives and replicates some of the Pragocentrism of their content. Czechoslovakism—the attempt that followed Czechoslovakia's establishment to create a hybrid nationality elevating the Czechs and Slovaks who lived in Czechoslovakia above all other ethnicities—was a political project that had been largely abandoned by the moment that *Red Tape* begins (one can hear its last traces in the postwar speeches of Presidents Eduard Beneš and Klement Gottwald, speaking alternately in Czech or in Slovak, depending on circumstance). Rather than an innately inclusive and cosmopolitan set of policies, scholars have rightly pointed out some of the project of Czechoslovakism's inbuilt inequalities, anti-German sentiment, and other shortcomings.[9] It is not in this political tradition that I opt for the term "Czechoslovak" over the pages that follow. The book deliberately uses the term "Czechoslovak," however, to avoid lazy use of the term "Czech" as a shorthand for events and debates that were shaped by and affected those beyond the Czech lands too.

Ultimately, radio in Czechoslovakia and Czechoslovak Radio never came to mean quite the same thing. While state radio staff and government functionaries sincerely wished that Czechoslovak citizens would tune into the state broadcaster to the exclusion of all else, listeners did nothing of the sort. Not only did audiences station-hop, they employed their foreign listening habits, as we shall see, to secure the programming they desired from the Czechoslovak state broadcaster. By thinking about the transnational nature of reporters' radio work and listeners' radio use, I show the complex back-and-forth that shaped "national" political debate in postwar Czechoslovakia and foreground some perhaps surprising, and highly generative, Cold War "philosophical geographies" that did so much more than point slavishly to Moscow and longingly to an Anglo-American "West."[10]

## Propaganda and Its Limits

On November 28, 1954, the celebrity travelers Jiří Hanzelka and Miroslav Zikmund spoke to the radio news, fresh out of the polling station in Gottwaldov (today Zlín), about casting their votes. Western onlookers would rightly judge these elections to have been both coercive and ultimately falsified. In the bid to encourage voting, Jiří Hanzelka told listeners to the radio news that "our travels . . . were the best form of political education, which helped convince us of the correct orientation and strengthen this conviction . . . Today's elections gave us the opportunity to proclaim out loud where we belong and what we are working for with heart and soul: for socialism, and for peace for all mankind."[11]

Some scholars have taken a rather broad view of propaganda. One of its finest theorists, Jacques Ellul, for example, has shown how instruments of propaganda can work in concert, and thus aspects of propaganda can take many different forms, from architecture, to face-to-face conversations, spanning visual imagery, radio broadcasts, and even the clothes one wears.[12] Ellul's theorization helpfully illuminates the broader social framework in which propaganda works, and rightly shows that no one work of journalism is, in itself, sufficient to shape a listener's worldview. But I take a much narrower view of propaganda here, understanding it—as professional journalists in postwar and socialist Czechoslovakia did—as a specific journalistic task that formed part of their job. Hanzelka and Zikmund's articulate radio explanation of why voting was necessary provides one such example of propaganda work.

8    Introduction

*Propagace*, which might be translated into English as either "propaganda" or "promotion," was championed by officials at the Communist-controlled Ministry of Information from the first days following the Second World War. Journalists were encouraged, sometimes downright directed, to participate in propaganda/promotional campaigns as diverse as drumming up support for the five-year plan, compelling citizens to cut their alcohol intake, or to collect scrap paper or metal. Most notoriously, radio listeners were impelled to eradicate the "American" potato beetle fomenting capitalist counterrevolution in Czechoslovakia's fields throughout the early 1950s.[13]

If propaganda was a journalistic task, then it was not necessarily one that journalists relished. It tended, in socialist Czechoslovakia's newsrooms, to be allocated to those at the bottom of the pecking order. In her memoirs, reporter Věra Šťovíčková recalled being allocated such dogsbody's tasks as trumpeting fulfillment of the economic plan in the state's collective farms, and indeed knocking on doors to persuade people of the value of Stalinism, on account of her junior status at Czechoslovak Radio in the early 1950s.[14] In the Soviet newsrooms which were supposed to serve as a model for Czechoslovakia's, meanwhile, Natalia Roudakova finds that designated "propagandists" were handed tasks that others "did not want to do." These included, "praising the party and its policies, denouncing the party's enemies home and abroad, [and] writing welcoming speeches for official events."[15]

Propaganda, then, meant the promotion to order of a specific government policy or objective. But the term "propaganda" (rather than its Czechified equivalent, *propagace*) came also to be used by both Czechoslovak journalists and listeners as a term meaning "bad journalism," serving as a foil to the "professionalism" of domestic journalistic output which was held in higher esteem. The postwar period did not represent a zero hour in this regard, as some of the negative connotations held by the term "propaganda" were a result of the wartime experiences that audiences had had under one of its most vocal champions, Joseph Goebbels. This distinction between "professional" journalism and scorned propaganda reveals discernment among journalists and listeners in a socialist state, but still requires further nuancing. As we have already seen, for example, the same individuals could produce both (though not every journalist was as forthright about this in retrospect as Šťovíčková).

The way that listeners received Hanzelka and Zikmund encouraging voter turnout was different from the manner in which they received the pair's travel accounts decrying colonialism in Africa. For a start, the former generated less of a trail of fan mail for the archives. While the latter lauded "progressive" politics where the travelers found it on their journeys around the globe, Hanzelka and Zikmund's Africa reports were in fact received as a refreshing break from propaganda by many. One pseudonymous listener wrote to the pair describing their reports as "a green oasis in the desolate, boring desert of Prague radio" during Stalinism. "They are the only thing I listen to," continued the listener, "because it is impossible to listen to any more propaganda and brass music."[16]

Reflections such as this listener's show the complexity of citizens' views of state media in state socialism: constituencies both inside and outside media institutions understood that radio could simultaneously produce propaganda and professionalism. Approaching propaganda production as a routine journalistic task rather than more abstractly as the main purpose of state broadcasting brings such nuanced listening on the part of the Czechoslovak public into focus. Listeners could be quite aware that journalists, like the vote-casting Hanzelka and the door-knocking Šťovíčková, produced propaganda at times, but they could still like and trust these reporters despite this. Western accounts of Communist media during the Cold War discounting its sum total as propaganda cannot begin to explain the discernment and journalistic ranking systems of media actors and audiences in Communist societies, let alone the affection that listeners could feel towards voices coaxing them, among other things, to eradicate imperialist potato beetles.[17]

If the sum total of Czechoslovak Radio's reports was not propagandistic, then it was certainly political. But this politics could extend far beyond the question of party politics. In socialist institutions like Czechoslovak Radio, personnel were judged, ranked, and issued orders according to factors beyond their publicly stated political loyalties. Professional hierarchies operated alongside, reinforced or, at times, undercut political affiliations.[18] By pinpointing just a few of the different political registers deployed by journalists and then decoded and reflected by listeners, I show the repertoire for political action within a socialist state that was so much richer than a Communist/anti-Communist binary, even at the most restrictive of moments. The case of Jiří Hanzelka's politics amounts to more than his propaganda

## Introduction

work loudly casting a symbolic vote in rigged elections. The same Hanzelka who dutifully encouraged voter turnout in 1954 was vaunted by Czechoslovak ministers as informing their Africa policy in 1961 and then ran for political office himself on a ticket of reforming socialism at the end of that decade.[19] The profile and the following he had created at the radio made this change of career possible.

### Reappraising Old News

At the heart of this book you will find research into the audio files preserved in the Czech Radio archive in Prague. I first came to know them in minidisc format as a junior reporter almost two decades ago. I was first interested, simply, in what such audio might be able to tell today's listener about the past. Over the past decade, I have been granted unprecedented access to the institution's sound archive, which is continually expanding as new recordings from the Communist era emerge from private collections. Even with these additions, however, the picture that this archive presents of the socialist period is far from complete. For example, neither audio from Hanzelka and Zikmund's experiences voting, nor very much audio at all from their first travels around the globe, remains. To round out the picture, I used transcripts and monitoring reports made by Western stations of Czechoslovak Radio programming, alongside reporters' scripts and correspondence, as well as diaries, literature, and films from the period, reflecting radio listening at the time.

The audio housed in the Czech Radio building tells us a lot about how socialist society was built and maintained in Czechoslovakia over the first two postwar decades. As Czechoslovakia's dominant medium at the time, radio established a presence in almost every household, as well as an audible role in the country's factories, city and village streets, institutions, and even, with the rise of the transistor receiver, in its meadows and fields.[20] During its second golden age, from 1945 until 1969, radio served, moreover, as the leading medium to which audiences turned for expression and support when making demands on authorities. These listener appeals are housed in the Czech Radio archive in the form of thousands of pieces of mail written to the reporters whose voices have been preserved there.

As a publicly disseminated medium which made its way across the Iron Curtain during the Cold War, the radio sound archive certainly does not represent a revelation for historians of socialism in the same way that the previously off-limits Communist Party or secret police archives might. But a systematic analysis of the social valence of audio that was made for all to hear then is no less—and perhaps indeed more—revelatory of state-society relations in postwar Czechoslovakia. Through its ubiquity and the sheer volume of audience feedback it garnered, radio provides historians with a unique way of thinking through how citizens, cultural elites, and top-ranking politicians encountered and addressed each other on a daily basis during state socialism outside of formal governmental institutions.

I define radio as an assembly of technology, content, and listening practices, which came to be associated with a particular set of personalities and voices in postwar Czechoslovakia. Perhaps "Communist radio" was understood by Western onlookers at this period as an instrument to frighten or demoralize listeners, but I show instead how it constituted a site of negotiation between Communist officials, a cadre of experts empowered through work with sound (chief among them broadcast journalists), and audiences.[21] My study ultimately charts the social dynamics that radio in Czechoslovakia either muted, amplified, or backgrounded.

Studies of radio in Cold War Eastern Europe have often focused on American-sponsored broadcasters—above all RFE—to understand the media environment and everyday lives of Eastern Europeans.[22] While this research informs my own, I nevertheless insist that it is crucial to understand the radio content, broadcast infrastructures, and fluid listening practices being generated within the Eastern Bloc itself, as this approach credits Czech and Slovak citizens and journalists with a more active role in their own history.

What follows is not a uniquely Eastern European story of technological lag. By emphasizing the importance of radio in the decades following the Second World War, I stress the capacity for mainstreamed technologies to fundamentally shape and reshape daily life, showcasing what historian of science David Edgerton has called "the shock of the old."[23] This approach can then inform contemporary assessments of the long-term effects of media that are now widespread, in some senses taken for granted, and no less significant for this, such as the internet and social networking platforms. A great deal of impressive scholarship has been written about radio, its uses and abuses in the interwar and wartime periods.[24] But what happens when attention moves on to the next big thing and a medium becomes in some ways "standard" or unremarkable for its users? Here, I argue emphatically that this backgrounding makes a medium no less influential for the societies in which it is used. It perhaps also challenges some of our chronologies of socialism: socialist journalists and officials placed greater importance on entertaining citizens through radio at an earlier period than might be suggested by the rich scholarship on socialist television (which only began broadcasting in Czechoslovakia in 1953).[25]

Grassroots actors have played a formative role in the largest of the twentieth century's infrastructural projects. This can be seen, for example, in the way that socialist ministers acknowledged and made use of Czechoslovak citizens' foreign radio listening techniques. Considerations of audience approval, moreover, inflected the decision-making of reporters analyzed throughout this book. Audiences thus actively contributed to debates about how radio was supposed to sound and on what the social function of radio might be. While perhaps sometimes perfunctory, the references to listeners that arose in the ministerial and institutional files examined here certainly refute the idea that socialist state radio disregarded its audiences' sensibilities and preferences, and replace the picture of a didactic hegemon with that of a reactive, at times even populist, broadcaster. Even during Stalinism, meaningful, multidirectional communication occurred between audiences and state-controlled media. But the attention to listeners' concerns and behaviors was generally repaid with a bid to harness it and entrench the status quo. The overall picture that emerges here is of how sound has historically been employed, and has imperfectly served, as a tool for governance.

The sources in this book are weighted such that the earliest chapters prioritize the perspectives of officials on radio in Czechoslovakia, before zooming in to the experiences of reporters who broadcast over the medium. As the book progresses, more and more space is given to listeners: both citing what they had to say and showing how they were represented on air. While the shift in emphasis from officials to the general public over the pages that follow reflects a change in state broadcaster Czechoslovak Radio's sound between 1945 and 1969, this shift does not indicate a devolution of power away from Communist elites and towards radio listeners. For while technologies diffused the venues of radio recording and listening, they consolidated and in some ways centralized the management of sound.

## History through the Radio

An amalgam of territories from the former Habsburg Empire broken up by the victors of the First World War, Czechoslovakia came into being in 1918. The young and self-described "modern" state, which made a point of embracing new technologies, was among the first to champion radio: Radiojournal (a private enterprise in which the state quickly purchased a 51 percent share) made its first broadcasts from an airfield on the outskirts of Prague in 1923.[26] Early broadcasts were frequently disrupted by chickens running into the tent in which recordings took place.[27]

By the 1930s, its poultry problems resolved, Radiojournal, now housed in a monumental functionalist building designed for this purpose in central Prague, broadcast to more than one million registered radio sets (each with multiple listeners) in a state of nearly fifteen million. Domestic commentators called this the radio's "golden age," referring to the creative work being written especially for the radio by the state's finest dramatists and the technical breakthroughs broadening, through cheaper equipment, the radio's geographic and demographic reach.[28] But, as David Vaughan has noted, Radiojournal's workings were hampered by the tribalism that blighted the democracy of this Central European state. Antagonistic political parties ran the institution's various news desks as their own fiefdoms. The Agrarian Party, for example, controlled "farmers' radio," while the Social Democrats managed "workers' radio." Partisan radio staff deemed cooperation undesirable, if not downright impossible.[29]

However, Radiojournal was not the only broadcaster in town. German elites invested massively in wireless technologies and radio news in the interwar period both to circumvent British control of global wired communications, such as the telegraph, and to promote German interests beyond Germany.[30] By failing to engage them with German-language current affairs broadcasting, Radiojournal progressively lost many of Czechoslovakia's three million German listeners to stations from the Nazi-controlled Reich.[31] In consequence of this first "radio war," the Czechoslovak administration's interests were drowned out at the national, and also the international, level.[32]

Having lost the battle of the airwaves, Czech and Slovak voices again failed to resonate at Munich in 1938. Notoriously, Czechoslovak diplomats had no say when the Great Powers of France, the United Kingdom, and Italy ceded a portion of Czechoslovakia to Hitler's Germany. The Nazi annexation of Bohemia and Moravia (the Czech lands' two component parts) and the declaration of a separate independent Slovak state followed in March 1939. The Czechoslovak government, headed by President Eduard Beneš, resigned and relocated in large part to London, where it would claim to rule in exile in Czechs' and Slovaks' name over the airwaves of the British Broadcasting Corporation (BBC) during the Second World War.

But while closing universities and repressing mass gatherings, the Nazis in fact stimulated radio listening in the Protectorate of Bohemia and Moravia and also in the newly formed Slovak state. Under Joseph Goebbels's watchful eye, administrators built new transmitters, distributed radio receivers for free, and kept radio concession fees deliberately low.[33] Many familiar voices from the interwar period continued to broadcast on Czech Radio during the war, now, however, in a mix of German and Czech. If the Protectorate, which provided weaponry and equipment to the Nazi war machine, had a relatively "good war," then the soundtrack to this was provided by classical symphonies and arias that Czech and Slovak Radios relayed.[34]

However, if radio played a central role in Nazi plans for the Protectorate and Slovakia, then it also played an important role in the framing of anti-Nazi resistance—at least in hindsight. The population of the Protectorate and the Slovak state found ways to use the enhanced radio infrastructure to tune into émigré broadcasters from London and Moscow, which, as the conflict progressed, brought down penalties as serious as the death sentence.[35] Following the war, however, contemporaries perhaps over-remembered their foreign radio listening practices, to the detriment of reflection upon the more usual experience of quite legally listening to and being entertained by the musical offerings and sometimes anti-Semitic cabarets of Czech and Slovak Radio, broadcast in workplaces and public spaces, as well as in private homes.[36] One unimpressed onlooker concluded that, after the fact, "everyone had fought the Germans by listening secretly to news on the radio and sharing it with their friends. Why they shared it with their friends I don't know, because these friends also wrote that they had listened to the news. So they shared it amongst themselves and their resistance activities were virtually nil."[37]

An important boost to Czechs' resistance credentials did come in the final days of the Second World War on May 5, 1945, when an uprising took place in Prague, fatally involving thousands of local people and hundreds of Nazi troops. Much of this fighting took place around what was now officially Czech Radio's headquarters, incited allegedly by reporters' calls to the citizenry to rise up and fight. This gave birth to the idea that Czechs had actively battled to liberate their state from the Nazis and that the radio was at the heart of this struggle. The Slovak story of resistance had a rather different chronology (it took place earlier) and was certainly commemorated in its own right, but lost ground to the Pragocentric story of the "radio revolution" in the popular imagination of the reconstituted postwar Czechoslovak state.

That postwar state, the Third Czechoslovak Republic, was envisioned as a democracy ruled by a coalition government consisting of four political parties, in which a number of right-wing parties that had played an important role in the interwar period were banned. Interwar president and Czechoslovak leader-in-exile Eduard Beneš again served as its head. The American, British, and Soviet troops who had liberated the territory withdrew in the winter of 1945. In democratic elections held in May 1946, the Communist Party won the largest share (more than 30 percent) of the vote. From the start in this left-leaning state, key industries such as film and weapons production were nationalized, but radio broadcasting was not. Czechoslovak Radio, as it was now called, returned to its interwar configuration of 49 percent private and 51 percent state ownership in 1945.[38] There were means other than ownership, however, by which Czechoslovak Radio quickly became a Communist institution. In its staffing, many radio employees—like many Czechoslovak citizens at large—had shifted their opinions leftwards during the war and immediately following the conflict.[39] Moreover, internal works committees dismissed journalists and technicians accused of collaborating or harboring "rightist sympathies," which were, at times, understood to amount to the same thing. The Communist-run Ministry of Information oversaw the radio and had the power to vet staffing and censor particular topics in broadcasts (powers, archival documents suggest, it very rarely "needed" to use).

Coalition partners bickered over the radio, but it was not here that cooperation ultimately broke down. Protesting Communist foul play in the police force in February 1948, the non-Communist members of the coalition government handed their resignations to President Beneš, expecting him not to accept them. In the face of mass rallies addressed by Communist Prime Minister Klement Gottwald, amplified by Czechoslovak Radio, with workers' strikes shutting down industry and, menacingly, "people's militias" publicly displaying their arms in marches in Prague and elsewhere, Beneš accepted the resignations and Communist plans to constitute a new government staffed with ministers either directly from their own ranks or sympathetic to their cause. The Communist takeover of Czechoslovakia had occurred.

Leading members of the Czechoslovak Communist Party then downplayed the "National Road to Socialism" that they had previously vaunted in favor of pursuit of "the Soviet model." This could, however, mean different things to different people—at least until in 1952 when Soviet advisors restructured Czechoslovak Radio.[40] Even in this peak moment of deference to the Soviet Union, however, Czechoslovak Radio broadcasts emanating from its headquarters on Stalin Avenue never elided totally with their Soviet counterparts.[41] Instead, Czechoslovak journalists wedded Soviet directives to historic practices that had been regionally developed and styles and ideas gleaned from Western radio spillover. This became particularly apparent in the broadcasts of Czechoslovakia's Stalinist show trials—which led to the conviction of thirteen non-Communist politicians including Milada Horáková and then fourteen Communist functionaries (of whom ten were trumpeted as being "of Jewish origin") and the execution of fifteen of those charged between 1950 and 1952. The coverage of the trials, which were in large part overseen by the Soviet Union, drew upon Czechoslovak journalists' experiences reporting from the Nuremburg trials and the domestic postwar prosecutions of prominent Nazis. Their manicured sound was furthermore shaped in part by the technical possibilities presented by the medium of tape, with which radio staff were experimenting—sometimes with strikingly similar effects—in lighter broadcasting in the West. Czechoslovak reporters' work during the late 1940s and early 1950s, the Stalinist period, shows that Sovietization and deference both to institutional traditions and "progressive" Western techniques were not, in fact, mutually exclusive. By reconstructing this, *Red Tape* contributes to scholarship charting the interplay of both domestic and Soviet influences during the Stalinization of Eastern Europe.[42]

Stalinism (defined by Stephen Kotkin as "not just a political system, let alone the rule of an individual," but instead as "a set of values, a social identity, a way of life") stubbornly persisted in Czechoslovakia longer than in neighboring states, historians of the region have tended to claim.[43] To be sure, Czechoslovakia did not have a revolution, like Hungary, in 1956, nor mass protests, like in neighboring Poland. Stalin Avenue, on which Czechoslovak Radio stood, was only renamed Vinohradská Avenue in 1962, the same year that the largest statue of Stalin in the world was dynamited on a hill overlooking Prague's new town. A focus on the radio, however, reveals a shifting "set of values" long before: a marked drop in incitement to violence, coupled with an appeal to listeners to trust reporters', and their own, assessments in a world in which law enforcement was assigned a less significant role. While legal and political reform were slow in coming, state media broadcasts in Czechoslovakia already promoted a somewhat different "way of life" during the presidency of radio journalist Antonín Zápotocký as early as 1954. "De-Stalinization," which sought to remove Stalinism from Eastern Bloc citizens' "set of values, social identities [and] ways of life," was not a linear, nor a one-way, process. To point to its early origins in Czechoslovakia does not imply that its course was somehow derailed. It merely foregrounds elements that were already being widely promoted, with consequences for listeners if not the political DNA of the state, under a Czechoslovak leadership that is rightly understood to have been politically rather conservative, long before Soviet leader Nikita Khrushchev's cataclysmic "Secret Speech" denouncing Stalin at the Twentieth Congress of the Soviet Communist Party in 1956.

Containing the former Habsburg monarchy's industrial heartlands, Czechoslovakia inherited the biggest economy of the empire's successor states in 1918.[44] After the Second World War, its economy was markedly larger than ravaged Austria's (which was frequently the comparison that mattered to Czechoslovak politicians and listeners deep into the Cold War).[45] During the mid-1960s, however, it rapidly lost ground, leading President Antonín Novotný, who had succeeded Zápotocký following his death in 1957, to abandon the third five-year plan. The country's infrastructure and economy were still, suggested the CIA, comparable with parts of Western Europe and abounding with consumer products like radios—averaging "more than one set per household."[46] But the economy's perceived underperformance had knock-on effects on citizens' sense of their own productivity

18    Introduction

and their ability to get their hands on goods. This was a catalyst for thinking through economic reforms like a lifting of price controls and a devolution of decision-making away from central party structures and towards managers.

Hand-in-hand with this drive towards economic reform came outright appeals for political reform. In 1967, at the Writers' Conference in Prague, speakers called for a reappraisal of the Communist Party's central role and an abolition of censorship. This, so the story goes, finally spurred Czechoslovakia's laggard politicians to address the crimes of the past—including the gruesome radio hits of fifteen years prior, the show trials.[47] The push towards political reform created change at the very top of the Czechoslovak Communist Party—long-time president Novotný was replaced by Ludvík Svoboda; Novotný ceded his position as general secretary of the Communist Party, moreover, to the young Slovak reformist Alexander Dubček in January 1968. This period of change at the top and reform came to be known as the "Prague Spring."

*Red Tape* traces an alternative derivation of the Prague Spring's shifts in public speech back to card-carrying Communist journalists in the censored newsroom of the state broadcaster. These important changes began to take place, moreover, during the 1960s administration of Antonín Novotný, who is often rightly understood to have been fervently anti-intellectual and culturally conservative. Whether broadcasters were or were not its progenitors, the Prague Spring in 1968 spelled some important changes for them, most notably the revocation of censorship in June. While the avowedly socialist journalists at the radio used their new freedoms with perhaps surprising restraint, censorship's lifting proved a particular bone of contention with Czechoslovakia's neighbors and was undoubtedly one of the factors leading Warsaw Pact armies to invade Czechoslovakia in August of that year.

Once again, the elegant Czechoslovak Radio building on Prague's Vinohradská Avenue became a key site of battle between Czechoslovak citizens and invading troops. The bullets whistling in the background of audio produced by the broadcaster in 1968, as they had in 1945, transmit clearly just how intertwined the history of the institution is with that of Czechoslovakia. A range of dubious radio stations simultaneously popped up, encouraging listeners to accept the invading forces into Czechoslovakia as invited guests, there to quash a capitalist-backed counterrevolution. Unable to continue broadcasting in the main radio building, the familiar voices of household names refuted such reports, urging calm and the passive resistance of Czechoslovak citizens, in underground broadcasts made from factories, cinemas, and other makeshift studios around the Czechoslovak capital.

On command, leading Czechoslovak politicians flew to Moscow. When they returned, and following a radio speech in which an audibly upset Dubček called upon listeners to help "normalize the situation in our homeland," calm resumed at the state broadcaster—no longer did its stars broadcast from secret bunkers around the capital.[48] But the radio was damaged by the "order" imposed, which saw the removal from the microphone of the personalities most associated with the broadcasts of the Prague Spring and the invasion. Then, when they did not recant for their actions over the past year—as the journalists focused on in this book overwhelmingly did not—they were removed from the radio to work in a range of blue-collar jobs. This process of "normalization," which extended deep into the 1970s and beyond, turned Czechoslovak listeners away from the defanged radio and towards the television, the rise of which has been captured by Paulina Bren in *The Greengrocer and His TV*.[49]

Chapter 1 examines the myth of the "radio revolution" propounded by politicians and reporters after the Second World War. While they unified political and professional groupings, narratives of wartime radio listening and the subsequent "radio revolution" marginalized the state's ethnic Germans, its Slovak population, and female listeners past and present—with consequences for the Third Czechoslovak Republic and the radio's standing in that state. Following the Communist takeover in 1948, radio broadcasting and indeed radio listening became, according to many accounts, subject to particularly stringent official diktat. Chapter 2 examines how radio broadcasting and listening changed between 1948 and 1953, taking the example of the show trials—often singled out as the quintessential Stalinist radio genre—to do so. Stalinist radio was, however, a multifaceted medium, in which there was room for playfulness directly alongside murderous anti-Semitism. To demonstrate this point, chapter 3 analyzes the simultaneous radio travelogues made by Jiří Hanzelka and Miroslav Zikmund in Africa and Latin America between 1947 and 1952 and their popular reception, which also challenges the notion of a closed East opposed to an open West in the first decade of the Cold War.

By the mid-1950s, those inside and outside of Czechoslovak Radio began to implement cautious reform. Chapter 4 analyzes the drive to "vernacularize" the broadcaster that took place during the years that President Antonín Zápotocký held power. The redefinition of who should enjoy a radio presence, and how they should sound, struck many listeners, however, as "inauthentic" and cultivated a stance of ironic detachment on the part of some. Disaffected listeners tuned out. Chapter 5 charts the history of German-language radio listening in postwar Czechoslovakia. It shows how the grassroots listening practices devised by Czech and Slovak listeners in these circumstances were then coopted by Czechoslovak state actors through a range of high-profile international media coproductions. Chapter 6 tunes into the official voice of Czechoslovak Radio overseas: its foreign correspondents. It charts the careers of Jiří Dienstbier, Karel Kyncl, and, above all, Věra Šťovíčková, who were considered Czechoslovak Radio's reporting elite during the 1960s and who insisted upon their own international expertise to influence the foreign policy of Czechoslovakia, a state that Western onlookers regarded as a mere Soviet "puppet." The leverage and social capital of these journalists, however, had its limits: every one of them was dismissed as a result of the role they played at Czechoslovak Radio during the Prague Spring and Warsaw Pact invasion of Czechoslovakia in 1968. Such events form the focus of chapter 7.

Exposing how institutions such as Czechoslovak Radio and technologies like radio can become guarantors of social discourse as well as social control, *Red Tape* underscores the point that *all* media are social media. The book's conclusion recaps how radio simultaneously represented state power and created conditions for its rearrangement in socialist Eastern Europe. Finally, I reflect on the lessons held here for those seeking to understand current fake news debates and the Facebook and Twitter politics of our own times.

# 1  The Radio Revolution

**WITH THE ASTROLOGICAL CLOCK,** Charles Bridge, Mucha paintings, and beer crossed off the list, Prague tourists often end up at the TV tower in Žižkov. In fact, it is hard to avoid, as it towers over the city skyline. Czech Tourism markets the structure apologetically, understanding its placement on the horizon as a blight and representative of the undemocratic nature of the Communist regime that built it.[1]

Prague inhabitants talk about the capital as "the city of a hundred spires," perhaps alluding more to the religious architecture of the Old Town than the communications infrastructure of the New Town. But it was the juxtaposition of both on the city's skyline which enraptured one American tourist when he visited over seventy-five years ago: "Prague is a graceful city, baroque and gothic," rhapsodized Norman Corwin for the benefit of American listeners in 1946, "with a skyline of radio transmitters and cathedral spires."[2]

Corwin was far from alone in wondering at Prague's radio transmitters alongside its cathedral spires in 1946. In the Czechoslovakia he visited, radio's importance during the Second World War and in ongoing postwar reconstruction was broadly accepted. The radio masts which dotted not just the capital's horizon were testament to wartime survival rather than viewed as carbuncles, or threats to birds as campaigners might complain today. With the country's roads, rails, and concrete communications badly damaged at the end of the war, electronic communications like radio were charged with creating linkages that otherwise would not exist between Czechoslovakia's people and towns. Politicians, reporters, and ordinary listeners looked to the medium to rebuild the state at a time when there was a lot of building to do.

This first chapter tells the story of radio in that process of postwar rebuilding. It recovers the hopes that Czechs and Slovaks, like Corwin, attached to Prague's "graceful" radio transmitters and placed in the deployment of such radio infrastructure beyond Prague—to the corners of the republic. This one story is, in fact, two: I examine how Czechs and Slovaks used and discussed radio at the national, and then at the international, level. In each instance, the study of radio tells us much of the society administering it and leads to a reappraisal of the political landscape of the Third Czechoslovak Republic, lasting from May 1945 until February 1948.

I first look at the role played by radio in rebuilding the Czechoslovak state at a time that other forms of communications, be they roads and bridges or the country's discredited newspapers, were recovering from war damage. I then turn to the idea of "radio revolution" which the state's radio reporters propounded to explain their own wartime work broadcasting Nazi-sanctioned programming. I conclude this section on radio's national importance with some reflections on why the officially promoted rhetoric of radio revolution resonated with Czech and Slovak listeners during the Third Republic and on the constituencies that such rhetoric marginalized.

Next, this chapter places Czechoslovakia into the context of a continent whose infrastructure had been decimated by war and examines the state's radio output from an international perspective. It notes the emergence of a network of foreign correspondents at Czechoslovak Radio before examining the work of one in particular—František Gel. Gel embodied the faith in technology that characterized the age, insisting that an ability to navigate overseas communications infrastructures formed a part of the reporter's "specialization."[3] As a "pioneering" journalist among an elite group of reporters at the Czechoslovak state broadcaster, Gel was dispatched to cover the highest-profile radio events of the era: the Nuremberg trials and domestic court proceedings against the Czech Protectorate's Nazi rulers.[4]

The Third Republic defined itself in distinction to the wartime Protectorate and Slovak state and as a new type of technologically managed society. In positing a radio revolution ending the ignominies of war and ushering in a technologically mediated brighter future, Czechoslovak Radio staff embedded their institution into the foundation myth of the postwar Czechoslovak state. They did so at a time when the capital's radio transmitters drew admirers from far and wide.

### Radio's Postwar Restructuring and Shift to the Left

Czechoslovak Radio was founded as a private enterprise in 1923. When it ran into financial difficulties later that decade, the Czechoslovak state bailed it out, assuming 51 percent ownership of the institution. The broadcaster then split into Czech and Slovak Radio when occupying Nazi forces dissolved Czechoslovakia in March 1939. Both of these broadcasters answered to the Ministries of Propaganda and Public Enlightenment established in their territories according to a blueprint drafted under German propaganda minister Joseph Goebbels.

Immediately following the Second World War, officials reconstituted Czechoslovak Radio from its two component parts. The institution reverted to 51 percent state and 49 percent private ownership. If coalition ministers legislated as if the past six years had not happened, however, then some radio employees vociferously disagreed with their "traditionalist" approach. Miloslav Disman, a prominent radio reporter and chronicler of the institution, claimed he and colleagues sought the complete nationalization of the broadcaster instead.[5]

Disman was one of the most vocal left-wing representatives of an extremely left-wing institution emerging from the war. Through staffing changes, and the wartime shift leftwards of the bulk of the institution's long-term reporters, Czechoslovak Radio was a Communist-oriented institution as early as 1945.[6] Employees further to the political right were, in many cases, dismissed by the institution's works committee, of which Miloslav Disman was head.

The Third Czechoslovak Republic established at war's end was governed by a coalition known both as "the Košice government" (as its makeup had been determined in this Slovak town) and "the National Front." With rightist parties banned on grounds of having collaborated with the Nazis, the four remaining prewar parties divided the country's ministries among

24    Chapter 1

themselves. Overseeing the radio were the Communist-controlled Ministry of Information and the Ministry of Post, led by the center-right People's Party. While the Ministry of Information was responsible, in theory, for staffing and content, and the Ministry of Post was to oversee the technical side of broadcasting, there were, in fact, confusion and indeed conflicts as to which ministry should ultimately sign off on which matter. "Although they technically formed a united coalition," Melissa Feinberg notes, "the parties of the National Front soon began to viciously compete with each other for a greater share of political power."[7] The radio was one site over which such power struggles took place.[8]

The Ministry of Information, headed by the Communist politician Václav Kopecký, was, from the first days after the war, granted the final say on new hires at the radio. Its files suggest, however, that it very rarely overturned decisions made by radio staff. The Union of Journalists served as yet another barrier to entry, filtering out journalists with rightist sympathies from its ranks. Those without union membership were unable to work as professional journalists anywhere in the Third Republic.[9] But with professional entrance to the radio guarded most vigilantly at the institutional level by existing employees selecting their coworkers, Czechoslovak Radio's example shows how, in fact, the Communist takeover happened one institution at a time in Czechoslovakia, through the process of vetting, in some instances long before February 1948. The Communists to whom we should attribute this political shift, furthermore, were not merely interfering parliamentarians and policemen, but also journalists and professionals already established within each industry. In the Third Republic, when there was still space for quite dynamic public debate, Communist dominance of Czechoslovak Radio took the form of staffing, rather than centering upon the specific content broadcast.[10] The fairly loose criteria for Communists at the radio chimes with what Molly Pucci finds in other Czechoslovak institutions during the Third Republic. She concludes that "while ideological belief may have been meaningful from an individual perspective, it initially mattered little for the KSČ [Communist Party] from an institutional perspective."[11]

Communist reporters' establishment of a stronghold at the Czechoslovak public broadcaster did, nevertheless, allow Party members to frame key debates in the Third Republic on the country's international orientation, on how the end of the war should be interpreted, and on the forms that state-building should now take. Noting a similar phenomenon at Hungarian state radio following the war, Anne Applebaum understands this to be a case of Soviet "reliance" on the radio's Communist employees to "get the programming right."[12] While Czechoslovakia's postwar history was distinct from Hungary's, and Soviet advisors only took their place at Czechoslovak Radio many years after the Communist takeover in 1952, I read the journalistic autonomy that Applebaum detects in a different light. Communist journalists at Central European broadcasters were not merely doing the Soviets' bidding. In choosing their colleagues and creating programming promoting certain narratives about their own institution's role in the end of the war and the new state that had emerged, Czech and Slovak actors set out to make the case for Communism on their own terms and tailored to local conditions. Therein lay their legitimacy.

This was not a unique moment of media politicization in Czechoslovakia. The major political parties had all published their own newspapers, for example, in the interwar years (and resumed the practice of doing so after). Even interwar Czechoslovak Radio had consisted of warring spheres of influence, with the Agrarian Party controlling broadcasts to farmers, while the Social Democrats had been in charge of programming for workers.[13] In the immediate postwar period, however, the former Agrarian dominance of sections of the radio evaporated.

In shifting their sympathies leftwards, towards the Communist Party, a sizable cohort of radio reporters moved with their listeners. In elections in 1946, the Communists gained 38 percent of the vote, becoming the biggest party in the coalition government. Czechoslovak Radio staff certainly played an active role in encouraging voter turnout for this election and covered themes that were particularly close to Communist members of the coalition's hearts, such as the restructuring of the economy and Czechoslovakia's pivot towards the Soviet Union in its foreign policy.

But if the Communist Party was unique in the growing influence it enjoyed with Czechoslovak Radio staff, then the consensus that radio ranked above newspapers in the postwar media hierarchy spanned party lines. This shift had begun already during the Second World War.

During the conflict, newspapers had been hard for Czechoslovak politicians in exile to distribute to audiences across state borders. Print journalism's "heavy reliance on industries exhausted by the war (in particular chemical and paper production)" led to drops in production which continued into peacetime.[14] Paper remained rationed well into the Third Republic, and the country's periodicals additionally needed to undertake some work rebranding after playing the role of Nazi mouthpieces.[15]

The statistics that officials gathered indicated that their largest potential audiences were to be addressed through radio broadcasting. In this disrupted media environment, Eva Ješutová finds that "the number of radio listeners was higher than the number of those who read the daily press. On May 1, 1945, the authorities registered 1,083,208 radio license payers."[16] Politicians of every stripe duly unveiled and promoted their policies on Czechoslovak Radio, using the medium, furthermore, to burnish the image of Czechoslovakia abroad. Such a shift in politicians' media strategies is obscured when historians continue to piece together an understanding of the era from one of the discipline's favorite source bases: newspaper clippings. These sources often merely rehash pronouncements first made by ministers to much fanfare over the ether.

During the earlier interwar period, Czechoslovakia's first president, Tomáš Garrigue Masaryk (in office from 1918 until 1935) and his Foreign Minister Eduard Beneš had "believed passionately in the political power of the written word."[17] Under Beneš, the Foreign Ministry had produced a weekly radio program promoting Czechoslovakia abroad, but radio had ranked a very distant second behind newspapers in both his and Masaryk's approach to media.[18] At the time of the Munich crisis in 1938, Beneš—by then Czechoslovak president—overlooked radio as a means of influencing domestic and world opinion, judges David Vaughan, with disastrous consequences for the state that he led. Such an oversight allowed Nazi *Reichssender* to stoke the crisis, ultimately setting its terms.[19]

During the Second World War, the mindset of Czechoslovak politicians changed. Members of the Czechoslovak government-in-exile in London judged radio the best way to insist upon their legitimacy as leaders to Czechs in the Protectorate and Slovaks in the Slovak State. Ministers used the medium to announce and debate their policies in a back-and-forth with their Communist counterparts at Radio Moscow.[20] BBC broadcasts established and maintained Eduard Beneš's "charismatic authority" as head of the Czechoslovaks in exile.[21] The president-in-exile was "presented by his government colleagues as wise, universally respected and almost infallible in his ability to predict the outcome of events. His speeches were high-profile broadcasting events, repeated several times at different times of the day and analyzed in great depth by commentators."[22] A poem composed by the future Nobel laureate Jaroslav Seifert reflected nostalgically upon Beneš's wartime radio speeches as his finest hour. Through the medium of radio, Czechs and Slovaks had in fact felt "closest" to the president when he was furthest away—his voice making its way into Czech and Slovak homes "through the distant stars."[23]

In the postwar Third Republic, President Beneš cultivated a prominent radio presence. In speeches from dozens of provincial towns, he trumpeted local feats of Czech and Slovak anti-German bravery to listeners nationwide and justified his policy of expelling Germans from the state.[24] The president (who had belonged to the center-left National Socialist Party—no relation to the German Nazis—but who was now nominally above party politics in his presidential role) took to the airwaves, moreover, to address citizens of other lands. Speaking to CBS's Norman Corwin in heavily accented English in 1946, he claimed, for example, "The Americans don't quite know exactly what is going on here and we are [unclear] what is going on in America, what the conditions are . . . especially social conditions."[25] By presenting Czech and Slovak "social conditions" to Americans in the interview that followed, Beneš sought to diminish international knowledge divides, reflecting his belief in the capacity of radio to edify listeners.

Communist ministers likewise emerged from the Second World War with a higher opinion of radio's importance. In May 1945, Minister of Information Kopecký declared that "the government should inform the radio [of events] before the newspapers."[26] With his department overseeing both media, his preference for the former held significance. Under Kopecký's watch, "complete radiofication" was planned, which would result in households still without receivers gaining such equipment (thus righting class imbalances in radio listening) and parts of the country in which reception was patchy being brought wired radio (thus addressing geographic inequalities).[27] Kopecký was following a Soviet model here as in so many other instances: "radiofication" was a Communist project originating in the Soviet Union between the two world wars which, like "cinefication" and "electrification," sought to employ "modern technology . . . to transform the Russian

28   Chapter 1

experience."[28] Material constraints meant, however, that the Czechoslovak ministry's bid to redress regional inequalities remained at the level of rhetoric throughout the entire Third Republic.

Other Communist ministers also returned from Moscow with a newfound enthusiasm for radio. Education Minister Zdeněk Nejedlý secured a weekly Sunday show on Czechoslovak Radio following the war as well as broadcasting regular political commentaries in which he advocated for decisions that he and fellow cabinet ministers had made. Trade Union head and future Czechoslovak President Antonín Zápotocký directed "Worker's Radio" in the Third Republic and addressed radio journalists as colleagues at the first state radio conference in 1949.[29]

Beneath the cross-party consensus on the medium's centrality to statebuilding, however, Communist and non-Communist coalition members disagreed about the nature of radio's political oversight. In 1946, the non-Communist members of the coalition "criticized the radio, rejected its nationalization and proposed that its oversight move from the Ministry of Information to a governmental or parliamentary commission."[30] Such clashes over Czechoslovak Radio's direction took place in an environment of "increasingly bitter partisan warfare" which accompanied the first postwar elections in Czechoslovakia in 1946.[31] The Communist Party emerged the victors of these democratic elections but continued to rule in an uneasy coalition with the Social Democrats, the National Socialists, and the People's Party. In this setting, they were unable to implement all of their political objectives. For example, non-Communists prevailed on the issue of Czechoslovak Radio's ownership, with the broadcaster only nationalized in April 1948 following the Communist takeover of the state. But coalition partners, on the other hand, failed to wrest the radio from Kopecký's Ministry of Information, as they had hoped. Such partisan warfare took place precisely on account of the shift in emphasis from the written to the spoken word as an instrument of politics catalyzed by the war.

### Propounding and Disputing the "Radio Revolution"

Reporters at the radio actively contributed to political debates about their institution's social role. On May 5, 1945, Czech Radio had begun broadcasting solely in Czech (as opposed to Czech and German, as it had during the occupation). Shortly after midday, reporter Zdeněk Mančal had called "all

Czechs" to come to the radio's aid and defend the institution from Nazi SS troops.[32] Radio reporters later claimed that this had triggered the Prague Uprising (a four-day battle which saw thousands of Prague inhabitants and hundreds of Nazi troops killed). The call had constituted a radio-instigated revolution.[33] The "radio revolution" that reporters proclaimed over the following months and years allowed Nazi-developed infrastructure, technology, and terminology to be appropriated as Czechoslovakia's own.

Around Eastern Europe, argues Tony Judt, any features of statehood inherited from Nazi occupying forces were "necessarily denied, and the alternative myth of the revolutionary postwar transformation took their place."[34] In Czechoslovakia it was not the Soviets who withdrew in November 1945, but rather local actors like reporter Miloslav Disman and his colleagues who cultivated such heroic narratives. The case of radio in Czechoslovakia demonstrates how, according to Judt, "the historical reality, that the true revolutionary caesura came in 1939 and not 1945, could not be acknowledged."[35] It also reveals how integral wireless communications were to the foundation narrative—and thus self-identification—of the postwar Czechoslovak state.

For all the claims of a "revolutionary" blank slate, the Third Czechoslovak Republic inherited a comprehensive radio network, and some of the ways to think about that network, from the Protectorate's Nazi occupiers and the Slovaks' Nazi overlords. The idea of a radio revolution, for example, was not new in 1945. Nazi Propaganda Minister Joseph Goebbels championed the medium's "truly revolutionary significance for contemporary community life" in a speech in 1933. Indeed, as Heidi Tworek points out, German elites had poured great hope and large sums of money into developing wireless communications technology since the early twentieth century as a means of mitigating Anglo-American dominance of wired, cable news networks.[36] The radio and the airplane would establish German dominance of the air, and Goebbels identified both as essential to the success of the "modern German revolution." As the Nazis rose to power, the propaganda minister understood radio as a conduit through which the masses could "participate in the great events of the day."[37]

Mass participation through radio was fostered by Nazi administrators in the wartime Protectorate of Bohemia and Moravia in the same way that it was in the Reich, claims Peter Richard Pinard; "not only did the occupation

30    Chapter 1

regime not seek to roll back Czech radio listenership, but on the contrary, it propagated the spread of radio usage on a massive scale and to a similar extent as among the ethnic-German population of the Reich itself."[38] The regime encouraged radio listening by keeping radio license fees low, distributing hundreds of free radio sets to war widows, veterans, and other target groups, and through expanding the broadcast network—constructing new transmitters in Plzeň, České Budějovice, and Jihlava.[39]

The content of wartime radio may have been, as some contemporary listeners claimed, dire, with Czech Radio churning out a diet of stodgy marching music and German military victories.[40] But away from the microphone, the period constituted a golden age for radio network expansion. "Czechoslovakia emerged from World War II with a well-developed post and telecommunications system which suffered a minimum of war damage," concluded a CIA report written just over one decade later.[41] Historians have made this point in reference to the Protectorate's film infrastructure, which was expanded and enhanced during the Nazi occupation.[42] By recalling that such infrastructural development took place in the radio too, we acknowledge the strategic importance the medium held for Nazi administrators in the Czech Protectorate and the infrastructural wealth with which the Third Czechoslovak Republic was initially bestowed. The republic could not boast the same integrity for its road and rail networks, and oral histories stress that many of the country's bridges were blown up by retreating Nazi troops.[43] In an environment in which concrete communications were out of commission, electric communications such as radio and telegraph had to perform more of the work of connecting the state.

Those with political views that have not been classified as totalitarian had also sought historically to harness radio for the purpose of statebuilding too. Some Czechs and Slovaks on the political right had pondered radio's importance for the state before the war. Prominent businessmen in the 1930s had envisaged radio, in one example, as a tool to boost Czechoslovakia's private enterprise.

In a 1937 manifesto, *Budujme stát pro 40 000 000 lidí* (*Let's Build a State for 40 Million People*), entrepreneur Jan Antonin Baťa rued the opportunities radio presented that were currently being missed. "We have hitherto used radio, one of the most powerful technical inventions, for the most part merely for fun," he complained.[44] But the medium ought to be used "for

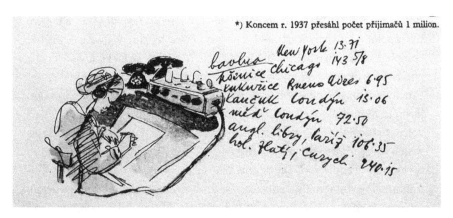

**FIGURE 1.** Illustration from Jan Antonin Bať a, *Budujme stát pro 40 000 000 lidí* (*Let's Build a State for 40 Million People*) depicting how radio might be used to communicate commodity import and export quantities to traders around the world. Source: Jan Antonín Bať a, *Budujme stát pro 40 000 000 lidí* (Zlín: Tisk Zlín, 1938), 118.

work, for trade, for advertising, for manufacturing, and mostly for the advancement of export."[45] If lawmakers followed his blueprint, Bať a insisted, Czechoslovakia would eventually need to send 20,000 salespeople abroad. Short-wave radio could ensure that these sales representatives maintained direct contact with their employers. Bať a sought to transmit cultural and educational programming overseas.[46] Cultural broadcasts would maintain expatriates' link with their homeland, while educational programming would train people in the changing technical aspects of their jobs.

It was the Second World War that led the Czechoslovak government to take notions such as Bať a's seriously. But by the time Bať a's dream became a reality, key industries and factories had been nationalized by the Košice government, and radio was now expected to promote Czechoslovak manufacturing as a state-run endeavor.[47] Czechoslovak Radio, for example, eagerly promoted the first two-year plan in 1947 and 1948.[48] By then, Bať a was exiled, discredited as a war criminal, and the industry that radio promoted, including the wares his former factory produced, fell increasingly into state hands.

Seasoned radio reporters were the chief proponents of the radio revolu-

32    Chapter 1

tion. Announcers first promoted the idea of a radio revolution in a collective apology for their wartime broadcasts aired in May 1945. As it posited complete change within the institution, such rhetoric in fact allowed for the persistence of practices and personnel from an earlier era. Josef Junek, Josef Cincibus, Adolf Mácha, Stanislav Kozák, Zdeněk Mančal, Ladislav Štorkán, Jaromír Matoušek, and Otto Kukrál expressed regret for "lend[ing] our voices to the damaging work of presenting news and political commentaries which we read with the utmost disgust."[49] They did so in anticipation of the revolution to come, explaining that "the order from the head of the revolutionary movement in the radio was clear: everyone hold on to your position, no matter what . . . Therefore, unreliable, national renegades [odrodilci] and mercenaries [zaprodanci] were not able to take advantage of these positions to influence the nation in a dangerous direction, as happened in two cases."[50] The "damaging work" the announcers had done, then, had been an exercise in damage limitation, leading to the moment when "we called you, informed you and encouraged you during the revolutionary days from Saturday May 5 until the evening of May 9."[51]

The broadcaster undertook a flurry of initiatives to commemorate and reinscribe its revolution over the years that followed. Miloslav Disman published the commemorative brochure *Československý rozhlas v boji* (*Czechoslovak Radio in Battle*) in May 1946, making the by-now standard assertion that "in the Prague May Uprising, the radio played the leading and at times decisive role. The appeals made by the revolutionary announcers were one of the most decisive commands to the Czech people in Prague and the countryside to rise up."[52] The brochure was translated into a range of European languages by the government-linked publishing house Orbis and presumably intended for widespread distribution beyond Czechoslovakia's borders. Radio revolution was good for export—something that, through print media, cultural functionaries sought to attach to Czechoslovakia's image abroad. May 5, 1946, also marked the first "Czechoslovak Radio Day," when employees were rewarded for outstanding work by Minister of Information Kopecký.[53] Such ceremony transformed May 5 into a moment of reset, the day that employees were to work towards each year, the implication being they had done so in 1945. As Bradley Abrams notes, Communist intellectuals in the Third Republic promoted May 5 as an alternative, and superior, independence day to the established October 28.[54] In declaring this

"Czechoslovak Radio Day," the broadcaster claimed this date and everything celebrated on it for itself.

Commemoration was solicited from broader circles still in May 1947, when readers of radio listings magazine *Náš rozhlas* were encouraged by reporter F. K. Zeman to send their memories of the "historic days of May 1945, in which we all participated."[55] This nominally future-oriented project ("we have to take care to capture everything . . . so that we have a thorough evaluation of our national resistance preserved and analysed for the future")[56] in fact asked magazine subscribers to reevaluate their past, framing their personal accounts of May 5–9 within a narrative of "the battle in and for the radio"[57] and "our national resistance,"[58] which Zeman used as synonyms. If, as Frederick Corney has argued on the basis of rival narratives of the Russian Revolution, "the effectiveness of the story relied on the ability of the storytellers to draw in, indeed implicate, the listeners in the telling of the story,"[59] then this was a play for their listeners' participation in the telling of the revolution on the part of Czechoslovak Radio staff.

Not everyone was convinced. One disgruntled listener complained in July 1945, for example, that the changes at Czechoslovak Radio had not been revolutionary enough. In a letter to the Ministry of Information, head of the National Committee in Prague-Podbaba, activist-citizen Karel Joch, demanded the dismissal of reporters Stanislav Kozák and Josef Junek. Stop Czechoslovak Radio from "enabling those two to further harass the ears of Czech listeners," he pleaded.[60] Likening the pair to "concentration camps" and Nazi-era jailers, Joch continued that "they were the biggest tyrants of the Czech people, with their shameless voices coloured and tuned by Nazism, and by the mockery of that which was dearest to us—the beloved president Dr. Eduard Beneš and his allies."[61] The ministry pointed Joch to the radio apology described above, which had "exonerated and cleared [Junek and Kozák] of the shadow cast upon them."[62] Alas, these assurances were insufficient for Joch; he still considered the radio's wartime reporters to be "polluting the free atmosphere of the republic."[63] To resolve the problem, Joch would "switch off the radio the minute I hear one of the voices in question, because I have lived through enough not to be willing to listen any further to the evil-profaned voices of the dreadful past in this new period of our liberation."[64] He sulkily concluded, "I won't be alone."[65]

In questioning Prague radio reporters' narrative of the revolution Joch certainly was not alone. Others asked whether the station had really been as responsible for unleashing anti-Nazi resistance as its employees liked to claim. Slovak reporter Gabo Rapoš suggested in 1946 that "the first revolutionary Czechoslovak Radio on home turf resounded on 27.10.1944 from a studio in our hills."[66] Rapoš argued that Slovak partisans preempted Prague by declaring a national revolution over the radio waves at the time of the Slovak National Uprising.[67] He thus disputed the Pragocentrism inherent in the prevailing radio revolution myth. And some who took part in the Prague Uprising also rejected radio's catalytic role. Herbert Jarošek swore years later that "the radio didn't play any role in it. Not at all. It was simply a spontaneous thing."[68] He recalled that the radio blaring from every window was irritating and concluded "whether the radio said something about it, I couldn't tell you. But that it initiated it? Not at all."[69]

### Radio Listening as Wartime Resistance?

Nevertheless, the myth of the radio revolution did find wider social currency, as it cast audiences (which is to say a large percentage of the country's citizenry) in a flattering light. Radio listening had been, after all, an everyday wartime activity and, if the medium had, as alleged, urged audiences to foment revolution, then the practice of listening had proven to be tremendously politically significant all along. By valorizing the nature of wartime radio listening in this way, Czechoslovak Radio staff elided their institution's wartime output with BBC broadcasts directed towards the Protectorate and Slovak State from London.

Czechoslovak Radio incorporated wartime staff and program genres from the BBC and Radio Moscow immediately following the Second World War. Prominent BBC journalists assumed high-ranking positions at Czechoslovak Radio: Bohuslav Laštovička became director in May 1945 while Jiří Hronek became the first head of the news division.[70] Radio news in fact emerged as a distinct department at Czechoslovak Radio as a consequence of journalists like Hronek's BBC experience. The first broadcast of *Rozhlasové noviny* (*The Radio Newsreel*) on September 19, 1945, "lasted an hour and had a modern structure which used jingles, a gong, sound effects as segues, and a theme tune."[71] All of this was borrowed straight from, and gestured aurally to, the BBC. The blurring of the BBC's wartime legacy with Czechoslovak Radio's postwar sound did not, however, erase the fact that listening to Czech and Slovak Radio had not carried the same risks as listening to foreign stations during the war.[72] This was because Czech and Slovak Radio had become official Nazi mouthpieces.

Tuning into stations of the Allied Powers in the Protectorate became illegal on September 1, 1939, when Reichsprotektor Konstantin von Neurath adopted the German "Decree on Extraordinary Broadcasting Measures." Thereafter, Peter Richard Pinard explains, "German broadcasting legislation and the punishments it foresaw, including the death penalty, also applied to the Czechs and were carried out."[73] A foreign radio listening ban only affected Slovakia with the declaration of total war in 1943.[74] Simultaneously, Protectorate authorities undertook a so-called *Kurzwellenaktion*, in which household radios were stripped of the ability to receive short-wave broadcasts, which often hailed from overseas. The Nazi authorities deemed this a more palatable alternative to confiscating radios. There were, however, workarounds, as Charles Heller recalls:

> Every radio that you saw during the war in Czechoslovakia—or in the Protectorate, there was no Czechoslovakia—had a paper tag on the front, attached to one of the buttons, which meant that it had been inspected and checked and gutted, gutted such that it could not get any international broadcasts. And . . . almost every Czech was smart enough to be able to fix it. They had this little bug . . . it was like a two-dollar item that you would buy at Radio Shack today, that they stuck in the radio so that they could all listen. And everybody listened to the BBC in Czech. Every night at a particular time . . . it was like 8:00 or 9:00, there was a broadcast and it would start out with Beethoven's symphony. It went *"boom boom boom, boom!"* . . . The first two words would be *"volá Londýn,"*—"London is calling." . . . At first, I would sneak behind the door and I would listen to these broadcasts, because it was the only truth we got about what was going on in the war. Because otherwise it was all propaganda and the Germans were always winning.[75]

Tinkering, or manipulating a technology to one's own ends, often fosters a bond of sorts between the user and that technology, claims Doug Hill.[76] Hacking one's radio set so that it could receive foreign frequencies thus generated a knowledge of, and maybe even an affinity with, this medium.

Technical expertise can, furthermore, create its own communities and a sense of group belonging.[77] Heller understood the community created by the practice of radio doctoring in overtly national terms, with "almost every

**FIGURE 2.** Radio with the "paper tag" that Charles Heller mentioned. On the red sign it reads: "Remember, remember, that listening to foreign radio is banned and punishable by prison or even death." Source: Wolfgang Sauber.

Czech [being] smart enough" to engage in such activities. With young boys encouraged in particular to gain technical knowledge through the construction and deconstruction of mechanical items when choosing hobbies in the prewar period, the community of "almost every Czech" that Heller referred to was perhaps, moreover, implicitly male.

Apologizing over the airwaves in May 1945, Czechoslovak Radio employees suggested a revolution of truth had swept their station. Never again would listeners have to stomach news of ubiquitous German success.[78] But by suggesting in the same apology that both they and their listeners had bided their time, waiting for the signal to rise up and attack occupying forces all along, Czechoslovak Radio's reporters collapsed Heller's neat dichotomy of a "truthful" BBC versus the "propaganda" of wartime Czech Radio. They posited the latent resistance credentials of listening to Prague during the war.

If radio reporters were waiting patiently to trigger the revolution, then their listeners were likewise poised to receive this command. Listeners duly adopted this rhetoric of resistant Czech Radio listening as a claim-making device. Communist Party members in the Prague suburb of Vokovice wrote, in one example, to the Ministry of Information about the opening of a new playground in 1948. Czechoslovak Radio should, they suggested, cover the event.[79] The letter writers' loyalty to the radio—both as listeners and its defenders—should guarantee this coverage. Two of those who had built the playground had fought for the radio in May 1945. While Engineer Tichý had been among the first to come to the radio's aid, Comrade Karel Fišer was decorated for his bravery in the battle that ensued.[80] With listening to and fighting for Czechoslovak Radio repeatedly elevated as the pinnacle of wartime anti-German resistance, the citizens of Vokovice used their record of both to extract coverage and material benefits from the broadcaster and the Ministry of Information.[81]

The Second World War created "conditions in which people could invest their 'subjective surplus'—which in peacetime had found outlets in the arts, in country walks, in nostalgia for 'history'—in 'everyday life' now suffused with history," argues Angus Calder.[82] For Calder, subjective surplus meant the emotions one feels that cannot easily be expressed through work or faith. Everyday actions took on heightened significance in wartime as one became convinced that one lived for the moment. Calder's reflections chime with how Czechs and Slovaks spoke of wartime radio listening after the fact. Oral history interviewees recalled the importance of listening to the radio at "historical" moments such as when the Munich Agreement was signed and when war began (in much the same way as people today can often narrate where they were when they saw images of 9/11 on the television).[83] But over and above this, the everyday act of listening to radio took on "historic" importance during the war. Cultural works in the Third Republic played upon this "historic" sense of importance that Czechs and Slovaks attached to wartime radio listening, and cast *all* radio listening at the period as essentially listening to the BBC.

Moreover, these representations frequently portrayed historically significant wartime listening to have been a male pursuit, in contrast to pollsters' findings that most contemporary radio listeners were female.[84] Women formed the majority of the electorate in the Third Republic and, as Melissa

38    Chapter 1

Feinberg notes, all of its political parties ran in the 1946 elections on a platform of upholding women's rights.[85] But beneath such politically expedient proclamations, cultural representations from the period told another story. Films and literature casting wartime radio listening as simultaneously resistant and male contributed to an erasure of Czech and Slovak women's roles in wartime resistance. The animated short film *Springman and the SS* (*Pérák a SS*, Jiří Brdečka and Jiří Trnka, 1946), for example, pitted an eavesdropping Czech collaborator against his BBC-listening Czech neighbor. The station was depicted visually through the London landmark of Tower Bridge (the station was known, as Heller notes, as "London" to listeners—in accordance with the place names found on radio dials). Its aural signature constituted the four beats (Heller's "*boom boom boom boom!*") which opened every program. In the cartoon, the broadcast's opening theme physically disturbed the eavesdropper by shaking his furniture. The listener, meanwhile, was represented as an old Czech man.

*Springman and the SS* shows the pettiness of the Nazi collaborator and makes a mockery of the overreaction of Nazi law enforcement. Following the arrest of the BBC listener, a canary chirping "Yankee Doodle Dandy" is put in chains and arrested too. The scene shows the absurdity of attempting to lock down something as free and ethereal as a bird or a radio broadcast. It also retrospectively naturalizes the behavior of the BBC-listening Czech. Just as it is comically absurd to arrest a bird for singing, so it is ridiculous to arrest this man for radio listening: only a terrible dictatorship could find such a normal, daily habit a crime. In poking retrospective fun at the strong arm of Nazi law, the cartoon naturalized "resistant" wartime listening habits and gave them a Czech, male face.

This image of the political male BBC listener lingered. In a novel written shortly after the Communist takeover, Josef Jedlička's narrator recalled dances at friends' houses towards the end of the war:

> We listened to old Armstrong records with the volume turned down, and sometimes we would roll back the carpet so we could dance. Toward evening the master of the house, returning home from the office, would poke his head in the door and say:
> "Is everyone having fun? Please, pardon me, I don't mean to interrupt. If I could just have a little quiet for fifteen minutes?"
> We all knew that meant he was going to tune in to London in the room next door. Only trusted friends were invited, although the caution was a bit overdone, since on the map hidden under the rug in the gentlemen's parlour, the

**FIGURE 3.** Still from Jiří Brdečka and Jiří Trnka's film *Springman and the SS* (1946) in which a Czech eavesdropper (albeit slightly Germanified with a Hitler moustache) strikes the table in frustration that someone in his building is listening to the BBC. Note the upturned chamber pot through which he listens, suggesting the filth attached to eavesdropping. Source: Jiří Trnka and Jiří Brdečka, *Springman and the SS* (1946).

**FIGURE 4.** The image of a BBC listener in *Springman and the SS*. The man lives alone in his Prague apartment (one floor below the eavesdropper). His white hair suggests his age. The doctored radio the character is using to receive London has the outward appearance of a bust of Adolf Hitler, taking the ability to tinker with objects so that they can receive foreign frequencies to a comic extreme. Source: Jiří Trnka and Jiří Brdečka, *Springman and the SS* (1946).

front line was always drawn circumspectly in accordance with the official reports of the German High Command.[86]

Through his use of tense, Jedlička suggests listening to London was a regular and punctual occurrence. It took place in the "gentlemen's parlour"—a masculinized space. Jedlička also styled BBC listening as a patriarchal pursuit by noting it was something that the "master of the house" did (as opposed to the household's younger members). The youth in the excerpt were involved in their own sorts of illicit listening, but instead to Armstrong records ("turned down" as dances were outlawed in the Protectorate—African American jazz was also frowned upon as "degenerate" music in Nazi eyes, though the genre was never quite as effectively banned as memory came to suggest).[87]

Literary depictions of foreign radio listening in working-class households similarly presented the practice taking place in a separate, and male, domain. The positive example of working-class political consciousness in *Life with a Star*, Josef Materna, listened to the BBC with his factory colleagues. In the absence of a gentlemen's parlour, the listening took place in Materna's bedroom—a modestly furnished space, containing a bed, a chair, and "a radio on the chest. It seemed to be the work of an amateur."[88] Materna and his coworkers also sketched maps of where they believed the frontline to be and discussed forms of anti-Nazi resistance. The book's narrator admires the bravery of each of these acts. The only woman to appear in this account is Materna's mother, who occasionally popped in to bring the men cakes and drinks.

Why would BBC listening during the war be remembered as such a male pursuit while radio programmers during the postwar years acknowledged the predominantly female makeup of their listenership? Oral histories show the extent to which women listened to foreign stations in the Protectorate too and were indeed persecuted for this.[89] Cultural representations like those analyzed above widened the scope of what could be considered anti-Nazi wartime resistance after the fact. Masculinized resistant listening could serve as a compensation for the compromised masculinity of occupied and subordinate Czechs. Such representations chimed, furthermore, with a simultaneous tendency to defeminize resistance (recasting female political prisoners as victims of Nazi brutality, for example, rather than as prisoners of conscience). Representations such as Trnka and Brdečka's, Jedlička's, and Weil's had the long-term effect of depoliticizing women's cultural consumption.

BBC listening was lionized in the Third Republic. That broadcasts from London had "stagnated," in Erica Harrison's telling, over the course of the conflict was forgotten; while "the spirit of the broadcasts seemed to falter and even listeners . . . appear to have lost interest as the conflict wore on," this was expelled from the postwar narrative of the importance of the BBC.[90] Furthermore, by eliding these broadcasts with those of Czech Radio (rather than Slovak Radio)—a mouthpiece of "constant German victories" as Charles Heller would have it, and "bad news and bad music" in Jiří Weil's words—Czechoslovak Radio staff flattered their listeners and amplified the resistance credentials of a practice which most people undertook daily during the Second World War.[91] Through the transformation of radio listening into an anti-Nazi activity, and the attendant transformation of radio in the Protectorate into the BBC, "everyone sought," as Tony Judt has noted, "to identify with the winners—in this case the Allies and those who had sided with them before the final victory."[92]

### Rebuilding the State over the Radio

A portion of the connection that reporters and listeners felt with Czechoslovak Radio during the Third Republic may have stemmed, then, from a form of agreed-upon false consciousness. But there were other important reasons to feel an attachment to the broadcaster following the end of the Second World War too: communications media played a central role in postwar reconstruction. "With the country's infrastructure failing and train, telephone, telegraph and postal connections not working, the radio became the organizer of public life," argue Petr Bednařík, Jan Jirák, and Barbora Köpplová.[93] In such an environment, Czechoslovak Radio broadcasts "helped recruit workers for agriculture and industry, with the supply of parts and materials essential for manufacturing, with organizing work brigades, in improving the morale of farmers during requisitions, and in political and moral-educational [*mravněvýchovné*] campaigns," Eva Ješutová explains.[94] Radio professionals understood music programming to constitute part of their "moral-educational" work, explaining that " classical music contributes to the deepening of life and is one of the factors in which the creative spirit of the nation expresses itself" to rural listeners who complained about the large number of symphonies the broadcaster aired.[95]

Broadcasts which sought to bring people displaced by the recent conflict back in touch formed a key (and particularly memorable) component of radio state-building. These were not unique to Czechoslovak Radio: the BBC also broadcast the names of Central European concentration camp survivors internationally. Nonetheless, such programming on Czechoslovak frequencies showed how integral people were to official and journalistic conceptions of the postwar Czechoslovak state. Shows seeking to reunite families in the public interest also pointed to a continued endorsement of first Czechoslovak president Tomáš Garrigue Masaryk's view that "rodina je základ státu" (the family is the foundation of the state). In a sign of how invested audiences were in such broadcasts, not to mention the scale of the issue of displacement at war's end, in one such program Czechoslovak Radio broadcast 38,000 messages in three weeks in 1945.[96]

Heda Margolius Kovály suggests such programs held great importance for her as a listener. "Every day I listened to the radio, anxious to hear news of liberated prisoners," she recalled.[97] The radio spoke to her personally, broadcasting upon occasion "a familiar name" and "summoning [my] father who had not been alive for a long time."[98] Holocaust survivor Kovály suggested the radio gave her cause for hope and even the chance to fantasize. Once, announcers broadcast details of a man who shared her father's name. She knew from wartime experience that her father had died, but nonetheless "jumped up from my chair and, in an instant, was in the street, limping furiously downhill toward the radio station" (resorting to such a journey as "public transportation had not yet been restored in the shattered city").[99] Kovály gained access to the "kindly" reporter's office, where he suggested that he would mention her father's name again in an upcoming late-night broadcast. The journalist followed up with Kovály two days later, suggesting nothing had come from his announcement.

Kovály's account shows just how personal the attachment to radio broadcasts, and the interaction with radio journalists, was for some at this historical juncture. Far from a disembodied voice, Czechoslovak Radio transmitted messages agreed upon in person with reporters whose "kindly" characters listeners felt they knew. The mention of familiar names over the ether almost served to evoke the physical presence of long-lost relatives (and, in the case of those luckier than Kovály, did actually result in their physical reappearance). The reporter-listener relationship sketched by Kovály here was then formative for the way that Czechs and Slovaks would engage with the wireless over the decades to come.

Radio was, furthermore, a go-between in Kovály's budding romance with another displaced Holocaust survivor, Rudolf Margolius. In Germany, Margolius had heard the messages that Kovály had sent her father in vain. Margolius had thus been prompted to write in to Czechoslovak Radio with a message for Kovály. She was given a heads-up that she should listen on a fixed date by the "kindly" reporter. She did so in a romantic haze. The act of simultaneous radio listening—even across state borders—fostered an intimacy between Kovály and her future husband: "That evening I sat again by the radio thinking that at the very same moment, somewhere in a camp high up in the mountains, Rudolf was sitting and listening too, hearing the same voice, the same words."[100] Like the best romantic ideals, Kovály's failed the test of reality—a power outage had cut off the radio announcement at Margolius's end. The tale thus shows both the very real affections placed in radio in the Third Republic and the technical limitations which tempered such emotional investments.

Radio commentator and Communist poet E. F. Burian claimed that such tracing messages formed the most rewarding aspect of his job. In fact, these messages were rather associated with Czechoslovak Radio journalist F. K. Zeman (in all likelihood the "kindly" journalist to whom Kovály referred), who was in charge of the radio's "special tasks department," charged with forging such person-to-person connections.[101] Perhaps to commandeer the legacy of such broadcasts for himself, Burian published a script of the sort of tracing message frequently heard on air in 1945, in which he asked: "Can Jan A. Řepka, Moravská Ostrava, Přívoz, Trocnovská 8 contact Prague Radio? His brave daughter would like to hear news of her family. Is that alright, Zdenka?"[102] He then turned to the news of one Klara Levková, née Kantnerová, who "greets her husband and daughter with happiness and is looking forward to her return." In conclusion, he mused, "What more to say? It is music to listen to this. I think that I'll never write anything better in my life!"[103] Burian positioned himself at once as the author of this speech ("I think I'll never write anything better") and merely as the intermediary. He posed both rhetorical and actual questions to his audience, asking Jan

Řepka to contact his relatives and his listeners at large how such radio could be surpassed. Publishing his radio speeches including this stylized tracing message, Burian blurred the boundaries between ephemeral radio and great literature.

Kovály provides one example of how listeners could feel a closeness to radio broadcasts made by Communists such as Burian and Zeman who, at times, wore their Communism quite audibly. Across the border in Dresden, Victor Klemperer provides another. Throughout his diary he complained that East German radio in the immediate postwar period "lied"—about the behavior of Soviet troops, for example, and the "rosiness" of the current situation.[104] But he found the vehicle of such lies sweet. In fact, he judged that even in such circumstances, "the wireless, substitute for cinema, car, reading, has recently given me a great deal."[105] When a fuse blew in his radio set in August 1945, he complained that "the house feels as deserted as after the murder of a child."[106] The radio did not bring Klemperer's family back together. Instead, it became a member of the Klemperer family. Personifying it as a "murdered child," Klemperer styled his wireless as a particularly boisterous, cheerful, and innocent family member who left a painful silence with its passing. The metaphor amplified the sense of loss and grief felt by the survivors of the broken machine.

Kovály's and Klemperer's recollections shed light on the multiple ways contemporaries felt that radio both rebuilt the state and their own lives following the Second World War. Klemperer looked to the radio as a substitute for other forms of entertainment and travel which were infrastructurally (and indeed for his shattered body, physically) impossible. Kovály on the other hand cited the medium's role in her courtship and subsequent marriage. While not necessarily identifying with the sum of its output, both listeners utilized the medium to their own personalized ends. Perhaps Kovály's and Klemperer's experiences contributed to their postwar conversion to Communism, but it would be wrong to style this as a case of passive manipulation or "brainwashing" by the medium, as histories of postwar East Central Europe have, at times. Kovály's and Klemperer's memoirs show how both were active in the creation of the radio content they heard. And both authors drew quite personal, and sometimes surprising, conclusions from broadcasts (for example, Klemperer once noted that he was initially unhappy to hear of his namesake's survival on air, as it triggered insecurity).[107] Lastly, KKKKKKováKly and Klemperer both document how tuning in to radio at this historical moment fostered their critical listening skills, rather than leading them to abandon their critical faculties altogether.

### The Radio's First Foreign Correspondents

Czechs and Slovaks engaged in cross-border radio listening both during and after the Second World War. The practice of listening and broadcasting across borders was formalized by Czechoslovak Radio following the Second World War, when it sent its own foreign correspondents overseas for the first time.

Foreign reporting had already gained prestige around Central Europe through the work of newspaper journalists. German-speaking Czechoslovak interwar journalist Egon Erwin Kisch had been a trailblazer in this regard.[108] A cohort of foreign correspondents had furthermore descended on Prague (and indeed Czechoslovak Radio, from which they had transmitted many of their reports back overseas) at the time of the Munich Crisis. But David Vaughan laments the inability of Czechoslovak Radio to learn from their example and dispatch its own reporters abroad in 1938.[109] In the wake of the war, it finally did. This led to shifts in the forms that foreign reportage took as a genre, discussed in chapter 3.

"Pioneering" among the radio's first foreign reporters was František Gel.[110] Born František Feigel in Albrechtice u Krnova on the Czechoslovak-Polish border, he fled to Britain where he worked as a military reporter during the war. His Jewish parents remained in the Protectorate and were murdered by the Nazis. Gel returned from London to work at Czechoslovak Radio in 1945, contributing to the institutional commingling between the BBC and the Czechoslovak state broadcaster. A former court reporter for the respected First Republic newspaper *Lidové noviny*, he was sent to report on the Nuremberg Trials, penning dispatches twice daily from November 1945 until April 1946.

Biographer Rudolf Kreśťan calls Gel's Nuremberg reporting "legendary."[111] Gel's former student additionally characterizes his mentor as "a creator of radio features, a translator, witness [to esteemed interwar paper] *Lidové noviny*, erudite author, and broadminded teacher."[112] Gel took on this last role when he was eventually sidelined as a broadcast journalist following the Communist takeover. Remaining at Czechoslovak Radio, Gel trained

46   Chapter 1

a new generation of reporters behind the scenes. When Jewish journalists were targeted around the time of the Slánský trial in 1952, Gel left journalism and made a living as a translator. This lasted for five years.[113] Thereafter, Gel took a job teaching journalism at Prague's Faculty of Social Sciences, where he left such an impression on Krešťan.

For early foreign correspondents, navigating Europe's damaged postwar communications networks was as much a part of the job as pondering how best to formulate the news.[114] Czechoslovakia's communications infrastructure may have been left largely intact by the war; the same could not be said for neighboring Germany's. In Dresden, a few dozen kilometers across the border, Victor Klemperer complained for example that "the lack of means of transport and communication is, in literally every respect . . . the basic problem."[115] Gel's dispatches from nearby Nuremburg initially went through English-language telegraphists to New York and then on to Prague. Thus, Gel complained, they ended up in the Czechoslovak capital practically unreadable.[116]

Gel managed to find a way to transmit his dispatches directly to Prague. While "all other news reporters sent their dispatches through the [American] military mission," Eva Ješutová recounts, "Gel managed to discover an old cable leading from Lisbon to Vladivostok through Prague and thus achieved the nearly impossible."[117] As Gel himself reminisced, "I went to the ruin of the Nuremberg post office . . . I found the cable in the plans. After a minute, quite clearly and in Czech [*po našem*] a melodic female voice said: 'Prague-Žižkov, intercity, here.' Never in my life has any woman said anything sweeter to me."[118] Here, Gel presented himself as someone whose passion was his job; the loveliest words he would ever hear were uttered by an operator putting him through to his employer. He also styled himself as an investigative journalist—where the object of investigation was how to transmit the news to its intended audience instead of the report's content. Detective work spared Gel's reports non-Czech-speaking telegraphists. By removing one layer of intermediary from the transmission process, the final form of his dispatches was, in his and his biographers' opinions, improved.

On the basis of this experience, Gel insisted that a knowledge of technology formed part of the reporter's job. A mental map of the cables crisscrossing the globe belonged in the foreign correspondent's toolkit. Such knowledge had distinguished him from the other reporters at Nuremberg and ought to be understood by his students as a part of "the reporter's specialization."[119]

FIGURE 5. Journalists' conditions in Nuremberg. Here, Gel's Polish colleague, Marian Podkowiński, works among "a litter of hastily thrown aside hats and coats" in the press work room. Source: Imperial War Museum. Reprinted with permission.

Gel's experiences in Germany gave journalism a concrete case of the *zlaté české ručičky* (golden Czech hands) of popular lore: his reports became legendary as an example of a technical ingenuity that was supposedly uniquely Czech. The tale also revealed much of its time: when journalism demanded a knowledge of technology, Gel's mastery of this as well as the literary side of his vocation assured his leading position in the field. If each age has its own networks associated with news, then Gel operated in an age marked by rebuilding and the forging of new connections (or the employment of old connections to new ends). He technically understood his medium at a time when technical expertise was highly valued.

Gel's stardom reached such heights that he was recalled from Nurem-

48  Chapter 1

berg before the trials' conclusion to report on 1946's other big radio smash—the prosecution of Bohemian and Moravian Reichsprotektor Karl Hermann Frank.[120] His story demonstrates how Czechoslovak Radio dispatched its finest reporters to cover trials and undertook expensive and "pioneering" international experiments to convey their proceedings and outcomes. The Third Czechoslovak Republic was a highly judicial state—few European countries could compare, notes Benjamin Frommer, "when it came to punishing [their] own citizens."[121] As the official mouthpiece for that state, Czechoslovak Radio committed its top human and technical resources to raising the profile of domestic and international court proceedings. By recalling that Nazi trials became a broadcast priority and thus a familiar genre in postwar Czechoslovakia, we can reappraise the Stalinist show trials of the early 1950s as less of a purely Soviet import. Viewed in this light, the airing of the show trials also represents the Czechoslovak state broadcaster banking on a "winning" format it had honed and popularized under the political plurality of the Third Republic.

## Conclusion

Czechoslovak Radio and the Third Czechoslovak Republic both defined themselves through backward-looking narratives about the Second World War and forward-looking narratives of technological progress. As technological developments were supposed to ensure a better life and a better state, so too a revolution spearheaded by radio must surely supplant the bourgeois newspaper revolutions preceding it. This revolution would erase the terror, humiliations, and shortages of the Second World War (although it drew on Nazi infrastructure and rhetoric to do so, and such terror, humiliations, and shortages were constantly being evoked as its justification). By attempting to draw listeners in to the rhetoric of "radio revolution," reporters cast their institution as the catalyst for the Third Republic, embedding the radio in the foundation myth of this particular form of Czechoslovak state.

In proclamations such as this about the radio revolution, as well as the implicit discrediting of the interwar First Czechoslovak Republic that accompanied it, we can see how reporters did promote, and even shape, narratives that chimed with the Communist Party's own rhetoric. But if Czechoslovak Radio was a Communist institution at this period, then this was predominantly on account of the political loyalties and party membership of a large portion of its staff, rather than its broadcast content. To be a Communist at this moment did not entail sticking steadfastly to a prepared party line.

And if the institution itself was largely Communist, then the story of radio in the Third Czechoslovak Republic is not exclusively so. Reporters and politicians of every stripe shared the belief that radio could rebuild the Czechoslovak state. The messages, apologies, news bulletins, and trial proceedings that radio broadcast all had a role in this process of reconstruction. But as much as they unified disparate political and professional groupings, myths surrounding wartime radio listening marginalized particular constituencies such as the state's ethnic Germans, its Slovak population, and female listeners past and present.

From poet Jaroslav Seifert to lovestruck listener and memoirist Heda Margolius Kovály, listeners often spoke of their closeness to radio during this period. Listeners participated in the creation of programming by asking the public service broadcaster to reunite their families, feeling at times that they had cultivated personal relationships with reporters. Far from an impersonal, disembodied voice which some depictions of Nazi radio had suggested the medium to be, postwar radio resided in a concrete location to which listeners turned when they sought particular people or goods, and the medium demonstrated its capability to evoke the physical presence of loved ones through its tracing shows.[122] Such programming constituted the most memorable means through which Czechoslovak Radio rebuilt the state.

This chapter has posited the immediate postwar years as a moment of particular preoccupation with technology, making the case for historicizing faith in nonhuman actors, such as Prague's "graceful" radio masts, Victor Klemperer's "childlike" radio set, and František Gel's telecoms cables from Lisbon to Vladivostok. Ambivalence about technology—which Doug Hill has argued is a historical constant when analyzing American attitudes— reached a remarkable low in this particular place, at this particular time. Even those who disagreed with the notion of the radio revolution in postwar Czechoslovakia merely quibbled with the nature of the event, rather than a technology's ability to catalyze historic change and transform society. The importance and hope that Czechs and Slovaks placed in technologies reveal much of the political climate and social realities of the time—notably a *lack* of faith in human actors on the basis of the man-made destruction recently and palpably wrought during the war.

"Legendary" reporter František Gel embodied this faith in technology: he argued that a mastery of infrastructure constituted a central part of the radio reporter's job. His own dexterity navigating international communications networks singled him out among an already prominent new cohort of foreign correspondents at Czechoslovak Radio. In his role as one of the institution's premier journalists, he broadcast from several high-profile postwar trials. There were plenty more of these to come, and they form the crux of the next chapter.

# 2 "The Brain Becomes a Phonograph Playing a Disc over Which It Has No Control"

*Show Trials and Stalinist Radio*

**IN FEBRUARY 1948,** the Czechoslovak coalition government fell apart. Non-Communist ministers protested the underhanded tactics of their Communist coalition partners by resigning en masse. Under political pressure and with armed "people's" militias marching in support of the Communists, President Beneš accepted the resignations. Communist leader Klement Gottwald was invited to put together another coalition which, while nominally cross-party, was in fact overwhelmingly stocked with Communist sympathizers (with a few exceptions—most notably Jan Masaryk, the son of the former president, Tomáš Masaryk). These events came to be known as the Communist "coup" by their detractors and "Victorious February" by their defenders. Over the following years, as the Communist hold over politics and media grew, radio broadcasting and listening—at least according to some accounts—became subject to particularly stringent official diktat.[1]

Here, however, I trace the limits to such understandings. Taking the example of the show trials—often singled out as the quintessential Stalinist radio genre—I chart the way broadcasting and listening did change between 1948 and 1953. But while politics certainly affected the broadcasts of these trials, at least some of the changes identified in subsequent histories as politically motivated were actually instigated by radio personnel for a wide variety of reasons resulting from changes in technology and broadcasting techniques. These shifts were taking place around Europe and not just in the socialist East. By excavating the radio trial genre back to its roots in the pre-Stalinist, immediate postwar period in Czechoslovakia, this chapter shows, moreover, how the radio personnel involved in this reworking were actors in their own right, who brought their own professional agendas to proceedings. Ultimately, I argue that some of the changes in broadcasting in the period that have been understood as manifestations of suppression were actually conceived to create a better listening experience for the audience.

This chapter first reflects on what the show trials and their broadcast can, and cannot, tell us about Stalinist radio in Czechoslovakia. It then situates these trials in a broader analysis of contemporary radio listening conditions. The venues for radio listening expanded in this period, leading sound scholars like R. Murray Shafer to complain that socialist listeners' ability to hear critically was being diminished. [2] On the contrary, I show how this expansion resulted in a diversification of listening techniques. Next, the chapter turns to the experiences of radio professionals at state broadcaster Czechoslovak Radio, considering what constituted editing and what constituted censorship in the extant tapes of the show trials, which were subject to both. This discussion sheds some light on everyday journalistic conditions at Czechoslovak Radio during Stalinism and highlights the agency and contribution of radio staff to the broadcasts of the show trials, which have consistently been underplayed in historiography. The chapter then revisits and analyzes the sound recordings themselves, examining the ways they gestured aurally to and differentiated themselves from each other. In so doing, it points to the deliberate continuities in the ways these trials were presented as a counterpoint to the changes in the justice system taking place altogether less obviously in Czechoslovakia in the Stalinist period. I conclude that the increased curation of these sound recordings over time, and their increasingly prescriptive presentation to listeners, did not result in more of a consensus regarding their meaning—something that government officials repeatedly took to the radio waves to attempt to correct.

Much has been made of what was "shocking" about these trials—and this is understandable from the perspective of the legal aspects that are at odds with today's procedures in, for example, other European countries, and in fact the current day Czech Republic and Slovakia.[3] Certainly, when it happened, the rounding up and arrest of a number of the highest-ranking politicians in the country did make for shocking news. But in this chapter, I try to get beyond the shocking to the continuities and what would not have sounded shocking at all to listeners in Czechoslovakia in the early 1950s. This is not an apologia for the methods employed by or the final verdicts of the trials. Instead, it can start to explain how these trials sought to establish their legitimacy with listeners and perhaps even their partial acceptance on the part of some.

### Using the Show Trials to Understand Stalinist Radio

The show trials examined here did not occur immediately after the Communist takeover and only later became synonymous with Stalinism.[4] Muriel Blaive rightly shows how historians' fixation with these trials, which persecuted many of those involved in the Communist takeover of power in 1948, served in fact in retrospect to recast some of the most important political actors in postwar Czechoslovakia as defenseless victims.[5] Of course we should bear in mind that Central Europeans involved in the shaping of institutions and political and social life in the postwar period could be both "perpetrators" and victims, and play other roles besides.[6] But while I recognize the potential pitfalls of boiling down the Stalinist period to these trials, I argue that they do grant us a particularly privileged window onto the workings of Czechoslovak Radio over the Stalinist period, as they left a rich trail of official documentation and that rarest item from the early 1950s: magnetic tape. The wealth of research that the historiographical bias towards them has spurred furthermore contextualizes the trials' radio presentation.

The show trials provided the occasion to pilot new techniques of control and censorship at Czechoslovak Radio. But if they ushered in a temporary state of exception at the broadcaster and anticipated long-lasting institutional changes, then their presentation, on the contrary, reflects enduring broadcasting conventions and important continuities on the part of radio reporters. I therefore argue that we should hear these tapes as in some ways "typical" of radio at the time, rather than as shocking exceptions. Indeed, the legitimacy that these broadcasts sought to foster with contemporary lis-

54    Chapter 2

teners stemmed precisely from the way in which they adhered to judicial reporting conventions and existing radio customs.

There is no consensus on when Stalinism actually took place. I agree with scholars who trace its beginnings to the disavowal of the idea that there could be a "national" Czechoslovak path to socialism. Prague politicians uttered this disavowal after the Communist takeover of power in 1948, coinciding with Soviet leader Stalin's condemnation of alternative models of socialism after his split with Yugoslav leader Marshall Josip Broz Tito.[7] Stephen Kotkin understands Stalinism to be a particular political culture, system of social values, and ultimately a "way of life" that was contributed to, through speech and actions, by people far beyond the ruling elites in socialist states.[8] With the political culture, modes of speech, and ways of life invoked in radio programming shifting remarkably in the mid-1950s under the presidency of Gottwald's successor, Antonín Zápotocký, I am a proponent of Stalinism ending sooner in Czechoslovakia than even many eyewitness accounts would claim (for more on its demise, see chapter 4). In this, I agree with Molly Pucci, who dates the end of Stalinism in Central Europe to when "the curtains fell on the show trials" towards the end of the first half of the 1950s.[9] Importantly, Czechoslovak Stalinism was not purely an import of a Soviet model developed some twenty years prior. In fact, the study of Czechoslovak radio presented here shows clearly how a concerted effort to "Sovietize" broadcasting could operate hand-in-hand with deference both to institutional traditions and "progressive" Western techniques—achieving its own distinctive audio results.[10] By examining audio of the show trials, this chapter therefore contributes to scholarship charting the interplay of both domestic and Soviet influences during the Stalinization of Eastern Europe.[11]

Both before and after the takeover, politicians such as Minister of Information Václav Kopecký vaunted "the Soviet model" as the path that Czechoslovak Radio should take, but this could be, and was, "marshalled to support mutually exclusive sides of an argument" in Czechoslovakia in the late 1940s.[12] Czechoslovak Radio was finally rearranged into four different sections, following the example of Radio Moscow, in 1952.[13] If action committees inside each workplace intimidated and thus sought to discipline employees in Czechoslovakia around the time of the Communist takeover, then memoirs (albeit rose-tinted) written from the perspective of radio reporters who enjoyed professional success at the time converge on the idea that Czechoslovak Radio was not a particularly "fearful" place until the period's end. These describe instead a hardening of attitudes and institutional practices accompanying the coverage of the last of the show trials in 1952.[14] Having successfully insisted upon both their left-wing, "revolutionary" credentials and their importance in the founding of the postwar Czechoslovak state during the Third Republic, radio staff thus managed to shield their institution from some of the purges and reforms that followed the Communist takeover.

Changes taking place outside of the radio were harsher. Communist officials organized a series of show trials which set out to consolidate the new regime and discredit its rivals. Most notoriously, the former Social Democratic politician Milada Horáková was tried alongside twelve other defendants in 1950; she and three others were sentenced to death. Two years later, the former general secretary of the Communist Party Rudolf Slánský was then tried alongside thirteen others. Some of the defendants in this trial, for example alleged ringleader Slánský, had played prominent roles in the Communist takeover of power in the first place. All were found guilty, and eleven were sentenced to death. These trials have come to be seen as the low point of Communist justice, including by later cohorts of Czechoslovak Communist officials themselves in the 1960s.[15] The media presentation of these trials was perhaps not quite as "Communist" as the judicial methods employed, however; it was inspired instead by high-profile trials which took place in the political pluralism of the Third Czechoslovak Republic.

The role played by Czechoslovakia's secret police in shaping the show trials has been widely researched. Radio professionals' input less so. And yet historians Karel Kaplan and Marek Janáč show how radio technicians' evaluations of the footage they recorded provided the initial framing of the trial of Milada Horáková, around which later textual and even judicial understandings were then created.[16] And with radio staff removing audio footage from the show trials and then reintroducing it to the Czechoslovak Radio archive years later, we gain another example of how they exercised influence to shape subsequent interpretations of the trials through their privileged position with audio.[17]

Here, I revisit the three highest-profile trials which remain in Czech Radio's sound archive—those of Reichsprotektor Karl Hermann Frank in

56    Chapter 2

1946, former Social Democrat politician Milada Horáková and codefendants in 1950, and then Communist Party secretary Rudolf Slánský and codefendants in 1952. Through their examination, I seek to understand the way the genre of radio trial was consolidated at the state broadcaster in the postwar and early Communist period. I note a shift increasingly towards the implicatory power of the words of defendants themselves. While Frank more or less refused to speak at his trial and Czechoslovak Radio largely broadcast his defense through the mediation of his lawyer, large sections of Horáková's cross-examination (but none of her defense) were broadcast, while Slánský's deposition, coming in at over three hours in length, was broadcast in full. This point leads me to a second change over time notable in this audio, from the "liveness" of the Frank trial to a more highly edited, and polished-sounding presentation of the Horáková trial. In the Slánský trial, the long, seemingly unedited deposition of the main defendant proved the exception; a far less hands-off approach was employed when presenting the others charged. The trial's chronology was, furthermore, openly altered by radio broadcasters, who spliced morning and afternoon court sessions together in their recaps of proceedings and sometimes saved witnesses from the previous day for later broadcast. Despite these shifts towards increasingly audible cutting and editing, the continuity of language and radio depiction of a courtroom setting invited the listener to feel at home hearing the broadcasts and rendered the "fantastic truths and compelling lies" of the trials' content familiar.[18]

The increasingly audible curation of these trials has been attributed by historians to Communist authorities' ever-growing drive for control—of media and of listeners' minds.[19] This is not necessarily wrong, but it fails to account for shifting radio aesthetics and technological changes simultaneously audible in the Eastern Bloc and beyond. These recordings took place at what Michael Denning has called the dawn of the "tape era" in which magnetic tape took over from phonographs as the medium on which audio was preserved and disseminated. Denning dates the tape era from 1948 until 1980.[20] The magnetic tape changed radio staff's and listeners' expectations for sound. For music, "the ability to splice and mix recordings, to bounce and layer tracks, and to create effects in the studio, led to an era that was less about recording specific musical performances than about making musical recordings."[21] In this view, the musical performer ceded some of his/her authority to the producer, and audio expertise apparently shifted away from the person at the microphone and towards the sound technician. The end recording sought less to capture a specific place and time and more to make the best possible output, which could select elements recorded at quite different times. Despite an initial dependence on Western Europe and the United States for supplies, the tape era which Denning discusses was redefining the nature of recording and hearing behind the Iron Curtain at this moment too. What this tape era meant for Czechoslovak Radio, and specifically the recording of large-scale public trials, was a similar shift away from capturing the genius loci and towards flawless audio. The increasingly audible curation of the trial broadcasts marked a shift in focus away from the voice at the microphone and towards the producer which Denning notes for musical performance.

The tapes I used to analyze these trials are different in nature. All of them have been digitized by Czech Radio and, during the covid pandemic, made remotely available to researchers to hear, as many contemporaries did, at home. The Frank and Horáková audio derives from the radio's original trial broadcasts. In Frank's case, large amounts of audio are missing, and the broadcasts merely point towards additional summaries of proceedings aired at other times, which are no longer available. In the case of the Horáková trial, the evening news program *Rozhlasové noviny*'s (*The Radio Newsreel's*) full coverage has been preserved. Conversely the Slánský tapes are obviously homemade, as indicated by interference and other stations whispering in the background in numerous Central European languages (sometimes audibly mentioning Slánský, as a sign of the trial's reach). In its less pristine and interrupted audio, the Slánský tapes perhaps present a more representative example of how the trial sounded to Czechs and Slovaks following proceedings at the time. But there are unanswered questions about who recorded them and where, which render these sources in some ways less categorizable than the radio recordings of Horáková and Frank. Finally, not all such high-profile radio trials have, to date, been preserved in the radio archive. For example the footage of the "extraordinarily mediatized" trial of the wartime leader of the Slovak State, Monseigneur Jozef Tiso—who was found guilty of treason and collaboration by a Czechoslovak court and executed in Bratislava in 1947—is nowhere to be found.[22] In other words, the examination of the audio sources that follows is far from exhaustive.

58   Chapter 2

These tapes tell us several things that other sources produced at the time of the trials cannot. For example, the radio recordings contain dialogue and information that court typists missed.[23] Furthermore, the voices of the trials' participants themselves provide us with information: contrasting Slánský's tired voice with the relentless energy of his prosecutor, two very different pictures of the state of socialism in Czechoslovakia in 1952 are presented. On the one hand, one is directed towards hearing the exhaustion of the old guard who helped build Czechoslovak Communism in the interwar period and worked towards the takeover; on the other hand, one hears the zeal of a new cadre of defenders of the socialist order. In its audio framing, atmospherics, and radio presentation, the Slánský trial evokes earlier depictions of law on the radio, therein assuming some of their authority. Last but not least, by comparing audio from the trials with court transcripts and other texts, historians can follow what radio staff edited out and thus learn more about radio editing practices.

### Listening to Radio in Stalinist Czechoslovakia

On the eve of the show trials, radio ownership in Czechoslovakia had doubled from its postwar rate of just over one million license holders. By 1948, more than 2.1 million Czechoslovak homes paid the radio license fee.[24] The number of radio listeners was even higher, as listening remained a collective activity, and multiple members of a household would gather round a single, licensed radio set. Czechoslovak Television only began regular broadcasting in 1954 and even then dedicated large sections of its schedule to Czechoslovak Radio programming—in particular the latter's news.[25] The television played a peripheral role in urban life, suggested literary accounts of the period such as Josef Jedlička's, while radio formed the backdrop to city dwellers' home life and social standing in the community (on the basis of the expense, complexity, and newness of one's radio set).[26]

Radio was not just a domestic medium. As it had been during the Second World War and in the Third Czechoslovak Republic, its programming could be heard in in the factories and streets of Stalinist Czechoslovakia during the day. Factories combined Czechoslovak Radio broadcasts from Prague with their own announcements and programming.[27] Municipal radio also alternated with centralized programming, blaring through loudspeakers attached to lampposts in cities and villages alike.[28]

Czech and Slovak journalists, accordingly, aimed their daytime programming at predefined social collectives in public spaces, which distinguished their output from that of their peers elsewhere. In Great Britain, for example, reporters sought primarily to mitigate domestic isolation in their daytime programming.[29] While housewives formed one constituency of daytime listeners in Czechoslovakia—as in Britain—the CIA noted in the mid-1950s, they shared this title with workers male and female, who were often targeted with "talks on Marxism and Leninism, on improvements of . . . proficiency and productivity, and on the desirability of collectivized agriculture"—topics the report's authors judged to be less than popular with audiences (while Marxism and Leninism featured altogether less frequently on the BBC's *Women's Hour* and *Housewives' Choice*).[30] Collective audiences were also anticipated by Czechoslovak Radio in its daily programming for students in the classroom. Such collectives were explicitly acknowledged in daytime reporting at the time of the Slánský trial, when reporters read out resolutions from groups of factory workers and schoolchildren, calling for the defendants to receive the harshest punishment.[31] Reflecting journalists' understanding of their audiences, listeners were addressed in groups, rather than individually, in daytime programs soliciting engagement with the trials.

While some theorists have argued that the permeation of radio into an increasing number of spaces homogenized or dulled the listening experience, representations of radio listening in Czechoslovakia from this period suggest instead that radio's expansion into ever more areas of life generated an assortment of listening modes. The doyen of sound studies, R. Murray Schafer, understood radio in postwar Eastern Europe as a "totalitarian" tool of "culture-molding."[32] He suggested the "cacophonies of patriotism and spleen" that he had heard "on station platforms and public squares throughout Eastern Europe" created a "wall of sound," cutting the listener off from the sounds of nature that underlay such programming, and limiting the listener's ability to think clearly or connect meaningfully with others.[33] But while the sound of radio might have been ubiquitous in Stalinist Czechoslovakia, the practice of listening was far from uniform. Two filmic representations reveal the wide array of different approaches that Czechoslovak citizens took to the medium, as well as ways in which the medium could foster social relations or rend them asunder.

60    Chapter 2

The documentary *They Shall Not Pass* (*Neprojdou*, Zbyněk Brynych, 1952) provides an example of daytime listening to radio at the workplace. It presented an idealized, prescriptive picture of radio audiences in Czechoslovakia. The film profiled the country's border guards on Czechoslovakia's westernmost frontier with Germany. Army conscripts from all over the country bonded with each other and, it was implied, the rest of the country by listening collectively to the May Day celebrations taking place in Prague. In the first scene in which the radio appears, a troop turns the dial of the radio receiver until the voice of Czechoslovak Communist President Klement Gottwald comes clearly through the speaker. There is no interference on the audio track of the film, which suggests both the impeccable audio quality of Czechoslovak Radio's May Day broadcasting and the perfection of the soldier's tuning skills. The guards are clearly pleased by what they hear as they smile at each other; their weapon cleaning going more smoothly thanks to the soundtrack. That this form of listening was patriotic was indicated, rather bluntly, by the country's flag flying proudly in the background of the scene. That such listening trained the guards' vigilance was suggested by their detention of a West German smuggler crossing the country's border in a high-drama sequence at the end.

*They Shall Not Pass*'s ideal radio soundtrack consisted of the uninterrupted, lone voice of the Czechoslovak president. Power here was monoglossic, and the film perhaps set out to sculpt an "aural dimension" of the leader cult that Stephen Lovell detects emerging on Soviet radio during Stalinism.[34] Such a soundtrack was in keeping with Information Minister Václav Kopecký's view, articulated in 1949, that Czechoslovak Radio should be "constantly at the disposal of the president and the head of government."[35]

But even at the height of Stalinism, Czechoslovak Radio's two national stations, Prague I and Prague II, were characterized by the "cacophony" of voices that had offended Schafer's ears and which were audible in each of the trial broadcasts, rather than a solitary leader's endless drone. If a leader cult was constructed around Stalin by these stations, it was certainly not through recourse to the generalissimo's voice. In an oral history, Jana Švehlová, who was born in 1943, recalled:

> I was home with tonsillitis listening to my beloved radio—we had two stations. And suddenly they announced that they would be singing Stalin's favorite song, "Sulika," and we all knew from school that this was Stalin's favorite song. I was

in bed with scarves and everything around my neck to keep warm. I pulled them all off. I was maybe 10 years old, 11 years old. I stood to attention, nobody told us ever we needed to stand to attention when they sing "Sulika" [but] I stood to attention and I was listening to "Sulika" from the radio . . . Because Stalin in a way was my temporary father and I just never know how to explain it to people. I had no other input. That's what I believe, that that guy, who sent my dad to prison, became my temporary father.[36]

Attempts to establish something of an aural leader cult for Gottwald on Czechoslovak Radio fared less well. Each year, the broadcaster retrieved his voice from the archive and broadcast his address to the masses on Prague's Old Town Square at the time of the Communist takeover to commemorate this event.[37] The late president's image was furthermore bolstered through the recollections of those who knew him: Slovak contemporaries, for example, remembered him fondly on Radio Bratislava on April 1, 1953.[38] But the "Sulika" effect was never achieved by the un-radiogenic Gottwald, whose own mother appeared to find his broadcasts eminently forgettable when quizzed about them on air.[39] The idealized image of Gottwald as the voice of Czechoslovak Radio at the Czechoslovak border presented by *They Shall Not Pass* is wishful in several ways. Just as Czechoslovak Radio shared the ether with and often lost out to foreign stations in these regions (see chapter 5), so Gottwald's voice shared the ether with and was often drowned out by others on Czechoslovak Radio's frequencies. Additionally, listeners like Jana Švehlová certainly could listen to the radio with as much vigilance as the guards depicted in *They Shall Not Pass*, but other films in which radio listening appeared suggested altogether less socially condoned modes of listening existing simultaneously in Czechoslovakia.

No law banned foreign radio listening per se in Communist Czechoslovakia, as was the case in the other People's Democracies.[40] The criminal code introduced shortly after the Communist takeover in 1948 outlawed "incitement against the republic" and sought to punish those who "deliberately or through negligence allow or facilitate the spread of seditious speech."[41] The new penal code in 1950 then mandated a sentence of between three months and three years for those who "knowingly enable or facilitate the spread of seditious speech."[42] Collective listening to or discussion of foreign broadcasts could therefore be punished indirectly and was.[43] If they had made radio listening a matter of the law, however, then early Communist author-

62    Chapter 2

ities may have shown up their limited ability to implement their own legislation. Their solution to the problem was thus extrajudicial. Punishment for listening to Western radio may not have taken criminal form, but such behavior may have had professional repercussions if it ended up in one's personnel file. Instrumental in detection of any transgression were the hundreds and thousands of citizens listening vigilantly to their neighbors' radio habits. As one farmer who was quizzed after emigrating to West Germany in 1954 summed it up: "People aren't scared of punishment, but one doesn't listen to foreign radio in front of people one doesn't know. If someone pops up unannounced, then you switch it off."[44]

The social, rather than legal, condemnation of Western radio listening in the early Communist period is demonstrated well in the 1958 film *Citizen Brych* (*Občan Brych*, Otakar Vávra, 1958). Itself a product of de-Stalinization, it is a retrospective source and, in hindsight, critical of the excesses of these first Communist years. Western radio listening formed the crux of a discussion between the eponymous Citizen Brych and his neighbor. Brych's neighbor comes to pick up his young daughter, who has snuck into Brych's flat and thus possibly saved our protagonist from throwing himself off his balcony in despair. The neighbor is thankful for the child-minding and apologizes for the noise produced by his newborn child (whose crying on the other side of Brych's walls has so far contributed to the dissonant soundtrack of the film). Brych responds politely "I don't hear it," to which the neighbor replies with a warning—equally polite in tone—"yes, of course, when you are listening to that radio."[45] The protagonist bristles and responds, "Is it banned?" To this the neighbor, also in a more clipped tone, suggests "no, not if someone wants to listen to their slander." After a moment, and in a more conciliatory tone, Brych's neighbor suggests that they have always lived alongside each other well. When Brych responds that this was true, pointedly using the past tense, his neighbor gives up and signals to his daughter that it is time to leave.

The scene shows the legal status of foreign radio listening at the period, as well as the mechanisms by which such radio listening was policed. In telling his neighbor to mind his own business, the audience understands that Brych is making trouble for himself, because his sympathetic neighbor is giving Brych a signal in this conversation that his radio listening habits are audible to the outside world. We understand the neighbor *is* sympathetic as he does not use such a threat to extract something from our protagonist. By saying the neighbor should mind his own business, Brych in turn is communicating that he does not care. Ultimately, Western radio listening constitutes a low-level misdemeanor for which a repentant Brych can and will redeem himself. But this is not before he has attempted to cross the border into Western Germany, a decision for which he has been primed by listening to the BBC.

Czechoslovak radio listeners used a range of verbs during the Stalinist period to describe their more or less socially condoned techniques of radio listening (ranging from the standard verb *poslouchat*, to listen, to the less standard term *odposlouchávat*, to eavesdrop).[46] This varied vocabulary was born of both the increased possibility to tune into radio and the complex social codes surrounding this action at the time.

If listening to municipal or factory radio were a collective, daytime event, then short-wave foreign broadcast listening such as Brych's would generally take place in the evening. The CIA understood this latter practice to be "widespread" in Czechoslovakia in the mid-1950s, specifying that "the usual audience for Western broadcasts is the family circle, although some intimate acquaintances are sometimes included."[47] Western broadcasts experienced stiff competition in the evening hours, however, from Czechoslovak Radio's most popular show, *The Radio Newsreel* which featured "news, on-the-spot reports from factories and public gatherings, sports news, weather forecasts, and comments on local and foreign political events."[48] Even if listening to Western stations were widespread, Melissa Feinberg rightly notes in her study of Radio Free Europe's coverage of the Slánský trial that this broadcaster's ability to shape understandings of events was extremely limited.[49] RFE was not alone among media outlets in its impotence to mold popular conceptions of the trials.

### Changing Journalistic Conditions at Czechoslovak Radio

The Slánský trial offered opportunities to pilot new censorship techniques that later became standardized at Czechoslovak Radio. It will therefore be examined here as an important instance of institution building. But censorship was not the primary reason why every cough, confusing or inaudible passage, or even sizeable chunks of defendants' depositions were cut from these trials ahead of their broadcast. Previous analyses of the Horáková and

64   Chapter 2

Slánský trials' media coverage have equated any cutting of the original trial tapes with censorship.[50] In so doing, authors have overlooked the work manipulating sound undertaken by radio employees themselves and some of the non-party political reasons they may have engaged in this. Here instead, I reveal how these trial broadcasts were simultaneously censored *and* subject to editing processes that had little to do with protecting state secrecy or "workers' interests."

Certainly, censorship was up and running as a practice at Czechoslovak Radio—and throughout the Czechoslovak press and arts—by the time the Horáková and Slánský trials were broadcast. As one recent exhibit on the history of journalism in the Czech lands puts it, censorship was the norm, rather than the exception, in the history of the profession up to and including the second half of the twentieth century.[51] However, it is important to note ways in which the phenomenon changed, as shifting censorship practices changed the ways that journalists went and felt about their jobs. And of course, Communist politicians had more subtle tools than censorship to heighten their prospects of favorable coverage—for example through the selection of ideologically suitable personnel in the first place. As a technique of control actively being built out in the Stalinist period in Czechoslovakia, however, I choose to focus on censorship here (and its limits) to better understand radio practices of this particular moment.

Following the Communist takeover, Czechoslovak authorities "radically" expanded the modes of censorship they had applied in the democratic Third Czechoslovak Republic: the Ministry of Information, and now the Central Committee of the Communist Party, gained a greater influence over mass media, including Czechoslovak Radio.[52] The different institutions overseeing censorship often had, however, "different motivations and interests and often did not pull in the same direction."[53] This point is exemplified by the souring relationship between the heads of the Ministry of Information and the Communist Party's press department, Václav Kopecký and Gustav Bareš. The sense that one was meddling in what was rightfully the other's domain contributed to this growing acrimony, claims historian Jiří Knapík, who charts Kopecký's ultimate sidelining and the closing of the Ministry of Information in 1953 as a result of this clash.[54]

In the first years following the Communist takeover, Party influence over the press took two forms in particular: firstly, the Central Committee issued instructions about what should, and should not, be discussed. Secondly, and perhaps most crucially, the Party had a say in the choice of editor-in-chief of each news outlet and radio department. By choosing those with "impeccable political credentials," functionaries sought to solve problems "before they ever occurred."[55] Censorship then took place within the news department, at the hands of the editor, who was (ideally) well apprised of which topics were currently in favor and which were out of bounds. The editor then bore ultimate responsibility for the output of his/her department.

On the eve of the Horáková trial, Ludvík Aškenazy was the editor at Czechoslovak Radio and, in this remit, the censor. His subordinate, reporter Jan Petránek recalled that Aškenazy was both "respected" by his radio colleagues and "terrible" in his role as monitor.[56] Aškenazy "went into a writerly trance right from the start of his shift," meaning that he did nothing to "approve the content of the news."[57] He was permitted this idiosyncrasy on account of his impeccable Communist credentials and status as a decorated Red Army veteran. His staff did not share his sense of security, in particular those just embarking upon and eager to improve their own careers. According to Petránek, those under Aškenazy's tutelage panicked about their own lack of preparedness and exposure as the evening news was recorded in the studio. Aškenazy was "nonchalant" in the face of his subordinates' panic.[58] The atmosphere changed and became altogether less "nonchalant"—and more fearful—at the radio simultaneous to the Slánský trial in 1952. At this time, Aškenazy was removed from his post at the radio, like many other reporters identified as Jewish by the authorities.

Undoubtedly nostalgic, the picture Petránek paints of the early Stalinist years at Czechoslovak Radio is nevertheless one in which the lack of editorial censorship characterized radio production and inflected output—even creating some headaches for those lower down the professional and Party ranks. Such headaches were reinforced by complaints from government officials disgruntled with the radio's output.[59] Furthermore, ranks of "eager amateur" censors often listened more vigilantly than those in the newsroom and did not hesitate to write in to Czechoslovak Radio and the Ministry of Information demanding redress for their complaints.[60] Such instances introduce the tyranny of the listener—or listeners' anticipated preferences—as a factor informing what journalists chose to write.

The show trials of Horáková and Slánský created the conditions in which future censorship methods could be piloted. Employees from the Czechoslovak Justice Ministry installed themselves at Czechoslovak Radio to oversee the versions of the trials prepared for broadcast.[61] Their presence on these two occasions preempted the creation of a distinct, fixed censor's office within the radio—the *Hlavní správa tiskového dohledu* (HSTD, the Head Office of Press Oversight)—which would, from its creation, be manned by state security personnel, rather than internal radio staff. This office was created according to the template of the Soviet censorship bureau, *Glavlit*, and came into full-time operation in 1953. In the radio too, then, as Molly Pucci finds in the Czechoslovak secret police, the show trials ushered in "a period of institution-building as well as repression."[62] They facilitated the transformation of an always imperfectly translated "Soviet model," (here *Glavlit*) into a daily reality with its own bureaucracy.

But if we were to follow the practice of censorship even further, until the end of the Stalinist period in Czechoslovakia, we would find that even the institutionalization and securitization of censorship did not serve to homogenize, nor completely to harden, the practice. Petr Šamal has rightly characterized censorship throughout the socialist era as a process of negotiation, in which "actors on the one hand fulfilled orders from above, but simultaneously followed their own goals. These could have very varied forms, from attempts to promote a specific aesthetic or ideological concept through efforts to publish a concrete . . . work or a simple attempt to secure one's own material success to conscious subversion of the system of censorship."[63] This negotiation sometimes took place explicitly with a censor on the police payroll; at other times such debates remained internal to an institution or a news desk, or indeed took place on the initiative of cultural producers themselves.

Well into the late 1950s, newspapers and magazines—and *not* radio— remained, for Dušan Tomášek, the "main battlefields of censorship."[64] Here, he suggested that the same content had a different chance of making its way through the censors depending on the medium. The radio's allegedly revolutionary credentials provide one potential explanation for this. Moreover, new censors from outside the radio ranks had particular difficulties with the material specificities of radio tape and film, which they had to "listen to vigilantly and watch even more vigilantly, so that nothing got past them."[65] This process took more time than skimming through a written text and proved even more time-consuming still if there were questions that led to the rewinding and replaying of a tape. While censors felt competent to strike through and rewrite the written word, they were painfully aware that "the experts [at the radio] held the scissors and glue for them."[66]

As one such scissor-and-glue-wielding expert, radio employee Věra Homolová describes the personal relationship that she fostered with the censor following the latter's installation at Czechoslovak Radio in the early 1950s. Their understanding was based on each limiting the workload of the other:

*Did the censors intervene a lot?*
"No, because we knew . . . We knew what we could not say, and so we didn't say it."

*And what were the things you absolutely couldn't say?*
"Nothing about the functioning of the Czechoslovak Communist Party, and no negative comments about the Soviet Union. This had to be discussed positively.
"There was a really nice woman we brought our texts to, but we tried to make it so that she wouldn't score things out of our texts, of course. Because then you had to do it again . . . She really was quite a nice woman."

*In what way was she nice?*
"She behaved well towards us. If we hadn't known that she was from the secret police, you know? . . . She was pleasant and behaved well to us. This was right in the radio building and before reports were broadcast they had to be approved."

*What about the interviews you did with other people, because you couldn't censor what they said?*
"No, you gave them the tapes to listen to. Everything that was broadcast was approved by the StB."

*Did you ever broadcast live?*
"No."[67]

In their first interactions instigated by the show trials, the relationship between radio personnel and visiting justice staff could not, of course, have been as familiar, let alone as convivial. But an awareness of what was expected, coupled with a desire to conserve energy by not deliberately provoking the censor, certainly could have already been cultivated by radio staff through their earlier work under Aškenazy and other editor-censors prior to the Horáková and Slánský trials.

Several articles have already considered what precisely was edited out of the show trials. In the Horáková trial, for example, the defendants' final speeches were never broadcast on radio. Karel Kaplan and Marek Janáč have argued convincingly that they were censored to stop the defendants from sounding too persuasive and sympathetic to listeners.[68] Petr Blažek has compared, meanwhile, legal transcripts with tapes from the Horáková trial to show that sections of Záviš Kalandra's cross-examination in which dates and names were repeated were cut from the radio broadcast, alongside a section in which the prosecutors mocked a Western contact of the defendant, one Helen Fisher.[69]

Were all of these edits censorship—or manipulation on the part of the trial's organizers? We will likely never know for sure. But based on the conditions at Czechoslovak Radio discussed so far, I would question whether some of the most repetitive passages of the trials were censored out of the broadcast at the behest of a member of law enforcement. Such decisions are rather suggestive of the aesthetic choices that radio broadcasters made to enhance the listening pleasure of the other programming they aired at the time. The conflation of editing with censorship has downplayed journalistic agency in Stalinist Czechoslovakia. Censorship was a daily reality at Czechoslovak Radio, which journalists who wrote text and edited tapes like Petránek and Homolová negotiated in changing but constantly generative ways. The national security nature of the alterations to the tapes discussed has long been stressed, but in the section that follows, I listen to the trials with an ear for what made them both conventional and compelling radio. This reinterprets the tapes as products of institutional traditions and simultaneously the state of the radio art, over and above mere proof of the existence of censorship in Communist Czechoslovakia.

## The Trial Broadcasts

While the Horáková and Slánský trials took place in a Communist-dominated Czechoslovakia following the takeover, the Frank trial did not—it was undertaken and broadcast years earlier, in the politically plural Third Czechoslovak Republic. As it established, however, the style in which the defendants and the law were presented in subsequent court cases, it is examined alongside those later proceedings here.

As the radio trial of Nazi police chief in the Protectorate of Bohemia and Moravia, Karl Hermann Frank, began, the announcer Miroslav Oplt took listeners on a virtual tour of the courtroom. Having described the interpreters' booths, the section for foreign journalists, and pointed out some of the famous people assembled in the room, Oplt then included Czechoslovak Radio's sound equipment in the roll call. He drew listeners' attention to the gallery on which, he noted, "our apparatus and machinery resides."[70] This suggested Czechoslovak Radio's prominent presence in the courtroom, and gave the radio's equipment credit for bringing the trial to listeners both at home and in attendance (with the machinery, he explained, also projecting audio into the grand room during proceedings).

The Frank trial started with the appearance of the accused in the dock and his questioning to ascertain biographic details and the amount of property he owned. Then the experts scheduled to testify gave details of themselves and swore an oath. There were long pauses, filled largely by coughs from the audience and mumbling among participants. After nearly twenty-five minutes, presenter Oplt reappeared with an apology and more details of the technical set-up: he explained to listeners that the amplification of the trial within the courtroom was being taken care of by Czechoslovak Radio through their sound system, meaning that he could not interject during such pauses as this too would be broadcast to the court. The apology again flagged the way that the very course of the trial relied upon Czechoslovak Radio's technological capacity but also underscored that technology's limitations.[71]

Radio conventions made for slower-sounding programming in the immediate postwar years and indeed throughout the socialist period. Eva Ješutová notes, for example, that announcers were trained to pause between sentences to slow down the tempo of each broadcast, perhaps also having the effect of enhancing their authority.[72] Veteran broadcaster Jana Peterková moreover recalls that "no one ever ran in the corridors of Czechoslovak Radio," as nothing—no breaking news—required such urgency in newscasters' eyes.[73] But even by the era's more ponderous standards, the recording of this and other trial proceedings was marked by long silences, passages of mumbling, and procedural lulls. It is hard to imagine "the whole

70    Chapter 2

nation follow[ing] the radio news from the courtroom with baited breath," as journalist Jaroslav Skalický has suggested.[74]

When the audio set-up permitted, Miroslav Oplt filled these gaps with details of how Frank looked, flagging unpleasant aspects of his appearance that, he insinuated, served as external markers of Frank's character.[75] This "aggressive and cutting language" (for example, radio reporters referred to Frank as a "disgusting subhuman") set a precedent for the way defendants were to be described in the Horáková and Slánský trials.[76]

Commentator Oplt here then turned to trial protocol (how long the trial would last each day, how long the trial was expected to last overall). He provided background on the judges and, to create the impression that he was particularly well-placed to report upon the event, behind-the-scenes information on the possible size of the charge sheet brought against the defendant. An impression of shared confidence was created by Oplt almost whispering into the microphone.[77]

Despite Oplt's best attempts to bring the proceedings to life, the format of the trial clashed with existing radio norms in several ways. For example, the prosecution's enumeration of paragraphs of the Czechoslovak legal code which Frank was accused of having breached made for a long litany of numbers without any subsequent explanation. Just such speech eschewing tangible objects in favor of concepts harder to visualize like numbers had been explicitly cautioned against by radio pioneer František Kožík in his recent handbook on making good radio, *Rozhlasové umění* (*Radio Art*).[78] In response to the prosecution's opening speech, the defense then provided a range of procedural reasons why Frank should not be tried in a Czechoslovak court at all, which were far from apparent to the lay listener and which even the panel of judges had to adjourn to mull over. As the court adjourned, Oplt gave a short explanation of what, in fact, was going on but left the legal wrangling and jargon of the past one hour largely without commentary.[79]

The difficult listening of parts of this trial suggest that it was not for listening pleasure alone that audiences tuned in. In his commentary, Oplt directed listeners to summaries of proceedings broadcast by Czechoslovak Radio journalists later in the day, which perhaps did a better job of condensing and communicating information about the trial. So why, then, tune in to at turns bewildering, and perhaps even rather boring, radio trial coverage spanning hours? The unabridged version of the Frank trial, in its length, suggested both the scale of the defendant's misdeeds and the thoroughness of the court trying them. Much of the trial reporting over the days that followed showcased witness statements, which perhaps sought to foster identification with and solidarity among listeners, who were encouraged to recognize their own wartime suffering in statements the witnesses made. The location of the daily trial broadcasts within the courtroom encouraged listeners to feel like they were there and participating in Frank's punishment, while the liveness of the broadcast vouchsafed its authenticity. The chance that Frank may not, after all, be found guilty perhaps added tension to the proceedings. That the Czechoslovak court trying Frank was meticulously going through the right motions was shown, and made into a show, by the radio broadcasts.

Twice when framing the trial for listeners, Oplt mentioned Nuremberg. The courtroom was set out "just like Nuremberg," Oplt claimed, suggesting that what was taking place in Prague in March 1946 was a small-scale replica with more local resonance (when Frank was in fact being tried according to Czechoslovak, and not international, law). And the status of the Frank trial as an offshoot of Nuremberg was reinforced with special reference to the presence of Doctor Bohuslav Ečer who, it was noted, had been a key participant at Nuremberg.[80] With reporter František Gel replacing Miroslav Oplt as a commentator after these first broadcasts, the trial moreover came to sound like Nuremberg through the voice guiding listeners through proceedings. Links consciously made to Nuremberg served to legitimate the international validity of the trial and its verdict, and also the media treatment of the trial. In both cases, reporters stressed their presence on the scene, deriving some of their authority through their status as eyewitnesses. This was unlike the trials to come, in which announcers in a radio studio provided commentary on proceedings, deriving their authority from the pristine sound quality of their pronouncements and perhaps even the distance they maintained from proceedings.

When Communist officials planned the media coverage of the trial of Milada Horáková and twelve other defendants in 1950 on treason charges, they drew on František Gel's experience with the radio genre. They additionally asked veteran reporter Josef Cincibus to advise on and cover proceedings.[81] The case positioned Horáková, a left-wing women's rights activist and social reformer who had spent time in Nazi concentration camps on account of her role in the wartime resistance, at the head of an international spy ring, working with Czechoslovak émigrés in the West and the Western powers to bring down the new Czechoslovak "people's democracy."[82]

If reporters had used "aggressive and cutting" language in their broadcasts to discredit Frank, then they were even less subtle in their construction of a critical standpoint when commenting upon the Horáková trial.[83] In their reproaches of the defendants and ostensible disbelief at the scale of their crimes, Czechoslovak Radio's announcers barely followed the premise of innocent until proven guilty. When Horáková once claimed not to know details of what the prosecution was implying, for example, the announcer interjected that Horáková was merely "pretending."[84] After the verdict was announced, reporters concluded that the "right" verdict had been reached.[85] While radio staff had apologized for their inability to interject at the Frank trial, the question-and-answer-like set up of the Horáková trial's reporting—which saw clips from proceedings interspersed with Czechoslovak Radio commentary—offered radio staff much more frequent a say on events as they unfolded.

There were also more fundamental ways in which the Horáková trial broke from the coverage of those that preceded it. Certainly, this was the case in its behind-the-scenes preparation ("aided" by the presence of Soviet advisors), which other scholars have already researched thoroughly.[86] Some differences were audible too. While there was very little of Frank actually recorded (he spoke little and in German, and largely through his defense lawyer and interpreters at his trial), the first day of the Horáková proceedings resulted in hours and hours of edited footage of the main defendant making it onto the air. She defended herself in this footage. Unlike the Frank trial where the defense's legal argument was expounded on air at eye-watering length, one never heard a word broadcast in defense of Horáková and the others accused, and this despite them having defense lawyers, whom they thanked in their final speeches—which were likewise cut from the radio coverage.

A lawyer by training, Horáková was warned by her judges at the start of her cross-examination not to speak in a "lawyerly" way.[87] There was no place for legal language in this court, which, as noted, had hardly proved conducive to easy listening at earlier radio trials. This chastisement of Horáková pointed to the nonexpert audience at which this trial was aimed. Directing

Horáková to speak as a nonlawyer indeed cast the nonexpert radio audience as the ultimate judges and jury in her case. This onus reflected the opinion of the justice minister at the time, Alexej Čepička, that "the new legal order must be understandable to everyone."[88]

Clips of Horáková's deposition were strung together and narrated by an announcer sitting in a studio, as opposed to there being any pretense at live courtroom reporting. At moments, the narrator took over, ostensibly to make the point that Horáková was articulating with more concision. At other times, he would underscore the gravity of what Horáková had just said through repetition. Everything was prerecorded, including the announcer's voiceover.[89] Footage of the trials was edited so as to "arouse the worst possible impression" of the defendants in the eyes of the public, but measured, demure, and articulate throughout, it is not clear that Horáková incriminated herself through the sections of her speech that were aired—instead the paratext provided by the prosecution and Czechoslovak Radio staff better served this purpose.[90] Worked into the format of the nightly news, the hand of the editor was certainly clearer here than at earlier radio trials.

The decision to prerecord and then broadcast the Horáková trial chimed with what Stephen Lovell has called "new standard practice" on Soviet radio following the war, ushered in by the increased availability of magnetic tape.[91] The introduction of magnetic tape fostered both new spaces for experiment and forms of control on Soviet radio: as tape allowed the finished sound of a program to be vetted before airing, it reduced the need for a script.[92] In Czechoslovakia, the "tape age" was written formally into law in 1953, when officials ruled that all artistic, sporting, and musical events could now be recorded and broadcast on the state broadcaster Czechoslovak Radio without charge. In other words, cultural life in Czechoslovakia was ripe for recording; recorded sound was the property of the state, and the state broadcaster had free access to the tapes that, more often than not, its employees had made.[93] Here as was the case with censorship, the show trials gave radio staff the opportunity (if "opportunity" is the right word) to pilot techniques that would later become standardized into media law.

Tape was nevertheless in short supply at Czechoslovak Radio in the postwar and early socialist years. This was not in small part because the Soviet Union had requisitioned a trainload of the stuff from the broadcaster at the end of the war.[94] One employee described the lack of tapes as "critical" in 1951, elaborating that "Czechoslovak Radio does not receive any quality tape from the West and only receives insufficient deliveries of bad tape (so called C-tape) from East Germany."[95] Czechoslovak manufacturers had set to work solving the problem, but their first fruits—magnetic tape and tape recorders from Optikotechna in Přerov—allegedly created such a din when switched on that the recordings they made were unusable.[96] Dreams of pre-recording everything, then, remained dreams throughout the early Communist period, and tape was only allocated to events deemed particularly important, such as the Horáková trial.

These shortages formed a constant of the early socialist period, with Czechoslovak Radio reporters implored to economize on tape well into the mid-1950s. In the shortage economy that was allegedly of Rudolf Slánský and co-defendants' making, a circular insisted to reporters that, while the delivery of new tapes was well assured, it was nevertheless important to remain "conscious that this is a material imported from abroad. By squandering it, we deprive our economy of hard currency."[97] Saving tape constituted part of a broader efficiency drive at Czechoslovak Radio with employees beseeched not to switch on too many lights and in which energy-guzzling electric heaters were prohibited from radio property.[98] Shortages and poor quality tape may start to explain why so little direct field recording was broadcast and so much was edited and revoiced in a studio. It does not, however, account for why the defendants' final speeches in the Horáková trial were not broadcast at all—this is frankly impossible to justify as a question of technical shortcomings.

Whether tape was used to broadcast from an event or not, the aesthetic outcomes of the tape age were far-reaching. As radio shifted its reporting norms to suit the tempo of the technology, a "slowing down of the passage of information to the listener" occurred.[99] As well as indicating what was said by defendants at the show trials, as some historians have used them to understand, tapes from proceedings thus can reveal a great deal about how events were framed, ordered, and conceptualized in the first place.[100]

The "rehearsed" nature of the entire proceedings, which has so often been taken as an element of the trial's horror, speaks as much to radio conventions of the late 1940s and early 1950s—East and West—as it does to the controlling hand of the trial's coordinators. Some listeners at the time likened the Horáková trial to "theatre."[101] But if the Horáková trial sounded theatrical, and hammy even in some parts, then this was in keeping with much else on the radio schedules at this moment, and by conscious design. At the first Czechoslovak statewide radio conference in January 1949, for example, Communist prime minister and erstwhile radio journalist Antonín Zápotocký had berated his former colleagues for "shoving the microphone beneath workers' noses" and expecting the latter to present their most articulate selves without any preparation.[102] In Zápotocký's view, preparation and scripting helped everyone—but in particular those without a formal radio training—present themselves in the most authentic way. This was particularly important as tape recorders began to grant new people in new venues their first experiences of being recorded. Simultaneously, the Ministry of Information's technical staff began to complain to reporters that the sound they were sending back from their field recordings sounded "unclean."[103] Historian Emily Thompson has called the blank, echo- and atmosphere-free audio background that these technicians so desired the "soundscape of modernity," which had become engrained in American radio reporting and the public ear by the 1930s.[104] Nearly two decades later during the time of the Czechoslovak show trials, politicians and radio professionals were likewise on the pursuit of "pure" sound, bearing as few markers of the time and location of its recording as possible. Such "imperfections" could be minimized by preparing the speaker to sound as polished as possible and controlling the surroundings in which the recording was made.

Listening to her husband's testimony in the Slánský trial on the radio, Rosemary Kavan noted that "there was something unnatural in his speech." It took a moment before she understood what was wrong, then it dawned on her: "he made his speech in written language . . . in the language of a newspaper's lead article."[105] This was a most unusual way to hear someone with whom one shared one's home speak, but it was far from unusual for radio voices at the time. Across the Iron Curtain in neighboring West Germany, Hans-Ulrich Wagner has pointed out that radio was understood by broadcasters and cultural functionaries to serve as a "language school" of sorts for listeners in which finessed, written forms of speech were championed well into the 1960s. "The public and radio programmers were skeptical about 'adventures into free discourse,'" he concludes, stressing that even programs that sought to provide a platform for listeners' voices were "dominated" by written correspondence, which was first "improved" by radio

76    Chapter 2

staff before being read out on air by professionally trained actors.[106] In the United Kingdom, Siobhan McHugh notes a similar phenomenon.[107] Wagner characterizes this polished, rehearsed, at times even slightly hammy style as "the sound of the fifties," which marked public broadcasters across West Germany.[108] It is this audibly rehearsed, and at times melodramatic, style that likewise marks the Horáková and the Slánský trials, which may seem unusual for a courtroom, but certainly did not sound out of place on Central European radio frequencies at the time.

The show trials were theatrical in the range of overarching literary tropes they employed. The prosecutors and witnesses, for example, explicitly suggested that they symbolized entire constituencies (and were thus invested with the moral authority of those constituencies) rather than speaking as mere individuals. Miner Vojtěch Břečka, brought on during the Horáková trial to testify against defendant Oldřich Pecl's conduct as a manager, claimed to speak on behalf of his profession, as well as for all workers who had struggled during the First Czechoslovak Republic (and, in so doing, perhaps echoed the solidarity-fostering function of the witnesses in the Frank trial).[109] Ludmila Brožová-Polednová was tasked with speaking for the prosecution on behalf of all women, epitomized in her concluding remarks when she asked the three female defendants—Milada Horáková, Antonie Kleinerová, and Františka Zemínová—for "women and mothers" everywhere, where had their hearts gone?[110] Procurator Juraj Vieska and judge Karol Bedrna brought the Slovak language to the proceedings, and thereby indicted and condemned the defendants on behalf of all Slovaks. If "all of the participants except the defendants rattled off their roles according to a script devised by the secret police in advance," then they did so according to criteria and generic conventions pioneered by radio staff.[111]

Two years later, Czechoslovakia's largest and final show trial, with former Communist Party first secretary Rudolf Slánský and thirteen other defendants, received "saturation radio coverage," making it much like the Horáková trial, and unlike the majority of "ordinary" trials which took place in Czechoslovakia at this period, whose content remained classified.[112] As in the case of Horáková and codefendants, prime-time favorite *The Radio Newsreel* was extended on nights that proceedings were covered.[113]

On the first evening, listeners were presented with the prosecution's opening remarks (delivered by Josef Urválek, a familiar voice from the

Horáková trial, where he had played a similar role). The defendants and their lawyers were then presented—a long and dry process left in the radio broadcast to serve as a form of opening credits, as well as to suggest that this was a trial which dutifully stuck to official protocol.

Czechoslovak Radio announcers played a markedly more hands-off role here than they had in the Horáková trial, but when they did interject, it was to brand the defendants "traitors and conspirators," just as they had then.[114] The three-and-a-half hours that followed were then given over to Slánský's testimony from earlier that day. Slánský was given the longest time in the dock of any of the radio trial defendants to testify. The ostensibly unedited presentation of his testimony, in a news program lengthened to accommodate it, served to underline that, as Melissa Feinberg states, "the real evidentiary basis of all show trials was the confession," rather than forensics, witnesses, or expert testimony.[115]

If trial planners had sought "to create a simple story with clear heroes and villains that corresponded neatly to the ideological sides of the Cold War," then it is not clear that listeners received it this way.[116] Instead of taking what they heard at face value, many embarked upon their own form of sleuthing, engaging with the trial by seeking clues in the defendants' tone and timbre. Slánský sounded tired and subdued, while codefendant Rudolf Margolius spoke in an "odd monotonous voice," according to his wife, Heda Margolius Kovály.[117] Rumors swirled that "'drugs,' 'pills,' 'injections,' 'narcotics' and 'chemicals' were responsible for [defendants'] abject performances."[118] No less than the head of the CIA, Allen Dulles, engaged in this pursuit, wondering in a Princeton speech whether a "lie serum" was responsible for the sound of Slánský and Clementis's recent confessions.[119] Such speculation, rife in Czechoslovakia, did not constitute anti-Communist "resistance," historian Kevin McDermott rightly notes, but did indicate "that the 'regime had lost the capacity to control the manner in which many of its subjects perceived . . . affairs.' "[120]

The resignation and exhaustion in Slánský and other defendants' tone contrasted strikingly with the vigor and the energy of their cross-examiners. This contrast was perhaps not unwelcome to those preparing the trial for radio broadcast, as it pitted the exhaustion of the old guard audibly against the energy and zeal of socialist Czechoslovakia's current caretakers. But, in fact, not every defendant did sound so very monotonous. Here, witness

Marie Švermová sounded audibly upset.[121] And previously, in the Horáková trial broadcasts, defendant Jiří Hejda had sounded positively chipper, forcefully and emotively countering some of the charges levied against him by prosecutors (though not, notably, the main indictments of espionage and treason).[122] Also in that trial, defendant Františka Zemínová had sounded both spirited and perturbed when faced with the charges laid against her.[123] If the robotic quality of some of the show trials' testimony has been stressed, then such passionate-sounding radio speech becomes, and perhaps sounded at the time, all the more remarkable.

Following Slánský's confession, a number of witnesses were presented to the audience of *The Radio Newsreel*, including Jaromír Kopecký, whom listeners may have recalled playing an identical role indicting Horáková. Czechoslovak Radio's announcer interrupted this testimony more often, at times paraphrasing outright what a witness had said. Unlike the Frank trial, the Slánský coverage clearly did not set out to foster identification with witnesses who had allegedly suffered as a result of the defendants' crimes. Witness testimony may not have proved as effective an indictment of Slánský as the international, antistate networks he allegedly belonged to that the announcer sketched for listeners.

The Slánský trial has rightly been described by historians as egregiously anti-Semitic. Slánský was a Czechoslovak citizen "of Jewish origin," as prosecutors underscored time and time again. Ten of the other defendants also had Jewish backgrounds. Slánský and codefendants stood accused of collaborating with a cabal of American Jewish bankers, Jewish aid organizations such as HIAS and the Joint Committee, and the state of Israel to undermine the nascent Czechoslovak "people's democracy," their loyalties instead leading them to seek rapprochement with the capitalist West. The anti-Semitic tone of the trial broadcasts was established by the Czechoslovak Radio announcer from the very first day of proceedings, when he introduced one witness and only one witness, the Israeli citizen Mordechai Oren, by commenting on his appearance (dubbing him "little" and "an Apache").[124] Singling those not recognized as nationally Czech out for such description served—as it had when native German speakers were introduced at the Frank trial—to underscore their peculiarity to listeners and mark them out as physiologically different.[125]

Day two began with former Communist functionary and Czechoslovak

Radio foreign service head Bedřich Geminder taking the stand. A transcript made of the radio broadcast by Western analysts noted that his testimony was presented: "Only in recorded extracts, linked by a few words by the radio commentator. Geminder spoke with a strong German accent and was at times difficult to understand. The Court apparently suffered from the same difficulty and the Presiding Judge had to ask Geminder several times to speak into the microphone."[126] Geminder's testimony has been presented in literary depictions of the trial as the moment when the anti-Semitism of the court was laid bare. In *The Confession*, written by defendant Artur London upon his release from jail and emigration to France, Geminder was harangued by the judge, who asked repeatedly whether he needed a translator in order to complete his cross-examination.[127] The radio framing of Geminder's cross-examination was certainly anti-Semitic, with the announcer introducing the defendant as "deracinated" and Geminder then referring to himself as a "cosmopolitan."[128] But Czechoslovak Radio appears to have avoided any overt questioning of their former employee Geminder's language skills, editing out any such back-and-forth with the judge. What followed was an accented, but carefully articulated deposition, with Geminder reminded of the technical set-up, rather than of his nominally humane but in fact deeply stigmatizing right to an interpreter, when his account became hard to hear.[129]

Nevertheless, the framing of native-German-speaker Geminder's testimony may have inflamed listener prejudices. The anti-Semitic language of the Slánský trial did have a broader social resonance: some of Czechoslovakia's Jewish citizens expressed concern for their own safety at the time of the trial's airing.[130] The Czechoslovak secret police, moreover, detected a spike in anti-Jewish sentiment statewide in the trial's wake.[131] Certainly, Paul Barton has argued that the Slánský trial set out to mobilize anti-German attitudes that had been stoked during the Third Republic, not least through radio trials such as Frank's.[132] The anti-Semitism of the Slánský trial was supposed to build upon such anti-German sentiment (with Jews represented, in particular in Geminder's case, as bearers of the German language and German culture in Czechoslovakia). As Michal Frankl has noted, a perceived lack of Czech-language proficiency had in fact served as an incriminating factor in even earlier legal trials—as far back as in the interwar First Czechoslovak Republic.[133] In a concerted drive to "de-Germanize" the radio, voices such as Geminder's which indicated that Czech was the speaker's second language were largely banished from Czechoslovak Radio in the postwar years, and therefore sounded increasingly remarkable when they were to be heard.[134]

While certainly contributing to the anti-Semitic nature of the trial, official instructions to Geminder to speak clearly served, perhaps above all, as a reminder that the audience was not primarily those assembled within earshot. The treatment of other defendants underscores this point. In fact, it was Vavro Hajdu who appeared to have the most difficulty delivering his testimony. He was ordered most frequently to speak into the microphone, an exhortation which carried no comment on the level of his native Slovak.[135] Such appeals demonstrate how, as Melissa Feinberg has argued, "once the proceedings had begun, the most important interaction was not between the state and the defendants, but between the state and the audience, the people who listened to the trial on the radio or read about it in the newspaper."[136]

Historians agree that the Soviet Union played a key role in the trial. Paul Barton deemed it the "director" of proceedings, reasoning that many messages conveyed by the trial were in fact to be understood overseas. For example, it heralded a shifting Eastern Bloc foreign policy towards the Middle East, with the Soviet Union announcing an abandonment of attempts to ally with the state of Israel, as the latter shifted closer to the United States. Furthermore, the trial served to discredit the members of the interwar International Brigades—incriminating in the process functionaries in neighboring countries, which would surely have led to a diplomatic spat if it were not for the Soviet Union's supervision.[137] Others have rightly noted the formative presence of Soviet "advisors" in the Slánský trial's organization, which ensured a harmonization of the Czechoslovak and other regional judicial systems, leading to "a consistent set of messages [being conveyed by the show trials] no matter their country of origin."[138]

But if the Soviet Union were the director of these show trials, then Czechoslovak Radio set the scene. Soviet state radio did not, for example, provide the media platform to unveil and resolve the contemporaneous "Doctor's Plot"—a campaign overseen by Josef Stalin targeting a number of predominantly Jewish physicians whom, he believed, were trying to kill top Soviet officials. Direct Soviet radio templates, then, were unavailable for import, unlike investigation methods, which most certainly were. The impetus to promote the Horáková and Slánský proceedings on the radio, and the experience of working with trial genres on this medium in the past, belonged to a preestablished Czechoslovak media culture.

The show trials did carry specifically Czechoslovak messages too, and there were winners and losers at the domestic level. The Horáková trial set out to discredit non-Communist politicians associated with Czechoslovakia's traditional left-wing parties. The Slánský trial suggested that former president Eduard Beneš was no longer to be discussed with the respect that had traditionally been afforded those who had occupied this post. And Marián Lóži has argued that the Slánský trials furthermore targeted a particular "charismatic" sort of Communist leader embodied by another defendant Otto Šling, who had amassed great power at the regional level.[139]

Far from having such proceedings foisted upon it, state broadcaster Czechoslovak Radio dedicated some of its biggest names (like interwar celebrity Josef Cincibus and František Gel) and finest time slots to the coverage of a genre with which it was by now quite at home.[140] Harnessing its best technical equipment which, as complaints from within the radio make clear, was in critically short supply, the radio mobilized its resources to make these trials radiogenic, thus striving to maintain the institution's relevance in the changing political conditions of the early socialist Czechoslovak state.

Audio of court proceedings was not the only means by which Czechoslovak Radio sought to raise awareness of the trials. The broadcaster, in addition, aired workers' resolutions related to the trials and reported on their content and social fallout in programming and features beyond *The Radio Newsreel*. One of the remaining tapes of the Slánský trial coverage, for example, contains a male and female announcer discussing workers' responses to the revelations that their station was broadcasting. Workers at the Koh-i-Noor factory in České Budějovice—mentioned previously in proceedings as a site of sabotage and mismanagement—held a meeting in the wake of such revelations to pledge that they would meet their plan targets regardless. One sawmill worker, Antonín Trojan, apparently visited the Czechoslovak Radio building in Prague in person to deliver a letter on behalf of his colleagues at Středočeské pily articulating the same desire. A recording was then played of a scientist, Eduard Bělík, talking about how the defendants had sabotaged penicillin production. Such programming added the testimony of lay workers, outside of the formal court setting, to the charge sheet against Slánský and codefendants.[141] It also suggested that the fallout caused by the defendants' nefarious deeds ran deep into the lives of everyday listeners, and therefore mattered to more than a limited group of legal experts and exemplary workers assembled daily in the court.

But while insisting that the government's and Czechoslovak workers' goals essentially aligned, coverage of the Slánský trial made the gulf between party elites and those they claimed to represent more apparent. The trials exposed the Communist Party to scrutiny from below.[142] Miners in Blovice, south of Plzeň, for example, met the trial broadcasts with consternation, asking who had been lying to them and who was telling the truth. When a Communist Party representative came to address their concerns, it was alleged, they threw him out of the pub.[143] Citizens voiced their shock that senior apparatchiks could have allowed such evildoing to take place for so long, directly under their noses, in the very institutions that they ran. Whether such complaints constituted a cleverly calibrated means of using official language to criticize authorities or genuine shock at the carelessness of the Communist ministers still in power, they underscored the distance between the lay listener and Communist Party officials' behavior in the wake of these allegations.

Responses to the trial were "more diversified" and "critical views were more frequent," claims historian Kevin McDermott, than media coverage suggested at the time of Slánský's condemnation.[144] Within a single community, as a woman quizzed by RFE astutely noted, attitudes to the broadcasts could be mixed. In Liberec, Communist Party members were allegedly happy that a "traitor" was being punished, while anti-Communists, meanwhile, were displeased that a plot to damage the existing government had been foiled. Members of the city's Jewish community were perturbed by the anti-Semitic language granted an airing at the trial.[145] State media and government officials succeeded at stimulating "extensive popular" interest in the Slánský trial.[146] But the interest sparked did not always stick to an official script and led upon occasion, in fact, to Communist ministers taking to the airwaves to engage in damage control.

Rumors about those implicated in the trial swirled at the time of its airing and immediately in its aftermath, suggesting that officials and radio broadcasters did not have a stranglehold on the narrative of proceedings. There was speculation that two protagonists, Rudolf Slánský and Bedřich Geminder, had, in fact, escaped execution and were instead receiving privileged treatment in prison.[147] Others suggested that Slánský's wife had subsequently been arrested in connection with her husband's case.[148] Still others apparently saw one of the defendants roaming the streets of Prague freely after his conviction.[149] Such speculation betrays the lack of satisfaction with official media accounts of the trial and its conclusion.

Furthermore, Communist officials feared that the anti-Semitism stoked by the trial was escaping their control. Having planted many of the seeds of this interpretation themselves, functionaries then followed increasingly violent rhetoric from some Czech and Slovak citizens with consternation. A party memorandum on the trial's reception among Prague workers concluded, notes Kevin McDermott, "that the 'race question' was so acute that it demanded immediate political intervention in order to avoid 'race hatred.'"[150] The form that this "political intervention" took is housed in the Czech Radio archive today. In one instance, Culture and Education Minister Zdeněk Nejedlý used his regular Sunday morning broadcast to refute that the trials were anti-Semitic in nature, as Western media charged.[151] Radio Free Europe certainly did make such claims about the Slánský trial, which rankled ministers such as Nejedlý, but we can understand Nejedlý using RFE here as a foil in order to "correct" popular attitudes closer to home. In this broadcast he insisted that the Slánský trial made Czechoslovakia's anti-Zionist stance abundantly clear, while in no way indicating a lack of acceptance of Jews per se.[152]

Not all of the credit for promoting the trials went to Czechoslovak Radio, as Zdeněk Nejedlý rightly pointed out. RFE simultaneously dedicated extensive coverage to the trials, and announcers in Hungarian and German can be heard discussing Slánský in the interference picked up on the tapes examined here.[153] Czech and Slovak listeners did not confine themselves to radio stations broadcasting in their mother tongues for information, even in the Stalinist period, as chapter 5 shows. And, of course, Czechoslovak print media carried trial developments on their front pages every day, varying in their emphasis, tone, and wording. But in their invectives about the wrong interpretations of the trials, often aired on Czechoslovak Radio's frequencies, government ministers like Nejedlý and Václav Kopecký appear to have

84   Chapter 2

identified radio as both the problem and the solution to questions raised through the trial coverage.[154]

Czechoslovak Radio rode the wave of popular interest in the show trials. But while they shaped some of the ways in which proceedings were discussed, radio staff and government officials could not always keep control of these broadcasts' interpretation. This was not least because the further roll-out of radio infrastructure in Communist Czechoslovakia was simultaneously generating new, increasingly varied, modes of listening. A comparison of the extant radio footage and its reception has shown that the increasing effort to provide an approved reading of proceedings was not accompanied by a broader social consensus on these trials. Instead, it provided the material supporting rumors about the treatment and fate of defendants, a basis on which to critique the regime for its lack of vigilance at a key moment for socialism's construction, and fodder for "race hatred," directed by some Czechoslovak listeners towards Jews.

## Conclusion

In a Princeton speech in April 1953, CIA head Allen Dulles captured the crucial role played by sound media in shaping the formulation and subsequent understandings of Central and Eastern Europe's show trials. Explaining Slánský and codefendants' "brainwashing," Dulles described how "the brain under these circumstances becomes a phonograph playing a disc put on its spindle by an outside genius over which it has no control."[155] Dulles identified the phonograph as the technology best placed to describe defendants' psychological preparation for the trial, while I have argued that the reel of tape was firmly in the minds of radio staff planning these trials' temporal and spatial framing, shaping much of their subsequent sound, and even aspects of their reception.

Conversely, a focus on these trials can tell us much of shifting practices of radio broadcasting and listening in Czechoslovakia during Stalinism. As radio events structured around tape recordings, the Horáková and Slánský trials broke with their predecessors, which had derived their legitimacy from their broadcast location and live relay. No longer did reporters such as Oplt have to apologize to listeners for the lulls and long silences that live trial broadcasts produced. Technologies are not politically neutral. Nevertheless, the aesthetics of the tape age which increasingly came to mark these trials—culminating in Slánský's—were certainly far from Communist, inflecting sound recording and radio broadcasting on both sides of the Iron Curtain, and more globally, at this particular moment. While scholars have focused on the ways that sound media were employed to stifle trial defendants, radio staff, and audiences, I have argued here that some of the broadcast changes that the show trials showcased were conceived instead to create a better listening experience. The Slánský trial represented the peak of the individual confession's incriminatory power, but the overall significance of proceedings derived from the way that this confession was cut, presented, and framed as part of a much larger patchwork of conspiracy. These enormously complex proceedings were offered a sense of order by the triumvirate of tape, scissors, and glue wielded by the "radio expert," rather than any "outside genius" police interrogator changing the record in Slánský, or Clementis's, or Cardinal Mindszenty's psyche.[156]

To focus upon what went on behind the scenes of Stalinist justice is to miss the crucial role—if limited agency—of the radio professionals who worked to turn these trials into "shows." By recognizing radio staff's input, our understanding of the show trials changes in several important ways. Firstly, if Stalinist justice had already been reshaped under the tutelage of Soviet advisors by the time that Horáková and Slánský came to trial, then Stalinist media had not. Czechoslovak Radio was only to be restructured according to the Soviet model as the Slánský trial climaxed in 1952. A focus on the trials' dissemination, therefore, underscores the active and decisive role played by Czechs and Slovaks themselves. Their media presentation—and the way they were received—was, in turn, built upon earlier Czechoslovak radio coverage of trials predating the Communist era: if the technical set-up relaying trials to audiences was new, then some of the derogatory language, dog-whistling, and strategies to other those implicated in proceedings were not. Such conclusions underscore Muriel Blaive's findings that "genuine Soviet responsibility" for aspects of Czechoslovakia's political history during the Stalinist period "does not [abnegate] the involvement of Czechoslovak elites—nor of the population."[157] By understanding these broadcasts as a mix of different impulses, we in fact get a better picture of Stalinism in Czechoslovakia between 1948 and 1953, which was itself an amalgam of Soviet influences, local traditions, and pan-European modernizing trends.

By focusing on the editing, presentation, and dissemination of these

86    Chapter 2

proceedings, furthermore, a clearer picture of how such trials sought audience approval has emerged. Listeners were actively asked to engage by trial announcers, with some of these strategies seeming to work more or less on broadcasters' own terms, while others quickly evaded control. Czechoslovak Radio succeeded in stimulating listeners' interest in the trials, but the broadcaster enjoyed far less success creating cohesion around a single, orthodox interpretation of proceedings. This "failure" has left its own trail of tape, with speeches by Communist functionaries such as Zdeněk Nejedlý attempting to correct misconceptions filed in the Czech Radio archive alongside the depositions of Slánský and others. By reconstructing state radio's limited ability to impose an orthodox interpretation of such high-profile media events, this chapter has underscored the diversity of listening attitudes, techniques, and approaches to media which continued to exist, and which were indeed generated through the expansion of radio listening venues, during Czechoslovak Stalinism.

If the show trials constituted, in some ways, "conventional" radio following the Communist takeover, then radio broadcasting at the period cannot, however, be reduced solely to them. Sharing the nightly news with the foreign plots they unveiled were dispatches from Czechs and Slovaks promoting their state overseas. These tremendously popular radio travelogues constituted the flipside of the isolationist and xenophobic messaging that crescendoed in the show trials; both were attempts to harness radio to define Czechoslovakia's role in a shifting postwar order. It is to these overseas dispatches and the stars that they created that this book now turns.

# 3   When Travelogues Became News

*The Africa Reporting of František Foit,*
*Jiří Hanzelka, and Miroslav Zikmund, 1947–1952*

**BANGUI, ON JULY 6,** 1948, and František Foit was having car trouble. Foit was finding it difficult to source spare parts for the Czechoslovak-made Tatra he was showcasing on a year-long tour around Africa.[1] In Central Africa, he was running out of cash and, worse, Czechoslovak Radio was broadcasting none of the materials he was sending them from abroad. His correspondent at the Czech Ministry of Information, Bohuslav Horák (the husband of Milada Horáková), assured him that things could only get better:

> Unfortunately, extensive coverage of the *slet* [a patriotic, large-scale gymnastics event] and the current holiday period mean that no report about your trip has yet been made. The radio is still broadcasting Hanzelka and Zikmund's reports, although the pair left Africa long ago and are now traveling to Brazil. Their last letter from Cape Town I received was dated June 20, 1948. And so I don't expect any report about your expedition to be realized on Czechoslovak Radio before September.[2]

Things did not improve. In January 1949, Horák wrote to Foit in Irumu, Congo, apprising him of staff changes at the Ministry and apologizing for "the continued difficulties with the radio. Not nearly as much of your material is being used as we would have expected. We will talk to them again."[3] Foit's voice remained absent from the air.

FIGURE 6. Article from *L'Alger Républicain* about František "François" Foit's second African tour. Foit is described as a passionate and experienced student of the continent. His Tatra car (in front of which he and his wife, Irena, pose) is praised as the "triumph of Czechoslovakia's [postwar] industrial reconstruction." Source: NA CR box 63. Ministerstvo Informací, 1945-1953. Doc. 60403, dated January 16, 1948. "Konsulát ČSR v Alžíru zasílá ČRSS výstřižek z deníku 'Alger Républicain.'" Reprinted with permission.

This was not František Foit's first tour of the African continent. As Sarah Lemmen has pointed out, Foit belonged squarely to a group of middle-class Czech men who had traveled beyond Europe during the interwar period on a mission to boost Czechoslovak trade and simultaneously prove the wonders of Czechoslovak science.[4] Postwar journeys such as Foit's built upon an interwar tradition that stemmed from Czechoslovakia's need, "as a newly created state, . . . to develop trading partners as markets for its manufactured products and as a source for raw materials in order to grow its export-oriented economy."[5] In receiving a second round of Ministry of Information funding in 1947 to foster Czechoslovak-African relations yet further, the sculptor František Foit was representative of what film scholar Alice Lovejoy has called "the persistence, in the first half-decade after the war, of political and aesthetic projects of the 1930s."[6] He would also become representative of such projects' failure.

In a journey from Cairo to Cape Town undertaken in 1932, Foit had paired with the zoologist Jiří Baum in a Czechoslovak Tatra car. This second time around there was competition. Crisscrossing the continent, the gentleman-adventurer and his wife, Irena, were competing with two younger explorers, also sponsored by the Czechoslovak firm Tatra and also documenting their travels of Africa for Czech and Slovak audiences. Unlike Foit, this pair had plans to continue on to South and North America on what was "above all, a business trip" to sell Czechoslovak products which began in 1947.[7]

Foit's rivals, Jiří Hanzelka and Miroslav Zikmund, became famous almost overnight. Their travel reports, which spanned from before the Communist takeover in 1947 until the height of Stalinism in 1952, "belonged to the most listened-to programs on the radio. The broadcasts . . . numbered more than 700 in total and familiarized the listener with 48 countries."[8] Jiřina Šmejkalová explains the pair's meteoric rise as a case of "command celebrity."[9] By this, she indicates that Hanzelka and Zikmund became famous as a result of their powerful patrons, most notably Information Minister Václav Kopecký. Media histories of this period indeed often characterize the relationship between the Communist-run Ministry of Information and Czechoslovak Radio as one of "command," in which the former issued orders to which the latter slavishly adhered.[10] But the case of Foit, Hanzelka, and Zikmund challenges this view: Ministry of Information files show that the luckless František Foit received exactly the same level of state support as Jiří Hanzelka and Miroslav Zikmund. Yet while Foit could not get his reports aired, reflections from Hanzelka and Zikmund's travels were "broadcast without interruption over a five-year period."[11] The difference between these explorer-journalists was not, then, in the top-down government support they received; it lay instead in their dealings with state-broadcaster Czechoslovak Radio.

Born in 1920 and 1919 respectively, Jiří Hanzelka and Miroslav Zikmund belonged to a generation of new recruits at Czechoslovak Radio immediately following the Second World War. Their contemporary, reporter Věra Šťovíčková, reflected that a cult of youth reigned at the broadcaster after the

90    Chapter 3

war and that her biggest advantage when she started there was her lack of a past and dearth of "experience from the First Republic." She and her peers "only knew the war and the occupation," which suited her employers well.[12] Czechoslovak Radio had propounded the idea that it had initiated a "revolution" in Czechoslovakia in May 1945. While Czechs and Slovaks mentioned the similarities in personnel and sound of the broadcaster in letters and listener polling, Czechoslovak Radio adamantly insisted that all had changed. If the radio helped Hanzelka and Zikmund rise to prominence by addressing millions of listeners, then it can equally be said that the duo helped the broadcaster make a clean break with its dubious wartime past.

The Communist takeover in February 1948 only ever partially affected the pair's radio work. In letters to their editor at the time of the takeover, they repeatedly voiced their ignorance as to the nature of the change that had taken place.[13] They insisted that Czechoslovak Radio broadcast their backlog of reports and specified, in July 1948, that they expected the radio to air their Kilimanjaro dispatches (written before the takeover at the start of that year) exactly as they had been composed.[14] Following a brief interruption at the time of the takeover itself, Czechoslovak Radio did resume the broadcast of Hanzelka and Zikmund's reports in their original form. The pair later reflected that their first experiences of battling with censors only came in the process of writing their books, after the radio had finished broadcasting their travel reports.[15] Moreover, Miroslav Zikmund explained, the pair's nascent celebrity granted them the "privilege" to broadcast "what others would not dare."[16] Their case reinforces the last chapter's findings that censorship at Czechoslovak Radio worked somewhat loosely at least until its institutionalization at the end of the Stalinist period.

Hanzelka and Zikmund's travelogues occupied the same wavelengths and schedules as the anti-Semitic and xenophobic show trials of Rudolf Slánský and Dutch national Johannes Louwers. They shared a prime-time billing with invectives against emigration by government ministers like Václav Kopecký and the Culture and Education Minister Zdeněk Nejedlý. Hanzelka and Zikmund's travelogues constituted the flipside of such isolationist and xenophobic broadcasting; both were attempts to harness radio to define Czechoslovakia's role in a shifting postwar order. While historians (and chapter 2 of this book) have foregrounded the former type of programming, Hanzelka and Zikmund's sensationally popular dispatches bringing the world into the Czechoslovak living room have, until now, gone largely unacknowledged.[17] Their analysis challenges the idea of a closed East as opposed to an open West in the first years of the Cold War.

This chapter first spotlights the business remit of Foit, Hanzelka, and Zikmund's travels, stressing that there was nothing deemed contradictory about representatives of socialism advertising their state's products overseas. Examining in particular how the three men wrote about their Tatra cars, this section explores further the men's relationships to the Czechoslovak technologies that they sold and to the potential foreign buyers of these technologies. It then turns to how Hanzelka and Zikmund established themselves as celebrities—something that the middle-aged Foit, struggling to reach mass audiences over the radio, could only have dreamed of. If thousands of listeners gushed in fan mail that they wanted to be, or be with, Hanzelka and Zikmund, then Czechoslovakia's novice Communist ministers also identified with the pair. The duo's example, then, reveals radio in Stalinist Czechoslovakia to have been a medium that seduced apparatchiks and "ordinary" listeners alike, rather than a tool used by powerful ministers to seduce and thus disarm a listening public.

I next turn to the content of Hanzelka and Zikmund's reports. By considering how they reworked the generic conventions of travel writing so as to fit in with the nightly radio news, I show how they made ideas and values that dated from the interwar, bourgeois First Czechoslovak Republic palatable and relevant for the altered conditions of socialism. This was something that František Foit—the inspiration for so many of Hanzelka and Zikmund's reports—himself struggled to do. The games that Hanzelka and Zikmund played with different media and types of writing, furthermore, make clear the room there was for playfulness on the state broadcaster's frequencies during Stalinism. Lastly, I reconstruct the picture of Czechoslovakia's global reach with which the pair flattered listeners, and which provided a counterpoint to broadcasts excoriating Czechs' and Slovaks' contemporaneous decisions to speak with foreigners or migrate overseas.

### Traveling Salesmen of Czechoslovakia and Its Wares

Foit, Hanzelka, and Zikmund set off on government-supported missions to foster Czechoslovak trade relations in what is today termed the Global South. Using radio reporters to establish trading contacts in Africa in 1947

92   Chapter 3

was "particularly desirable," Ministry of Information officials reasoned, as "German links with Africa disrupted by the war have not yet been resumed."[18] Their thinking had interwar precedents: as Sarah Lemmen has noted, Czechoslovak politicians had pondered how to take over German trading links (and maybe even inherit former German colonies) following the First World War.[19] Hanzelka and Zikmund themselves understood and wrote about their journey in business terms. In addition to their radio work, the pair published a weekly double-page spread in the magazine *Svět práce* (*The World of Work*), "an economic weekly," akin, Zikmund later explained, to *Hospodářské noviny*—the present-day Czech equivalent of *The Financial Times*.[20]

In their focus upon trade, Foit, Hanzelka, and Zikmund represented Czechoslovak attitudes towards the African continent in the immediate postwar years. Czechoslovakia had long sought to develop "markets for its manufactured products and . . . source[s] for raw materials."[21] This form of economically driven diplomacy was expanded following the end of the Second World War, with Hanzelka and Zikmund dispatched alongside Foit by Czechoslovak officials in 1947 to foster trading relationships.[22] That economic relations between Czechoslovakia and African states were significant in volume at the time of the Communist takeover is stressed by Philip Muehlenbeck who finds that, after it took place the following year, "85 percent of all Soviet bloc exports to Africa were from Czechoslovakia."[23] He argues that the takeover initially had little effect on such links, "as inertia kept Prague's diplomatic, consular, and economic relations intact."[24] Accordingly, Hanzelka and Zikmund's route did not change on account of the takeover—in fact it followed the interwar journey made by František Foit on his first trip.

The pair spent a considerable amount of time in Egypt—a key prewar trading partner of Czechoslovakia, although in the immediate postwar period relations were strained.[25] From there, they traveled through Sudan (then under British control) and into Ethiopia, where they met Emperor Haile Selassie and where "shortly after the end of World War II, Czechoslovakia began to aggressively market its industrial products . . . and in the late 1940s . . . arms manufacturer Považské strojírny opened an ammunition factory."[26] If the Czechoslovak-made cars and tires they used on their journey were the industrial products they foregrounded in their reports, then the men also advertised, rather more discreetly, the weapons which made Czechoslovakia the world's seventh-biggest arms exporter upon its establishment in 1918.[27]

Hanzelka and Zikmund finally changed course at the same moment the Czechoslovak government did—in 1950. The pair were denied visas to continue their travels from Latin America into the United States. As the Cold War finally caught up with their route, they returned to Czechoslovakia. At this same moment, claims Muehlenbeck, the Communist Party of Czechoslovakia began to "follow Moscow's Stalinist line of insular foreign relations."[28] Hanzelka and Zikmund spent the next two years broadcasting details of their trip—filling the Czechoslovak airwaves with tales of distant lands for almost the entire Stalinist period.[29] Their example underscores that socialist internationalist ideas found media sponsorship and were widely audible in the Eastern Bloc before the Khrushchev era, which is frequently taken as the starting point by historians of Cold War Second-Third World relations.

The promotion of Czechoslovak trade on the African continent undertaken by the three men signals the Communist Party's outward-looking perspective in its first years in power. The new regime actively helped the travelers, relaying their letters home, for example, in the Czechoslovak diplomatic post bag. The cash-strapped explorers additionally stayed in embassy accommodation where it was available.[30] While the three travelers certainly provided information to Czechoslovak authorities, it would be wrong to categorize them as stooges of the Czechoslovak secret police. As Molly Pucci has deftly shown, in the years leading up to and immediately following the Communist takeover, the Czechoslovak police were attempting to fix an institutional line and rid themselves of personnel not deemed "revolutionary" enough.[31] In other words, the secret police were occupied first and foremost with matters closer to home. The sorts of standardized practices implemented to garner information from those traveling abroad which we will encounter in future chapters were yet to be developed. Foit, Hanzelka, and Zikmund did not so much slip the net as point to the fact that the net was not yet there to slip.

Through letters to ministers and discussions with diplomatic officials, Foit, Hanzelka, and Zikmund nevertheless did shape ministerial outlooks on the places they traveled. Czechoslovak foreign policy, Linda Piknerová

94   Chapter 3

rightly concludes, "was established parallel to these adventurous expeditions."[32] One decade later, in a meeting with their Soviet counterparts, Foreign Ministry officials vaunted Hanzelka and Zikmund as an outstanding source of Czechoslovak expertise on Africa and living proof of their country's historic engagement with the continent.[33]

The tone of Hanzelka and Zikmund's 700+ radio reports was relentlessly optimistic about technology. Using their Tatra car, they expounded their views on technology more generally. The duo achieved a delicate balance between elevating the vehicle as a brilliant example of Czechoslovak industrial production, while initially cultivating doubts that their Tatra could successfully get them through their adventures.

In fact, the way that Hanzelka and Zikmund structured their journey—and much of their writing—around their car owed a great deal to Foit, who had in the interwar period come up with the idea of gaining corporate Tatra sponsorship to underwrite his journey around Africa with natural scientist Jiří Baum. As Sarah Lemmen points out, Foit and Baum had sought to prove that a normal Czechoslovak car was capable of succeeding at a journey which usually only specially customized French cars were used to undertake.[34] In addition to providing them with transportation, Foit and Baum had niftily converted their car into lodgings and had even created a darkroom in their Tatra, in which they developed thousands of images from their trip. Visual artist Foit described and indeed included images of these transformations in his diary from his first trip, *Autem napříč Afrikou (Across Africa by Car).*[35]

Hanzelka and Zikmund copied Foit in gaining sponsorship from the firm Tatra. Such sponsorship was facilitated by Jiří Hanzelka's father, who worked at the firm.[36] These family connections were not played up in reports, unlike, of course, the Tatra car itself. Some listeners found the way Hanzelka and Zikmund foregrounded their vehicle gimmicky. Audience members in Moravia advised the pair, "you would save at least two minutes if they didn't open your news with a caricature of your car honking, natives drumming and you revving your engine, and if they didn't end it in the same needless way."[37] These fans complained that the pair were not given enough time on the air and argued that such cheesy sound effects had to go. Meanwhile Mrs. L. Stříšková was happy that they did not; she listened with her twelve-year-old daughter in "suspense" to the pair's reports, while "even my seven-year-old boy gives us at least a moment of peace when he hears the

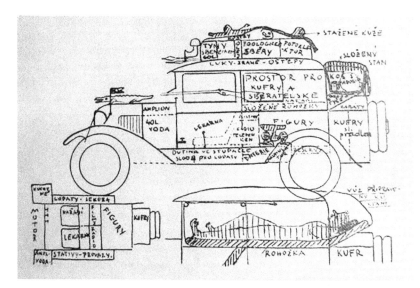

**FIGURE 7.** Foit's sketches of how he and Jiří Baum customized their car. Source: František Foit, *Autem napříč Afrikou: deník jedinečné cesty z Prahy do Kapského města, díl 1* (Prague: Self-published, 1932), 7.

sound of your car."[38] Střišková thus suggested that the car sounds were a large part of the appeal of their broadcasts for her young son.

Hanzelka and Zikmund likewise foregrounded their Tatra in their first film, which opened with shots of the pair touring the nationalized Tatra car factory. Extensive footage of Hanzelka and Zikmund peering over the shoulders of workers assembling their vehicle followed, alongside the assertion that the travelers had to see how it was made in order to use it to travel the world. As it had in the case of earlier travelers Foit and Baum, the Tatra here represented Czechoslovak science and industry and, as Sarah Lemmen relates, "the superiority of Czech products, which could compete ... on the world market" with Renault, or Mercedes, or Jaguar.[39] Hanzelka and Zikmund repeatedly suggested that their car turned heads: Czechoslovak automobiles were envied by the people they met around the world. But not only were Hanzelka and Zikmund promoting Czechoslovak industry through their Tatra; they were now promoting a mode of *nationalized* industrial production in which a centralizing state was responsible for such scientific and technological achievements.

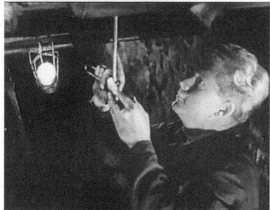

**FIGURES 8, 9, AND 10.** Stills from the film *Africa, Part I* in which Hanzelka and Zikmund visit "national enterprise Tatra" to learn how their vehicle is assembled "down to the last screw." The pair also apprenticed in a repair shop, because they would "not be able to rely on foreign help" to fix their vehicle during their travels. Source: Jiří Hanzelka, Miroslav Zikmund, and Jaroslav Novotný, *Afrika I. Část – Z Maroka na Kilimandžaro* (1952).

Yet the functioning of their Tatra constituted a source of tension in their reports. This is most apparent in a series of five broadcasts in which Hanzelka and Zikmund drove their way across the Nubian Desert.[40] The pair never downplayed the capabilities of their car but did build in doubt whether they would be able to make it. They tired themselves out constantly having to dig their car out of the sand and repeatedly found that their chosen through-route was impossible because of rock formations they had failed to spot in time. To heighten the suspense, they serialized their four-day journey across the desert. The pair divided the narrative into four parts, broadcast over two weeks. Each report began with an itinerary, a series of plans and distances for the day, and in the first three reports, the plot largely turned on how such plans went awry. In each instance, the pair almost cultivated hubris, suggesting their intention to achieve a particular goal that each time, to dramatic effect, came undone.

Hanzelka, Zikmund, and Foit set out to show how Czechoslovak science and technology could conquer Africa; Foit did so in his postwar reports using rather more outmoded terms. In an article titled "The Little Silver Tatra among the Wild Babinga," Foit described using his car to rush to the aid of a group of Congolese villagers, who marveled at the "bottles, boxes and tubes" he carried in a first-aid kit onboard.[41] Foit and his wife Irena then proceeded to debunk witchcraft by administering two pills to an ailing village chief (whom they addressed using the informal or childish *ty*).[42] In this scene, medicinal practices and village hierarchies were dismissed and denigrated by the presence of Czechoslovaks in a state-of-the-art vehicle wielding cures. Czechoslovak medicine was thus introduced and overwrote its local equivalents.

Foit then used his vehicle to abduct a "dwarf" whom he sought as a model for one of his sculptures. When this man entered his Tatra, Foit used racialized stereotypes to play for laughs. Employing a well-worn literary cliché, he stressed the fear his model felt at the prospect of the car (presented as a point of ridicule here for the Czechoslovak listener). In a slapstick scene, Foit described the way his chosen model entered the vehicle "on all fours, like a monkey."[43] Foit then recounted how he closed the car window so that the terrified passenger could not jump out, seemingly negating any evidence of consent involved in the exchange.

Foit strove for comic effect at the expense of the Africans he met, using already deeply cliched notions of their fear of technology and "animal-like"

98   Chapter 3

nature. Relying as they did on assumptions of racial hierarchies that Foit had employed in his interwar writings, but which had since been widely discredited, or at least rendered taboo, through their association with Nazism during the Second World War, Foit's reports were never broadcast.[44] While Hanzelka and Zikmund suggested that black Africans could constitute a potential market for Czechoslovak goods, Foit's reports, on the contrary, cast black Africans as foils to which he could contrast the modernity of Czechoslovak industrial production.

By stressing their own limitations and the limits of the technology that they used, Hanzelka and Zikmund masterfully cultivated drama and suspense in their reports. By insisting upon racial hierarchies which placed him at the very top of the pecking order, Foit on the other hand reduced drama to the commonplace. Discussing in the same report the dangers of being run off the road on his way to Bangui, Foit suggested that "to meet a black driver on a bend or even on such a narrow road is always dangerous."[45] In positing the risk as constant, and by attributing this risk to a racialized deficiency on the part of those with whom he shared the road, Foit cast a potentially dramatic situation as a normal occurrence.

Beyond their Tatra, Hanzelka and Zikmund stressed the crucial importance of, but recognized the potential for malfunction built into, other technologies they used throughout their journey. Indeed, a focus on the limits to the technology facilitating their trip was exploited for comedic effect. In the pair's final broadcast, "Opět v Československu," ("In Czechoslovakia Once More"), which is one of the two audio recordings from their first trip that remains, Hanzelka and Zikmund's reunion over the telephone is performed by Karel Pech and Jaromír Spal (Hanzelka flew home early from Mexico, having broken his arm, while Zikmund was responsible for driving the Tatra home by himself).[46] When Zikmund ostensibly spoke into the receiver in Poland (in fact as clear as a bell in a studio in Prague), a distant-sounding Hanzelka suggested he could not hear his fellow expeditionary properly over the line. The deliberately garbled sound perhaps alluded to the distant nature of the pair's connection with the listener throughout; it certainly pointed to the precariousness of their entire trip at the hands of technology, which could now, upon their safe return, be presented in humorous form. If Foit had mocked the Africans he met, then Hanzelka and Zikmund here poked fun at themselves and their inability to master the technology that had underwritten their whole journey.

## Hanzelka and Zikmund as Projections of Czechs' and Slovaks' Desires

Hanzelka and Zikmund became vocal representatives of the newfound public prominence of youth in postwar Czechoslovakia—something that forty-something František Foit could not hope to achieve.[47] Young people enjoyed newfound privileges and respect in the postwar Third Czechoslovak Republic.[48] The voting age was lowered from twenty-one to eighteen, which meant a whole new swathe of young people, at a stroke, became politically significant.[49] The state was characterized by a notably younger population than in the interwar years.[50] An older generation of Czechs and Slovaks, meanwhile, had been discredited on account of the positions of authority they had occupied at the time of the Munich Agreement and during the war. The popular attention that the young reporters commanded, and their ultimate success, was symptomatic of a broader European valorization of youth in the immediate postwar period.

Youth, as Mischa Honeck has pointed out, however, need not be the prerogative of minors—if Hanzelka and Zikmund were spokespeople for Czechoslovak youth at this moment, then they were also, equally, "boyified men." Honeck flags the conservatism inherent in such modes of self-presentation, calling the decision on the part of an adult to present oneself as a child "a social performance employed to sustain existing power relations by shrouding them in the emotionally uplifting valences of youth."[51] Hanzelka and Zikmund certainly insisted upon their youth to justify their redeployment of older, First Republic—and even Habsburg-era—literary forms and ideas. "The image of youthful, energetic, and attractive masculinity" that the duo projected, moreover, proved, in Jiřina Šmejkalová's telling, "conducive to the acquisition of their celebrity status."[52]

Converging with the blank-slate narrative that Czechoslovak Radio was cultivating about itself was the myth of the new nature of Hanzelka and Zikmund's stardom. Newspapers cultivated this myth, according to Pavel Skopal, to justify the pre-socialist nature of elements of the pair's fame.[53] Reports stressing the duo's hard work suggested that they had become celebrities through their own merit, rather than as products of a capitalist-style star system which allegedly elevated stars for lesser reasons, such as their appearance or personal connections to industry chiefs. Czechs and Slovaks were assumed to be familiar with such a system from their experiences of the interwar First Republic.[54] Under socialism, "in the absence of commercial media, celebrity was based mostly on merit and achievement," Anikó Imre argues.[55] Contemporary celebrities in capitalist states, however, justify their fame on these grounds too. Specific to the Third Republic and early socialism was the promotion of such a fame-through-hard-work narrative in a society which explicitly conferred citizenship rights to those in employment alone and thus elevated the political significance of work.[56] Hanzelka and Zikmund were not *Stakhanovites*, but in the image they constructed of themselves on air, and the image constructed of them in newspapers, they were an advert for the results that government-sponsored hard work could bring, both for the state and the individual as part of a team.

Hanzelka and Zikmund's radio fame hinged both on their destinations', and their own, allure. While František Foit's unbroadcast reports recycled tropes about Africans' particular physicality and "sex appeal," fan mail in particular from teenage female listeners suggested that Zikmund and Hanzelka themselves held the main appeal in their radio dispatches.[57] Both were unmarried—seemingly available—and thus invited to numerous provincial secondary-school classrooms upon their return so their adolescent female fans could get to know them better.[58] A near "tragedy" was caused by a stampede of teenage girls assailing the men in Gottwaldov in 1952.[59] In a relatively representative letter posted in 1951, Věra and Marie from Nymburk near Prague asked for a photo of the two pin-up adventurers, as they had appreciated pictures of the men on their travels in *Svět Práce* but, over and above this, "if you could send us your, really your own, photos" Věra and Marie specified, "we would be grateful."[60] While this and the exposition of fan mail that follows is striking in its heteronormativity, Hanzelka and Zikmund's archive yields fewer letters sent by teenage male fans, and those preserved betray less of an ostensibly erotic subtext.

Female students from a vocational school in Děčín, North Bohemia, wrote to Hanzelka and Zikmund aghast that they had been traveling around Africa "unaccompanied and without a translator"; they asked the pair to reply at their earliest convenience to say it was really so.[61] The eight signatories attached portraits alongside their own personal messages to the travelers, imploring them among other things "don't disappoint our great hope!" and "don't throw this in the bin!"[62] The teenagers additionally enclosed a collective love poem to the traveler-reporters. The poem was addressed to "Two enterprising men/ Who racked their brains/ How to promote our products/ They found their way to Tatra."[63] Three years after the Communist takeover, the authors of this poem still lauded the idea of Czechoslovak foreign trade and indeed Hanzelka and Zikmund's "entrepreneurship." The authors ended their letter with the staple socialist sign-off *práci čest* (honor to work), underscoring the fact that listeners versed in the language of the new regime did not understand the original, business purpose of the men's trip as something inconvenient to be subsequently obscured. Both ministry officials—"for reasons of economics"—and students at the vocational school in Děčín were rooting for Hanzelka and Zikmund's success selling Czechoslovak products abroad.[64]

In their second stanza, these Bohemian rhapsodists then turned to the pair's departure from their mothers and adventures on the road; they introduced the medium of radio and how the pair used it to tell people about their experiences in the third stanza. Next, the girls described Hanzelka and Zikmund's appearance, referring to the pair as *krasavci* (heartthrobs).[65] This was followed by the versified appeal "Please, write to us too/ Lower your elevated gaze towards us/ There are enough of us here—you have a big selection/ We are beside ourselves when we hear your signature theme."[66] This stanza invited the pair each to choose a single girl and to choose based on their gaze (perhaps the unnamed portraits in the poem's margins were to help?). Contact was to take the form of writing, sought twice more in the poem through the imperatives *Napište nám!* (Write to us!) and *pište!* (write!). Finally, the authors suggested that each time they heard Hanzelka and Zikmund's signature theme (*znělka*) on the radio they became excited. This pointed to the highly anticipated and episodic nature of Hanzelka and Zikmund's broadcasts and to some listeners' passionate fixation on the pair.

The pair's voices were never mentioned in the poem, and this could be because, in spite of what evolved into a prime billing at 21:00 on Tuesdays and 18:00 on Saturdays, Hanzelka and Zikmund were never actually heard.[67] Their reports were read by radio announcers, first by Karel Pech who handled their correspondence, and then by Pech in tandem with Jaromír Spal, in imitation of a dialogue between the two men.[68] For a Christmas special in 1947, Hanzelka and Zikmund recorded a message in their own voices and sent this disc from Addis Ababa to Czechoslovak Radio for broadcast. But their voices never became central to their renown: upon their return from their first trip in 1950, they decided that Pech and Spal should continue to play them on the radio and indeed narrate the film version of their travels, as they judged the announcers to be better than them in front of a microphone, and this was more in keeping with the image they had honed so far.[69] In fact, on the poster for their first feature documentary, *Africa, Part I*, Pech and Spal were given a prominent credit for their narration.[70]

It was far from an oddity to have radio announcers read Hanzelka and Zikmund's reports. As the last chapter made clear, it was standard radio practice in the 1950s, East and West, to read out letters sent to broadcasters in the pristine conditions of the studio. With political speeches often reread by professional announcers in the Czechoslovak Radio studio at the period, moreover, Hanzelka and Zikmund were hardly alone in receiving this treatment.

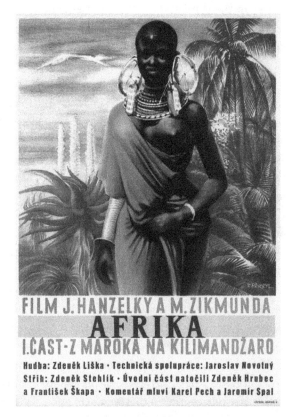

**FIGURE 11.** Poster for *Africa, Part I* at Prague's Sevastopol Theatre. Source: Museum of Southeast Moravia in Zlín. Reprinted with permission.

In spite of their nominal muteness, Hanzelka and Zikmund were directly involved in the evolution of their sound. A letter dated October 10, 1951, reprimands Pech and Spal for a lackluster performance.[71] Hanzelka and Zikmund situate their criticism in the context of overall happiness with Pech and Spal's work, but continue: "It was difficult to understand Jarka [Jaromír Spal] and, don't take offense, but in several places even you sounded different from usual. We both felt like you read it in a rush, without a prior readthrough or preparation. Maybe you were very tired. The dialogues . . . were unnatural, unbelievable, and artificial. On other occasions we feel as if we are saying it ourselves."[72] Hanzelka and Zikmund sought comprehensibility, clear preparation reflected in the reading style, and dialogues which evoked "discussion among a group of friends" in the presentation of their reports.[73] When Pech and Spal were at their best, Hanzelka and Zikmund suggested they approximated the latter pair's relationship and speech. If stardom was more "provincial" and "intimate" in socialist Eastern Europe than it was in the West, with audiences considering stars to be "extended family members . . . or people with whom one can strike up a conversation on the street," then Hanzelka and Zikmund actively sought here to convey their approachability by striking a friendly, familial tone.[74] If the duo remained largely voiceless on the air, then the physical aspect of their celebrity rested on their appearance. But their correspondence suggests the importance they placed in their audio profile as well. How Pech and Spal voiced them fed into their celebrity status. Mindful of this, Hanzelka and Zikmund played an active role crafting their audio personas.

Teenage girls were not the only group pouring their fantasies into Hanzelka and Zikmund. What the pair referred to as their "most dedicated fans" placed very personal hopes on Hanzelka and Zikmund, which was exactly what high-ranking Communist functionaries did too.

It is an oversimplification to conclude that the two travelers represented a fantasy of escape from Communist Czechoslovakia. The duo were frequently asked to bring small aspects of the foreign *back* to Czechoslovakia to satisfy their listeners: Jan Číp in Nová Paka asked for a mineralogical specimen, Josef Hanka in Turnov desired a foreign coin, and Prague Zoo sought information about animals to boost their existing collections (here too Hanzelka and Zikmund found themselves in competition with Foit, who spent much of 1948 looking into the procurement of a chimpanzee for the attraction).[75] In a rather heartbreaking letter, meanwhile, Hanzelka and Zikmund explained to school pupil Kamila Kováčová that they could not bring a small child they described in one report home, as this would separate him from his family, he would have to travel through a range of other countries with them before reaching Czechoslovakia, and "we would only be helping one little boy, when there are so many poor children in the world. We want to help them all."[76] The two travelers encouraged "Kamilka" to work hard at school and suggested that if adults became involved in the "boj za mír" (fight for peace), then child poverty could be eradicated in its entirety.[77] No response from the pair has been archived, however, to Karel Hesek's request that Hanzelka and Zikmund bring him "a young Arab, Indian or even a black woman" to marry, "as women here play so hard to get."[78] One can only presume that no radio-order bride was transported to the Kladno region to be "cultivated" by the lovelorn Mr. Hesek.

Hanzelka and Zikmund voiced their frustration that so many listeners sought material tokens from their travels. In a letter to Lída Humlová at Czechoslovak Radio in 1950 they pleaded, "Please ask Karel [Pech] to pass on our heartfelt thanks to those who write in . . . Can he somehow explain to them that we can't send them stamps, nor monkeys, snakes or baby elephants? Sometimes we really would like to make the most dedicated fans happy . . . But we don't have the time, nor the money."[79] Whether seeking baby elephants or personal photos, stamps or life partners, Czechs' and Slovaks' desires were directed towards and mediated in the figures of Hanzelka and Zikmund as a result of their prime-time radio presence. Hanzelka and Zikmund embodied the hopes of Communist officials establishing themselves following the war and the hopes of students at the vocational school in Děčín, Karel Hesek near Kladno, and the fifth-grader Kamila Kováčová alike.

Historians Jiří Knapík and Martin Franc posit a binary framework pitting the listener against the regime in their analysis of Czechoslovak media between 1945 and 1956, arguing that Czechoslovak Radio's listeners pulled towards entertainment, while the regime preferred educational programming designed to ensure cultural elevation.[80] Functionaries such as Bohuslav Horák certainly did champion radio's capacity to uplift Czechoslovakia's citizens, celebrating the medium as a tool of "beneficial violence"—presumably pummeling listeners with opera arias and educational lectures—in the years following the war.[81] But the case of Hanzelka and Zikmund nuances the picture of listeners versus officials. Listener mail and ministry documents present a picture of convergence, suggesting that high-ranking and "ordinary" Czechs and Slovaks were basically in accord. Jiřina Šmejkalová describes Hanzelka and Zikmund as posing a "challenge" to "the binary distinction between 'the people' and 'the elite' by providing a space for movement and interchange between the two."[82] But, in fact, their case presents us with no binary at all. Hanzelka and Zikmund did not become celebrities because the regime decreed it, nor because they somehow embodied a form of entertainment that was anti-regime. Instead, it was precisely this convergence of fantasy (albeit for extremely varied reasons) in the figures of Hanzelka and Zikmund that assured their success.

Even socialist celebrity might be about the procurement, possession, and consumption of material items—such as personal photos or exotic minerals—deemed important by the fan. But Hanzelka and Zikmund's celebrity was equally about that which one cannot assuage through consumption: suspense, belief, anticipation, and hope. The duo had a clear timetable and route, but there always remained the question of whether they could truly pull it off. They nurtured and played with this seed of doubt masterfully in their radio writing. It was the same satisfaction of fans' hopes tempered by doubt which explains the excitement of Děčín's schoolgirls when Hanzelka and Zikmund's signature theme really did come on at 18:00 on Saturdays, and the delight of Information Minister Václav Kopecký when the two travelers really did return to Czechoslovakia rather than resettling abroad in 1950.

### Making the Travelogue Newsworthy—Hanzelka and Zikmund's Ascent of Kilimanjaro

If František Foit's writing had, in some ways, fallen out of fashion by the Third Czechoslovak Republic and the early socialist period, then it still provided inspiration for Hanzelka and Zikmund's radio reports. Foit's travel diaries, *Across Africa by Car*, had been "exceptionally successful" upon their release in 1932.[83]

Hanzelka and Zikmund drew inspiration from even earlier, Habsburg-era travelers too. Captivated by the nineteenth-century explorer Emil Holub's "enthusiasm and verve," they extended their voyage into Southern Africa "out of fascination with his story."[84] Their reporting remediated the genre of travel writing specifically for radio. Remediation takes place when a newer technology "defines itself in relationship to earlier technologies of representation."[85] Rather than attempting to present an immediate window onto the sights and events they witnessed in Africa, Hanzelka and Zikmund imitated earlier travel writing and considered how to reinvent the genre through sound.

Among the best received of Hanzelka and Zikmund's reports were those in which the pair recounted their adventures scaling Mount Kilimanjaro to plant a Czechoslovak flag on its summit.[86] In this sequence of reports, they explicitly stated that they followed in the footsteps of František Foit and sought indeed to catch up with and overtake him in their successful trip to the mountain's peak.[87] They surely recognized the potential appeal of this stage of their travels, as they devoted a rare stock of color film to recording their ascent.[88] The pair then used their experiences climbing Kilimanjaro to advertise their first film, *Afrika I: Z Maroka na Kilimandžaro.*

Hanzelka and Zikmund discussed filming this footage in a radio report in 1948. Writing, like Foit had, in the form of a travel diary, the pair suggested their day on the ascent of Kilimanjaro began by leaving their hill hut and taking "some rewarding photographs and film footage."[89] After describing some of the flora they observed, Hanzelka and Zikmund posited their incongruity because, in this rocky, deserted landscape, "the crouched, hairy figure of a hunter from the stone age would fit better than modern climbers with tropical helmets and film cameras."[90] Film cameras were the instruments which distinguished them from the hunter as modern. While the hunter scoured the landscape in search of food, so the pair scoured the landscape in search of the perfect shot. The caveman may have "crouched" because of congenital posture, while Hanzelka and Zikmund bent over on account of the burden of heavy camera equipment which they transported to the summit. At such moments, the duo played with the idea that the radio was not the full extent of their work overseas and that the radio could not be the only way to document their travels, due to its limitations as a medium. Pointing beyond the medium, however, constituted an integral and formulaic part of their reports.

"Promontory descriptions" such as Hanzelka and Zikmund's ascent of Kilimanjaro are a staple of exploration writing.[91] Analyzing Victorian-era British travel literature from Central Africa, Mary Louise Pratt suggests that such descriptions served to "render momentously significant what is, especially from a narrative point of view, practically a non-event."[92] The non-event consisted of Europeans visiting a site and asking local inhabitants to take them to a place where the former could proceed to discover what the latter already knew. For Pratt, the construction of such a narrative required three things: firstly, an aestheticization of the landscape; then, an insistence on said landscape's density of meaning.[93] Finally, the "relation of mastery between the seer and the seen" needed to be demonstrated to establish the climb's significance.[94] All of these elements are at play in the five dispatches Hanzelka and Zikmund authored on their ascent of Kilimanjaro.

The pair began to aestheticize the Kilimanjaro landscape by explaining that the mountain's name meant "radiant hill" in Swahili.[95] They then focused on the light and sparkle of all they encountered on the mountain. They thus suggested the harmonious nature of the entire scene and intimated that the site presented something of an optical illusion for the uninitiated traveler. The mountain streams twinkled, so did the local banana-growers' teeth, the sun danced on the coffee bushes and it took an "iron will" not to stop and be seduced, but instead to continue upwards "with the automatic precision of a machine."[96] The peak of the mountain glittered at them during their ascent and, once at their first hill hut, they used light as a means of communicating with those down below.[97]

To convey density of meaning, Pratt points to the copious use of adjectives in a text alongside "referents which all . . . tie the landscape explicitly to the explorer's home culture."[98] The description of the rivers as "crystal" and "silver," and of the summit as "sparkling" and "magisterial," served this purpose.[99] As too did purple sentences describing "a soft carpet of grass fork[ing] upwards. Thousands of golden flowers of African edelweiss are interwoven with the azure of tall lobelias."[100] The explorers referenced their home culture when they likened the clouds, unconventionally, to hermelín cheese, and when the peaks they reached on their second day climbing were equated with the summits of the Austrian Alps.[101]

Finally, Hanzelka and Zikmund mastered the landscape by resisting the urge to stand and gape at the seductive scenes of the foothills. Their "iron will" led them to the summit. They reported to Czechoslovak Radio listeners, after a series of dispatches stressing the physical difficulty of scaling their "rival" the mountain, that "at 11 o'clock East African time, the Czechoslovak flag flew over the summit of Kilimanjaro. We planted it with joyful pride."[102] Opening with the time the event took place, and in the passive construction that followed, this formulation echoed the sound of the radio news bulletin. Thus the "non-event" described by Pratt was transformed, through the narrative strategies employed, into an item of news.[103] Hanzelka and Zikmund then inserted themselves into this scene of national conquest, speaking of their "pride" at planting the flag.[104] Blending the conventions of the evening radio news with the travel writing staple, the promontory description, Hanzelka and Zikmund encouraged listeners to "acknowledge the medium [of radio] as a medium and to delight in that acknowledgement."[105]

Jiřina Šmejkalová has described Hanzelka and Zikmund's cross-referencing of literature and film in their radio reports as a "pioneering example of the media franchise model," tailored to the economic conditions of socialism.[106] The references to other genres and types of media dropped into Hanzelka and Zikmund's radio scripts were not only a promotion of different products that the travelers made but also a comment on their ongoing sonic experiments and games with the medium of radio. Jay David Bolter and Richard Grusin have termed moments when new media acknowledge older forms of media representation as cases of "hypermediacy."[107] They highlight the playfulness of texts and other media which employ such a technique. Following them, Hanzelka and Zikmund's "hypermediacy" showed that there was the possibility for playfulness—on the state-controlled airwaves, no less—during the period in which Czechoslovak culture was being Stalinized.

While Hanzelka and Zikmund were producing report after report conveying the "density of meaning" of African landscapes, the Ministry of Information was also encouraging František Foit to enrich the descriptions of the sights he saw. As Hanzelka and Zikmund scaled Kilimanjaro, Bohuslav Horák complained in a letter that "a description of the countryside, nature, atmosphere and so forth," was "lacking" from Foit's journalism. "I cannot imagine these things here very well," Horák continued, "and reporters only rarely look for sources in travelogues, according to which they can depict the mood of the African landscape and the whole environment there."[108] Horák indicated here that the "remediation" of travelogues as radio reports was more than theoretical; when they had the time to enhance programming that arrived too bare from the location itself, radio employees inserted older travel writing into contemporary travel reports. Authenticity here could be demonstrated by showing that a text fitted into a series of generic expectations held by the Czech or Slovak listener, rather than by dint of it having been authored overseas. Listeners like Horák tuned in to radio travelogues for descriptions of African landscapes and nature, expectations of which had already been established by pre-socialist literature about the African continent.

## Czechoslovakia's Global Reach as Presented by Hanzelka and Zikmund

If the interwar First Czechoslovak Republic had shaped aspects of all of these men's literary output, then it also inflected how they understood the social realities of the places they visited. To make sense of the colonial societies they encountered on their travels, Hanzelka and Zikmund drew from what some in the Czechoslovak metropole had understood to be an interwar project of domestic colonization. Between 1918 and 1938, the easternmost region of the republic—Sub-Carpathian Ruthenia—was repeatedly likened to Africa in literary and political depictions, in a bid to justify a Prague-spearheaded civilizing mission.[109] In a dispatch from Egypt in 1947, Hanzelka and Zikmund inverted this trope, likening the Africans they met to Ruthenians: "there is no big difference between the life of an Egyptian fellah and smallholder or shepherd from Carpathian Ruthenia after the First World War," they explained.[110] The pair continued by likening "the primitive, often insufficient clothing" of both groups, alongside "the simple, stereotypical diet, the basis of which is one's own produce, [and] the primitive clay dwellings which often double up as grain-stores, and where all living creatures sleep together during the cold winter."[111] They mused on the lessons from a Czechoslovak past for an Egyptian present, with Ruthenia no longer a Czechoslovak territory—belonging now to Soviet Ukraine. They also inverted and exported some of the features of earlier domestic Czechoslovak travel writing to fit an international frame.

Czech and Slovak travel writing in the early twentieth century had displayed an ambivalence towards colonialism, argues Sarah Lemmen. By comparison, Hanzelka and Zikmund's later reports were more enthusiastically neocolonial in tone. While František Foit's and companion Jiří Baum's interwar travelogues had exhibited a "form of orientalism . . . not based on

110   Chapter 3

direct or explicit colonial interests or overseas possessions,"[112] Hanzelka and Zikmund's reports went as far as praising the Czechoslovak "colonial" efforts they witnessed on a trip to Batadar, Egypt, in October 1947.[113] "The young Czechoslovak does not employ the old colonial methods of the large nations against the natives," the pair explained here, stressing Czechoslovakia's difference from but also comparability with Western Europe.[114] The Czechoslovak colonizer "does it in our way," they continued, explaining that "he himself grew up in a village in modest conditions. He implements in Batadar the social possibilities typical in our country, but wholly unknown in Egypt."[115] The Egyptian king himself enjoyed visiting, the pair concluded, to witness "the results of pioneering Czech work" in the town.[116] What the pair referred to as Czechoslovak "colonial" efforts were based upon empathy, it was implied, rather than brute force, with all parties sharing a modest, rural background and united by the fact they did not belong to a great imperial power.

Discussing here a company town built to service the Baťa shoe dynasty, Hanzelka and Zikmund indicated that enterprise, rather than government, may be the best agent of colonialism. That "social possibilities" should be attached to Egyptians' employment and thus conferred through work was endorsed by the pair. Here Hanzelka and Zikmund's own role as salesmen should be remembered, not to mention the "world domination" that they themselves embodied took the form of one sales contract after another. Hanzelka and Zikmund's praise of the Baťa business empire was squarely rooted in the industries and traditions of the First Czechoslovak Republic, but broke from the "noncolonial orientalist" tone of earlier Czechoslovak travel writing. The text having been struck through, it is likely that this section of their report was never broadcast; as no audio remains, there is no way of verifying. Hanzelka and Zikmund's enthusiasm for "pioneering" Czechoslovak colonialism through enterprise appears to have exceeded the bounds of conventional travel writing and official opinions at the time.

Hanzelka and Zikmund's reports from Egyptian towns like Batadar established the pair's self-reliance. There was both an implicitly national, and inexplicitly international, boy scout–style element to the pair's self-sufficiency. The claim that the two men would "not be able to rely on foreign help" articulated in their first film was patently false. They were led up Kilimanjaro by guides and provided with both local and Czechoslovak diplomatic help when they crashed in Libya in 1947.[117] But their systematic downplaying of external help, alongside their frequent insistence that the resources they used on their journey were made in Czechoslovakia, did resonate with listeners. The patriotic nature of their fan mail peaked when they arrived at the summit of Kilimanjaro to plant the Czechoslovak flag. In one representative example, Mrs. M. Kudrnová wrote, "I'm shaking your hands in spirit for your difficult ascent of Kilimanjaro . . . and for planting our flag on its summit. I found it beautiful to listen to and, as a Czech, I am proud of you."[118]

In cultivating an image of self-sufficiency, Hanzelka and Zikmund moreover piqued the interest of young listeners involved in the scouting movement (which was permitted in Czechoslovakia between 1945 and 1948, before disappearing underground following the takeover). They thus repurposed some of the values found in the adventure stories of Jaroslav Foglar, which had achieved tremendous popularity in interwar and postwar Czechoslovakia following their serialization in scouting magazines. Miroslav Zikmund later cited Foglar as one of his literary influences.[119] Regretting never having been a scout himself, Zikmund reflected that some of the same values had been inculcated in him by his childhood membership in the YMCA.[120] As a movement, finds Mischa Honeck, twentieth-century scouting "crossed borders without subscribing to an ideology of borderlessness, respecting and reinforcing all kinds of boundaries that separated nations, races, age groups and sexes."[121] The respect and reinforcement of boundaries that Honeck finds underpinning the international scouting movement can certainly be found in the "boys-only" adventures that Hanzelka and Zikmund authored and in the ways the pair wrote about race.

Hanzelka and Zikmund avoided assertions such as Foit's that black Africans were innately less capable when it came to certain tasks like driving on account of their race. In one dispatch about conditions in a South African mine from 1948 the pair suggested that white engineers and black miners were somehow rendered equal through their work, as "in the depths of the earth, danger knows no difference."[122] The story of the mine suggested certain spaces allowed connections between European engineers and African miners to be forged. That working could level out differences of race, class, and nationality—leading ultimately to the workers of the world uniting— was a tenet of socialist internationalism predating the Cold War, which

112   Chapter 3

continued to be espoused on Czechoslovak Radio well into the Stalinist period.[123] In singling out the profession of mining as a site of racial harmony, Hanzelka and Zikmund presented a profession to which the Czechoslovak government sought to attract more recruits in a particularly flattering light.

Hanzelka and Zikmund's was certainly no postracial world, however. Their reports frequently stressed phenotypic difference. They attributed, nevertheless, the meaningful differences they described between peoples to culture instead of biology. People went astray when they tried to move from one culture to another: Hanzelka and Zikmund lamented black Africans wearing ragged European clothes and adopting European customs rather than keeping their own.[124] Theirs was a world of contiguity rather than integration, akin to the ethnicized world of incompatible nationalities that Chad Bryant describes the postwar Czechoslovak state to be.[125]

If Hanzelka and Zikmund complicated and pluralized Czech and Slovak listeners' received understandings of race, then two orthodoxies underpinned their work: Africa was full of Czechs and free of Germans. The total omission of the latter distinguished Hanzelka and Zikmund's work from the interwar writings of František Foit, who had allowed for the presence of Germans in Africa, often describing them, however, in negative terms.[126] The frequent mention of Czech and Slovak expatriates in Hanzelka and Zikmund's work created an overall aural impression of a global Czechoslovakia, whose representatives had already reached every corner of the earth, an image which listeners found extremely gratifying. As they explained in a letter to Karel Pech in 1948, they were traveling on a shoestring budget (of 302 crowns a day, on average) and often stayed with local Czechs and Slovaks in a bid to limit expenses.[127] They frequently discussed their hosts in their reports, as well as the Czechs and Slovaks they met along the route (whom they hierarchized from excellent representatives of the country abroad to probable former collaborators, and therefore no loss to the country).[128] Listeners responded warmly to these reports: large numbers sought expatriate pen pals.[129] So many listeners attempted to track down long-lost relatives that the duo drafted a template response to such requests.[130]

In hindsight, both Zikmund and Hanzelka suggested that they regretted not writing *more* about the Czechs and Slovaks they met around the globe. They suggested that some of the comments they wanted to make about Czechoslovak expatriates began to be censored when they drafted their third book of travelogues in 1953.[131] Certainly, their earlier radio reports are full of discussions of Czechs and Slovaks abroad. They thus offered listeners an image of the familiar, or themselves, on the other side of the world—of successful Czech world domination.

The tendency to focus on Czech and Slovak emigrants in Hanzelka and Zikmund's radio work is less apparent in the pair's films. This suggests a difference in generic convention (while texts about Africa and Latin America could allow for the appearance of European actors, films—in order to appear strictly ethnographic to Czech and Slovak audiences and to the Czechoslovak Ministry of Education which commissioned them—had to erase any trace of Africans of European origin). The proliferation of images of Czech and Slovak expatriates in their radio work suggests that Hanzelka and Zikmund felt more comfortable infringing the norms of the genres they employed in their radio writing than in their filmmaking. While their films might be read as somewhat more conventional, their radio work played with the conventions of how Africa and Latin America should sound.

Reports about the lives of Czech and Slovak expatriates settled around the Global South came at exactly the same time as Hanzelka and Zikmund's sponsor, Czechoslovak Information Minister Václav Kopecký, took to the airwaves to excoriate those who had left the country following the Communist takeover, suggesting there was room still for a plurality of views regarding emigration on the state broadcaster's frequencies.[132] Hanzelka and Zikmund's descriptions of their countrymen and women stationed overseas continued to be broadcast into the era of Czechoslovakia's anti-cosmopolitan campaign, championed by the radio's supervisor Kopecký, which singled "rootless" Czech and Slovak emigrants out for opprobrium alongside Jewish Communist Party functionaries, most famously, Party General Secretary Rudolf Slánský.[133]

Hanzelka and Zikmund later suggested that their families were then holding a sweepstakes on whether they would, in fact, return to Czechoslovakia.[134] Dušan Segeš has estimated that around 23,350 Czechs and Slovaks left the country while Hanzelka and Zikmund toured the globe, over the first three years of Communist rule.[135] In 1950, the year of the duo's return, the American-sponsored and émigré-staffed radio station, Radio Free Europe, began promoting emigration as an honorable and indeed patriotic activity in programs such as *Zvolil jsem svobodu* (*I Chose Freedom*) and

*Češi a Slováci ve svobodném světě* (*Czechs and Slovaks in the Free World*).[136] The numbers of Czechs and Slovaks who left during the early Communist period were by no means insignificant, but the symbolic value of this out-migration was arguably more significant than the numbers of migrants themselves. As Segeš has argued, "the [Czechoslovak] regime had a fundamental problem explaining why a citizen would take life-threatening risks and prefer capitalism to the achievements of socialism."[137] Correspondingly, US authorities promoted the idea that citizens who left socialist countries were "voting with their feet." What Tara Zahra has termed "celebrity defectors"—the likes of which Hanzelka and Zikmund would most certainly have been—were a particular prize for Western, and in particular American, authorities when they settled in the West.[138] Accordingly, by the early 1950s, Czechoslovak Radio began to call for "vigilance and attention" when sending employees abroad. All trips were to be approved by management at least three months in advance; reporters who had visited the West must not then be deployed to the socialist East and vice versa; and "social origin, political maturity, attitude towards the republic, expert knowledge, character, behavior and the importance of the trip" were all to be scrutinized thoroughly before approval was given.[139] This closed the window of opportunity which had propelled a new generation of overseas reporter to fame . . . for a while.

### Conclusion

How had Hanzelka and Zikmund achieved fame in the first place? The pair were transformed into celebrities in postwar Czechoslovakia as a result of the treatment they received at the hands of the state broadcaster, Czechoslovak Radio, rather than through the maneuvering of any all-powerful Communist minister. In fact, the case of their rival František Foit suggests the limits to the influence of tastemakers at the Czechoslovak Ministry of Information during the Third Republic and into the Communist era. A study of Hanzelka and Zikmund, and the hapless František Foit, has therefore challenged the idea that stardom worked by government decree at the time of the Communist takeover in Czechoslovakia.

Czechoslovak Radio championed the two men because their personalities and dispatches helped the broadcaster sound new and different following the Second World War, and thus enabled the radio to distance itself

When Travelogues Became News   115

from the output it had produced in the Nazi Protectorate. Their "different" sound took to the airwaves in 1947 and did not change substantially following the Communist takeover (with the pair insisting that the broadcaster leave their Kilimanjaro reports, of which they were particularly proud, untouched in mid-1948). With their reporting and their route both largely unaffected by the takeover, the story of Hanzelka and Zikmund is much more one of continuity than change.

The dispatches that Hanzelka and Zikmund sent the radio needed less tweaking than those provided by František Foit; their texts did not need to be augmented by passages from existing travel literature. We can therefore understand their foregrounding as a practical drive to limit work on the part of Czechoslovak Radio's employees. In their radio reports, Hanzelka and Zikmund remediated earlier travelogues; they played with the conventions and expectations of listeners who were used to the writings of interwar adventurers like František Foit.

Hanzelka and Zikmund were at once a break from the past (in their ostensible youth and skill with new media) and proponents of older, interwar ideas (such as poaching German trade in Africa). As such, they helped their listeners think through the contradictions innate in the project of socialist revolution. They were able to resolve these contradictions, unlike Foit, on account of their lack of association with Czechoslovak media under earlier regimes and their ability to speak in a less biologically deterministic way about race.

In their radio work, Hanzelka and Zikmund alluded to other media, such as the films they were simultaneously making. What Bolter and Grusin would term the "hypermediacy" of the pair's reports shows how there was space for play on the socialist airwaves during Stalinism. By reducing the output of state radio during Stalinism to the show trials, which some histories of Czechoslovak socialism have done, we lose sight of the possibility for lightness and playfulness in state-sponsored culture of the time.

The role that Foit, Hanzelka, and Zikmund played in promoting Czechoslovak trade on the African continent should lead us to reevaluate a fledgling Communist government's stance towards advertising its products (through hardworking heartthrobs, no less) and its outward, even cosmopolitan, viewpoint in its first years in power. As Linda Piknerová points out, these three travelers indeed influenced the foreign policy of a "satellite"

Soviet state through the contacts they fostered overseas and the writings they made about their travels.

If this chapter has charted the meteoric rise of Hanzelka and Zikmund, then its last word, like its first, belongs to František Foit. The two expeditions differed in their demographics and written output, but their single biggest difference resided, fittingly, in each trip's conclusion. If Information Minister Václav Kopecký was hoping yet doubting that Jiří Hanzelka and Miroslav Zikmund would really return from their explorations abroad, then the same can be said of his ministry's other protégé, František Foit. And while Hanzelka and Zikmund did come back, to cheer and celebrity and acclaim, Foit never returned. Because he and his wife stayed abroad, they were subjected to an erasure: while the National Technical Museum celebrated seventy years in 2017 since Hanzelka and Zikmund set off on their first journey, very few Czechs and Slovaks know today that, at the same time, a man called František Foit ever traveled abroad to promote their state.[140] Foit may have represented the "political and aesthetic projects of the 1930s" and their ultimate failure in the form of his defection from a Stalinizing Czechoslovakia.[141] But his story is not merely one of failure: while Foit has found little commemoration in Prague, a sculpture in Nairobi honors his life and legacy in the Kenyan capital, while his name survives as one of his students, the Kenyan sculptor Morris Foit, took his surname out of respect. Moreover, it was precisely such Czechs and Slovaks who traveled or remained abroad who honed the unofficial radio voice of Czechoslovakia at stations such as Radio Free Europe. In the next chapter, I explore how these emigrants then helped shape journalistic and political debates inside Czechoslovakia over the years that followed.

# 4   De-Stalinization Disturbs Listening

DE-STALINIZATION WAS A PROJECT in which radio played a key role. It began with changes to the very public speech audible on state broadcaster Czechoslovak Radio's frequencies, some years before Soviet leader Nikita Khrushchev made an altogether more "Secret Speech" denouncing Stalin in 1956.

This chapter focuses on one particular radio genre which aired on Czech- and Slovak-language media on both sides of the Iron Curtain specifically during this period: the émigré press conference. It uses the reception data that exists to consider why audiences responded to this genre with the cynicism that they did. Contemporary accounts often depicted the period of de-Stalinization as a moment of disillusionment more generally, and the work of state media certainly contributed to that. But I argue here that an analysis of the cool response that such press conferences garnered underscores most of all how Czech and Slovak radio listeners could simultaneously express their lack of enthusiasm for programming that struck them as overtly propagandistic *and* engage with content on the very same frequencies that they deemed professional, correct, and/or otherwise entertaining.

As any historian of media would attest, understanding reception is hard. But as state radio reporters in socialist Czechoslovakia were always engaged in an albeit uneven dialogue with their listeners, we must try to do so, in order better to understand the nature of their back-and-forth. The sources examined here that point to how people heard radio in Czechoslovakia during de-Stalinization are either literary artifacts, and so reflect the views of a cultural elite, whose opinions were sometimes more akin to those held by the radio reporters who, at this moment, frequently were puzzled at the gap that existed between themselves and "the people." Or they were generated by rival broadcaster Radio Free Europe, whose institutional biases are evident in the questions they asked Czechs and Slovaks abroad in order to better understand when Communism might crumble and where its weak spots lay. The critical picture these sources combine to create is certainly not absent, however, from the letters sent to Czechoslovak Radio about the content it produced and must be acknowledged alongside the fan mail that formed the focus of the last chapter.

Listeners held critical views towards the Czech- and Slovak-language broadcasts that they heard emanating from both sides of the Iron Curtain. In the cynicism listeners voiced towards what they heard both on Czechoslovak Radio and the American-sponsored station RFE, we see how listeners' own party-political convictions did not always provide the primary lens through which they evaluated content. Instead, listeners tended to reject broadcasting that they judged heavy-handed, that confused them, and/or that they found to be overly moralizing—particularly if what was being condemned was a behavior they recognized in themselves. By showing how listeners clearly articulated such negative standpoints and nevertheless looked forward to and praised other aspects of these broadcasters' programming, this chapter makes clear the discernment of media audiences in even highly restricted media environments.

## Defining De-Stalinization

If Stalinism was a set of values and "way of life" shared—which is not to say wholeheartedly endorsed, necessarily—by those both in and beyond the corridors of power, then de-Stalinization was the shifting of this set of values and way of life.[1] It was a much more multifaceted process than simply removing the image, the mention, or the doctrine of Stalin from existing practices. The process consisted of three important pillars: legal reform, professional reform, and changes to the language Czechs and Slovaks used to discuss their relationship to socialism and each other. Each of these three things shifted slightly, if less emphatically than in neighboring states, under the presidency of Antonín Zápotocký (1953–1957). Czechoslovakia is often described as having come late to de-Stalinization, but precisely on account of these limited shifts, I join scholars who date the first signs of de-Stalinization to Zápotocký's time in office.[2]

As Kevin McDermott notes, "a measure of liberalization did occur" within the Czechoslovak penal system after the almost simultaneous deaths of Stalin and Czechoslovak President Klement Gottwald in 1953.[3] Most strikingly, "grandiose show trials" were "eventually eschewed," changing the public presentation of how justice was administered.[4] Moreover, a number of those who had been implicated in the trials, such as Artur London, Vavro Hajdů, and Marie Švermová (discussed in chapter 2) were quietly released from prison. Importantly, however, such "liberalization" did not extend to all of those condemned in the show trials—most of those who remained in prison were pardoned just as quietly by President Antonín Novotný in 1960, and their full rehabilitation only came during the Prague Spring in 1968.

Other amnesties were more far-reaching and trumpeted more loudly. On May 9, 1955, president Zápotocký announced an amnesty which sought to woo Czechs and Slovaks abroad back to Czechoslovakia. Previously, those who had left "illegally" or had remained abroad for longer than their visa allowed had anticipated a prison sentence and a large fine upon return. The remigration campaign that ensued blasted from Czechoslovak Radio's frequencies (which officials were sure Czechs and Slovaks overseas tuned into), as well as deploying print materials, word of mouth, and guilt-inducing letters from relatives to achieve its ends. This all took place under the watchful eye of the Czechoslovak secret police (StB).

Not all of the impetus for de-Stalinization, however, came from the upper echelons of the Communist Party and the secret police. Analyzing journalism in Poland, Jane Curry defines de-Stalinization as an attempt by journalists to take control of their own profession, speaking for it instead of taking their cues from politicians, and seeking, through specialist organizations, to regulate the profession's membership and practices for themselves.[5] She dates its origins to a meeting of journalists in Warsaw in November 1953.[6] In Czechoslovakia, change arrived slightly later and took the form of "polemical essays and discussions" in the Union of Journalists' periodical *Československ-*

120  Chapter 4

*enský novinář* (*Czechoslovak Journalist*), alongside "conflicts of opinion" aired by journalists about themselves in ever more public venues.[7]

Another strand of scholarship has stressed de-Stalinization as a linguistic project. To understand it, Marci Shore examined Czechoslovak writers' professional address of one another at meetings of the Writers' Union. She identifies a gradual shift in their speech away from evocations of "the people" and towards a society made up instead of person-to-person relations: this envisaged a different role for the writer vis-à-vis the collective.[8] The de-Stalinization of language resulted in some writers shifting away from denunciations of each other and towards reflection upon their own "responsibility" for the earlier course that Communism in Czechoslovakia had taken.[9] The way they framed their involvement did not use ritualistic language in fact to atone for blame and so diverged from earlier styles of self-criticism. Their reflections, moreover, suggested the important role played by the individual as a meaningful driver of historical change. Examining the speech of Communist Party members in East Germany, Poland, and Czechoslovakia, Pavel Kolář comes to a similar conclusion: he understands what he calls the "post-Stalinist" period to constitute to a new discursive environment. In this, the individual, alongside or perhaps instead of the vanguard of the Communist Party, could prove a motor of history.[10] Mistakes were both possible and reversible, and society was no longer structured around a central antagonism pitting Communists against anti-Communists (but indeed sometimes Communists against one another).[11]

Kolář dates "post-Stalinism" to the aftermath of Soviet leader Nikita Khrushchev's "Secret Speech," made at the Twentieth Congress of the Soviet Communist Party in February 1956. Marci Shore identifies the de-Stalinization of language taking place even later in the Czechoslovak Writer's Union—over the course of the 1960s. But antecedents of the changes both identify can be found in broadcasts on Czechoslovak state radio's frequencies in highly public, and highly stage-managed, performances over the years of Zápotocký's presidency. The analysis of such linguistic shifts that follows then suggests that the Zápotocký era constituted an important moment of ideological gestation.

I focus here on one radio genre—the émigré press conference—as the epitome of de-Stalinization on Czechoslovak Radio, defined by the triumvirate of legal reform, professional reform, and the language people

De-Stalinization Disturbs Listening    121

used. As it relied upon and rubber-stamped the period's limited judicial reforms, it is a genre that is particular to de-Stalinization. Airing debates among journalists about what constituted good and bad journalism, these press conferences showcased, moreover, the tentative steps towards professional reform that journalists in Czechoslovakia undertook at the time. These events, broadcast between 1954 and 1956, contributed to the shift in language taking place: they appealed to audiences to judge their wayward fellow citizens in less violent ways than the show trials had. Furthermore, the press conferences deliberately downplayed the role of law enforcement in the Czechoslovak media and reattributed the role of those best placed to discern the truth to the press. The protagonists of these events, the returnee emigrants at the microphone, ultimately provided templates by which listeners were encouraged to narrate their changing relationships to socialism after Stalin's and Gottwald's deaths.

## De-Stalinization at Czechoslovak Radio

As well as broadcasts of genres specific to the period, such as the émigré press conference, de-Stalinization at Czechoslovak Radio took two important forms: firstly, it entailed a concerted attempt to incorporate the voices of the Czechoslovak people (*lid*) into broadcasts and, secondly, it constituted a drive to professionalize the radio's spoken and musical output. Both of these initiatives were championed by radio staff in order to create more open, interesting, and persuasive forms of radio in Czechoslovakia, which would speak to the state's citizens and foster their sense of identification with the broadcaster. Such alterations to programming took place in the absence of deeper structural change at the institution itself, which in fact experienced a moment of organizational stability during the Zápotocký years.

Radio staff had long been exhorted by government ministers to get closer to "the people" in their broadcasting.[12] During President Gottwald's time in office, radio had responded with a set of socialist-realist studies penned and read by postal-worker-turned-newsman Jaroslav Bažant. In one example, Bažant assumed the character of a factory worker to eulogize his "first and greatest love . . . a drill."[13] Instructive, socialist-realist worker narratives such as Bažant's lingered on Czechoslovak Radio well into the Zápotocký years. But they increasingly had to lean on the speech of those who were not radio professionals to claim legitimacy. The first episode of *Okénko lidových autorů a vypravěčů* (*A Window onto Folk Authors and Raconteurs*) in 1955, for example, showcased a performance by Wallachian storyteller Františka Smolková alongside what was patently an actor's cheesy impersonation of a trade-school student describing her first failed attempts on the production line.[14] The spot-on political messaging of the student's account lent a suitable political framework to Smolková's tale. Conversely, Smolková's highly colloquial account of her fellow townsfolk's reluctance to board the train (which she likened to "a wild boar") when it first arrived in her region lent folk credentials to the official-sounding narrative that followed.

Speech showcased in programming explicitly for and about the Czechoslovak "people" was sanitized and, indeed in some cases, censored outright. In Czechoslovak Radio's local branch in Ostrava, for example, journalist Věra Šejvlová toned down the religious elements of the folk music that she prepared for broadcast, changing any reference to Jesus (*Ježíšek*) instead to the more neutral but rhythmically similar *děťátko* (little child). She also recalled fastidiously replacing any mention of stables in Bethlehem in Christmas carols with more local references to stables in the nearby Beskid Mountains.[15] Reporters thus strove to "improve" the image of the people that they presented on air.

Reporters' attempts to clean up the images of the people they claimed to represent in broadcasts were part of the radio's simultaneous professionalization drive. One listener complained to Radio Bratislava in April 1956 that "in broadcasts from factories or workshops, the radio reporter often interrupts the working people, who want to talk about their own experiences in their own words. Honestly it sometimes [gives] the impression that the reporter himself were employed in the factory and knew its problems better than the workers!"[16] In response, the radio announcer suggested that this was indeed the case, claiming that reporters, through the sheer number of enterprises they visited, gained a "specialization" of which the lay worker could only dream: "in this way," the announcer insisted, "reporters gain a perfect knowledge about their fields, which enables them to ask objective questions" (and, it appears, answer them on workers' behalf).[17] Parallel attempts to professionalize radio output could be found in the broadcaster's music policy: Czechoslovak Radio assembled at this moment permanent orchestras of professional musicians to present "folk [*lidová*] music and song at the highest artistic level."[18] A final facet of the radio's professionalization drive saw news reporters debate best practices and reappropriate genres of programming that were audible on frequencies broadcasting from the West.

For all their vehement rebuttals, radio staff did worry that the sanitized view of "the people" that they aired in their programming may, in fact, be alienating listeners. At a crisis meeting in Bratislava in November 1956, just after citizens of neighboring Hungary had instigated a revolution, the same reporters who had vaunted their own "specialization" just a few months prior suggested that they needed to improve their offerings—and fast. They had received many listener letters condemning the violence in Hungary, and the state broadcaster had to do a better job disseminating the population's opinions.[19] Moving closer to the listener, they agreed, would be possible by implementing four particular changes. Firstly, the broadcaster must reveal facts about which it had previously remained silent (Czechoslovakia's decent foreign trade figures, hitherto a state secret, were cited as an example). Secondly, it needed to adopt a more critical line, following the enactment of policies and their social effects, rather than merely declaring their roll-out. Thirdly, more roundtables with listeners and experts, broadcasting differences of opinion, should be aired. Finally, the radio had to "serve the public" meaningfully, in addition to serving the Communist Party. This meant talking listeners through bureaucratic procedures so as to make their lives easier.[20] Those present felt that radio should attempt less to hold a mirror to the people than to present its public with a set of tools to navigate state institutions. When "the people" had been represented on the radio until now, they had been questioned and mediated by journalists. Now these Bratislava journalists suggested that the radio would move closer to the people only when it allowed radio staff to answer directly to the listeners themselves.

As these Bratislava journalists' reflections made clear, Czechoslovak Radio's attempts at vernacularization, on the one hand, and professionalization, on the other, were projects marked by their own internal contradictions. The vernacularization drive jarred with reporters' continued conviction that radio should serve primarily as a tool for audience improvement, combined with a dose of snobbery and their fear of broadcasting *brak* (junk or penny fiction). Attempts to present an "improved" image of the Czechoslovak folk led state radio staff to wonder, moreover, whether they were not, in fact, talking over and above the heads of the very people their

124   Chapter 4

medium claimed to represent. The broadcaster's professionalization drive, meanwhile, was complicated by the simultaneous appeal—and danger—of adopting practices closely associated with Western journalism. On the one hand, radio staff creatively reappropriated genres audible on Western frequencies, tailoring them to specifically socialist ends. On the other hand, Czechoslovak Radio's endorsement of techniques and voices associated with Western radio raised the question of where the difference actually lay between Czechoslovak Radio and its stated rivals on the other side of the Iron Curtain.

The vernacularization and professionalization drives taking place at Czechoslovak Radio during de-Stalinization did not do so in a vacuum. Instead, debates about how the "voice of the people"—and professional radio—should sound unfolded in the context of a Cold War dialogue between radio stations broadcasting on either side of the Iron Curtain. This lively conversation between Eastern and Western broadcasters took place at a time when official dialogue between the blocs was strictly limited.[21] Austria and West Germany were, as the next chapter shows, the points of comparison that a large number of Czechs and Slovaks used to define themselves and their place in the world. Simultaneously, however, official media encouraged Czechs and Slovaks, both journalists and listeners, to understand themselves in contrast to a Cold War ideological "Other" epitomized in the American-sponsored broadcasts of RFE. The symbiosis between rival Cold War radio stations becomes clearest in the press conferences analyzed below.

De-Stalinization on Czechoslovak Radio arguably ended up producing the opposite audience response to the one its journalistic patrons desired. Czechoslovak Radio and RFE's attempts to deploy the same materials, media forms, and even the same voices to apparently incompatible ideological ends—all the while insisting upon the unique believability of their own programming—led some listeners to assume a position of ironic detachment from both stations. The cynicism that Czechoslovak listeners cultivated towards some of the media they tuned into at this moment may have contributed to a broader "apathy" that some commentators suggested typified the Zápotocký age.[22] Here, however, I focus on such attitudes to showcase the possibility for simultaneous detachment *and* engagement on the part of Czechoslovakia's discerning listeners.

## The Returnee Press Conference

In 1955, a voice which had risen to prominence precisely through the vernacularization drive spanning Czech- and Slovak-language radio swapped its daily staple of reports on workers' issues at RFE for an altogether more extraordinary press conference in Prague. Before he became a journalist, Vladimír Kučera had been a miner from near Kladno. His accent was similar to that of the garrulous president, himself no stranger to the microphone, Antonín Zápotocký.

Kučera's voice had first been amplified when he left Czechoslovakia for West Germany and was tapped there as an expert on workers' affairs by the American-sponsored, Munich-based radio station RFE—also seeking to represent Czechoslovakia's blue-collar workers in the sound of its output. He received still more space at the microphone following his decision to return to Czechoslovakia as part of an amnesty for emigrants seeking to repatriate.

In the late 1940s and into the 1950s, as Matěj Kratochvíl explains, "workers partially replaced peasants as the nation's main representatives"—including on the radio.[23] This shift reflected the widespread conviction that industrial workers were the primary support base of the Communist Party and should be the focal point of its efforts to inculcate political consciousness. Industrial workers, miners in particular, became a key focus for programming at Czechoslovak Radio. As it sought to mirror (and thus replace) domestic Czechoslovak media, RFE also began to create programming addressed to blue-collar workers.

Having left his job and returned to Czechoslovakia, Vladimír Kučera then proceeded to reveal the structure of his former employer's Czechoslovak news desk to those assembled at the Czechoslovak Press Office in Prague. At a press conference on June 6, 1955, Kučera unmasked his former colleagues (with RFE reporters often broadcasting under pseudonyms) and recounted personal anecdotes to call their character and reporting into question. In a strong Central Bohemian accent, Kučera stressed his own experience falsifying reports as "Tonda Horník" (which one might translate as "Tony Miner"). On the other side of the Iron Curtain, RFE analysts quizzed those who had known Kučera from the Valka displaced persons camp near Nuremberg for their opinions on his radio performance.[24]

In response, RFE broadcast a recording of Kučera in which he claimed he would never return to Czechoslovakia voluntarily. This broadcast pro-

126 Chapter 4

voked a second Czechoslovak Radio appearance from Kučera.[25] At a town hall meeting in Švermov near Kladno on June 21, moderated by Czechoslovak Radio correspondent Květoslav Faix, Kučera suggested he had been forced to record the audio *kompromat* that RFE had just aired. Its creation and RFE's subsequent decision to use this footage amounted to yet more of the station's dastardly tricks.[26] The Švermov meeting was nominally to discuss the current international situation. Kučera—a new inhabitant of the mining town—was its guest of honor. However, the only audio that Czechoslovak Radio then broadcast from the meeting was Kučera's explanation of how he had been tricked into recording such incriminating materials for RFE. Colleague Otto Graf had allegedly threatened him into recording such a statement. Graf had furthermore plied Kučera with alcohol before making the compromising tape.

At the Švermov town hall meeting on June 21, several inhabitants called for their new fellow citizen's forgiveness and acceptance back into Czechoslovak society on account of the work he was willing to do to contribute to its growth. This reiterated what Kučera himself had requested in his press conference in Prague two weeks' prior. An elderly woman closed this Švermov broadcast with a polemic against politicians from the interwar First Czechoslovak Republic who had, she judged, done little for the working class when they had been in power and now, in emigration and in positions of prominence at RFE, continued to use members of the working class like Kučera as pawns to further their own reactionary agendas.

Kučera's case is bewildering. While he did return to Czechoslovakia of his own accord, judges historian Prokop Tomek, the verbal sparring between stations that ensued certainly confused this point.[27] Beyond questioning Kučera's volition, these radio debates also turned on, and undermined, Kučera's character. Could someone really change his/her character over time and find redemption at the hands of the Czechoslovak regime? Domestic Czechoslovak Radio suggested that Kučera should be given a chance to atone for his regrettable actions at RFE. Radio Free Europe stressed, on the other hand, their erstwhile reporter's incorrigible drunkenness and deep-seated moral deficiencies. In their view, Kučera—presumably always a spy—had not changed at all: since appearing on Czechoslovak Radio he had merely revealed his true colors. Consequently, the redemption he was ostensibly being offered in Zápotocký's Czechoslovakia was nothing more than theater. After a period of respite, debates about Kučera's character were again ignited when he stabbed two people and attempted unsuccessfully to flee to the West again in 1956.

Whatever the nature of Kučera's character, and no matter how willingly he returned to Czechoslovakia, most important for our purposes is the lively debate (or radio "ping pong") that his return unleashed.[28] His Prague press conference was met with an archival recording of Kučera speaking against the likelihood of his voluntary return, which was in turn met with a town hall assembly in which he undermined the conditions in which he made such a statement. Such radio back-and-forth, which took the form of a conversation that Kučera held with himself over two radio stations, confused listeners then (as it does historians with declassified documents at their disposal now). Such attempts on the part of both Czechoslovak Radio and RFE to use the same voices and media forms to champion two different agendas may have contributed to an erosion of Czechoslovak listeners' trust in all media.

Kučera commandeered the microphone undoubtedly in part because of his own charisma, but also because his profile, twice over, fitted with the recording priorities of officials and journalistic elites in Central Europe during the early Cold War. Firstly, Kučera had granted RFE its own anti-Communist "voice of the people" along the lines simultaneously being promoted in Prague. Secondly, as a returnee to Czechoslovakia, he had an allegedly unique perspective with which to compare both blocs and was thus seemingly in a position to articulate things that few in Czechoslovakia could say. Media profiles of remigration were an important tool used to "define the script for life in socialist Czechoslovakia," argues Paulina Bren.[29] Returnees' "media savvy or else officially shaped" performances articulated the way state authorities hoped that Czechs and Slovaks might define themselves—in contradistinction to the West.[30]

### Echoes of the West

Emigrant press conferences such as Kučera's, however, borrowed some techniques straight from the very West that they, in theory, rejected in toto. Press conferences were not simply a Western import to Czechoslovakia: they had been held with film stars and politicians, for example, in the interwar period and indeed into the socialist years. But press conferences profiling those who had crossed the Iron Curtain were championed first and most voluminously by American-sponsored news agencies during the Cold War, constituting a key feature of US-sponsored "Cold War pageantry," judges historian Susan Carruthers.[31] Such media events played a crucial role, moreover, in American "domestic mobilization."[32]

Media events with returnee emigrants were likewise designed to mobilize domestic audiences on the other side of the Iron Curtain. In Czechoslovakia, Western media techniques of profiling emigrants were reappropriated and deployed to wholly socialist ends. The broadcasts from such events show, therefore, both the indelible ways in which stations such as RFE (which often aired the Western versions) inflected the output of rivals like Czechoslovak Radio and the creative work that Czechoslovak journalists did harnessing "capitalist" media forms to fit their own goals. Furthermore, they prove Marie Cronqvist's point that media forms and personalities need not necessarily promote a stable agenda or a single form of politics. Just as cartoon character Unser Sandmännchen was transformed from a "calm socialist hero" in East Germany into "an outspoken and sometimes rude capitalist in Sweden," so too these press conferences could promote very different ideas and value systems in the different societies in which they were aired.[33]

The first Czechoslovak conferences took place in late 1954. Their protagonists were former Social Democratic politician Bohumil Laušman and the erstwhile RFE journalist Bruno Folta—or "Jožka Rybárik," as he had been known on the station. While the two men's experiences of return to Czechoslovakia were extremely different (with the former having been kidnapped by the secret police, while the latter was detained returning to visit his family), their narratives were not: both downplayed the role of law enforcement, stressing the ease of return to Czechoslovakia, presumably for the ears of those considering such a move themselves. They were joined in 1955 by Vladimír Kučera and, the following year, by yet another RFE broadcaster (and former starlet), Helena Bušová-Kasalová.

A total of 1,169 people returned to Czechoslovakia as part of the re-emigration campaign, judges Tara Zahra.[34] It appears that only a few of these voices were singled out for the press conference treatment, however. There was a strong preference given to former employees of RFE in the organization of such events. While the remigration campaign was far from a numerical success for the Czechoslovak regime, "Western governments took these amnesties and redefections seriously [as] migrants from the West were embarrassing."[35] The symbolic value of migrants outweighed their numbers, and both Czechoslovak Radio and RFE sought to deploy this symbolic capital to suit their own ends.

The structure and aesthetics of these Czechoslovak press conferences mirrored American-sponsored profiles of Eastern Bloc defectors. For example, a film reel of a conference with Eastern Bloc escapee Victor Kravchenko, held in Paris in 1949, showed the protagonist first reading a prepared statement before fielding journalists' questions and facing a media barrage of lights and cameras. Czechoslovak events with Bruno Folta and Vladimír Kučera, which were likewise recorded for the weekly Czechoslovak film newsreel, followed this statement/question and answer/photo opportunity structure and enjoyed similar film coverage, juxtaposing well-lit close-ups of the protagonist's face with wide-angle shots of dozens of scribbling journalists indicating the intense media interest in the event.[36]

There were, however, also crucial differences between the Eastern and Western versions of such events. Firstly, while Western press conferences tended to place a great deal of emphasis on the method by which the defector escaped, which pitted "clever escapes (embodying the capitalist values of individualism and resourcefulness) against a socialist system governed by buffoons and automatons," Eastern Bloc press conferences largely downplayed the process of transit itself.[37] Instead, they focused on the abysmal conditions and moral bankruptcy that speakers had witnessed in the West firsthand and showcased speakers' change of heart which culminated in their decisions to return to Czechoslovakia.

While Western escapees such as Kravchenko furthermore became "celebrity defectors," Czechoslovak returnees never did.[38] For Kravchenko and other defectors to the West, book deals and other opportunities to cash in on their newfound fame often followed. In Czechoslovakia, meanwhile, the book contracts to tell all about conditions on the other side of the Iron Curtain went, most often, to the journalists quizzing re-emigrants, rather than to the re-emigrants themselves.[39] Indeed the media coverage of Czechoslovakia's press conferences suggest that, to some extent, the speaker at the lectern was not the point at all: with film footage lingering on the crowds of journalists assembled and radio broadcasts airing their original questions in full (before providing a Czech or Slovak translation of what had been asked), the stars of these events were the international cohort of Eastern Bloc journalists quizzing the returnees and not the returnees themselves.

The Czechoslovak events followed a highly standardized format. As Petr Vidomus finds in his analysis of the simultaneous media treatment of the Wards, an American family who defected to Czechoslovakia in 1954 and whose case was handled similarly: "A half-hour recording of the press conference was broadcast on Czechoslovak Radio on the day of its occurrence, extracts from it made their way into the Czechoslovak Weekly Film Bulletin and the [protagonists'] statement was printed . . . in all of the main Czechoslovak newspapers and, through the Associated Press Newswires, in many foreign publications."[40] In the press coverage the following day "there was no room for deviation, and the announcement was published in absolutely identical form."[41] The Wards authored their own statement, judges Vidomus, as did press conference protagonist Bohumil Laušman, argues his biographer Pavel Horák.[42] With this, both researchers rightly stress that such events were not the product of secret police puppet-mastery alone. But the exact extent to which these and other speakers authored their own testimony is ultimately unknowable and, I would argue, less important for our understanding of media in Zápotocký's Czechoslovakia than the messages that their accounts sought to convey.

Ultimately, these press conferences broadcast the clemency, not the vengeance, of the Zápotocký regime. While they were coordinated by the Czechoslovak secret police (StB), they relied upon the StB remaining in the wings of the Czechoslovak Press Agency—the stage generally chosen for such events. If Western press conferences profiled individual initiative and the initial euphoria of having made it to the West, then these Czechoslovak returnees foregrounded the moral degeneracy of the West and the superiority of material, social, and political life in Czechoslovakia. They also showcased a form of Czechoslovak humanitarianism which allegedly extended to Czechs and Slovaks no matter where they might be. An unimpressed onlooker, the Catholic RFE journalist Pavel Tigrid, described the protagonists of these spectacles as "prodigal sons." For Tigrid, these productions set out to transmit the unfaltering love of the benevolent father, Zápotocký, for his errant children.[43] They occupied radio schedules alongside the very last of the trials to be highly mediatized in Communist Czechoslovakia, but they reflect a concerted shift away from "terror" and towards "persuasion" in propaganda methods following Stalin's death.[44]

By the second half of the 1950s, historian Eleanory Gilburd finds that more and more Western culture was translated and adapted to fit the linguistic and social conditions of Eastern Europe (her focus is on the Soviet Union). This led to particular cultural artifacts understood by Eastern European audiences to be "Western" being simultaneously adopted and claimed by such audiences as their own (she references the literary work of Ernest Hemingway as an example).

Whether it was adopted by Czechoslovak audiences or not, these returnee emigrants' testimony carried a great deal of weight on account of the limited possibilities that audiences had to visit countries in the West themselves.[45] While business and even personal travel to countries like West Germany and Austria were not negligible (as the next chapter shows), for the majority of the Czechoslovak population at the time, images of the West were mediated, coming through radio, other forms of journalism, and perhaps letters from relatives. The organizers of these press conferences with returnees hoped that listeners would turn to these media spectacles to glean their information about the West, rather than to stations broadcasting directly from Western states.

Perhaps more important than the lessons these events encouraged listeners to learn about the West, though, was the template they offered Czechs and Slovaks narrating their own changing relationship with socialism in their country at the dawn of de-Stalinization. Return to Czechoslovakia offered those who undertook it the chance to start again: a "new, better life," as reporters and re-emigrants put it.[46] This suggested the humanity and benevolence of Czechoslovak state officials vis-à-vis returnee emigrants *and* the possibility, more broadly, of self-reinvention and reset within society on the part of citizens—and maybe even on the part of Communist elites.

Speaking in the mid-1950s, Bruno Folta, Bohumil Laušman, Vladimír Kučera, Helena Bušová-Kasalová, and others utilized their press conferences to engage in ritualistic self-criticism. Set phrases were preferred to individual introspection in these speakers' accounts. At their press conferences, many returnee emigres cited "adventure" as the catalyst for their emigration.[47] This extenuated their decision to leave, dismissing any form of consideration behind it with recourse to a biologized rashness often alloyed

132  Chapter 4

to the speaker's youth. Other speakers attributed their decision to leave to "ignorance."[48] Listeners were not invited to delve into speakers' motives beyond this. The fix was presented as simply as the problem. The ability to expiate one's wrongdoings came through work done well and towards the right cause. Work was hard to find in the West, a chorus of re-émigrés insisted. Thus there had been no way to integrate into society there and raise oneself up through gainful employment.[49] There was work, however, for everyone who wanted to work in Czechoslovakia, allowing "even" ethnic Germans who returned to the Czech lands to "work honestly and live humanely."[50] Re-emigrants' intentions would ultimately be revealed, the newspaper *Rudé právo* (*Red Right*) claimed, through the approach they took to their work.[51] Work was the ultimate criteria by which returnees sought to, and should, be judged.

In the enthusiasm they expressed for building socialism through work and the optimistic future that work in Czechoslovakia promised, these re-emigrant narratives differed from those produced during the 1970s and 1980s examined by Paulina Bren. This later testimony stressed the relative ease of work in Czechoslovakia in comparison to the backbreaking labor and inhumane hours demanded in the West.[52] At the time that Folta, Laušman, Kučera, Bušová-Kasalová, and others spoke, work completed diligently all but guaranteed a better future for the narrator and for listeners alike. In their bid to reintegrate into Czechoslovak society, moreover, many of these returnees pledged to become "model" workers.[53] In so doing, they somewhat changed the picture of who a model worker might be, away from the exemplary *Stakhanovite* and towards those in society judged to have been the most fallible or susceptible.

There were ways in which these press conferences contributed to a linguistic environment which Pavel Kolář has termed "post-Stalinist." This was marked by three characteristics.[54] Firstly, a new "system of inclusion and exclusion" was built, in which antagonism no longer worked purely along socialist/capitalist lines but instead allowed for the ostracism of "bad" Communists too.[55] Secondly, Khrushchev's condemnation of Stalin's "mistakes" paved the way for a new understanding of history that could incorporate contingency and false paths alongside (and perhaps within) the relentless, irreversible course of Communist progress.[56] Thirdly, the individual was reintroduced into history and its making, with "the vanguard of the party" losing its role as the supreme, and sole, historical actor.[57] As a result, "ordinary communists were no longer to be given their history and identity from above, but rather should adopt it themselves through self-narration."[58]

Several years before Khrushchev's "Secret Speech," Czechoslovak returnees were already trying out elements of the rhetorical shifts that Kolář outlines in very public speeches. Re-defectors such as Bruno Folta and Bohumil Laušman blurred the lines between good socialists and bad capitalists.[59] The "deviousness of the imperial West" framed Folta, Laušman, Kučera, and Bušová-Kasalová's narratives, but the road to ruin was no longer one way; each returnee's message was that a person could right him/herself and occupy different positions on the good socialist/bad capitalist spectrum at different moments in time. These press conferences furthermore provided prime examples of Czechs and Slovaks adopting their "history and identity" though "self-narration": among others, Laušman and Folta furnished instructive templates for individuals narrating their own changing relationship with the socialist world following Stalin's death. We might therefore read Khrushchev's speech as a product and endorsement of just such a rhetorical environment, rather than its progenitor.

This is not, of course, to argue that Khrushchev took his cues from a handful of Czech and Slovak returnees. Instead I am suggesting that Folta, Kučera, and Bušová-Kasalová's speeches were, in their turn, indicative of broader changes in both linguistic and journalistic practices following Stalin's death. These took place, in the Czechoslovak context, during the presidency of Antonín Zápotocký and as a consequence of his administration's decision to promote re-emigration. The image we glean from these press conferences qualifies our picture of his time in office as a stale prolongation of the policies and general atmosphere of the Gottwald and Stalin years.

## Journalistic Professionalization Debates

Press conferences like Kučera's granted Czechoslovak reporters a public forum to debate what good and bad journalism sounded like. In their testimony, former RFE employees like Kučera focused in on bad practices at their erstwhile place of work. Kučera compared the station's news output to cheap fiction. He claimed he had compromised the accuracy of his own reports about mining in order to spur the emotions of his listeners.[60] Bruno Folta, meanwhile, suggested that the station scoured West Germany's refugee camps both for "vulnerable" refugees to employ as journalists and news about life in Czechoslovakia for broadcast.[61] Stories about "Bolshevik terror, hunger and poverty in Czechoslovakia" were those for which RFE paid the most.[62] Folta thus described a system of news capitalism in which tales with a totalitarian tinge were the most lucrative for emigrants to tell. "The bigger the slasher story [*krvák*], the bigger the reward," Folta explained, insinuating that the literary quality of the best-selling stories was also the lowest.[63] Having thought up such *historky* (yarns) himself, Folta referenced his own experience to authenticate his claims.[64]

Journalism here came to symbolize the rival bloc's social, political, and economic systems—and the perceived ills thereof.[65] In each of their accounts, returnees insisted that money was the axis upon which RFE ultimately turned. Helena Bušová-Kasalová charged, for example, that her former colleagues would work for the devil, if the money was good enough.[66] Kučera meanwhile allegedly cited a colleague who claimed "it's dirty work, but the dollars don't stink."[67] Their pronouncements verbally evoked the dollar sign atop Pavel Tigrid's microphone in earlier polemics against RFE.

When asked by a Czechoslovak Radio correspondent to describe journalistic practices at RFE, Vladimír Kučera responded that the station doctored interviews to make working conditions in the West sound better (inflating worker's salaries, for example, by translating them into Czechoslovak crowns).[68] Most damningly, when it rained, Kučera's colleagues whiled away the hours conversing in the canteen instead of venturing out of the radio building to record. To compensate, reporters then penned commentaries bereft of any additional sound.[69] They were thus out of contact with the events that they covered and belonged to a chattering class that mistook its opinions for news.

Kučera's was implicitly a class critique, recycling earlier written dismissals of Czechs and Slovaks in exile as "coffeehouse loafers."[70] RFE was staffed by the First Republic's leisure classes who continued with their earlier practices of idling in cafes. In Kučera's telling, RFE preserved many of the problems of the interwar republic—such as its inequalities—as well as the vanished state's values (of "freedom," "truth," and "democracy") that its reporters vaunted loudly on air.[71] In his critique of RFE's workings, Kučera suggested, alongside the human resources departments of Czechoslovak media institutions, that class background was a factor affecting reporters' believability.

FIGURE 12. Cartoon of Pavel Tigrid from 1953. Tigrid was described here as a "cheerleader" for an "American war." His violent intentions are indicated by his apparent use of an axe or tomahawk to beat the drum he holds before the microphone. Source: Čestmír Suchý, Jiří Hochman, and Jiřina Brejchová, *Emigranti proti národu* (Prague: Mladá fronta, 1953), 135.

Press conference coverage itself contrasted RFE's "lazy" reporters with the image of their socialist peers. Footage of these events depicted men and women of action quizzing returnees about their experiences.

By suggesting the work of the socialist reporter was more intense than that of journalists in the West, these events juxtaposed the decadence and languor of professionals whose employment was protected on account of their social standing in the West with the vitality and energy of their peers in the East.

Kučera, Folta, and Bušová-Kasalová all stressed the remove between RFE reporters in West Germany and the United States and the Czechoslovak conditions that they claimed to expose. This remove began, according to Kučera, with reporters' reticence to stir from their office seats. Folta and Bušová-Kasalová took a different tack: they voiced their surprise as former

**FIGURES 13 AND 14.** Journalists questioning Bruno Folta at his press conference. Source: *Československý filmový týdeník*.

reporters at the scale of their own ignorance, which they only grasped upon returning home. Both reveled in the picture of plenty that greeted them upon their return.[72] Their delight at Czechoslovakia's material abundance signaled to listeners that they ought not to believe that the grass was greener in West Germany mid-*Wirtschaftswunder*. Here, Folta, and Bušová-Kasalová also indicated discrepancies between the information they had been privy to in Munich and the realities on the ground in Czechoslovakia. In this, they targeted and amplified the reservations articulated by some RFE listeners: as we will see, the isolation of its staff from the society on which they reported was indeed a factor tempering some listeners' identification with the station.

Question-and-answer sessions like this with disillusioned RFE journalists show how, during the first decade of the Cold War, "propagandists and pundits on both sides positioned journalism as the symbol of their respective social and political systems."[73] In them, Kučera and his erstwhile RFE colleagues were elevated to the status of experts on the West and Western journalism at precisely the moment when work trips abroad for Czechoslovak reporters were most restricted. Contemporaneous Czechoslovak Radio policy dictated that foreign reporting trips were to be approved a quarter of a year in advance, while those granted permission to travel abroad in the Eastern Bloc were not then to be sent to the West and vice versa.[74] On the one hand, Kučera and his colleagues presented an unparalleled view of journalistic styles on both sides of the Iron Curtain; on the other, the negative example of journalistic practices they embodied helped Eastern journalists articulate their own professional aspirations and raison d'être in ongoing domestic professionalization debates.

In the back-and-forth between media outlets across the Iron Curtain that ensued, reporters in Czechoslovakia carved out more professional autonomy. But while they granted journalists a stage to codify appropriate professional behavior, these events also sowed disillusionment among audiences. Inadvertently, they showcased voices such as Kučera's that had first presented one set of viewpoints on RFE and subsequently quite another on Czechoslovak Radio. Such speeches, perhaps more than Khrushchev's secret one never intended for "ordinary" listeners' ears, provided the soundtrack to de-Stalinization and its discontents in Czechoslovakia.[75]

### Czechoslovakia's Cynical Listeners

Radio Free Europe was not the most popular foreign station in Czechoslovakia in the 1950s and 1960s, as the next chapter shows. It came, nevertheless, to inflect the state's broader media environment, not least in the ways that state media sought to respond to its claims and repurpose some of its programming to fit their own ends. The deployment by both RFE and Czechoslovak Radio of near identical types of programming and, at times, the same voices to champion quite different ideas could lead, however, to disillusionment on the part of some listeners with both of the broadcasters

138   Chapter 4

concerned. This contributed to what writer Vojtěch Mihálik referred to as a more general apathy which had become "characteristic of Czechoslovak society" by the early 1960s.[76]

Reception data suggests that press conferences such as Kučera's certainly challenged some listeners' faith in RFE. In 1956, a Czech surgeon urged the station to air more "informative talks on the fate of Czech and Slovak emigrants . . . for people would like to hear refuted the statements made by the exiles who returned to Czechoslovakia."[77] He still credited RFE with the dissemination of "information," but suggested the station had some work to do refuting the seed of doubt planted by these returnees' exposés in Czech and Slovak listeners' minds. Audiences knew and maybe even trusted the voices of Folta, Kučera, and Bušová-Kasalová from RFE broadcasts; the deployment of their voices in this different context critiquing RFE—and the attendant questioning of their character in RFE reports—served to create reasonable doubt about the claims to authority they had made on the station.

While some questioned the credibility of RFE as a result of returnees' testimony, others evaluated the veracity of the press conferences themselves. Inmates at the Bytíz forced labor camp reportedly spent "several days" debating Bohumil Laušman's appearance on Czechoslovak Radio.[78] Prisoners fell into two groups, the first believing that Laušman had returned to Czechoslovakia of his own accord. The second group judged (rightly) that Laušman had been kidnapped and suggested that clues could be found in his testimony. In the latter group's view, Laušman "only parroted what the StB had written for him in advance."[79] His speech did not sound sufficiently personal, leading the skeptical listeners in Bytíz to claim "we have heard it all before." They dubbed what they heard "a propaganda trick to stupefy those who don't know about conditions in Czechoslovakia." In so doing, they displayed their awareness that a portion of the broadcast's intended audience resided over the Iron Curtain. Mistrusting inmates also questioned the speech's timing, arguing Laušman's propaganda value dwindled by the day: "the more time it takes, the firmer the opinion becomes that Laušman has been adequately prepared for his task, and then really no one can possibly believe him."[80]

These reception reports are marked by hearsay, with the Czech surgeon vaguely mentioning "people" seeking reassurance in light of Folta's revelations, and the informer in the second source having an unspecified relationship to the inmates in Bytíz. But RFE-solicited sources such as these still reveal traces of respondents' emotions about their daily circumstances, if not the indisputable facts of those daily circumstances themselves.[81] Importantly, such sources provide us with some sense of how those who did not end up publishing memoirs or diaries felt about the radio they listened to at the time.

They betray the suspicion that Czechoslovak listeners could feel towards some of the programming they listened to in Zápotocký's Czechoslovakia. The surgeon here articulated a wish that RFE might provide the truth combined with a doubt that it could. The Bytíz source depicts two groups of listeners attempting to read between the lines of a Czechoslovak Radio broadcast while agreeing fundamentally that the state broadcaster ought, in this instance, not to be taken literally. Both betray a general disenchantment with programming that sounded to them like "propaganda," in the Bytiz inmates' telling.

If such media events set out to contrast the shoddy journalistic practices of RFE with the "professional" world of Czechoslovak journalism, then they appear not have had quite the desired effect. While they contributed to a media landscape in which RFE was taken with a grain of salt, they hardly bolstered confidence in Czechoslovak state media. Czechs and Slovaks jumped between RFE and Czechoslovak Radio, and the rejection of one station did not lead simply to the endorsement of its rival. Instead, the circumspection that Czechs and Slovaks cultivated towards media during the Zápotocký era came to typify more than the media environment of the age.

Many in Czechoslovakia, like the surgeon quizzed here, listened to RFE at least upon occasion.[82] Musician Jan Rychlík attested to this in a diary entry from March 28, 1955:

> There's a lot of traveling going on at the moment. It isn't, however, a mass thing for the time being. Mostly it is those who weren't poor before and who were somewhere else before who are traveling. And so the public's interest is focused on the lottery. If you hand in enough junk [sběrné suroviny] and enough old paper, you can win a motorcycle, television or pen collection. The hope that you'll win is one in 30,000. But you need to know how to count a bit to figure that out. And hope after all, is hope. So what with the level of probability? The whole thing got off to a slow start. People didn't know about it, because few listen to our radio and read the daily papers. It was not until Radio Free Europe gave it a proper boost. They mentioned the lottery unfavorably in their broad-

casts and now it's up and running. There isn't, after all, anything treasonous in winning a telly for a few kilos of old paper.[83]

Rychlík's account is dripping with irony. The Communist revolution has led to the same old elites undertaking the same luxurious activities, while the brighter future it envisaged consists of the Czech and Slovak masses picking up junk. In an atmosphere approaching, he suggests, domestic press boycott, RFE had furthermore done the Czechoslovak government's bidding by publicizing the existence of a lottery in return for citizens' recycling efforts. By positing that there was nothing "treasonous in winning a telly," Rychlík insinuated that RFE listeners adopted the station's moral message when they saw fit and discarded the political nature of their own behavior when RFE's criticism cleaved uncomfortably close to the bone. The listening stance that Rychlík described was one of ironic detachment.

The station elicited violent antipathy in other listeners, in Bohumil Hrabal's telling. In "Ingots," a short story marked by graphic violence against everyone but in particular women, two characters discuss the accelerating arms race and chide RFE for its triumphalist coverage of the American nuclear bomb. Singling out announcer and wife of section chief Slavka Peroutková, one character states: "That cow, Peroutková, really got up my nose when she said that the Americans bombing Prague at the end of the war was just a teensy little foretaste, and that this time around it would be a different kettle of fish. Listen here, Peroutková, you silly cow, fuck your Radio Free Europe, because what kind of life will I have if you blow it to smithereens?"[84] Hrabal suggested—like all of the press conferences' protagonists— that RFE's reporters had a credibility problem stemming from their foreign broadcast base.

RFE disseminated "new knowledge about the destructive capacity of thermonuclear weapons" which, Melissa Feinberg argues, sparked increasing fear among those the station questioned by the mid-1950s.[85] If one of RFE's aims was to demobilize its listeners in Eastern Europe through fear, then the short extract of "Ingots" suggests a visceral and verbally explosive response, situated in a broader context in which Czech and Slovak citizens took their sense of frustration and impotence out on each other—in the most extreme form described in this story, by committing rape.[86]

Hrabal and Rychlík's accounts suggest that there were many reasons listeners might feel less than enthusiastic about RFE's reports—the station could point out the moral failings of Czechs' and Slovaks' behavior or strike fear into its listeners. Its reporters did so from a position of remove, in West Germany and the United States, where listeners believed the same forms of civic participation were not required of them and where they were apparently sheltered from the violence they could at times trumpet. Both of these accounts nuance histories of RFE suggesting the station was unreservedly welcomed by listeners around the Eastern Bloc.[87] They certainly show the fertile ground onto which revelations such as Folta's and Kučera's fell.

Heda Margolius Kovály concludes that listeners were ultimately primed to uncover Radio Free Europe's falsehoods in Zápotocký's Czechoslovakia. She disagreed with Rychlík about the scale of RFE listening, writing:

> Very few people listened to foreign broadcasts such as Radio Free Europe or the BBC, partly out of fear, but mainly because the broadcasts were so effectively jammed that it was almost impossible to understand what was being said. Occasionally someone would catch a few words out of context, surmise the rest, and pass it on. That first bit became further distorted by repetition until people dismissed it with a wave of the hand, "Now you see how they lie!"[88]

Distortions that made their way into the oral transmission of RFE news were attributed to the broadcaster itself and seen as proof of its untrustworthiness. This was far from a given and reflected listeners' preexisting notions of the station. Compare, for example, Kovály's account to the way that contemporaneous Algerian listeners responded to the heavily jammed broadcasts of the Voice of Algeria, according to Frantz Fanon:

> The listener, enrolled in the battle of the waves, had to figure out the tactics of the enemy, and in an almost physical way circumvent the strategy of the adversary. Very often only the operator, his ear glued to the receiver, had the unhoped-for opportunity of hearing the Voice. The other Algerians present in the room would receive the echo of this voice through the privileged interpreter who, at the end of the broadcast, was literally besieged . . . A real task of reconstruction would then begin. Everyone would participate, and the battles of yesterday and the day before would be re-fought in accordance with the deep aspirations and the unshakeable faith of the group. The listener would compensate for the fragmentary nature of the news by an autonomous creation of information.[89]

Both sources describe a station's patchy reception and subsequent reconstruction at the hands of listeners. But while Czechs and Slovaks found proof of RFE's "lies" therein, these same reception problems led to the "creation of information" by Voice of Algeria listeners, underpinned by their "deep aspirations" and "unshakeable faith." The nature of the conflict that both stations reported on was quite different, with Peroutková and colleagues allegedly championing the possibility of war, while the Voice of Algeria reported on battles and casualties taking place in the listener's state. As chapter 1 discussed, wartime can make the act of radio listening seem particularly meaningful. Contrasted to Fanon's listeners' "aspirations" and "faith," Kovály depicts radio listening in 1950s Czechoslovakia as meaningless. She evokes listeners' deep cynicism: Czechs and Slovaks sought to find their worst impressions of foreign broadcasters corroborated. The preexistence of such bad impressions speaks to the success (for all of the reservations that listeners articulated) of anti-RFE propaganda campaigns such as the returnee press conferences.

It is worth repeating, however, that such cynical attitudes were not only born of suspicion towards foreign stations like RFE; Czechs and Slovaks continued to have major questions about the quality and character of domestic radio too. These likewise attached themselves, above all, to programming that struck listeners as propagandistic. When one Austrian listener criticized the output of his local station in Linz, an indignant Slovak listener wrote in, advising the dissatisfied Herr Prybil to "turn the dial on his radio a few centimeters further, so that he can spend the whole day listening to Prague, where he can find such 'interesting' programmes are broadcast about how many people have undertaken voluntary work that day, for example, or how the plan was fulfilled, or which new machines have come into use in Poland or Bulgaria, and so on."[90] A Brno-based fan of Radio Vienna concurred. She begged the broadcaster to continue transmitting its programming on frequencies that she could receive. It was her "only possibility" to hear good programming, as "apart from music, Czechoslovak Radio airs lectures on peace and on plans that remain only that: plans."[91]

The cynicism these listeners articulated here was directed in particular at programming that struck them as proclamatory, predictable, and hollow. They both wrote about it, like Rychlík had before them, in deeply ironic ways. They suggested that such programming, in its predictability, bored them. But the second of these disgruntled listeners—like many others who voiced their frustration with Czechoslovak Radio over these years—built important caveats into her complaint. Here, music was Czechoslovak Radio's saving grace; elsewhere, it had been, somewhat vaguely, "really interesting reporting," or broadcasts from the radio exhibition MEVRO, or the reports of Jiří Hanzelka and Miroslav Zikmund.[92] As the Brno-based listener cited here was writing to an Austrian Radio station, it is not likely that she was attempting to be polite or otherwise compelled to find a positive in Czechoslovak Radio's programming. Indeed, the structure she employed here of "with one exception, Czechoslovak Radio is dreadful" is mirrored in the fan mail sent to Jiří Hanzelka and Miroslav Zikmund and examined in chapter 3.[93] This very formulation shows the possibility for coexisting attitudes of disenchantment and enchantment directed towards state socialist radio.

### Conclusion

Competing cynical and engaged listening attitudes could coexist in socialist Czechoslovakia, and listeners could prove, at times, quite reflexive about this. These only ostensibly contradictory attitudes attached themselves to broadcasts emanating from both sides of the Iron Curtain, as the criticism of the émigré press conferences here makes clear, suggesting that listeners' own party-political convictions were not always the primary lens through which they evaluated (and rejected) content.

Listeners' cynical attitudes came to fasten themselves to particular types of programming, above all broadcasts that struck their audiences as proclamatory, predictable, or hollow (which is to say at odds with listeners' own empirical findings). Confusing journalism such as Vladimír Kučera's dialogue with himself across radio stations in 1955 also elicited a negative response. Czechoslovak Radio and RFE's attempts to deploy here the same media genres, and even the same voices to apparently incompatible ideological ends—at the same time as insisting upon the unique believability of their own programming—constituted the sort of confusing journalism that could elicit a stance of ironic detachment on the part of listeners. The allegations that Kučera made may not have proven utter bombshells to audiences mired in the mudslinging of the early Cold War, but they certainly did not foster trust in those same quarters. They constituted strikingly public discussions in Czechoslovak socialist mass media about how radio was made behind the scenes (which focused on the negative example of RFE's alleged malpractice). While occasions such as this did provide journalists with important opportunities to codify their own professional standards, listeners hardly appear to have reflected upon these moments in retrospect as lifting their overall estimation of journalism.

144   Chapter 4

There were ways in which the cynical listening attitudes examined here were products of de-Stalinization. For example, they were connected to genres of programming such as the émigré press conference that came to exist in connection with the period's limited legal reforms. Moreover, Czechoslovak Radio's attempts to vernacularize and professionalize its output—the two ways in which the broadcaster sought to undertake de-Stalinization during the Zápotocký years—created their own forms of backlash. The same Bratislava journalists who had defended reporters' right to speak over the workers they interviewed on account of the radio professional's "specialization," themselves rued a few short months later that the radio's venacularization and professionalization drives were resulting in the opposite of the more engaged audiences for which they had hoped. And if cynicism and apathy were themselves key characteristics of the period of de-Stalinization in Czechoslovakia, then this chapter has shown how radio broadcasts certainly contributed to this.[94] In stressing this point, this chapter has delved into some of the particularities of the period between 1954 and 1963 in Czechoslovak history, which Muriel Blaive has suggested is often "glossed over" on account of the ostensibly minimal change taking place in the upper echelons of the Communist Party at the time.[95]

But there are ways, too, in which the coexistence of negative and positive listening attitudes articulated by listeners here were not at all specific to de-Stalinization. The Brno listener's complaint to Radio Vienna that, "with the exception of one thing, all Czechoslovak Radio's output is awful" echoes the formulas that listeners had used when writing to Jiří Hanzelka and Miroslav Zikmund in the late 1940s and early 1950s. Therefore, this chapter has made the case for the endurance of such discerning attitudes on the part of Czechoslovakia's radio listeners throughout, and beyond, the first decade of Communist rule.

If this Brno-based listener drew on a widespread template when she articulated her partial enjoyment of Czechoslovak Radio, then she also conformed to another, far more widespread trend, when it came to where she turned when Czechoslovak Radio programming failed to entertain. Austrian stations such as her addressee, Radio Vienna, enjoyed a sizeable audience alongside other German-language broadcasters in socialist-era Czechoslovakia. The next chapter examines why.

# 5 Listening in on the Neighbors

*The Reception of German and Austrian
Radio in Cold War Czechoslovakia*

**PRESENTER ERNST HILGER** raised a laugh when he suggested to a live radio audience in Linz in 1965 that he would translate effortlessly what his cohost in České Budějovice (Budweis) had just said to audiences across the border in Czech. Despite Hilger's ironic dig at the incomprehensibility of the Czech language, his joke indicated a degree of fellow feeling across borders between Austrians and citizens of Czechoslovakia. It came as part of a broadcast of *Alle Neune*, a radio game show coproduced by Austrian public broadcaster ORF's (Österreichischer Rundfunk) regional subsidiary in Linz and Czechoslovak Radio's local station in České Budějovice. The program, which aired on both state broadcasters, featured live audiences in both locations showing how much they knew about each other's culture—in one round, the Austrian and Czech teams both had to guess which Strauss waltz and Smetana polka they had just heard. Additional rounds of the game show (on famous Europeans or canonical dramatic texts) pointed out how much both constituencies had in common.

The program was a celebration of radio technology and infrastructure—through radio, the inhabitants of České Budějovice could answer questions posed by people in Linz, and their answers could be heard in Prague and

Vienna, where stations relayed the program. Listeners from both countries were encouraged to participate by mailing in their answers to a question posed especially for them; those who wrote in were promised a book, whether they correctly guessed the answer or not. One round of the game show paid homage to the Linz-České Budějovice railway—the first horse-drawn railway in Europe built in 1825. While the railway was invoked as proof of Linz and České Budějovice's historic connection, the program demonstrated how the technology had been superseded and radio could now transfer information between the two locations more quickly. At the end, hosts Jiří Stuchal and Ernst Hilger concluded that radio built bridges, and guests in both locations clapped their approval.

Coproductions such as *Alle Neune* have been examined for what they show of changing international politics at the elite level during the Cold War.[1] But here, I argue that *Alle Neune* constituted Czechoslovak and Austrian state endorsement of "grassroots" listening practices that both parties already knew existed and that were not particular to the liberal 1960s. Czechs and Slovaks listened to German-language radio from Austria and West Germany in the thousands during the postwar period. By officializing Czechoslovak listening to, letter writing to, and participation in Austrian radio, Czechoslovak Radio sought to claim, through *Alle Neune*, some of these practices' popularity for itself. Thus institutional, infrastructural projects such as *Alle Neune* should not always be understood to constitute dirigiste attempts at shaping citizens' perceptions and solidarities; by embarking on such projects, state actors could also take advantage of and formalize networks already created by their citizens.

The scale of Austrian and West German radio listening is made apparent in surveys conducted by Radio Free Europe about listening habits in the Eastern Bloc. RFE reception polls throughout the 1960s found that Radio Vienna was the most popular foreign station with Czechoslovak listeners. The American-sponsored broadcaster instigating such surveys was, perhaps to its own analysts' chagrin, frequently the runner-up to German-language radio in the contest for audiences. Such conclusions find reinforcement in the Communist Party's own reports from the 1950s and 1960s and in the first systematic Czechoslovak radio polls from the end of the 1960s.[2] German-language radio listening thus emerges as a constant of radio's second "golden age" in Czechoslovakia.

Cross-border, German-language listening during the Cold War mattered, then, not only between the Germanies, but also in Central Europe, where listening habits were shaped by the multilingual heritage of the region. Focusing on this, rather than on the experience of listening to RFE which most scholarship on foreign radio in Czechoslovakia has done to date, additionally reveals the enduring significance of German as a language of regional communication, the continued importance of cross-border contacts (in particular in border regions), and the significance of light entertainment in Central Europe during the Cold War.

While the "ability to receive radio and television from neighboring countries was not specific to the case of divided Germany," Frank Bösch and Cristoph Classen have claimed, "it had particular significance within the context of the German-German rivalry because there were no language or cultural barriers that had to be overcome."[3] But historians have wrongly assumed linguistic barriers between citizens of different Central European states in the postwar era. Instead, language barriers had to be *created* between Czechs, Slovaks, and Germans—which led to generational divides emerging between media users at the onset of the Cold War. Exploring first who listened to German-language radio, how, and when, this chapter overturns the notion that Europeans held linguistically homogenous media preferences after the Second World War. Czechs and Slovaks may have lived in an increasingly ethnically homogenous state, but they did not forget the languages they had learned in school and had used (no matter how grudgingly) in daily encounters with the state and other citizens during earlier regimes. Following this sketch of listening techniques and venues, a short section on language politics in postwar Czechoslovakia maps in more detail the rise and fall and rise of German as a language of regional communication.

I then turn to the way that radio was used by listeners in Czechoslovakia to maintain and rework cross-border contacts, particularly in border zones. Analyzing above all Czechs' and Slovaks' experiences of listening to Austrian stations, I show how their actions at once retooled cultural practices established under the Habsburg monarchy and reflected broader contemporary media consumption trends. Next, I take the Austrian driving show *Autofahrer Unterwegs* as a case study in how Czechoslovak listeners remediated contact with German speakers. Finally, I investigate the significance of

148 Chapter 5

such light entertainment during the Cold War, returning to the game show *Alle Neune*.

Devised by ORF to celebrate "all nine" of Austria's federative states and their historic international connections, *Alle Neune* shows the enduring infrastructural importance of regional interchanges long beyond the demise of the Habsburg Empire and into the Cold War. That Linz and České Budějovice (and not Prague and Vienna) were chosen for this high-profile production shows how infrastructures tend to, as Lisa Parks and Nicole Starosielski point out, reutilize former connections, "depending" on previous networks for their routes while creating new cultural, economic, and societal configurations.[4] The Linz-Budějovice nexus of this radio link also attests to the significance of provincial, borderland radio interconnections, which are frequently overlooked, argue Carolyn Birdsall and Joanna Walewska-Choptiany, in transnational radio histories which wrongly "privilege radio produced by national broadcasters in capital cities, located at the heart of 'media capital,' and invested in reproducing the image of 'media centrality.' "[5]

If media histories rarely focus on borderlands as key sites of media use, then Central and Eastern European historiography frequently takes them as its focus. Czechoslovakia's postwar borderlands have been researched both as sites of ethnic cleansing and as a ground zero for Communist modernization.[6] Revealing how local populations used foreign media (and modern technologies) to renegotiate their relationships with native German speakers, I qualify the extent to which the "new" societies forged in the borderlands following the war completely broke with past practices of association. I also question the characterization of such spaces as *"former* contact zones."[7] Instead, inhabitants reshaped contact with German native speakers to suit their own ends. Listening to Western radio did not constitute a failure to recognize the Czechoslovak state's sovereign borders. Rather, foreign radio listening diversified the ways in which Czech and Slovak citizens could position themselves within their own society. Their use of foreign media was ultimately appropriable by Czechoslovak state actors through initiatives such as *Alle Neune* and in this way came to impact centralized media programming.

The majority of scholarship on light entertainment's importance during the Cold War focuses on television.[8] This exploration of German-language radio reveals how governments and media professionals, East and West, placed such hopes in radio too and, moreover, at an earlier period than TV-centered scholarship might suggest. The image that emerges is of a reactive and populist Czechoslovak Communist regime seeking and only partially managing during Stalinism and de-Stalinization to cater to the radio preferences of its citizens. Where possible, I introduce the perspectives of listeners themselves into discussions of light entertainment, indicating how game shows, phone-ins, and Austrian pop provided opportunities for audience interaction and the possibility of inclusion in Cold War listening communities that hinged more upon musical taste than one's stance toward the Communist Party. The inclusion of listeners' opinions tempers Reinhold Wagnleitner's findings that Austrian radio helped establish American influence in postwar Europe: in interviews, Czechoslovak listeners repeatedly remarked upon the "Austrian flavor" of what they heard while remaining silent about the Americanizing elements of broadcasts such as adverts and news.[9] Rather than separating listeners out primarily by citizenship or ethnicity, I ultimately show how the solidarities fostered by shows such as *Autofahrer Unterwegs* and *Alle Neune* cut across national boundaries and divided people up by generation, geography, class, and technical dexterity.

An analysis of German-language radio reframes discussions of radio listening in Cold War Czechoslovakia, which have largely been shaped by historiography on the American-sponsored broadcaster RFE. Authors have adopted one of four strategies to justify this focus, each with its own drawbacks. Firstly, scholars have worked outward from RFE's articulated aims to understand the station's "success"—and indeed listeners' behavior. According to Arch Puddington, RFE sought to topple Communism through eliciting "acts of personal resistance" from listeners.[10] Did they or did they not do as the broadcaster hoped? The framing of this question necessarily leads to the conclusion that RFE enjoyed some measure of success (the debate becomes to what degree). But such analysis presumes a rather two-dimensional relationship between broadcasters and listeners, with the former telling the latter what to do, and the latter doing it (or not).

Secondly, historians have pointed to RFE's unique "popularity."[11] But such claims are directly contradicted by Prokop Tomek who finds, in his comprehensive study of the broadcaster, that "the majority of the Czechoslovak population did not listen to Radio Free Europe, nor was it the most popular foreign radio station" in socialist Czechoslovakia.[12] Tomek belongs

150  Chapter 5

to the third school, which explores measures the regime took against RFE to reveal the station's importance.[13] By positing RFE's social significance as a corollary of regime repression, however, Tomek employs a heuristic framework established by a regime he criticizes for its overreaction and out-of-touch nature to comprehend the society it claimed to represent.[14] The fourth and final strategy is to cite dissidents from the region saying how important the station was to them.[15] No one experience of Communism—dissident or otherwise—is, of course, more valid than another.[16] But there is a problem in taking the view of, say, Václav Havel, whose plight was regularly promoted by RFE precisely on account of his dissident status, to speak for Czechs and Slovaks in general (particularly in the face of data suggesting that, when it came to matters of the radio, he did not).

RFE analysts during the Cold War, and subsequent historians of the institution such as Puddington, Parta, and Johnson equated listening to RFE—and indeed Western radio more generally—with "resistance to communism."[17] Despite some fine scholarship nuancing this view, this interpretation has become more widespread in recent years on the part of listeners themselves, with memoirist Jan Šesták claiming, in one example, that listening to radio-relayed rock 'n' roll constituted anti-Communist "rebellion" in Czechoslovakia.[18] A recent Prague exhibit suggested that listening to Western radio during the socialist period contributed to Czechoslovakia's "freedom" from dictatorship.[19] Retroactively understanding foreign radio listening as innately anti-Communist fits in to what oral historian Miroslav Vaněk has called a year-on-year growth in "the number of alleged resistors or 'warriors against the regime'" to have opposed Communism after its demise.[20] Claims such as Šesták's overstate the risks of listening to foreign radio and reduce the politics of this activity to a question of party politics. Ironically, the reconstruction of a Communist/anti-Communist listening binary revives the logic of Communist functionaries during the Stalinist era, who sought to corral radio listening practices into narrow categories of political reliability and unreliability.[21] Such a party-political understanding overwrites the practical and personal reasons that people tuned into the West.

Here, I use RFE sources to tell another story. The interviews that RFE analysts gathered with emigrants and tourists in the West throughout the 1950s and 1960s provide unparalleled insight into Czechs' and Slovaks' listening techniques and attitudes towards radio. By taking their institutional biases into account when reading and rereading such sources, I reveal what they have to say about the enduring significance of the German language, cross-border connections, and light entertainment in Communist Czechoslovakia instead.[22] While RFE compiled "information items" to look for resistance to Communism and find signs of socialism's imminent downfall (and the station's role in this), their findings shed much more light on the cohesive effects of Czechs' and Slovaks' wide-ranging and esoteric media tastes in the 1950s and 1960s.

## Listening to German-Language Radio in Czechoslovakia

The practice of German-language radio listening in Czechoslovakia had precedents that predated the Cold War. Czech and Slovak listeners were used to hearing German on Czechoslovak frequencies both before and during the Second World War.[23] They were also used to actively seeking out German-language spoken films: Petr Szczepanik finds that German and Austrian "talkies" beat their Hollywood counterparts hands down in the box office in 1930s Czechoslovakia. He attributes this to the fact that, despite the state's changing geopolitical and technological circumstances, "audiences remained embedded in old cultural traditions of popular music and theatre" established under the Habsburg monarchy, when Vienna was the cultural center of the empire.[24]

Official German-language broadcasting in Czechoslovakia came to an abrupt halt following the end of the Second World War. Banishing German from the corridors of public service broadcaster Czechoslovak Radio, however, did not erase the sound of German from the republic's radio receivers. In the immediate postwar years, the Czechoslovak Ministry of Information acknowledged that it was easier to tune into German-language stations in some western and southern regions of Czechoslovakia than it was to pick up Czechoslovak Radio.[25] The reception of German-language radio stations became a matter of international diplomacy when Ministry of Information officials urged their counterparts in the Ministry of Foreign Affairs to include a clause on radio broadcasting in the postwar peace treaty they were negotiating with Germany; Prague sought to limit German broadcasting aimed at Czechoslovakia, which it understood as an enduring act of hostility on its neighbor's part.[26]

The efforts of the authorities failed to curb the reception of German-language radio on Czechoslovak soil. When those deemed ethnically German (and not sufficiently anti-fascist) were being stripped of their citizenship between 1945 and 1947, disgruntled Czechoslovak nationalists complained to the Ministry of Information about the continued presence of the German language in Czechoslovakia over the airwaves. According to such activists, Czechoslovakia's aural environment should be purged of German just as its physical environment was being cleared of Germans.[27] To solve the "problem" of German language radio, the government set to work building radio infrastructure in Czechoslovakia's border regions and attempting to roll out FM broadcasting (which suffered less interference from neighboring stations). Financial constraints, however, limited the speed of such infrastructural projects' implementation.

Czechs and Slovaks made the Ministry of Information aware of their own German-language radio listening to gain concessions from officials. In one example, a listener lamented shortly after the Communist takeover that "I am always somewhat ashamed when I catch a foreign station, for example Vienna or Budapest, and I hear lots of beautiful arias from our operas, while here amateur brass music prevails."[28] In this complaint, the listener couched her habits in the necessary language of shame and regret in a bid to alter Czechoslovak Radio's music policy. She suggested that her foreign listening practices were, in fact, patriotic, as both Vienna and Budapest played "our" operas, while Czechoslovak Radio allegedly shunned them in favor of oompah hits. Other listeners wrote to the Ministry outlining their foreign radio-listening habits in a bid to inspire an earlier start to Czechoslovak Radio's morning programming and a more "natural" style of reporting, such as one heard "in the West."[29]

The Czechoslovak government considered outlawing foreign radio listening but decided against such an idea, because prohibitive legislation had been highly unpopular under Nazi rule and had also proved almost impossible to implement.[30] Despite what might be argued from certain historical perspectives, the fledgling socialist regime was in no rush to have parallels drawn between itself and its Nazi forebears. Nor did it seek to expose its inability to monitor and control its citizens by imposing a law that would prove so easy to flout. Instead, the regime sought to nudge Czechoslovak citizens towards approved forms of domestic radio listening and to stigmatize unapproved forms of radio listening socially by dubbing them "German"—regardless of the language such stations broadcast in.

With RFE's first broadcasts in 1950, the grudging acceptance of Czechs' and Slovaks' foreign radio listening changed. To counter this station's Czech- and Slovak-language broadcasts, authorities placed their faith in the speedy development of new media; television broadcasts, Ministry of Information officials judged (in hindsight rather optimistically), "cannot be adopted from abroad, [and therefore] we want to focus listeners' interest on television and thus distract their attention from listening to foreign [radio] propaganda."[31] Again placing their faith in technology as a solution to the foreign radio predicament, the Czechoslovak authorities introduced jamming in 1952. Jamming was a means of interrupting foreign radio stations by broadcasting domestic programming, or simply a steady signal, on the same frequencies. This drowned out the sound of the stations targeted.[32] The phenomenon was known colloquially as "Stalin's bagpipes."

**FIGURE 15.** Cartoon from *Rudé Právo* in which Radio Free Europe's links to West German rearmament were insinuated. A caption suggested that the "lies of Radio Free Europe" provided a smoke screen hiding the work of German weapons producers. The cleanly shaven, smoke-blowing reporter resembles RFE Czechoslovak service chief Ferdinand Peroutka. Source: Czech Literary Bibliography Research Infrastructure. Reprinted with the permission of the Institute of Czech Literature of the CAS.

154   Chapter 5

People came up with their own ways around signal jamming, as RFE sources suggest. One Czech surgeon suggested that the practice sent people hunting for foreign stations that may not have been their first choice.[33] He explained that friends had devised a workaround, which relied upon their foreign language skills: with "transmissions of all the Western broadcasting stations . . . jammed for listeners in Prague," the surgeon's acquaintances tuned in instead to "BBC transmissions in German [that] had clear reception."[34] Another interviewee described himself habitually undertaking this very practice, calling himself "an enthusiastic listener to BBC programs, but mainly to those of the German service, from about 20:00 hrs onwards."[35] This listener followed German-language radio "for two reasons: firstly, it was not jammed, and secondly, he did not want his nine-year-old son to know what he was listening to."[36] This testimony shows how Czechs and Slovaks developed techniques to mitigate jamming's effects, relying upon their linguistic skills to produce a DIY solution to the problem jamming posed (with some generations more capable of this than others, to which the father of a nine-year-old fluent in Russian but not German could attest).

Czechoslovakia's Stalinist authorities, and the RFE analysts who quizzed Central European listeners, may have wished to present radio listening as an either/or practice: either one listened to "seditious"/ "freedom-bearing" foreign broadcasters or one listened to "truthful"/ "propagandistic" domestic Czechoslovak Radio. But both constituencies understood very well that listeners in fact station hopped, as the last chapter made clear. In the early 1950s, indeed, a range of programs sought to cater to such inconsistent listeners. On RFE, *Rub a líc* (*The Other Side of the Coin*) set out to "overturn" the lies that listeners were assumed to have been heard first on Czechoslovak Radio, while Czechoslovak Radio meanwhile broadcast numerous commentaries about why the claims made on Radio Free Europe were wrong.[37] Such mudslinging over the radio mistook elites' chief rivals for the foreign radio that actually mattered most to Czech and Slovak listeners.

In 1955, the CIA judged that "listening to Western stations is widespread, and even Party members admit that they have listened to some Western broadcasts."[38] The report continued that "intellectuals" listened to "German broadcasts from Switzerland (Beromuenster), RIAS (Berlin), and Red-White-Red (Vienna), whose reception is clearer than [the] Czech and Slovak broadcasts of the Western stations."[39] For the CIA, German-language radio listening in Czechoslovakia was a matter of class; professionals were apparently happy to listen to radio in a second language in a way that blue-collar workers were not. The report rejected the premise that foreign radio listening constituted "resistance" to Communism, with listening habits cutting across party political affiliation. It also acknowledged that listening ease constituted an important reason why Czechs and Slovaks might tune into such broadcasts.

Jamming was expensive and, in the 1960s, cash-strapped Czechoslovak officials scaled it back. Despite registering a "shift in listenership from Czechoslovak Radio towards more entertaining and topical broadcasts by neutral states' stations, particularly from Austria and Switzerland," Politburo members redoubled their efforts to restrict RFE and RFE alone.[40] They singled it out as the sole foreign broadcaster for jamming, ultimately deploying the practice against only certain shows. While officials fulminated against German-language media and the unflattering mirror they shone on their Czechoslovak counterparts, they clearly continued to deem such stations less of a personal existential threat. "Entertaining and topical broadcasts" from Austria and Switzerland were much less likely than RFE, after all, to report upon discord and malfeasance within the Czechoslovak Communist Party's ranks.[41]

Meanwhile, RFE listener surveys found that Radio Vienna was the most popular foreign station with listeners in Czechoslovakia throughout the 1960s. The American-sponsored broadcaster instigating such polls was frequently the runner-up. In 1962, 35 percent of interviewees said they listened to Radio Vienna (as opposed to 33 percent who followed RFE). From 1963 to 1964, some 39 percent of Czechs and Slovaks said they tuned into Radio Vienna (as opposed to 37 percent who listened to RFE).[42] And in 1965, some 71 percent of those questioned said they listened to Radio Vienna (as opposed to 43 percent who listened to RFE).[43]

German-language listening practices then informed how Czechs and Slovaks approached television. During the 1970s, described by Paulina Bren as the start of the television age in Czechoslovakia, German-language programming made its way onto the television sets proliferating in the border regions where German-language radio listening had long been widespread.[44] Informed by their experiences of radio jamming, Prague officials also decided not to jam these signals, reasoning that such a (costly) step

156  Chapter 5

may have interfered in domestic Austrian or West German broadcasting and therefore caused an international dispute.[45] With a now customary mix of anxiety and impotence, functionaries worried that satellite television would extend coverage to other parts of the country too, addressing citizens hitherto unaware of German-language media's attractions.[46] That those able to tune into Western television did so is indicated by the high sales of Austrian Communist newspaper *Volksstimme* in Czechoslovakia. In addition to its ostensibly high-quality reporting, more importantly the publication included the daily Austrian television schedule. By the end of the 1980s, the Czechoslovak press resorted to publishing Austrian television listings themselves.[47]

### German in Postwar Czechoslovakia

Noting what he calls Radio Vienna's "surprising" popularity in RFE listener polls which endured through the 1970s and 1980s, Prokop Tomek explains that "only a third of Czechoslovak adults, in particular those in older age groups, understood German."[48] What Tomek refers to as "only" a sliver of the population amounted to, by this calculation, over three million people. Older generations were used to German in the classroom, in the media, on street signs, and in public institutions, and some may have even participated in a *Kinderaustausch* (child swap) with a German-speaking family during their childhood. Following the war, the public use of German was restricted, and the venues for speaking and hearing the language reduced. Before German-language television rose to prominence in the 1970s, even members of the state's remaining German minority struggled to "preserve" their German, according to Sandra Kreisslová and Niklas Perzi.[49]

But even during Stalinism, when restrictions ushered in following the war remained strong, official attitudes towards the German language were ambivalent. German allegedly benefited from a shift away from English teaching in Czechoslovak schools in 1951.[50] *Aufbau und Frieden*, a German-language weekly newspaper, began publication in Prague that year, renaming itself *Volkszeitung* in 1966.[51] It appeared at Czechoslovak newsstands alongside the East German daily *Neues Deutschland*.[52] A "general relaxation in language practice" was discernable to an inhabitant of Dolní Poustevna on the border with East Germany by 1952, with German increasingly to be heard on the town's dance floors and in pubs.[53] German, after all, was a language spoken by citizens of one of Czechoslovakia's socialist allies just meters down the road. German-language training was furthermore required in order to collaborate with East German experts posted to key Czechoslovak industries such as textiles and metallurgy, and indeed on exchanges overseas.[54]

Czechoslovak citizens might listen to the radio to learn German or, conversely, they might learn German to listen to the radio. Domestic broadcaster Czechoslovak Radio promoted the first of these two activities with German-language classes as part of its daytime *Školský rozhlas* (*School Radio*).[55] Citizens taught themselves languages directly through listening to foreign stations too.[56] Others learned foreign languages to better enjoy radio content: the DJs of Radio Luxembourg were Jan Šesták's "secret teachers" of English which he sought to learn to understand rock and roll.[57] If American and British music seem the only types capable of seducing Czechs and Slovaks into language learning, then the case of erstwhile king of Czechoslovak pop (and Austrian Eurovision star) Karel Gott is revealing. He claimed that West German music provided him with the initial impulse to learn German.[58]

In a state which dedicated limited resources to the instruction of foreign languages, radio could provide a readily available learning aid. Czechs and Slovaks used the medium to improve their German, English, and, less well remembered, to gain practice in the mostly widely taught foreign language of all: Russian.[59] That radio listeners such as Šesták used the medium to work on a language they were being taught in school qualifies the extent to which we should understand such radio usage to constitute "linguistic disobedience." But decoding what a beloved singer was saying or using radio to heighten one's chances of acing a class test both certainly subsumed the mass media available in Cold War Czechoslovakia to one's personal interests and ambitions.

## Radio in the Provinces

While many of the sources evaluated so far bear a Pragocentric bias, Ministry of Information files and Czechs' and Slovaks' own testimony of Cold War radio listening (not to mention the experience of driving about the Czech and Slovak Republics today) show that borderlands were the key site of foreign radio "spillover," where foreign radio listening was the most commonplace.[60] Focusing on how local inhabitants actively remediated earlier connections they had had with their neighbors qualifies the extent to which we should view Czechoslovakia's "cleansed" border regions as "former contact zones," now "hobbled by decaying infrastructure."[61] It was in these "peripheral" locations, at times overlooked by elites in Prague's ministries and media historians more generally, that radio listeners used the infrastructures available to them to renegotiate contact with their German-speaking neighbors in ways that benefited them practically and in ways that came to inflect centralized Czechoslovak media content.

The Ministry of Defense's jamming maps for RFE reveal that the state's jamming power concentrated on areas of the country with the highest population density, leaving the state's periphery (where foreign signals were the strongest and the population frequently the most dispersed) relatively untouched.

For metropolitan visitors, the sonic experience of this map meant a holiday for the ears. Jan Šesták recalls how a trip to the North Bohemian mountains gave his hearing a break: upon return to Brno, his attempts to tune into Western radio were again marked by "music covered in static, music that would fade depending on the atmospherics."[62] And just as one might come to associate a particular song with one's summer holiday today, RFE sources suggest that listening to foreign radio stations was seen by some city-dwellers as part of, and subsequently synonymous with, the experience of vacations spent out of town.[63]

For local border region inhabitants, Western media reception was widespread enough that it created its own social allegiances and social divides. A Sudeten German from North Bohemia suggested that the RIAS signal was so clear in Jablonec nad Nisou that local German and Czech speakers alike tuned in to the station. While he petitioned RIAS to schedule more programming specifically for ethnic Germans living as minorities in socialist states (as he believed Czechs and Slovaks already had their own station—RFE—for this purpose), he nevertheless identified the shared experience of listening to RIAS as something that diminished differences between Jablonec's linguistic groups.[64] Shows such as *Schlager der Woche* may have brought people together, in his opinion, but they were also capable of driving neighbors apart. In České Budějovice's school yards some years after the end of radio's second golden age, Martin Matiska recalled that Austrian radio continued to confer a social prestige on its teenage listeners, stigma-

**FIGURE 16.** Map displaying the reach of RFE jamming in Czechoslovakia, September 1952. The country is split here into three, color-coded zones. The red areas are described as being "fully covered, enemy broadcasting does not penetrate at all." The green areas (which include vast swathes of Czechoslovakia's border regions) are deemed to be "partially covered, sibilants or some words are audible, but impossible to understand the sense of a sentence." Finally, the blue zones are "uncovered, out of the reach of jamming, everything comprehensible." Importantly, this map only shows the locations in which RFE was jammed, while the picture looked different (and less restrictive) for other Western stations. České Budějovice—later home to the broadcast of *Alle Neune*—is in a region in which RFE was successfully blocked. Here in South Bohemia, foreign stations transmitted from neighboring Austria were the easiest to catch. Source: Czech Security Services Archive. Secretariat of the Minister of the Interior (A 2/1), inv. no. 432. Reprinted with permission.

tizing those who failed to listen. Matiska explained that the Austrian pop chart broadcast weekly throughout the 1980s on Ö3 on Sundays, and those who missed it were subsequently pilloried for their lack of street cred in school on Mondays.[65] His listening habits and those of his peers explain the popularity of stars like Falco and Sandra in 1980s Czechoslovakia and their

160   Chapter 5

prominence on nostalgic radio stations playing classic hits in the Czech Republic today.[66]

Czechoslovak functionaries acknowledged the state's periphery as a site where "listening to West German radio and in particular the American station RIAS was widespread" throughout the 1960s. They understood these sites as key venues of Austrian and Swiss radio listening too.[67] It was such official recognition which paved the way for state-sanctioned cross-border initiatives like *Alle Neune* in 1965.

If "radio in the provinces" is a geographic term denoting listening habits in the Czechoslovak territories with the strongest Western radio frequencies, then it is also a generic term referring to a particular type of radio broadcasting. Austrian radio directors, for example, distinguished between metropolitan and provincial audiences when they fashioned the country's radio network into the statewide ORF in the mid-1950s.[68] With the restructuring of Austrian radio following the signing of the State Treaty, Vienna became a statewide broadcaster, tasked with burnishing the image of Austria as a "cultural superpower" domestically and to audiences abroad, while regional stations such as that based in Linz—producers of the aforementioned *Alle Neune*—were expected to broadcast more light entertainment, including game shows and popular music. Thus, less sophisticated regional offerings came to be broadcast on Ö2's frequencies, while Vienna was eventually rebranded as Ö1. Provincial radio was qualitatively and aesthetically different to that produced in the media capital, and letters to Czech officials about Vienna's arias aside, it appears to have been this light entertainment which proved a particular hit with Czechoslovak listeners. This point is made by and simultaneously obscured in the surveys used here, which bundled different Austrian stations together, asking their respondents to discuss their experiences of listening to "Vienna."[69]

Faced with the reality of large audiences at the peripheries of Central and Eastern European states, Western media programmers yearned above all to address metropolitan elites.[70] A well-remembered example of these attempts is provided by the *Stadtgespräche (City Talks)*—a Czechoslovak Television and ORF coproduction spanning 1963–1964. This short-lived set of TV discussions derived their weight from the "media capital" of their broadcast locations, Prague and Vienna. Invited guests discussed human rights and cultural politics, among other topics. Their host, Helmut Zilk, subsequently became the mayor of Vienna and modestly suggested in hindsight that the programs had served as the catalyst for the Prague Spring.[71]

Such debates about human rights and cultural politics were not, however, to everyone's taste. For television, Paulina Bren has claimed that the "majority of viewers who could turn to Western television did not do so for purely ideological reasons." Instead, they switched when programs were "too strongly adapted to the demands of the Prague intellectual elite" (imagine their dismay on the nights of the *Stadtgespräche!*).[72] Rightly or wrongly, media professionals and pollsters East and West came to think along the lines of two audience camps whose entertainment preferences suggested they had more in common with audiences across borders than fellow nationals. With some scholarly attention already paid to the metropolitan elites embodied by Zilk and the *Stadtgespräche*, I turn now to his colleagues at "Ö-Regional"—Walter Niesner and Rosemarie Isopp—and the mix of Austrian traffic news and music requests they presented in *Autofahrer Unterwegs*.[73]

### Autofahrer Unterwegs

When trying to understand Austrian radio's "evident popularity" in the mid-1960s, RFE staff attributed it "first and foremost" to "the popular daily 50-minute program *Autofahrer Unterwegs*."[74] Explaining that "traditional ties between Austria and the populations of Southern Bohemia, Southern Moravia, and South-West Slovakia" played an important role in Austrian radio's approval ratings, RFE analysts dismissed their findings that more Czechs and Slovaks tuned into Austrian radio than their own reporting as a historical relic. Such behavior, in this view, had more in common with the world of the Linz-České Budějovice horse-drawn railway than it did with the new Cold War world order in which these listeners found themselves.

But program format, evaluators conceded, was a crucial factor in attracting audiences at home and abroad. They concluded that *Autofahrer Unterwegs's* combination of "advice to the motorist," "human interest items," and "personal greetings and messages from drivers . . . sent to persons in Austria and other countries, including Czechoslovakia" proved singularly successful.[75]

Hosted by Niesner and Isopp, *Autofahrer Unterwegs* broadcast traffic updates and details of stolen cars alongside messages to drivers daily starting in 1957. The show served as a message board for matters not directly

**FIGURE 17.** *Autofahrer Unterwegs* film poster from 1961.

related to driving as well. It epitomized the "immense popularity of local classifieds" which Frank Bösch and Cristoph Classen suggest swept 1960s Central Europe, creating an audio version of the free newspapers full of such adverts which proliferated in the West at this time.[76] The tremendously popular show spurred its own eponymous polka and, in 1961, a film.[77] It ceased broadcasting after an impressive forty-two-year run in 1999.

In 2017, Isopp recalled that "everything was possible with this program . . . When someone had an accident and needed a wheelchair, we had one by the next day. We brought children who had run away home. And we found an antidote for a child who had been bitten by a snake and saved his life."[78] The sort of classified advertising service that *Autofahrer Unterwegs* ran extended into Czechoslovakia, with Isopp recalling that:

A woman from Bratislava called us crying during a broadcast. She begged for help, because she had had an eye operation and feared that she would go blind as she was running out of medicine. I announced this and a quarter of an hour later a pharmacist came along with medicine. But how to get this across the Iron Curtain? A member of the public stood up and said, "My name is Schnitzel, and I have a visa and can go there!" He left the recording studio to thunderous applause. Two days later the woman called in crying again. Her sight had been saved.[79]

Isopp's narration sounds dramatic, but Schnitzel's journey "across the Iron Curtain" was far from isolated during *Autofahrer Unterwegs*'s heyday. Hundreds of Czechs, Slovaks, and Austrians traversed the border legally for work or family reasons already in the 1950s.[80] The following decade, tourism in both directions further increased, with Czechs and Slovaks now visiting Austria en masse to see the sites.[81] Sport was another long-running area of contact between Czechs, Slovaks, and their German-speaking neighbors.[82] By the 1960s, football matches between inhabitants of the Czech and Austrian side of the border were even becoming an annual fixture.[83] And material goods such as newspapers, books, and clothing made their way across the border alongside the eye medicine that Schnitzel transported— although the flow of "finished" goods was stronger in one direction than the other.[84]

Isopp's recollections are inflected with a tinge of messianic Western humanitarianism, but she nevertheless places the story of the woman in Bratislava within a larger context of real personal connection and ad hoc aid fostered by the show. While RFE dismissed Austrian radio listening as a historic relic, Isopp's statement in fact shows how Czechs and Slovaks used new media (such as FM broadcasting, telephones, and personal cars) in savvy ways to overwrite earlier historic connections between Austria and their state. *Autofahrer Unterwegs* suggested a cross-border community of those ready to help and be helped, and a conversation that acknowledged Czechs' and Slovaks' material circumstances and difficulties (which is not to say that Czechs and Slovaks were "victims" of an underdeveloped consumer market, but rather that the very present grumblings about material shortages audible in Czechoslovakia at this time found international amplification through *Autofahrer Unterwegs*).

164   Chapter 5

## Light Entertainment's Value during the Cold War

Alongside *Autofahrer Unterwegs*, RFE cited the music played by Austrian radio and game shows like *Alle Neune* as key to Austrian radio's success.[85]

Austrian broadcasters had sought to "position [their country] with light classical music" through international broadcasts as early as the interwar period, claims Suzanne Lommers.[86] They continued with this strategy throughout the 1950s in explicit distinction to purveyors of jazz, like American Forces Network, and alleged purveyors of "amateur brass music," Czechoslovak Radio.[87] Vienna aired some two hundred hours of music a month by the 1950s, including "weekly concerts of the Vienna Philharmonic held in the Konzerthalle."[88] In a subtle bid to normalize American-style radio advertising, such concerts were sponsored, claims Reinhold Wagnleitner.[89] Perhaps this was so, but in the ears of the US officials overseeing them, the Austrian radio journalists preparing them, and the Czech and Slovak listeners quizzed about them, the weekly recitals became associated with an "Austrian flavor"—much more so than their subtle capitalist framework.[90] This association was perhaps shaped by enduring ideas of what Austria sounded like, cultivated by radio professionals of an earlier age.

Red-White-Red (RWR—ORF's predecessor broadcasting from the American zone of Austria until 1955) placed great importance upon the quantity and quality of music it broadcast to attract listeners to its news.[91] But it is not clear from listener testimony that it succeeded. Czech and Slovak interviewees, with the same discernment we found in the last chapter, singled out the music they had heard on Austrian frequencies to the exclusion of all else. One interviewee from South Moravia suggested, representatively, that RWR was "the most reliable station when one wanted to listen to good music."[92] Czechoslovak Radio broadcast "good music" too, but not reliably so, one barber explained. He continued that listening to domestic radio required "planning . . . so one does not tune in by mistake to some speech or *The Radio University*. One reads magazines to find out when a symphony orchestra or chamber music will be on. It is the only agreeable and unobjectionable listening possible."[93] Listening to music constituted relaxation to this barber, who contrasted it with the experience of following political speeches or overtly edifying programming. Interviews with RFE pollsters suggest that RWR's Czech and Slovak listeners may have been equally as selective in their preferences for music over the spoken word, raising the question of whether some were happy not to understand the nuance—or even all that much—of what they heard. For all their talk of "good music" on RWR, interviewees make no mention of the news accompanying it.[94]

Game shows were another radio format linked to the early days of RWR. They were introduced to Austrian radio on account of their popularity with American audiences and to present Austrians with an image of "good play" according to American rules.[95] But they also came to be wholeheartedly endorsed by socialist media from around the time of *Alle Neune*'s broadcast in the mid-1960s, explains Christine Evans, as they "performed the state's responsiveness to its citizens" and suggested the importance of citizen participation on "predetermined fields of play."[96]

Teaming up with regional Austrian radio, Czechoslovak Radio sought, through *Alle Neune*, to "gatekeep the foreign," presenting itself as, in fact, the best means to tune into foreign radio.[97] *Alle Neune* did little to "mobilize citizens towards the construction of socialism," which is what socialist game shows, according to Evans, set out to do.[98] It was instigated by ORF and followed a format that the creators had devised for earlier, intra-Austrian broadcasts. But the cooperation was no trojan horse for Austrian-style social democracy—it had several important benefits for Czechoslovak Radio and Prague officials too. It presented Czechoslovakia and Austria as technological equals capable of such broadcasting feats on account of both states' robust radio infrastructures. Furthermore, by introducing Austrian-style light entertainment into Czechoslovak radio schedules, *Alle Neune* facilitated the ongoing appropriation of radio genres familiar from the West onto Czechoslovak frequencies.[99]

Thus *Alle Neune* served the political purposes of Czechoslovak radio professionals and officials. But what about its listeners? Writing in to claim a free booklet, or to *Autofahrer Unterwegs* for a shout-out, was certainly not party political, but it was political in the sense that Michel de Certeau would understand it—in that it saw non-elites use mass media to their own specific ends. Procuring eye medicine or swotting up on the pop charts in order to impress one's peers in the schoolyard on Monday are but two ways that consumers of mass media can "make use of the strong."[100] To me, this represents the interesting ways that people actually go about incorporating mass media into their everyday lives, tailoring such media to their own ends.[101]

166   Chapter 5

Programs such as *Alle Neune*, *Autofahrer Unterwegs*, and the Austrian pop chart reveal the different and varied roles that radio can play for its listeners. RFE sought to furnish its audiences primarily with news, while the Austrian radio shows examined here set out to provide entertainment.[102] Correspondingly, Czechs and Slovaks did not turn to Austrian radio just because they were unable to tune into RFE. Instead, game shows, phone-ins, and Austrian pop provided different opportunities for audience interaction and the possibility of participation in different listening communities. The same listener could and did, of course, seek out news and entertainment in turns, but it was RFE analysts' nagging concern that the latter held more importance than their own offerings for Czechs and Slovaks (in terms of time spent listening, memorability, audience participation, and affection). This chapter has explored why, concretely, their concerns might have been justified.

### Conclusion

The director of ORF, Gerd Bacher, ruminated in 1967 that "for those with whom we lived for centuries in the same state, we [meaning Austrians] are, quite simply, 'the West.' "[103] It was a question of personal framing whether Czechs and Slovaks did indeed tune into German-language radio because they believed it represented "the West." Beyond debate is that Central Europeans entered the Cold War with their own radio traditions and understandings of media, which continued to develop over the decades that followed. While RFE may have been the ultimate foreign radio reference point for Communist politicians such as Information Minister Václav Kopecký, many Czech and Slovak citizens did not agree. This chapter has explored how, over the twentieth century, as Heidi Tworek argues, "many individuals, groups, and states challenged Anglo-American infrastructures, firms, and approaches to news"—and indeed their centrality to regional media environments.[104]

This chapter has disputed the particularity of the two Germanies' Cold War media history, arguing that cross-border German-language radio also mattered profoundly in Central Europe, where listening habits were shaped by the region's multilingual heritage. Surprisingly perhaps (and the teenagers of České Budějovice notwithstanding), older generations might be said to have proved more ingenious in their use of available media. Just as Petr

Szczepanik finds that cultural affinities with Austria survived geopolitical and technological shifts well into the 1930s, I have proposed that such affinities lasted even longer and that the "cultural barriers" evoked by Bösch and Classen were not yet thoroughly entrenched until deep into the Cold War—indeed the extent to which they are in place today is still open to question.[105] Analyzing German-language radio listening in Czechoslovakia has additionally shed light on the enduring importance of German as a language of regional communication, the continuing importance of cross-border connections, and the significance of light entertainment for Central European audiences during the Cold War.

*Alle Neune* officialized practices of which the Czechoslovak and Austrian authorities had been long aware—cultivated by shows such as *Autofahrer Unterwegs*. Rather than constituting the legacy of a bygone, Habsburg age, German-language radio listening saw Czechs and Slovaks use new technologies in sophisticated ways to overwrite and alter earlier connections between their state and their nearest neighbors. The Cold War certainly shaped the choices that Czech and Slovak listeners had available to them (in terms of what was jammed and which languages they knew), but it may not have shaped their approach to the German-language radio they heard. An altogether recognizable mix of self-improvement, longing for connection, peer pressure, habit, curiosity, a desire to vent one's grievances, and material aspiration appeared to inflect Czechoslovak listeners' preference for Austrian and West German radio during the Cold War—and we should not collapse this into the easy catch-all of "resistance to Communism," as some period RFE analysts and several recent memoirs and exhibits have done. Finally, I have indicated how the solidarities that German-language radio listening forged divided listeners up not by citizenship or ethnicity, which is often how media consumption in twentieth-century Central and Eastern Europe is framed, but by age, technological know-how, class, and geography instead. In contradistinction to the well-studied divide between East and West Berlin, Yuliya Komska has called the West German-Czechoslovak border "the Cold War's quiet border."[106] It turns out that it was anything but.

# 6   Spring in the Air?

*Czechoslovak Radio's
Foreign Correspondents, 1958–1968*

**IN 1963, VĚRA ŠŤOVÍČKOVÁ—ALREADY** a seasoned foreign reporter—
recalled her first encounter with a deadly poisonous snake:

> It was a mamba, the very first time I was in Africa, in Guinea. I asked one of my
> friends for help to take me to a bauxite refinery in Fria, because at that time I
> still didn't have a car . . . We flew into a bend . . . and there was nothing for it
> when we discovered that in front of us, and across almost the entire road, lay a
> thick black line. He slammed on the brakes, and after the black line we skidded
> and flew into a tree . . . We both realized that the skid had been caused by a
> mamba crossing the road. I looked for my camera and tried to get out of the car,
> and I owe my friend for saving my life twice over, because for a start he didn't
> crash headlong into the tree, and secondly he didn't let me out of the car. As he
> correctly supposed, a moment later a second mamba slid out of the ditch (be-
> cause mambas as a rule go in pairs), looked at its dead companion and waited
> until the guilty party came along to take revenge.[1]

Šťovíčková's brush with danger on the road to Fria came in the form of light
relief for listeners to Czechoslovak Radio.[2] She delivered the story as part
of a Christmas special of the foreign news desk's flagship program *Svět u
mikrofonu* (*The World at the Microphone*), which swapped jokes and anecdotes from the field for its usual staple of political commentary and analy-

sis. In the same program, French correspondent Ján Čierny showcased his flirting skills in an interview with a Dior model and, in a humorous example of a propaganda staple, Karel Kyncl lampooned American media advertising from New York.[3] The eighty-minute show was punctuated by Ella Fitzgerald singing "Lorelei," and 1963's cloister-to-charts sensation the Singing Nun performing "Dominique."

Members of the foreign section of Czechoslovak Radio were considered "an elite club" within the broadcaster between 1959 to 1968, argues Zdenka Kotalová.[4] Fellow radio historian Milan Rykl concurs; he suggests that foreign reporters were the broadcaster's most "erudite" employees who spearheaded Czechoslovak Radio's "renaissance," which he identifies taking place during the years discussed in this chapter.[5] Certainly, they were an active group, known for a host of other public appearances and experiments with genre elsewhere on Czechoslovak Radio's schedules.[6] Among them, Věra Šťovíčková was particularly well respected. In a Radio Free Europe information item from December 1967, she was described as: "The most popular [foreign] correspondent, together with [Karel] Kyncl. Her subject is Africa. She has already made a host of programs considered to be excellent. She is highly capable and liked by colleagues for her friendly disposition. She often travels abroad. Her programs are favourably received."[7] Šťovíčková's colleagues were described in much less flattering a light. Jiří Dienstbier's vanity and alleged proclivity for women who were not his wife was noted in the rival broadcaster's report, while Dušan Ruppeldt, Czechoslovak Radio's South American correspondent, was described as "unpleasant, an absolute communist" who always wanted the last word and was shunned by his colleagues.[8] One year's worth of Šťovíčková's fan mail retained in the Czech Radio archive seems to bear out Radio Free Europe's claims about her popularity: the correspondence culminates in a letter from Czechoslovak Television, informing her that she has been voted the personality of the year in one of their shows.[9]

Šťovíčková, Dienstbier, Kyncl, and Ruppeldt belonged to a group of around eight hundred employees fired from Czechoslovak Radio by 1969. Simultaneous to their dismissal, as Zdenka Kotalová explained "their traces were destroyed in the [radio] archive . . . Instead of documents, the memories of eyewitnesses were all that remained of many people and many things."[10] And memory has downplayed the role of news journalists in the years preceding the Prague Spring. Accounts of the cultural background to the Prague Spring commonly cite its progenitors to have been "playwrights, poets, and novelists," dating its origins in particular to the Czechoslovak Writers' Conference in 1967.[11] It is true that the Union of Journalists distanced itself from the writers' criticisms, but the journalistic profession was much more diverse (and reformist in attitude) than the leadership of its union would suggest.[12] This chapter shows how reporters worked to shift the discussion of politics and contemporary Czechoslovak affairs in ways that a mere examination of union policy does not reflect. Based upon reporters' scripts, I argue that the discursive climate that shaped the Prague Spring arose firmly within official structures, within the establishment long before 1968, and within the censored and monitored environment of the Novotný-era newsroom.

Memory has also served to code foreign reporting male. As Ulf Hannerz reflects, the "lingering stereotype of a foreign correspondent" is that of "a lonely, hardened man, graying and leading a not very wholesome life."[13] The macho (and highly questionable) stories of Šťovíčková's friend and travel companion Ryszard Kapuściński wrestling cobras have been recalled over her less dramatic tales of giving mambas a wide berth.[14] In their reporting and the way they spoke about their job, Šťovíčková's colleagues presented foreign reporting as a man's work. The consequence of this is that scholar Petr Drulák, in an otherwise excellent assessment of the work of Czechoslovak Radio's foreign reporters through the late 1950s and 1960s, can argue that the team constituted an "island of positive deviation" at the broadcaster, but when it came to the "extraordinary and intellectually independent personalities" who made up this group, it suffices Drulák to note Milan Weiner, Karel Kyncl, Luboš Dobrovský, Jan Petránek, Karel Jezdinský, "and of course Jiří Dienstbier."[15]

What can a focus on Věra Šťovíčková over and above her colleagues reveal? Firstly, the shifting forms that socialist internationalism assumed. Like socialist rule itself, socialist internationalism was far from a homogenous project; its venues and possible participants changed over the years. From the youthful and dexterous Jiří Hanzelka and Miroslav Zikmund "exploring for socialism" discussed in chapter 3, we arrive here at Věra Šťovíčková, an experienced female laborer fully integrated into the workplace in West Africa by the late 1950s. Šťovíčková periodically styled herself as one of the thousands of Czechoslovak experts sent to reside in Guinea following its independence from France in 1958. In her writing she suggested it was not enough to travel through a place if one wanted to understand it and that knowledge of people in foreign places could only be attained through work.[16]

Secondly, Šťovíčková provides a case study in how foreign correspondents relied upon, and were beholden to, state structures in Novotný-era Czechoslovakia while at the same time attempting to shape those very structures. Šťovíčková's interactions with her employer, Czechoslovak Radio, and other state institutions can be pieced together in fine detail thanks to her scripts and correspondence from 1958 to 1968, which she left to the Czech Radio archive following her death in 2015. Finally, her work shows how news journalists contributed to the discursive conditions that shaped the Prague Spring—slowly, continuously, and incrementally over the decade of Novotný's rule.[17] Far from a period of stagnation—following the economic outlook of the time, Novotný's reign is sometimes understood to have been—the decade prior to the Prague Spring can be seen as the incubator for such developments, sited in official and censored institutions such as the state broadcaster, no less.

These last two arguments point to a larger insight into journalists' limited autonomy from the socialist state. By her own account, Šťovíčková produced, at times, propaganda.[18] As she explains in her memoirs, she had been a card-carrying member of the Communist Party from the 1940s and was wholly invested in the project of reform of the Party, rather than its overthrow or abolition, in the 1960s.[19] In other words, it is far from clear that, given the freedom to write whatever she wanted, Šťovíčková would have pulled in a different direction. To posit a reporter-versus-state antagonism is unhelpful here. But within this symbiosis there was still room to maneuver and space for conflict. As Šťovíčková recalls, she was uniquely able among her colleagues to write what she wanted about her beat "because the Party line 'on Africa' was still not established and so it was not necessary to skirt around it."[20] In her limited autonomy, coupled with tangible points of obligation and reliance, I argue that we should employ Šťovíčková as a metaphor for the Czechoslovakia of Antonín Novotný within the Eastern Bloc and more specifically, the state's relationship with the Soviet Union in its Africa policy.

**FIGURE 18.** Věra Šťovíčková at work upon being posted to Guinea, circa 1958. Source: Věra Šťovíčková-Heroldová, *Po světě s mikrofonem*, 52.

### Reliance on State (Infra-)structures

Věra Šťovíčková was first dispatched to Guinea in 1958, following the country's declaration of independence from France and coinciding with Conakry's sudden importance to Prague.[21] After an initial, extended stay, she returned to Guinea to live for almost two years in 1960, using Conakry as a base to travel to and report from countries including Mali, Côte d'Ivoire, and Ghana. Identifying the inauguration of Sékou Touré's left-wing government in October 1958 as the start of a "euphoric period" of Czechoslovak involvement in Africa, historian Philip Muehlenbeck claims that "building upon Touré's fond memories of being a student in Prague and his inclination to distance himself from France or either of the superpowers, whom he feared might try to impose hegemonic influence over his country, relations between Czechoslovakia and Guinea continued to blossom into 1961"—the year that Šťovíčková left.[22] By the time Šťovíčková did return to Prague, Guinea had become, according to Muehlenbeck, one of the biggest customer of Czechoslovakia's state export organization. Prague sold automobiles, medical supplies, industrial machinery, and film and radio equipment to Conakry. It was paid in nuts and tropical fruit which nevertheless—and as memory has immortalized—remained extremely difficult to find in Czechoslovak stores.[23]

Czechoslovakia sent experts as well as exports to Conakry, and a number of those dispatched to Guinea during these years included journalists such as Šťovíčková.[24] From her memoirs one can infer that Šťovíčková certainly came into contact with institutions such as the Czechoslovak-sponsored school of journalism in Conakry and its students, even if she was not herself a full-time lecturer. She noted the presence of a large number of Czechoslovak experts in Guinea and surrounding countries through radio interviews and in her book *Afrika rok jedna* (*Africa Year One*).[25] In this publication she suggested that she was an expert worker like any other. Taking great care to differentiate them from the colonizers who preceded them, Šťovíčková suggested that the Czechs and Slovaks in Conakry at the time were less physically and morally repulsive than the agents of empire in whose footsteps they followed. The key to this was work.[26] The idyllic image of efficient, hard-working Czechs and Slovaks in Guinea she presented contrasted with the low productivity rates blighting the domestic Czechoslovak economy during the period, about which the readers of her books were most certainly aware.[27] In her description, Guinea was a tropical paradise, specifically, a paradise of meaningful work and work with tangible effects.

Šťovíčková's return to Czechoslovakia was surely a result of Prague's economic difficulties; it certainly constituted a bid on the part of the Central Committee to save valuable supplies of hard currency. Her recall to Prague and the decision to use her henceforth as a "parachute journalist" coincided with the expansion of Czechoslovakia's network of air routes and a concerted Czechoslovak attempt, claims Philip Muehlenbeck, to dominate African civil aviation.[28] Her reports served as something of an advert for this initiative, notably not extending to two fatal plane crashes on Czechoslovak Airlines' Prague-Zürich-Rabat-Dakar-Conakry route in 1961. Instead, the reporter recalled particularly memorable flights she had been on in the program *Sedmilháři*; she ranked the airports of the world through which she had passed in an article titled "Celnice je barometr" ("Customs Are a Bellwether"); and she reflected in radio commentaries upon how the flight schedule into and out of towns shaped the very fabric of her reporting, limiting her time, for example, in Abidjan, Côte d'Ivoire, resulting in her skipping a siesta and exploring instead an empty city, out of sync with its dozing inhabitants.[29] Fan mail suggests that listeners engaged with and responded warmly to her stories of jetting across the globe. Upon hearing a tale of the reporter missing the last plane out of a remote region and bursting into tears, for example, one Ksenia Ivanovová exclaimed that she finally

**FIGURE 19.** Hungarian-language poster for Czechoslovak Airline's Prague-Zurich-Rabat-Conakry-Bamako service from 1961. This was the route along which Šťovíčková and her recorded materials frequently traveled.

realized Šťovíčková was no "dry correspondent at all, but instead a woman with heart and feelings." Ivanovová then divulged that she was old enough to be Šťovíčková's mother, before fishing for an invite to the radio building to meet the reporter.[30]

As well as transporting the journalist herself, Šťovíčková's reports literally relied upon Czechoslovakia's state transport network during these years. Using a "stationary tape recorder the size of an old fridge" to record audio in Guinea, Šťovíčková then recalled: "I cut the tapes by hand and stuck white tape where I had cut them, as was the norm in radio at the time. I then sent the tapes to Prague by plane, because a Czech plane flew to Conakry once a week back then. Otherwise by boat. News was sent by telegraph, with the words joined together to save money."[31] In other words, transport schedules shaped the rhythm of Šťovíčková's reports and the classification of what was "news" as opposed to a feature in Czechoslovakia. Considerations of how long it would take to send the audio to Czechoslovakia apparently influenced the type of report that Šťovíčková chose to make. If it were audio-rich, then the report would not be broadcast quickly, and if it better suited the category of "news," then it would be read by another announcer in Prague.[32]

As well as material limitations created by the Czechoslovak state's technological capacity and overseas infrastructure (which, we should note, was world-leading in some aspects of technological and infrastructural development in West Africa—this is not a story, by any means, of Eastern Bloc backwardness), Šťovíčková was of course answerable to the state's political structures. Her reports were censored, although it is worth underlining that journalists largely knew what was appropriate to report and thus performed preemptive self-censorship to save themselves the work of reediting sound and rewriting text.[33] In some instances, such as the overthrow of Ahmed Ben Bella in Algeria in 1965, Šťovíčková suggested that she was furthermore subject to the censorship of the state she was reporting from, in addition to the one into which she broadcast.[34] And her very position at the radio and dispatch to West Africa were dependent upon her good political standing. Political background checking (so-called *kádrování*) was a facet of every workplace in socialist Czechoslovakia and particularly important in instances when an employee traveled abroad.

Nevertheless, Šťovíčková suggested that she "had a relatively free hand"

176    Chapter 6

to write what she wished in her reports because "the Party line 'on Africa' was still not established." [35] Lutz Mükke echoes her claim, concluding in his analysis of East and West German foreign correspondents during the Cold War that each individual's room to maneuver varied, affected by the relationship that the reporter's home country maintained with his/her destination.[36] Eastern Bloc correspondents who traveled to the West were extremely limited in the praise they could shower on the countries in which they were based, for example, while there was only limited room to criticize aspects of life in socialist bloc countries, with critiques of the Soviet Union almost completely taboo.[37] Where Czechoslovakia maintained no relationship at all with a country, either because the state in question was new or located in a geographic region in which Czechoslovakia had not previously maintained a blanket diplomatic presence, reporters had more of a say in how that relationship might sound.

The association her home state (and home bloc) maintained with her destination affected the welcome that Šťovíčková received abroad. Lutz Mükke refers to this as "indirect Cold War censorship" and explains that "journalist visas, accreditations, entry-, film- and work-permits were issued faster, with more difficulty, or not at all, depending on the camp to which one belonged."[38] This became particularly apparent during a short and abortive visit that Šťovíčková made to Congo in 1964. Following a tip-off that she was under investigation for spying—with her radio equipment further fueling suspicion—she beat a hasty retreat.[39]

### The Czechoslovak State's Reliance on Šťovíčková

Such fears on the parts of foreign correspondents' hosts were not completely unfounded. Reporters did amass different kinds of information during stints overseas, not all of it for broadcast. Eastern Bloc journalists gathered materials for mass distribution and additional information to be shared through official written reports and debriefing discussions with state security officials upon return home. In her memoirs, Šťovíčková recalls the process of filing such reports. Such bureaucratized procedures show how the Czechoslovak state developed structures to harness the knowledge of— and monitor—its foreign journalists, even if, frustratingly for them, party functionaries did not always follow the recommendations that correspondents made.[40] The information that news reporters provided, however, was not that of intelligence professionals, who often already had their own operations embedded in correspondents' host states.[41] The Czechoslovak secret police maintained an extensive presence in Guinea and Ghana, for example, with intelligence officers lingering after helping to establish local security forces.[42] Information that Šťovíčková provided was therefore supplemental to intelligence gathered by specially trained agents on long-term postings in both states. This point somewhat pours cold water on colleague Jiří Dienstbier's self-characterization as a sort of microphone-wielding James Bond discussed later on.[43]

On top of their work as journalists, Eastern Bloc foreign correspondents served as "state employees equipped with instructions," claims Lutz Mükke, who refers to this as their "double role."[44] Mükke focused on the role of East German reporters, who were in the particular situation of being posted to many locations that did not recognize their home state at all, and thus these destinations lacked any sort of formal diplomatic mission whatsoever. But Czechoslovakia likewise had a limited diplomatic presence on the African continent when Šťovíčková lived and traveled there; at the beginning of 1960, Muehlenbeck recalls, the country had diplomatic relations with five sub-Saharan African states (to the Soviet Union's two)—Guinea, Ghana, Congo, Ethiopia, and South Africa.[45] A leaf through Šťovíčková's scripts from that very same year shows that she traveled to and sent dispatches from the first three of those, as well as Mali, Côte d'Ivoire, and Madagascar, and additionally a number of North African states such as Algeria and Morocco. In other words, Šťovíčková often went where Czechoslovak state employees did not yet; the information she transferred back to Czechoslovakia about such places was among the only sources that Prague officials, and Czechoslovak listeners, had.[46]

Even in countries where a Czechoslovak diplomatic mission was present, Šťovíčková suggested to her listeners that the socialist reporter could play a special role. In a report from Tunisia in 1968, Šťovíčková described international relations in terms of interpersonal communication: "With many of our good friends, we *tykat* [use the informal 'tu' or 'Du' form]. Figuratively speaking, we *vykat* [use the formal 'vous' or 'Sie'] with Tunisia. This isn't so warm but on the other hand, it stops you from calling the other party a 'rascal,' because *darebáku Vy* ["you rascal," but using an oddly formal form] somehow doesn't work."[47] In this assessment the world was split in two,

178  Chapter 6

between those one *tutoie*-d and those one *vouvoie*-d, and socialist friendship was a literal project of switching from *vous* to *tu*—the friendly form
of address. This could happen, as the transition from *Vy* to *ty* normally did,
through dialogue and the familiarity it bred. In another radio interview,
Šťovíčková suggested that conversation was the prerogative and the spe-
cialty of the socialist reporter. She reflected that the work of the journalist
from a socialist country in Africa was to speak to as many people as possible: "whenever I go to Africa," she told Radio Prague's Sylva Součková, "I look
for truthful answers to my questions, from presidents and monarchs, at the
marketplace, in the Savannah, in ministries, at conferences—everywhere I
find someone willing to help me."[48]

## Writing about Czechoslovakia When Writing about Africa

Šťovíčková made direct claims on the Czechoslovak government in reporting she produced in the spring of 1968. Such critical reporting did not
come out of the blue. It derived from a sense of expertise on Africa which
Šťovíčková stressed she had cultivated in the decade she had spent reporting on the continent. Additionally, Šťovíčková already had a long history of
making claims about Czechoslovakia in her journalism—using Africa as a
backdrop to do so. Such claim-making about Czechoslovakia (in less and
less veiled terms) is one rhetorical precursor to the Prague Spring worth examining here.

Šťovíčková exoticized herself and her listeners to cultivate empathy
among audiences and to suggest that her comments might hold resonance
closer to home. One of her favorite tropes was to suggest that Africans,
Czechs, and Slovaks were all victims of the same outdated notions, and thus
that Czechs and Slovaks should know better than to voice such ignorant
utterances when they knew from personal experience just how ignorant
those utterances were. "A sensation-seeking European on the hunt for magicians and fetishes will make a Guinean just about as happy as a Czechoslovak becomes," she suggested for example in *Afrika Rok Jedna*, "when faced
with the disappointment of American tourists who have just found out that
we don't walk along the river on Sundays in ribboned folk costumes from
Kyjov, and we don't knock our shepherd's axes [*valašky*] against the Prague
paving stones."[49] Repackaging the same idea for a younger radio audience,
Šťovíčková argued that clinging to outdated ideas of magicians in Guinea

"would be just about as ridiculous as one very elegant Parisian woman, whom I had to persuade that we don't wear here in Czechoslovakia, and haven't for a long time, embroidered national costumes like [the folk dance troupe] SĽUK during performances."[50] In both examples, she suggested that Africans and Czechoslovaks were subject to Western prejudices and a lack of knowledge. She suggested the bar was higher for those on the Eastern side of the Iron Curtain, firstly because they could not feign such ignorance (primed as they were by her reports), and secondly because they knew from experience how ridiculous such ignorance sounded. Here she warned against taking first visual impressions to represent the whole; Czechoslovakia was much more complicated than a SĽUK performance. Such auto-exoticization worked both ways, if Czechs and Slovaks were supposed to see the plight of newly independent Africans in their own, then they were also being invited to see their situation in that of the states that Šťovíčková discussed.

James Mark and Péter Apor suggest that journalists drew such connections between Central European socialist audiences and their confreres in the decolonizing world in a bid to spark a younger generation's zeal for socialist revolution. Such comparisons demonstrated how closely connected Central Europeans were "to the vital new political movements springing up across the world."[51] Šťovíčková did certainly suggest that Czechs and Slovaks were united by revolution with their peers in socialist African states, but here she suggested they were joined in another way: both groups were othered by Western eyes. Šťovíčková understood herself and other Czechoslovak experts to be "Europeans" in Africa, but in such situations she stressed the gulf between the Eastern and Western halves of the continent. Czechs and Slovaks were joined with African citizens as objects of a Western gaze. Rather than scoffing at the prospect of being likened to Africans by this othering, Šťovíčková embraced the comparison, indicating that a particular type of knowledge could derive from these shared circumstances.

As a committed Marxist, Šťovíčková believed in an ineluctable, stadial course of historical development. Within this framework, Czechoslovakia was further along the plane of development than newly decolonized African states and could thus offer advice from further along the same process of transition towards socialism. This was certainly the message propounded time and again by Czechoslovak Radio's Anglophone Africa service since its

180   Chapter 6

inauguration in 1960, and in an interview with the station's Sylva Součková in April 1968, this was exactly the view that Šťovíčková herself articulated. Radio Prague's African listeners could learn from the trials and tribulations of Czechoslovakia on its road to development, according to Šťovíčková.[52] When asked what she "wished for African women," Šťovíčková responded she hoped that they "learned from the mistakes of European women, as we moved along the path to emancipation first."[53] She closed the interview with the proverb "once bitten, twice shy" suggesting—somewhat arcanely—that European women may have suffered the consequences of taking a wrong turn or two so that their African counterparts might not have to.[54]

The view that Czechoslovakia was further down the path to development of course categorized an African present as backward and posited, paternalistically, an understanding of precisely the course that decolonized states would now take. Šťovíčková here suggested that Czechoslovakia held lessons for an African future. She was not alone in this: in a meeting with their Soviet counterparts in November 1961, Czechoslovak Foreign Ministry officials argued exactly the same point.[55] Around Central Europe, as Mark and Apor note, it was axiomatic that the course of historical progress moved one way and "the potentially inspiring stories of violent struggle for national liberation in the Third World were seen as irrelevant as models for behavior in contemporary [Central Europe] where the Communist movement had overcome its enemies, [and] established a stable regime."[56] Employing this logic, however, Šťovíčková used such an understanding of historical development to analyze events the opposite way around: present-day Africa could shed light on Czechoslovakia's past. As Neal Ascherson has claimed when reflecting upon the output of Šťovíčková's Polish colleague and sometime travel companion Ryszard Kapuściński, "writing about distant lands in ways which instantly suggested domestic comparisons . . . was a classic way of evading the censors (another was the 'historical' novel which was really about the present)."[57] In reflecting upon elements of Czechoslovakia's history in an African present, Šťovíčková achieved the double whammy of spatial and temporal disguise.

This use of foreign people and places to critique events closer to home can be seen most clearly in a book of reportage titled *Bouře nad rovníkem* (*Storm over the Equator*) published on the basis of Šťovíčková's experiences reporting from Africa in 1967. The "storm" to which she referred in the title was created by a series of coups that took place since "the Year of Africa" in 1960. Šťovíčková examined the cases of Algeria, the Central African Republic, Ghana, and Nigeria, all countries in which progressive leaders favored by Prague had been deposed, to reflect upon revolution done right, revolution done wrong, cults of personality, and the limits to and possibilities for reform within established regimes.

In Algeria, she recounted how sidelined socialist leader Ahmed Ben Bella was criticized by the revolutionary council which deposed him for having fostered a cult of personality. Noting the pictures of him that lingered in Algerian shops and public spaces, Šťovíčková hinted at the former president's continued legitimacy (which certainly chimed with Prague's official stance). She then criticized Ben Bella's replacements for espousing a "cult of anonymity" as opposed to the cult of personality of which they accused him.[58] The author then recalled at length one of her interactions with an Algerian censor in the midst of covering the coup.[59] Publishing the details of her tiresome negotiations with the censor about what she could and could not say in Czechoslovakia—a country which itself still employed censorship—proved enlightening in its detail. In her telling, local Algerian censors were most fervently opposed to her plans to discuss the violence government forces had used against crowds of protesters at the time of the coup.

In a short article about the Central African Republic, Šťovíčková then called out those who had recently taken over from former leader David Dacko by saying they threw the terms "bourgeois" and "fascist" about too loosely.[60] She highlighted the hollowness and ultimate damage caused by the manufacture of a foreign, "Chinese plot" to justify the takeover from Dacko after the fact.[61] Czechoslovak readers would recognize such claims of foreign plotting from the time of the Slánský trials in the early 1950s. Here, she presented such rhetoric as a craven power grab on the part of one faction of a state's elite. In the process of looking at these and other revolutions that did not last, Šťovíčková examined some of the pitfalls that attended the establishment of socialism and critiqued them harshly. That Šťovíčková's writing about Africa allowed her to make arguments about Czechoslovakia was not lost on her Czech and Slovak readers. In a blurb for this very book, reviewer Zbyněk Kožnar exclaimed that the text was "perfectly Czech. More than once in the subtext can you read a trenchant irony, and parallels to

182    Chapter 6

domestic conditions."[62] Media discussion of the show trials and connected abuses of justice in Czechoslovakia is rightly understood as a journalistic development of the Prague Spring (discussed in more depth in the next chapter). *Bouře nad rovníkem* shows, however, how the Prague Spring's protagonists on the radio came to such direct discussions via less direct evocations through foreign commentary.

### Cultivating and Propounding Her Own Expertise

In an article for *Plamen*, the magazine of the Czechoslovak Writers' Union, published in 1965, Šťovíčková argued that socialist journalists had to date oversimplified African politics. Following the Communist takeover in Czechoslovakia, reporters had understood any reaction to colonial oppression to be "a priori progressive, almost pro-socialist."[63] "As had been the case with domestic news reporting," Šťovíčková continued acerbically, details that did not fit this framework were omitted and "only the positives" were stressed. Journalists still had difficulty capturing the nuance of African socialism's different ideologies. Here, she teased some of them apart. Šťovíčková introduced readers to Frantz Fanon, explaining the complete revocation of European and American influence he propounded in *The Wretched of the Earth* to be a result of the conditions of the Algerian war of independence in which he wrote. She then presented Nkrumah's idea for a United States of Africa and suggested that this had so far failed to gain traction with other African leaders. Šťovíčková described Nkrumah's political philosophy as the only form of African Neo-Marxism born of materialism. She contrasted it to Senghor's socialism which envisaged a revival of Catholic values, and Ben Bella's socialism, which was "authentically Marxist in its economics" but integrated aspects of Islam.[64] Writing for an erudite audience, Šťovíčková argued that Africa should not be understood as a unified political actor and reflected upon the different strands of Marxism emerging there. While the continent's colonial past and contemporary class structures marked it out as different from Central Europe, she argued that socialist thinking developing on the continent might, in fact, have something to offer contemporary Central Europeans after all. Šťovíčková presented herself as an intermediary for such ideas, offering further reading in a range of languages (Fanon in French and Tom Mboya's *Freedom and After* in English) for those seeking additional enlightenment.

Šťovíčková returned to the idea that not all socialist journalists were equal, hinted at in this report, later, when she explained to colleagues at Czechoslovak Radio that better and worse practitioners existed within her own field. The socialist reporter, just like any socialist state, had to go through his or her own dialectical development process. Šťovíčková explained what this meant in an interview with Sylva Součková in April 1968. Reflecting upon the task of being a "socialist reporter," Šťovíčková argued that it was a professional responsibility "to free oneself from romantic notions of Africa's mysteries and then in one's articles to shatter the old and long defunct illusions of newspaper and book readers, and radio listeners."[65] One "freed oneself" from such romantic notions through spending time in one place. "I had to go through the usual stages a European visitor experiences," she explained.[66] From the perspective of a land-locked Czech, it was necessary to overcome "the enchantment one feels when seeing the wonderful sea, the palm trees, the blue skies, when one hears the music."[67] Disenchantment followed enchantment, and only then could the socialist reporter do his or her job, which consisted of finding a synthesis incorporating "praise" of the continent with clear-eyed reflection upon its "painful development."[68] She suggested here that Czechs and Slovaks belonged to a European community of listeners and readers, primed by outdated notions of the continent, but that it was the "socialist" reporter alone who could liberate him or herself from such views.

In a few of her reports, Šťovíčková contrasted her work with the negative counterexample of reporters hailing from the former colonial powers or the United States.[69] While Šťovíčková sought answers to her questions indiscriminately "from presidents and monarchs, [and] at the marketplace," letting, in her view, the people whom she interviewed speak for themselves, an idea *not* betrayed in the high percentage of reported speech evident in her scripts, Šťovíčková profiled Western journalists arrogantly speaking over even the most powerful voices on the continent, assuming superior knowledge to those they interviewed.[70] Whether she did provide as much of a platform for her African interlocutors as she suggested, some colleagues at Czechoslovak Radio singled out her journalism as an example. Speaking in 2013, former foreign reporter Luboš Dobrovský suggested that not everyone had forgotten her work: "I would even say she created a certain form of journalism," he reflected, describing her style as a mix of "reporting and simultaneous analysis of her own knowledge."[71]

184   Chapter 6

Šťovíčková suggested that traveling across Africa was not the ideal way to gain knowledge of the continent, and to be a proper journalist of Africa, one could not be an explorer at all. She made this claim at precisely the moment when Czechs and Slovaks began themselves to travel in increasing numbers.[72] As Milan Rykl suggests in his analysis of Czechoslovak Radio between 1959 and 1968, the period was characterized by the first upswing in foreign tourism in Czechoslovakia following the Second World War.[73] In his analysis of Czechoslovak "penetration" of Africa, Curt Beck suggested Czechs and Slovaks were jumping at the chance newly offered to "travel abroad" offered by Prague's engagement with African states.[74] Here, Šťovíčková shifted the goalposts: by suggesting that a good journalist caught things that a visitor's eye (or ear) might not, she suggested a level of expertise on the foreign correspondent's part not accessible to the lay visitor.

If Šťovíčková was distinguishing herself and her role in opposition to that of a tourist in Africa, then she was equally differentiating herself from the journalists and explorers, not least her radio predecessors, Jiří Hanzelka and Miroslav Zikmund, who had previously written about the continent. When explaining to Součková, and by extension listeners of Radio Prague's Anglophone Africa service, how the socialist reporter needed to jettison his/her "romantic notions" of the continent, Šťovíčková continued: "please don't hold them against us, our whole childhood we read books about Africa and we always arrive there for the first time full of ideas, sometimes outdated, sometimes unrealistic, or simply naïve."[75] Herself a keen reader and avid translator of literature (such as James Frazer's *The Golden Bough*) that hailed from colonial powers at the peak of their imperial might, Šťovíčková clearly devoured the content of such works, which she nonetheless assessed to be a flawed written introduction to the societies she reported on. Such works contributed to a European's "romantic ideals," which ultimately needed to be overcome.[76]

In a program directed towards children broadcast on July 24, 1960, Šťovíčková suggested that the way Africa was being written about now in terms of "presidents and political parties, economic planning and school building" was difficult to square with what "travelers and authors of adventure stories have written about this continent for generations, indeed what Hanzelka and Zikmund wrote about their first journey a few years ago."[77] Šťovíčková argued that the gap between the literary canon and the reality on the ground could be attributed to the breakneck pace of change taking place in a decolonizing Africa, but she also suggested that the adventure stories about the continent that her young listeners loved were largely the products of colonial authors, in whose interest it was to "spread many false impressions in order to cover their own tracks."[78] Here, and in *Afrika rok jedna*, she gently insinuated that a lot of the language of this writing, which had served to shore up imperial projects, had been repurposed rather too wholesale by her radio forebears, Hanzelka and Zikmund.[79] Colonization was a backward system (now confined to Guinea's National Museum, which Czechs and Slovaks had helped build in order to contain it), but this backwardness was projected by the very people who instigated such a system onto this system's victims.[80] Yes, Šťovíčková said, one could still find people dancing to the tam-tam drums, if one really looked, but "every bigger village in Guinea now had a radio loudspeaker."[81] The soundscape of rural West Africa, then, had changed since the time of Hanzelka and Zikmund's radio broadcasts, which adopted African drumming in their opening theme. Old technologies now resounded alongside modern ones, and Guineans now received their news just like Czechs and Slovaks through radio.[82]

"In order to understand," she explained in more depth in *Afrika rok jedna*, "one must live, go shopping, make one's way through the streets, not with a photo camera but in a hurry, get up for work in the morning and on Sunday search for the most pleasant way to unwind. In short, to understand means to live like other people."[83] Working for a section of the radio called the "International Life" division, Šťovíčková, it appears, took the "life" part of her job description seriously. She proposed a form of almost anthropological journalism that posited understanding as a result of empathy, built by undertaking the same tasks as the person one set out to comprehend. This same logic had, in fact, informed the sending of gymnasium students and intelligentsia into Czechoslovakia's fields and factories—a practice that continued into the time of Šťovíčková's writing in the early 1960s.[84] In her presentation of the life of many Czechoslovak experts around the African continent at the microphone, in interviews with doctors in Tunisia or engineers in Egypt, Šťovíčková spoke to them as a peer. She was a representative of and promoted the alleged gender parity of Czechoslovakia's contribution to the socialist internationalist project by the Novotný years. She lived and worked as an expert in West Africa. While her colleagues' tools might be

186   Chapter 6

spirit levels and stethoscopes, the one she used to contribute to this project was a microphone.

### Foreign Reporting in a Man's World?

The 1963 Christmas edition of *Svět u Mikrofonu* in which Šťovíčková had discussed her happily limited exposure to poisonous snakes opened with French correspondent Ján Čierný's apparent struggle to stay on task when confronted with a beautiful woman in a designer dress. Interviewing a model at the Christian Dior fashion house, Čierný quizzed his interlocutor as to whether she liked cakes, as she was a "charming girl."[85] He followed up with a question about what "we men" could expect from Dior's Spring 1964 collection, musing hopefully on whether the décolletés would be lower and the skirts shorter. Čierný concluded by thanking his interlocutor for this "rendez-vous charmant," blurring the line between a work assignment and a pleasurable meeting.[86] The Parisian fashion piece that set the tone for the Christmas special profiled Čierný's incorrigible ways with an interviewee who played the straight woman to his outrageous flirt. On the one hand, this section of the program suggested that it was difficult for Čierný to conduct his job when faced with such overwhelming female beauty. On the other hand, the interview underscored the fact that such glamorous encounters with beautiful women *were* a part of Čierný's job (while poisonous snakes were a part of Šťovíčková's).[87]

Čierný appeared again later in the program discussing, on presenter Veronika Matějová's request, what made Brigitte Bardot the ideal woman.[88] Reflecting in hindsight upon his posting to France, he suggested that the unsuccessful pursuit of Bardot had consumed his four years on the job, although in this he was merely following editorial orders; here, he again deliberately conflated work with pleasure and identified pin-up stars as one point at which the two converged.[89] In *Svět u Mikrofonu*, Čierný's musings on Bardot's ideal qualities expanded to become something of an office straw poll, with presenter Veronika Matějová then turning to Jan Petránek in Moscow with the same question. Petránek suggested he had conducted his own survey of public opinion—beginning in a dentist's waiting room—and found that men younger than twenty-eight and older than forty liked slender, tall women with "modern haircuts and high heels."[90] In the age group in between, however, he claimed that the answer was more complex but failed to elaborate. Šťovíčková was then asked to comment on the topic by Matějová and refused to answer the question.[91]

At a time when filmic adaptations of Ian Fleming's *James Bond* books were enjoying massive box-office success in the locations in which many of these reporters were posted, if not yet the cinemas of Prague, Czechoslovak Radio's foreign correspondents styled themselves accordingly, suggesting that their extensive business travel lent them a connoisseurship of women, or indeed that a connoisseurship of women may in fact have been a part of their job.[92] Čierny could judge who was "simply breathtaking" and tell them so based on the discernment he had cultivated through his travels and work classifying information of every kind.[93] In this, Čierny was by no means exceptional. A string of Jiří Dienstbier's reports from his later stint in the United States demonstrate this same point further and in some more detail.

In "Fízlové, střezte se žen" ("Cops, Watch Out for Women"), for example, Dienstbier pondered whether, as a reporter from a Communist country, he was followed and bugged by the FBI. He then recounted how a quiet Washington neighborhood was recently shaken by the shooting of a Haitian chauffeur who had been, it transpired, a senior intelligence officer for Haitian President François Duvalier.[94] "The murderers were two well-known prostitutes," Dienstbier explained, going on to reflect that "women, the authors of many iniquities, were thus the downfall of this high-ranking officer."[95] Dienstbier closed the report by bringing the two seemingly disparate strands of his reflections together: in the absence of any tangible traces of FBI surveillance, and in light of what had just happened to this Haitian foreign agent, Dienstbier reappraised the many women he had met in his travels around the United States.[96] The tone of this report was whimsical; humor derived from the melodrama of Dienstbier's concerns, but the author used the opportunity to gloat on state radio—not so very elliptically—about his own considerable experience with women during his assignment in the United States (while diminishing his own role, as the women involved were all to be understood as femmes fatales). Indeed, if women were a sign of FBI interest in a subject, then Dienstbier pondered, not as ironically as he might, upon his own significance. Written in 1969, Dienstbier's report conformed masterfully to editorial objectives reinforced after the Prague Spring, highlighting both FBI's "dirty tricks" and crime in America. But the reporter sub-

188   Chapter 6

verted the radio genre of American crime story by seemingly implicating himself within this web of sleaze.

While it was axiomatic that the females these reporters judged attractive should have an aural public presence, courtesy, of course, of an interview with them, Dienstbier ridiculed the claims of women whose appearance he disdained to a role in public life. In a report on the Daughters of the American Revolution, Dienstbier lampooned the group's origin, its purpose, and its members to comic effect. Like all of the reports discussing women analyzed thus far, this piece, notably, was to be taken as a "joke." As with the females in Dienstbier's previous report, the women he discussed here were, at root, prostitutes: couching the claim in the telling of an unnamed bystander, Dienstbier described the "daughters" as "a dreadful bunch—they began as whores who followed Washington's army around and strengthened the fighting spirit. And they refused to sleep with the English."[97] He then went on to ridicule their members for their meaningless speeches.[98]

The greatest ridicule of all was preserved, however, for their appearance; for one, they were old. Dienstbier suggested he was not in fact sure whether they were "the same brave girls" his neighbor had described from the time of Washington's military campaigns.[99] And then he singled out one member for particular, grotesque description: the unnamed daughter wore "a flag pinned to her belly. She clumped on high heels like a well-trained horse in a ring and, as she shook, powder fell rhythmically from her face and her neck."[100] Dienstbier continued that the idea of women marching at all was in itself faintly ridiculous, and thus that a part of what made the scene so grotesque was the unwomanly activities these daughters undertook. The most uncouth activity in which they engaged was public speaking, an ignominy to which Dienstbier returned at the end.

If Dienstbier was styling himself as an international connoisseur of women somewhat akin to Fleming's James Bond, he was also writing within a specific Czechoslovak context, in which deeply misogynistic texts such as Kundera's *The Joke* had recently been released and adapted to film to widespread public acclaim. Kundera's novel likewise posited that public speaking defeminized the orator. It explored the physical and moral repulsiveness of one woman who insisted upon her right to a public voice—here, as a radio journalist. "Behind the veil of Helena's journalistic playacting," protagonist Ludvík mused when he first met news reporter Helena, "I saw a woman, a woman capable of functioning as a woman."[101] He thus suggested an incompatibility between the roles of journalist and woman, and saw self-delusion in Helena's claims to journalistic professionalism, and grounds therein not to take her seriously. Another leading character, Jaroslav, echoed these sentiments.[102]

Helena's bad journalism forged a leitmotif throughout *The Joke*. Upon first encounter, narrator Ludvík reflected that "it was clear to me that before coming to the institute she'd thought her whole report through and that all she needed from me was a few facts and figures, a few examples to prove her hackneyed points."[103] While the scientist Ludvík's knowledge of the world was based, or so he believed, on empirical evidence measured from the circumstances he monitored, Helena merely sought limited corroboration, indeed ornamentation, for the inflexible and tired scaffold that she had built in advance. Ludvík likened this "phrase-mongering, loud-mouthed, pushy woman" to a male political activist who had executed an act of great violence against him at the height of Stalinism.[104] While this latter character, Pavel, developed intellectually throughout the book, the stunted character of Helena never could. Her mediocrity and repugnance were reinforced later, when Ludvík supposed Helena must be "scurrying about the neighboring village with a tape over her shoulders, bothering the passersby with a microphone and silly questions."[105] The scorn and disgust Ludvik felt for Helena as a journalist was mirrored in the scorn and disgust he felt for her as a sexual object; she was already in her thirties, which the narrator gave as reason for cataloging aspects of her physique and movements which he found vile. Helena was superannuated, like the medium of radio she represented.[106]

Helena's "playacting" stood for the phoniness of de-Stalinization and the disingenuousness of socialist media in the Novotný era.[107] Šťovíčková, on the other hand, was one of those responsible for the contemporaneous "rehabilitation" of radio news.[108] By emphasizing immediacy, drawing on sources beyond the traditional newswires ČTK and TASS (such as AFP and Reuters as well as the Ghana News Agency and *Jeune Afrique*) and through the creation of new radio genres such as the self-reflective commentary and the call-in show, foreign reporters ushered the Prague Spring into Czechoslovak Radio, Milan Rykl claims.[109] In dismissing both the medium of radio and its key female voices under Novotný, Kundera claimed the rhetorical shifts of

190   Chapter 6

the years prior to 1968 for writers such as himself.[110] He also provided the image of Czechoslovakia's Communist journalists that endured in the West. Translated into English in 1982, *The Joke* shaped British and American perceptions of socialist media as staffed by fantasists and fools, spouting empty slogans to apathetic audiences.

That the notion that public speaking defeminized its practitioner was widespread in Czechoslovakia at this moment is attested by the attitudes of Věra Šťovíčková's fans. Ksenia Ivanovová's delight that Šťovíčková was no "dry correspondent at all, but instead a woman with heart and feelings" reproduced the same reporter-woman dichotomy that Kundera and some foreign correspondents promoted.[111] Such claims were made in a state where men and women were constitutionally declared to have achieved "the same standing in the family, in work, and in public activities" in 1960 and point to the gap between the official proclamation and lived experience of women's equality.[112]

At the time of her hiring in 1958, Šťovíčková's employers understood foreign reporting to be a man's job. As she recalled:

> Someone in Prague understood that the world situation was changing and that there should be a permanent [Africa] correspondent. For three months they searched for a man who spoke English and French, who was reasonably informed about Africa and willing to go there. After a quarter of a year some men were found who mastered the languages, but they didn't know anything about Africa, or they didn't want to go there. A quarter of a year later the radio bosses sighed and decided that in the end they would send me. I forgot to mention that I applied straight away for the first competition, but no one took it seriously.[113]

Throughout the 1960s, Šťovíčková's work environment remained male-dominated, which she dealt with by "accepting the predominantly male rules of the game . . . I was one of the gang and this atmosphere suited me well."[114] She cautioned listeners that being a foreign correspondent was not a job well suited to many women, noting that "the costs [to one's personal life] are much too severe to make this profession absolutely attractive to the majority."[115] Šťovíčková here alluded to the difference between her male colleagues' family circumstances and her own. She was a divorcée without dependents who traveled to her journalistic postings on her own. Her male counterparts, by contrast, were often dispatched with their families overseas, where their wives were expected to engage in full-time childcare (in what appeared suspiciously like a traditional bourgeois family set up). For all of the proclamations of the achievement of gender equality through socialism, it was unheard of that a husband would relinquish his work to become a primary caregiver abroad. Female foreign correspondents, Šťovíčková indicated, had to forego certain aspects of family life if they were to maintain their profession.

At times, Šťovíčková seemed to uphold precisely the value system that barred entry to other would-be female foreign reporters. She too could ridicule the superstitious beliefs about the African continent that, she assumed, were held by listeners' overly fussy and ill-informed mothers rather than fathers.[116] And she too could distance herself from the Czech housewives in Conakry who sought to transport the "family hearth" overseas and thus reject all local influences—Šťovíčková tellingly likened herself here to "the experts and the doctors outside of the capital who integrated quickly" instead.[117]

But, upon closer inspection, Šťovíčková played with the notion that public speaking defeminized its practitioner to refute sexualized stereotypes about herself, her female interlocutors, and in particular, the African women to whom she spoke. This last constituency had historically been hypersexualized in Czechoslovak travel literature and visual imagery and continued to be presented in this way in 1960s Czechoslovakia (with magazine *Lidé a země* [*People and Countries*], in one example, sending an image of topless African females as a new year's greeting to those on its mailing list in 1968).[118]

Šťovíčková integrated women's voices and stories into the main news, rather than reserving them for "women's interest" items or comedy Christmas specials. In so doing, she anchored their experiences firmly within mainstream radio reporting. She often interviewed African students in Prague as experts on their country of provenance and, in the case of Omoyele Gadagbé, a female student hailing from the Republic of Dahomey, this evolved into a longer-running cooperation, with Šťovíčková repeatedly inviting Gadagbé into the studio to comment on the weekly news round-up from around the African continent.[119] Similarly, in *Afrika rok jedna*, Šťovíčková profiled the enterprising Mrs. Kouyaté less as an example of the preservation of "old and traditional female crafts" but instead, alongside the collective of female dyers that she had established, as the prime motors of economic regeneration in a suburb of Kissidougou.[120]

192   Chapter 6

Listeners wrote to Šťovíčková about how she confounded their ideas of femininity. The aforementioned Ksenia Ivanovová exclaimed that Šťovíčková made her reappraise her stance towards female emancipation: "I don't like suffragette-style women, but you are so completely different!"[121] Jitka Novohradská latched on to Šťovíčková's courage in particular, proclaiming her "a brave woman, whose courage exceeds that of many professional soldiers."[122] In both cases, Šťovíčková defied easy categorization—firstly as a militant feminist and then as a woman (with professional soldiers coded thoroughly male in 1960s Czechoslovakia).

Another facet of Šťovíčková's character that fan mail often stressed was her intelligence. A Mrs. Němcová from Prague 3 wrote that she was proud when she heard Šťovíčková's reports "that we have such intelligent and educated women here. I'm still convinced that a woman should be beautiful and stupid if she wants to be happy, but I do know from my own experience the feeling of satisfaction a person derives from a piece of work well done."[123] Němcová's was one of the few letters that posited some kind of connection with or understanding of Šťovíčková. More often, correspondents' tone was one of marvel or awe from a position of remove. More conventional in this regard was Marta Bednaříková's missive which stated, in an interesting hierarchical ranking of knowledge gleaned abroad, "my mother always says how clever you are. And you know, her praise counts for a lot, because she was in the USA before the War and spent 10 years there."[124] Margareta Kalábová wrote to Šťovíčková in much the same vein, apologizing in so doing for her poor Czech as, she explained, she was schooled in German.[125]

And while Šťovíčková studiously avoided wading into cheerfully misogynistic debates on the air about who the ideal woman might be, listeners informed her in fan mail that their ideal woman was, in fact, her: a young girl who wanted to be a journalist when she grew up wrote to Šťovíčková for tips on how to become like her.[126] And Milada Přikrylová, a student from Kroměříž, confided in Šťovíčková in October 1968 "you are my example as a woman [*vzorem ženy*]" explaining further that the reporter's "character and behavior" provided Přikrylová with templates to follow.[127]

In downplaying her, and her interviewees', status as females, Šťovíčková may have contributed to the idea that foreign reporting was a man's world. This was certainly the message that her male colleagues conveyed repeatedly in their reports, not least through their voluminous appraisal of the women they brought before the microphone. But Šťovíčková's fan mail does suggest that her output and comportment confounded listeners' expectations of both a radio professional and a woman in striking ways. As Richard Dyer has noted, stars serve to "manage" or resolve contradictions in ideology.[128] As a supremely popular radio star throughout the 1960s, Šťovíčková embodied the contradictions between the theory and the practice of women's emancipation in modern Czechoslovakia. In theory, all women enjoyed the same rights as men and gender disparities no longer existed; in practice there were significant differences in Šťovíčková's work and lifestyle from those of her male peers which allowed her to posit this ideal. The vast amounts of female fan mail she received, not least from younger girls wanting to be like her when they grew up, points to her subverting, for a short period, the idea that foreign correspondence was a male undertaking.

## The Biafran Scandal

Šťovíčková relied upon Czechoslovak state structures in her reporting, and the Czechoslovak state relied upon her. Ultimately, Šťovíčková sought to alter Czechoslovak African policy in March 1968. She did so in a way that utilized existing communications networks and techniques established long before the spring of 1968, while attempting to leverage the new conditions of loosening press censorship, which was abolished by law entirely in June 1968. Her behavior should be read as a continuation of her previous practices of presenting her opinions embedded in information from the African continent to Prague authorities for consideration, coupled with a mounting expectation that she should be listened to on account of her own, by now decade-long expertise on the region.

"Restricted" topics such as arms dealing constituted taboos in Soviet news journalism well into the 1960s, suggests Simon Huxtable.[129] A leaf through Šťovíčková's scripts show how Huxtable's findings for the Soviet Union most certainly applied to Czechoslovakia too. But despite its absence from Šťovíčková's writings, arms dealing formed the backbone of Czechoslovak relations with the African continent throughout Šťovíčková's time as regional correspondent, a point stressed by Philip Muehlenbeck who dedicates a chapter of his monograph *Czechoslovakia in Africa* to this topic.[130]

Šťovíčková complained in her memoirs of being wrongly taken for a representative of the Czechoslovak state in Burundi in 1964, when she was mistaken for an arms dealer and asked by her hosts about the possibilities of facilitating a sale.[131] She suggested here that she had strong words for her superiors at the radio and those "higher up" upon her return about how distressing this wrongful conflation had been.[132] Given the terms she had used when filling out an "obligatory business travel report" at the end of her deployment, Šťovíčková recalled, "I expected some sort of racket [rachot]."[133] Instead, she mused, this was the last she heard of the incident.

Šťovíčková finally got her "racket" four years later when the Czechoslovak government began selling arms to both sides in the Biafran War. Šťovíčková first wrote to an unnamed "comrade," arguing that the sales of planes to Nigerian government forces should stop as it was damaging Czechoslovakia's reputation around the "developing world" and the country's claims to political legitimacy ("if it were willing to stand on the side of feudal lords rather than advanced tribes, if this brings in money").[134] Philip Muehlenbeck explains that the Czechoslovak government had a reasonable amount of autonomy from the Soviet Union to sell arms to whom it wished, with the exception of some larger deals, such as Egypt in 1955 and here in Nigeria in 1968.[135] Thus, Czechoslovakia had started out by arming Biafran separatists, but subsequently had been ordered by the Soviet Union to equip General Gowon's forces as well. "Thanks to Czechoslovak and Soviet arms," Šťovíčková continued, the conflict in Biafra "has become a war of extermination."[136] Any monetary gain the country made from the sale would be "outweighed many times over by the moral damage wrought," Šťovíčková concluded, citing her "own experience in Africa," to underscore her point.[137]

Šťovíčková used the threat of covering the event in the media to leverage officials, rather than immediately going to the press: "the Czechoslovak public is for the moment uninformed about this, because it has been subject to censorship. In these new circumstances [in which censorship was abolished] it will be difficult to keep secret much longer."[138] In other words, Šťovíčková continued to use an existing system of petitioning upwards for change, rather than deploying the tools of the mass media at her disposal to provoke change from the bottom up. Yet, it was on account of her "experience in Africa" and standing at Czechoslovak Radio that she sought to make these claims upon this Foreign Ministry official in the first place.[139] "I have listened to numerous critiques at the Organization of African Unity in Kinshasa last autumn, in Nigeria itself, and the same viewpoint is held by many of the listeners who write in to Czechoslovak Radio's Africa service."[140] Here, Šťovíčková leveraged listener mail as a source of public opinion and suggested the radio—through the letters and experts that it contained—was a repository of this, which officials would do well to consult. Šťovíčková's pleas were in vain, the sales continued, and she broadcast several exposés on the topic on both Czechoslovak Television and Czechoslovak Radio.[141] A newspaper article from April 1968 suggests that audiences responded by protesting outside the Czechoslovak Foreign Ministry.[142]

## Conclusion

These protests were only possible because of the lifting of press censorship in Czechoslovakia in 1968 and because a topic which had previously been off-limits—arms dealing—now made its way into Šťovíčková's reports. But it would be wrong to read the Biafran scandal as constituting a massive break with Šťovíčková's past journalistic practices. Over the previous ten years—Antonín Novotný's time in office—Šťovíčková had established herself as the Africa correspondent for Czechoslovak Radio, an institution with tremendous social capital (and whose capital she sought to leverage in correspondence with officials in 1968). She had cultivated through her reports an image of herself as an expert, both a socialist expert-worker in the field and an Africa expert in Czechoslovakia. It was on grounds of her own expertise that she petitioned the Foreign Ministry in 1968 to change its course towards Biafra. Repeatedly over the previous decade, Šťovíčková had used her reports and longer-form writing to make claims on Czechoslovakia, couched in analysis of the countries she visited. Increasingly, the veil of the foreign dropped from her reports.

By understanding the Biafran scandal as a culmination of practices that Šťovíčková had honed since her deployment to Guinea in 1958, this chapter has provided an alternative narrative of the Prague Spring's origins. Looking beyond the Writers' Union, and in particular its 1967 conference, it has traced some of the reformists' rhetorical foundations back to the depths of conservative leader Antonín Novotný's time in charge. Furthermore, it has sited these nascent cultural shifts in the newsroom—a fundamentally establishment institution subject to censorship until the spring of 1968.

Focusing on Věra Šťovíčková's career has moreover revealed the shifting forms that socialist internationalism assumed during the Cold War. In a departure from earlier socialist explorers, Jiří Hanzelka and Miroslav Zikmund (to whom she paid tribute but from whom she ultimately distanced herself in her reports), Šťovíčková stressed the importance of living and working in the locations on which she reported. She emphasized journalism as a form of Czechoslovak overseas work—like medicine or engineering— that could foster friendship and meaningful collaboration in places on the road to socialism. As a woman undertaking such expert labor, she was in theory indicative of the gender equality which Czechoslovakia as an established socialist country had already achieved and was now exporting. In practice, however, her initial struggle to be seen as a serious candidate for her position and her family life marked her out as different from her male colleagues.

By analyzing Šťovíčková's relationship with the state as one of its official mouthpieces, we can in fact unlock the nature of the relationship between Antonín Novotný's Czechoslovakia and the Soviet Union when it came to formulating Africa policy. Šťovíčková essentially espoused the same value systems and held the same aims as the state for which she spoke, which is not to say that this relationship was without points of conflict and particular points of obligation. So too, did Czechoslovakia share basic policy concepts with the Soviet Union, which is not to say that it had no intentions, investments, or ideas of its own. We should not, in hindsight, read moments of conflict between cultural professionals and the state as inherently anti-Communist on the former's part. Nor should we read differences in opinion between Czechoslovakia and the Soviet Union in 1960s Africa policy (for example on the matter of to whom to sell arms) as an inherently moral, defiant stance on the part of Czechoslovakia.[143] Šťovíčková had, in her own telling, significant room to maneuver coupled with several non-negotiable aspects to her job. This is how Philip Muehlenbeck characterizes the Czechoslovak state and its ability to pursue its own goals on the African continent: largely autonomous, but at several moments issued with orders to follow from Moscow. Western onlookers then and now have overestimated the centrally issued directives to which the socialist reporter, and the socialist satellite, had to adhere.

Finally, I have argued that these insights, which were available to Šťovíčková's peers and certainly to her listeners, have been lost; both through unofficial memory regimes, which have coded foreign reporting so very male, and through institutional attempts to remove almost all traces of Šťovíčková and her colleagues' voices from the radio archives following the Warsaw Pact invasion of Czechoslovakia in August 1968. It is to such dramatic events that I now turn.

# 7 All Together Now?

*Czechoslovak Radio during the Prague Spring
and Warsaw Pact Invasion in 1968*

**THERE ARE SEVERAL WAYS** to destroy a magnetic tape's contents, each with its own unique advantages and drawbacks. Shredding tapes with a blade relies upon readily available tools but requires elbow grease; demagnetizing (or degaussing) them takes less work but needs a strong magnet. Recording over tapes is probably the most environmentally friendly option but requires time, while burning such highly flammable materials works quickly but produces noxious fumes. Czechoslovak Radio's foreign reporters did not have long to ponder these options as they set about destroying their own sound archive after Warsaw Pact tanks rolled into Prague in August 1968. By doing so, they sought to make a sonic reconstruction of their work that year as difficult as possible. This will not deter us from trying over the pages that follow.

If the build-up to the Prague Spring at Czechoslovak Radio was slow and incremental, as the last chapter argued, then the changes that took place once the process of reform gathered pace in the first months of 1968 rang loud and clear. So much so, in fact, that the state broadcaster's output was cited as a reason to invade Czechoslovakia and roll back reforms by the summer of that year.[1] Scandalously or thrillingly, the way that Czechoslovak

198 Chapter 7

Radio's reporters aspired to contribute to social change was best captured in the transforming relationships that they articulated with politicians on the one hand and listeners on the other.

After sketching the events of the Prague Spring, this chapter reconstructs the radio listening practices of Czechs and Slovaks in 1968, before examining how state broadcaster Czechoslovak Radio's output changed over that year. Focusing on the broadcaster's foreign news desk headed by Milan Weiner, it considers how socialist journalists like him reevaluated their purpose and interests, highlighting their cautiousness and trepidation (a point missing from the polemics against Czechoslovak journalism audible at the time around the Eastern Bloc).[2] The chapter finally places the events of the Warsaw Pact invasion of Czechoslovakia in August 1968 into this context, arguing that the voices of the reporters in Weiner's team came to function as "vocal signatures" during the invasion, evoking these events for listeners (even in the absence of much surviving magnetic tape) for months, and even years, beyond.

The events of the Prague Spring were, as Melissa Feinberg writes, "part of the global protest wave in 1968, but . . . had their own dynamic."[3] They were driven forward, for example, by established political and cultural elites in the Czechoslovak Communist Party in a bid to consolidate socialist rule in Czechoslovakia, rather than by a younger generation of students seeking to undermine existing structures of power.[4]

For one of the political and cultural elites who gained in prominence that year, the writer-turned-reformist politician Pavel Kohout, the Prague Spring's goals were fourfold: federalization of the Czech and Slovak regions of the republic, rehabilitation for the victims of Stalinist justice, "democratization, and a new economic model."[5] Reformists, however, were a diverse bunch, and others added questions of political pluralization or a withdrawal from the Warsaw Pact and declaration of military neutrality to this. It was reformist economic thinking which had opened the door to broader political change in the first place, with the Czechoslovak economy in the doldrums since the period leading up to President Antonín Novotný's decision to abandon the third five-year plan in 1962. Novotný, in power as first secretary of the Communist Party since 1953 and president since 1957, had furthermore alienated Slovak functionaries and citizens through rejecting calls for increased autonomy as "bourgeois nationalism," including in the few public appearances in Slovakia that he did venture to make (he tried to avoid visiting the territory as much as possible).[6] Most recently, he had tarnished his image in further quarters still through the heavy-handed way his administration had persecuted writers—like Kohout—who had criticized censorship and the level of cultural life in Czechoslovakia at the Writer's Conference in 1967.

To spur the economy, some Communist Party functionaries had begun advocating for a loosening of price controls and the devolution of economic decision-making from the Central Committee to factory managers. One of the key architects of this, Ota Šik, argued that this economic reform could not take place without accompanying political reforms. In January 1968, the reformist wing of the Communist Party agreed, pushing Novotný out of power, and electing a relatively unknown young Slovak, Alexander Dubček, to the position of first secretary of the Communist Party in his stead. In April, the Politburo released an "Action Plan," outlining proposals to decentralize the economy and rehabilitate political prisoners from the Stalinist era.

If economic reform was fundamental to the way that the Central Committee conceived of and experienced the Prague Spring, then its focal points at Czechoslovak Radio lay closer to the concerns of writers such as Kohout. Czechoslovak Radio staff—chief among them editor of the foreign news section Milan Weiner and the foreign correspondents in his department—pushed for the complete revocation of censorship and for the full rehabilitation of victims of the Stalinist show trials (which had personally affected some of their number, including Weiner). These reporters—who described themselves as engaged and committed "communist journalists"—additionally sought to expose cases of corruption and the ongoing abuse of workers' rights in their reports, and reveal and eradicate latent anti-Semitism in Czechoslovak society.[7]

In March, the Communist Party "relinquished its control" over censorship, fundamentally altering the Czechoslovak media environment. Media outlets could now air "unrestricted debate, a clash of views," as well as opinions on "long-taboo subjects."[8] In June, the National Assembly outlawed censorship altogether by revising the press law.[9] The onus was now placed back on editors-in-chief like Weiner (as it had been on editors such as Aškenazy in the years preceding the show trials—see chapter 2) to make sure that state secrets were not being divulged in reports.

Hailed as "the only democratic achievement to [Czechoslovakia's] credit this year" by writer and radio journalist Ludvík Vaculík in June, the revocation of censorship was an important, if not the most important, pretext for the Soviet-led invasion of Czechoslovakia in August 1968.[10] Censorship's annulment drew what became almost "ritualistic" criticism from Czechoslovakia's socialist neighbors from the moment six of the bloc's leaders met in Dresden in March.[11] As Petr Andreas notes, "polemics with the pro-reform media regularly appeared before the invasion in the mass media of [Czechoslovakia's] allies and, after August 1968, they created a sizeable portion of . . . Vltava, a radio station broadcasting [in Czech] from the GDR."[12] It was not only foreign onlookers who railed at the changes they witnessed in the Czechoslovak media. Even if Novotný had been deposed, there were many retaining positions of power in the Czechoslovak Communist Party who were also perturbed by the move. In the "invitation to invade" they sent to Soviet leader Leonid Brezhnev in August 1968, Communist functionaries such as Alois Indra, Drahomír Kolder, and Vasiľ Biľak singled out media developments in Czechoslovakia as of particular concern.[13] Censorship was rapidly reinstated following the Soviet-led invasion in August 1968 as an explicit demand of the protocol that Czechoslovak leaders signed in Moscow.[14]

The discussions they tabled on air in 1968 did not make reporters rebels or defiantly anti-establishment. In fact, after two decades spent at the state broadcaster, journalists such as Karel Kyncl and Věra Šťovíčková were synonymous with the establishment, if not the establishment itself. In a country that had experienced two revolutions within the last half century, moreover, these reporters sought to shore up rather than tear down "cherished" institutions like their employer Czechoslovak Radio.[15] While Western analysts understood the abandonment of censorship in Czechoslovakia as a sign that the country sought to align itself with the West, Czechoslovak journalists used the new media environment they inhabited with perhaps surprising restraint, seeking to shore up socialism for generations to come. This chapter explores why they employed their newfound freedoms so cautiously, reconstructing how reporters censored themselves so as not to attract the censure of their office mates and peers. These by-now veteran journalists indeed stayed true to their own professional habits honed over the previous two decades of socialism, due to a belief in the reforms of the Prague Spring—including the revocation of censorship—which they felt that they in particular had the power to undermine.

Here, I focus on Czechoslovakia Radio's foreign news-desk as the "dominant" force introducing the Prague Spring to the broadcaster.[16] Foreign correspondents moved closer to Czechoslovak political elites at precisely the moment when the influence of the latter was removed from the workings of the newsroom. But the Prague Spring not only spelled a reassessment of relations with politicians: journalists rearticulated their role and responsibilities vis-à-vis the general public, too.

### Radio in Czechoslovakia in 1968

During the Prague Spring, radio was the most important medium in Czechoslovakia. Four million radio receivers furnished Czechoslovak homes in August 1968, judged the CIA, compared to 2.5 million television sets.[17] Taking portable transistor radio receivers into account, Eva Ješutová claims that there were as many as seven million radios in a country of fourteen million inhabitants.[18]

While media professionals understood television watching to be a group activity—given the expense and relative rarity of receivers, radio listening was increasingly becoming an individualized and mobile practice. Milan Rykl claims that the proliferation of transistor radios led Czechoslovak Radio management towards a policy of "differentiation between stations . . . directing them towards different groups of listeners." Rykl suggests that this increasingly personalized approach was a factor leading to the broadcaster's "renaissance" in the 1960s.[19]

Transistor radios had begun changing the venues of radio listening in the early 1960s, and thus the soundscapes of Czechoslovakia's towns and countryside. In an article for youth magazine *Mladý svět* penned in 1961, music journalist Jiří Černý complained about transistor radios' ubiquity and the "exhibitionism" of their owners. In "Tranzistorový teror" ("Transistor Terror"), he likened the radios to cars and suggested while the police took care of reckless drivers, it was a social obligation—currently going unfulfilled—to take care of reckless listeners. In this tongue-in-cheek piece, Černý acknowledged that the law currently prohibited loud radio playing after nine o'clock at night (and ten in the summer), but was otherwise powerless to control listeners' tastes and the venues they chose to indulge in their hobby. In an article suggesting radio listeners—rather than law enforcement—constituted a "terror" just years after this word had been used, at least by some Western onlookers, to describe Stalinist Czechoslovakia's judicial apparatus, Černý called ironically for increased policing of transistor use at tennis matches, in public spaces, and in Czechoslovakia's fields and groves.[20]

By the spring of 1968, the popularity of the transistor radio had risen higher still, in particular, it seems, in the Czechoslovak capital. Author and reform politician Pavel Kohout noted in May that the device had become "the most popular fashion accessory in Prague," implying that an element of each receiver's appeal lay in what it signified to onlookers in addition to the information that it could provide its owner.[21] Czechoslovak Radio's foreign news chief Milan Weiner, meanwhile, remarked that listeners were taking their transistors "into the cinema and the theatre" so as never to miss a word.[22]

One reason for the proliferation of transistor radios was their cost: they were cheaper than the larger stationary sets furnishing millions of Czechoslovak homes. The devices were far from universally accessible, however. When they first hit Czechoslovak stores, receivers like the Tesla T58 cost 460 Czechoslovak crowns—which amounted to more than a third of the average gross monthly salary.[23] Throughout the 1960s, their din remained loudest where "fashionable" people converged. Writing in the early 1960s, Černý associated above all a younger demographic with the devices. When Kohout and Weiner commented on their use at the decade's close, they continued to be associated with a youthful, relatively affluent, and culturally engaged demographic, able to spend a portion of its salary on cinema tickets and consumer electronics.

The vast majority of the country's radio sets were equipped to pick up foreign stations, which is not to say that everyone did. In 1968, around two thirds of listeners tuned into foreign broadcasts—a historic low, claimed Radio Free Europe (RFE), attributing this drop to the amount of information newly available on state broadcaster Czechoslovak Radio.[24] Western stations like RFE that had targeted Czechoslovak listeners since the immediate postwar years were joined by ever larger numbers of Eastern Bloc broadcasts. In one example, CIA analysts calculated that "Radio Moscow . . .

more than doubled its direct broadcasts in Czech and Slovak." Neighboring East Germany also considerably stepped up the volume of broadcasts it directed towards Czechoslovakia.[25]

That Czechoslovak Radio was commanding an ever-larger listenership was noted by foreign news chief Weiner, who described moreover a change in the nature of the relationship between the reporter and the listener. Newspapers had begun the Prague Spring at the start of 1968, he claimed, bringing the most information to their audiences.[26] Bursting with stories, they regularly sold out. Czechoslovak Radio, on the other hand, had lagged behind. It played too much music, listeners had complained, and offered too little commentary on current affairs.[27] Weiner and colleagues had adapted their work to accommodate listener demands. They had broadcast commentaries critiquing the words and actions of those in power and live interviews with politicians. Audiences had responded favorably to Weiner and colleagues' work. Now, enthralled listeners were allegedly glued to their radios.[28]

Czechoslovak Radio saw its "big competitor," according to Weiner, as television.[29] In a socialist country, different forms of media could, in this view, "compete" with one another—for attention, audience share, news exclusives, and talent. Rather than rival foreign stations on the same medium, Weiner indicated that radio employees in Czechoslovakia understood their competition by 1968 to be different domestic media. His judgment is indicative of the self-referentiality and the self-interest of the Czechoslovak media that year.

As the theatergoing transistor-listeners who "terrorized" Jiří Černý make clear, media audiences then, as now, used multiple media, sometimes simultaneously, to entertain and inform themselves and to participate in the events of the day. For all the "competition" between Czechoslovak Television and Czechoslovak Radio, audiences did not opt for one to the exclusion of the other. Czechoslovak Television also played a crucial, and complementary, role creating the tone, style, and aesthetics of the Prague Spring. Historian Paulina Bren acknowledges radio's primary status while demonstrating how television brought "disclosures and confessions" relating to Czechoslovakia's Communist past out of the literary (and journalistic) circles in which they had first been uttered and "onto the communist screen," which in turn sparked discussions on "the streets and eventually the upper echelons of the

204 Chapter 7

party."[30] Radio's prominence in Czechoslovakia in 1968 should be read less as a mark of East Central Europe's "backwardness" and more a comment on the continued importance of technologies whose use has become engrained and widespread long after the excitement of their invention has worn off. To stress the importance of radio to the events of the Prague Spring and the subsequent invasion is not, then, to present a uniquely Eastern European story of technological lag, but instead to present a more generally applicable study of what historian of science David Edgerton has called "the shock of the old"—the capacity for mainstreamed, mass technologies to fundamentally shape and reshape daily life.[31]

The year 1968 around the globe has been characterized as a time when "rebels" rejected "most institutions, political leaders and political parties."[32] Kieran Williams observes almost the opposite trend taking place in Czechoslovakia: he argues that Prague Spring reforms were intended to shore up "cherished" institutions rather than smash them down.[33] By harnessing the possibilities that the Prague Spring presented to comment on current political affairs, Weiner posited that he and colleagues were able to consolidate Czechoslovak Radio's preeminent standing as a state media institution in 1968.

Czechoslovak Radio's paramount position was not to survive the Prague Spring. An RFE survey from January 1969 found that the number of Czechs and Slovaks listening to Western broadcasts shot up in the months following the Soviet-led invasion. "After the country was invaded," it concluded, "almost nine persons in every ten tuned in to Western broadcasts."[34] Over the period of normalization that followed, dating approximately from 1969 to 1989, Paulina Bren has shown how television ultimately dethroned radio, with a majority of Czechs and Slovaks turning to radio's "big competitor" for their entertainment and news.[35]

### Czechoslovak Radio during the Prague Spring

Two major shifts shaped Czechoslovak Radio's output over the first months of 1968, as the Prague Spring found its audio form at the state broadcaster. Firstly, Czechoslovak Radio's foreign reporters, profiled in the last chapter, switched their focus to domestic matters, practically ceasing to report on foreign affairs. Secondly, if reporters like Šťovíčková had indirectly addressed aspects of Czechoslovak history in their reports up until now, then such reporters began to speak extremely frankly about recent Czechoslovak history—above all, the show trials of the 1950s (examined in chapter 2).

"In the last few months of . . . exceptional political activity at home," Sylva Součková explained to Czechoslovak Radio's international listeners in April 1968, "a number of commentators whose main business it is to discuss international affairs [have] centered their attention on home politics."[36] Foreign news desk chief Milan Weiner explained why. In March 1968, he addressed what he called a common listener complaint on air: audiences had long protested that "they knew more about Ruanda-Urundi than neighboring Hungary."[37] He uttered these comments in a "domestic political commentary"—a genre in which he frequently wrote in 1968.

Foreign correspondents had long discussed Czechoslovakia when talking about the rest of the world. They had done so, however, opaquely. During the Prague Spring, reporters mentioned the rest of the world if and only if it strengthened an argument they were making about Czechoslovakia. In another domestic political commentary, for example, Weiner—formerly the China correspondent for the Czech Press Agency ČTK—asked whether the path Czechoslovakia was traveling was similar to Beijing's in the run-up to the Sino-Soviet split.[38] Not at all, he concluded, Czechoslovakia was undertaking something quite original, rather than following in the footsteps of any previous deviator from the Soviet party line. Weiner's was, in fact, one of the few reports mentioning a fellow socialist country retained in the Czech Radio sound archive from 1968. While the picture is difficult to reconstruct because many tapes from that year were destroyed, it appears that, despite pledges to shed more light on "neighboring Hungary than Ruanda-Urundi," adjacent socialist countries continued to play a secondary role on Czechoslovak Radio, overshadowed by changes taking place at home.

As part of their shift towards domestic affairs, Czechoslovak Radio's foreign correspondents revisited controversial moments in Czechoslovak history.[39] In June 1968, for example, Karel Kyncl—formerly Czechoslovak Radio's US correspondent—made a two-hour program on the 1950s, simply called *Padesátá léta* (*The Fifties*). He spoke to survivors of the show trials, such as Eugen Löbl and Marie Švermová, as well as relatives of those who had been executed, for example the wife of Rudolf Slánský, Josefa Slánská, and the wife of Ota Šling, Marian Šlingová. Reports such as this, which drew on some of the only tape that Czechoslovak Radio had preserved from the

206 Chapter 7

1950s served, as Muriel Blaive has shown, to render the show trials synonymous with Stalinism in the memory culture of the period (and thereafter). Such broadcasts, moreover, "contributed . . . towards portraying the history of the 1950s as [above all] a history of political repression."[40]

In this radio documentary, Kyncl asked those affected by the show trials where they believed the trials' origins lay and why those persecuted had been selected. One respondent, Bedřich Kopolt, argued that the trials' roots lay in the Soviet Union. Kopolt stressed that not all Soviets were former Soviet police chief Lavrentiy Beria's henchmen—a group he characterized as having "sunk to the bottom of humanity." But his views, which Kyncl broadcast, came strikingly close to criticism of the Soviet Union, hitherto completely out of bounds in public speech.[41]

Kyncl interspersed interview footage with the original radio coverage of the Slánský trial. The buzz that the old recordings made when replayed morphed into discordant music composed specially for the program. This rendered audio that many listeners may have remembered hearing overtly disturbing to revisit. Archival footage of agitated, shouting prosecutors was contrasted with the thoughtful recollections of those who had been persecuted almost two decades ago. Kyncl featured the voices of his interviewees at length and did not interject when they spoke. He kept his own appearances to a minimum, distilling the question he had asked down to its simplest, one-word form—such as "roots," "who," and "why"—and then omitting his voice from the interviews that followed. As a result, the listener gained the impression that the victims of the trials were being granted an opportunity to speak for themselves.[42] In letting his interviewees speak at length on the radio without interruption, Kyncl mirrored and subverted the onus placed on defendant testimony to incriminate the speaker that was such an important element of the trials' original radio coverage (see chapter 2).

Kyncl suggested that those he broadcast here were initiating an overdue discussion in society in general, rather than speaking among themselves. By pointing out that these interviews addressed listeners, Kyncl hinted that they were implicated in a conspiracy of silence that had shrouded the show trials over the past two decades and asked listeners to take responsibility for this. Foregrounding voices which had been inconvenient or shameful for people to hear for too long, Czechoslovak Radio staff thus understood themselves to be contributing to the reevaluation of the country's history made possible during the Prague Spring. If listeners had originally been asked to participate in the show trials by writing into the radio demanding the harshest of punishments for defendants, then the participation that radio staff solicited of listeners now was to acknowledge, through discussion, these voices and the suffering that they had endured as a result of their pillorying.

Alongside amplifying the voices of show trial defendants and their families, Czechoslovak Radio retrieved from the archive recordings of others who had fallen into disfavor, such as that of former foreign minister, Jan Masaryk. The broadcaster additionally provided a platform for rehabilitated journalists to speak.[43] Former radio commentator Stanislav Budín made his return to state radio after being thrown out of the Communist Party in 1950.[44] And Milan Weiner himself, dismissed from the role of ČTK China correspondent at the time of the Slánský trial in 1952 on account of his Jewish background, became an ever-more prominent speaker gradually from the mid-1960s onwards after taking over the radio's foreign news desk.

Jettisoning their foreign focus, reporters such as Weiner and Kyncl redefined their own interests, roles, and responsibilities. Their turn inwards and the explicit rejection of foreign templates that Weiner articulated here are indicative of the sui generis nature of much of the Prague Spring. Foreign correspondents, like many of their listeners, were pushing back against decades of state-sponsored professions of solidarity with comrades in the East and South. With those who had formerly uttered appeals for international solidarity now scrutinizing Czechoslovakia in their reports, we gain an impression of how the Prague Spring consolidated itself "alone in its own cosmos, without links to international politics."[45] Indeed, these reporters' introspection constituted one of the biggest ruptures of the Prague Spring: its critics dubbed it, unfairly but on this basis, a time of "chauvinism" and extreme "nationalism."[46] Even less fairly, they argued that the reformist journalists around Weiner were not, in fact, Communists at all.[47]

## Weiner versus Záruba and the Discursive Environment of the Prague Spring

That these journalists were not anti-Communist, but instead invested in redefining what the role of an engaged socialist journalist should be, becomes clearest in the debates that they held on air during the first months of 1968.

208 Chapter 7

These culminated in a "memorable discussion" held between foreign news desk chief Milan Weiner and a concerned citizen—an "old Communist," in the words of one Radio Prague reporter—Comrade Josef Záruba."[48]

Weiner versus Záruba began in a domestic political commentary in March. In a monologue conventional for this radio genre, Weiner reveled in the plurality of views that had arisen about democratization in Czechoslovakia. He warned, however, that listeners at the more cautious end of the spectrum risked having their trepidation hijacked by "conservative elements putting the brakes on reforms." These "conservative elements" were not defending the interests of the working class. Weiner pointed to the material differences between high-ranking conservatives and the workers they allegedly represented: while the latter traveled to work "jammed into trams, if you'll pardon me, like animals," the former drove to their office jobs in luxurious Tatra 603s.[49] Thus while "conservative elements" currently had something to protect, the Czechoslovak working class had nothing to lose but their chains.

"I've been a journalist for more than two months," Weiner continued, "and so I know that journalists, when they want to, will always find four or five people in this republic with the opinions that they need: pro-Chinese, anti-Chinese, pro-American, anti-American, pro-Dubček, anti-Dubček." Merely citing a plurality, then, without analyzing whose interests this equivocation served, was not enough. The responsibility of the Communist journalist lay instead in refuting points made in the name of the working class that actually supported an existing system of wastefulness, cronyism, and capitalist-style inequality.[50]

Away from the microphone too, Weiner was seeking to reform the journalistic profession. Having founded a Prague branch of the Union of Journalists in 1968, he had advocated for less Communist Party oversight of the occupation. The only limit to the reporter's job "should be the socialist conscience of the journalist."[51] The individual rather than the Party, and conscience rather than the law, should define the limits of a journalist's work. Czechoslovak journalists should be faithful to the tenets of socialism in their writing. But this did not mean slavish praise of every action that had been performed in the name of socialism in the past. Rather, it necessitated the discussion of themes that protected the rights of Czech and Slovak workers. For Weiner, the journalist truly promoting socialism rejected violence, including (and perhaps especially) violence committed in socialism's name.

In the commentary culminating in his clash with Záruba, Weiner's words gained moral authority from his age and his life experiences—he could talk about journalistic practices from the Stalinist period firsthand. His seasoned-sounding voice, world-weary and even exasperated tone, and recurrent use of *anteoccupatio* added to the idea that he had seen this all before and that the debates of the Prague Spring were not necessarily in themselves all that new. Discussing such thorny issues on the radio, however, certainly was.

In a divergence from the usual format of a radio commentary, Weiner then dedicated the last three minutes of this broadcast to a phone exchange between himself and one disgruntled listener. Josef Záruba had taken issue with Weiner's commentary the previous day. The listener had called the radio to ask Weiner if he believed any good had come of Communist rule in Czechoslovakia, given the way he was allegedly rubbishing it on air. Záruba continued by inquiring whether Weiner was a member of the Communist Party. Weiner responded that he was, since 1942, when he joined in a concentration camp. The detail presented Weiner as a survivor of what was often styled as Western imperialism in its most distilled form: fascism. Weiner thus also foregrounded his Jewish background in a non-explicit way.

Záruba retorted that if Weiner was indeed a Communist, then he did not want to be in the same party as him and that perhaps two should be created. Weiner gleefully agreed, in a broader context in which Czechs and Slovaks were debating whether democratization could be managed solely by the Communist Party or in fact required political pluralization.[52] Záruba then called Weiner an "agent of imperialism." Weiner refuted this immediately and then again in his summary at the end of the piece.[53]

This was exactly the language used, Weiner suggested, to incriminate the defendants in the Slánský trial. While he was in no way working with Western powers to overthrow socialism, Weiner stressed that he was "honored," through this appellation, to be likened to André Simone (real name Otto Katz—a Czechoslovak Jewish journalist hanged as an "agent of imperialism" alongside Slánský in 1952).[54] By invoking the show trials, which had impacted his career too, Weiner again gestured to the abuses of justice he had survived. In conclusion, Weiner argued that it was time for a change: while proud to be likened to Katz—who was as innocent of Western plotting then as he was now—Weiner was no journalistic martyr and not prepared to go to the gallows, nor did he believe that anyone in Czechoslovakia

210  Chapter 7

should on account of their views. Weiner's experience showed instead that there was a direct link, embodied by Katz, between the stifling of freedom of expression and the "darkest moments of socialism in this country."[55] To avoid repeating the mistakes of the past, Weiner invited Comrade Záruba into the radio for a live debate the following Monday.

Years later, and with the vagaries of memory causing her to misname the outspoken Záruba, Věra Šťovíčková recalled what happened next:

> Opponents of the Prague Spring protested that we weren't giving them the space to talk—and that everything that was going on at the time in Czechoslovakia we were interpreting in our own way. Milan therefore invited the loudest of the unreconstructed [skalních] Communists, Comrade Zahrádka, to the microphone—who had himself asked for this exchange. Just the two of them sat down and talked together. Comrade Zahrádka had free rein, Milan didn't limit the time he had to speak or the topics he could talk about. And the meeting went smoothly. The response was thunderous. Despite wearing his Bolshevik heart on his sleeve, Comrade Zahrádka was totally defeated.[56]

In this telling, a battle was waged for the hearts and minds of listeners between Weiner, the voice of reform, and Záruba, the voice of Communist conservatism. For Šťovíčková, this debate had a winner and a loser, and victory was gauged by audience response.

The exchange took place in what Heda Margolius Kovály calls the "spirit of tolerance" that characterized the Prague Spring. As she recalls, "whenever someone dared to stand up in defense of the old order," à la Záruba, "people heard him out, with contempt perhaps but also with patience, and then repudiated his arguments and paid him no more attention."[57] Yet the debate between Weiner and Záruba was perhaps more a performance of even-handedness than an actual display of equality. Those associated with Czechoslovak Radio had a vast technological advantage when it came to creating, editing, and transmitting audio over those who were not. In other words, Weiner made a show of his own magnanimity by airing the phone interview with Comrade Záruba, but if it had been less flattering to him, he could as easily have left it out. Exposing Záruba's audible agitation in contrast to Weiner's studied cool may have indeed served to discredit the former. Weiner had the right to add the final word to the telephone call he recorded with Záruba, giving him the advantage of hindsight that Záruba did not have. Reformists in support of First Secretary Alexander Dubček deftly succeeded in painting their opponents as dogmatists, claims Martin Schulze Wessel.[58] Radio-relayed debates such as this were where the reformist camp achieved this feat.

Discussing Czechoslovak Television in 1968, Paulina Bren has argued that "the television stars that year were the ordinary people who appeared daily on the screen. As meeting after meeting was broadcast live, students and workers, men and women, made themselves heard."[59] The Záruba-Weiner debate qualifies this. Non-radio stars were certainly important referents in media broadcasts that year, and important to the overall aesthetics of such broadcasts, but their appearances were edited and styled by radio professionals—indeed often to make the point that reporters were aware of and understood their audiences. Weiner was not guilty of deliberate ill faith towards Comrade Záruba, and his approach—of debating and seeking to defeat his opponent—constituted a more openly engaged form of journalism than the mere splicing together of contradictory statements provided by the "four or five people in this republic [who are] . . . pro-Dubček, anti-Dubček" required of any journalist seeking to draw up a nominally balanced report. But while it delighted radio colleagues like Šťovíčková and Součková (the Radio Prague reporter cited at the start of this section) as a rhetorical victory for their cause, this debate hardly brought those alienated by contemporary media developments back into the fold.

Záruba was not alone in feeling that the Czechoslovak media propounded largely reform Communist views. In their "invitation to invade" Czechoslovakia, hard-line Communists Alois Indra, Drahomír Kolder, Antonín Kapek, Oldřich Švestka, and Vasil Biľak complained that they were finding it difficult to gain a platform from which to broadcast their standpoint, which, they added, was much less critical of the Soviet Union than that of the reformists.[60] And if reform Communists such as Weiner and his colleagues did well to paint Záruba, Indra, Kolder, and Biľak as yesterday's men, then these men, precisely through documents such as their letter to Brezhnev, arguably enjoyed even more success in painting Weiner and his radio colleagues as not Communists at all. Here, however, I have underscored how far away such claims were from radio staff's own understandings of the work they did.

## Shifting Reporter-Listener Relations
## through the Lens of Listener Mail

Czechoslovak Radio audibly wove into its reports the feedback that listeners like Záruba delivered over the phone. But writing letters to Czechoslovak Radio continued to be the method that most listeners used to communicate with the broadcaster.

Czechoslovak Radio had actively solicited letters since at least the 1950s. Then, writers such as the humorist Zdeněk Jirotka had mused that listener mail "was extremely valuable not just as material for programming, but also as an expression of faith in the radio on the part of listeners."[61] Letters could, and did, inspire radio journalists, but they also reflected—and created— radio's social standing. Writing a letter was an "expression of faith" in the broadcaster, and the broadcaster could then leverage this "valuable" faith when dealing with state authorities.

Addressed to individual journalists or news desks, letters were generally processed by a department at Czechoslovak Radio dedicated specially to handling listener mail. This was feminized work, with the task of respond- ing to listener correspondence understood at the radio to be secretarial (and secretaries in Czechoslovak offices in the 1950s and 1960s were overwhelm- ingly women). In 1955, section head, Mrs. R. Rollová, reprimanded journalists for being too slow to process letters, insisting that time was of the essence when it came to issuing a response. Dealing with listener mail should not be understood by journalists as "a pain," but letters instead represented the "innumerable threads joining a news outlet to life, to the masses."[62]

Reporter Karel Kyncl parodied the sense of obligation that journalists felt to listener mail in a radio play in 1961. In *Rozhlasová romance* (*Radio Ro- mance*), Kyncl—playing himself—was unwillingly dragged into a story of love gone awry when a letter from a jilted, pregnant lover reached his desk.[63] Despite his initial trepidation, colleagues guilted Kyncl into upholding his professional duty and seeing to it that the wrongly separated couple were wed. Kyncl mocked himself as a radio journalist who felt such attention to listener mail was beneath him (or who might just be lazy) in the play, which nevertheless affirms with its happy ending that there is nothing the radio cannot solve for its listeners.

By 1968, Kyncl's by-now boss Milan Weiner suggested that he was re- sponding to listener feedback in a different way. Rather than pulling strings with authorities behind the scenes, which Kyncl had done with military officers and the groom-to-be's family in *Radio Romance*, Weiner cited letters in commentaries as reasons he and his team needed to change their own output. Weiner's point was that listener feedback shaped the news team's agenda, and that journalists were intermediaries through which listeners could find themselves and their topics of interest live on air. While Kyncl's tale leveraged Czechoslovak Radio's social capital in off-record negotiations with authorities, Weiner suggested that the institution now derived its social capital above all from amplifying the listener's voice, which came in the form of the written and telephonic feedback radio staff gained from listeners.

Listener letters allow a "denser description than usually can be realized" when studying the content of socialist radio programming alone, argues Christoph Classen.[64] Concretely, they shed light on how socialist journalists' relationships with their listeners changed in the years running up to and including 1968. Certainly, journalists did not always type—or even author—the correspondence with listeners that carried their name. But these reporters suggested, as far back as Zdeněk Jirotka in the mid-1950s, how important such correspondence was for, firstly, understanding one's listeners and, secondly, the ability to leverage authorities on Czechoslovak Radio's behalf. What was new by the late 1960s was the insistence within programming that listener feedback served as the impetus for the journalist's choice of subject matter and even the questions that journalists posed to their interviewees. The shift signaled by the increasing insertion of references to listener mail was that reporters now performed a service for their listeners, although—in the way that reporters continued to gatekeep and edit the correspondence they received—there were certainly limits to this.

### Songs with a Telephone and the Reconfiguration of Political Speech

If the journalists around Milan Weiner sought to signal that their relationship to their listeners had changed over the course of the Prague Spring, then they also suggested that their relationship to politicians had shifted. The call-in show *Písničky s telefonem* (*Songs with a Telephone*) was an important venue in which the politician-reporter-listener relationship was loudly reconfigured. Inspired by the radio that foreign correspondents heard abroad, *Songs with a Telephone* constituted a "technically-demanding live program with telephone interviews . . . interspersed with songs."[65] From its inauguration in 1967, radio staff called officials with the request that they explain themselves and their policies live on air, and politicians, for their part, gained a "direct" platform to address media audiences.

**FIGURE 20.** Promotional shot for *Písničky s telefonem* (*Songs with a Telephone*) in which (from left to right) presenters Věra Šťovíčková, Jiří Dienstbier, and Sláva Volný posed with the eponymous telephones, showing off the technological mastery of the show. Source: Czech Radio. Reprinted with permission.

If radio were a mainstreamed technology in Czechoslovakia in 1968, then telephones were most certainly not. Indeed, many newsrooms were still not equipped with a single telephone at this period, which made coordinating meetings hard.[66] And while many recollections of the 1968 invasion begin with the narrator learning about the event over the telephone, many more recall that a lack of a telephone made it extremely difficult to contact relatives at the time. In 1970, the CIA judged that 1.8 million telephones were in use in a country of 14.5 million people.[67] The telephone so central to the title and the fabric of this program, then, continued to be an aspirational object, adding glamour to the show (as evinced in its promotional materials—see figure 20). Built upon conversations with those who owned telephones, a particularly urban, and relatively affluent, demographic was invited to have its say in this show.

The program featured politicians and journalists in the studio or over the phone, answering listeners' questions live. A typical script from March 1968 contained an interview with actress Jiřina Jirásková about her role in a new play by František Hrubín alongside a discussion with "progressive economist" Karel Štrégl, and feedback from Berlin correspondent Ladislav Porjes regarding comments made by East German politician Kurt Hager attributing Czechoslovakia's reforms to "West German imperialists."[68]

During the Prague Spring, reformist politicians increasingly turned to mass media such as Czechoslovak Radio to present and explain their policies to Czechs and Slovaks.[69] This marked a major shift in politicians' media presentation which, for Martin Štoll, constituted the very crux of the Prague Spring.[70] Previously, "normal people had no opportunity to set their eyes on government officials, let alone hear their opinions."[71] The only exception was at moments of official ritual, like the May Day parade, or the president's new year's speech. Pavel Kohout reflected on how dire he had found such events in his diary in 1968, joking ironically that former president Antonín Novotný's "annual off-the-cuff remarks at the end of the May Day parade, brought by radio to the most remote hamlet, [had] belonged to the golden fund of tape recordings." He recalled the "mediocrity" of the message unfailingly projected into the crowds by "this enthusiastic voice," summarizing it as "there will be meat, my female comrades! There will be meat!"[72] By the time that Kohout wrote these words, promises of a future full of meat no longer sufficed. Instead, politicians engaged in live Q&As on programs like

*Songs with a Telephone*—and in so doing broadcast the existence of differences in opinion within the highest ranks of the Communist Party.

The cornering of politicians in *Songs with a Telephone* could compromise journalistic standards, radio journalist Karel Lánský complained: "Even such a popular and listened-to show . . . could sometimes seriously overstep the mark. It would happen that its authors, in the holy fervor of communicating the most possible in order to gratify listeners, would call people at an importunate time and, wholly unprepared, would force them to express their opinions immediately and live on some burning or serious issue. I didn't consider this to be correct."[73] For Lánský, there was a tyranny to listeners' imagined need for information at any cost during these months and journalists pandered to it unprofessionally. *Songs with a Telephone*'s presenters were zealots in their belief in the Prague Spring's professional reforms, and their work bore traces of their "holy fervor." As Lánský's complaint makes clear, within Czechoslovak Radio, and even among reformist journalists, disagreement existed about what constituted good journalism during the Prague Spring.

Did journalists succeed in soliciting new forms of speech from politicians or, on the contrary, in shows like *Songs with a Telephone*, did they end up doing reform politicians' bidding? Scholars have suggested that reformist politicians around Dubček sought to curry favor with journalists in 1968 so as to ensure their unfettered access to media.[74] On the other hand, Petr Andreas has suggested that, when censorship was reintroduced during the normalization period, those working as censors were envisaged at least in part as "bouncers" to protect politicians from journalists.[75] Whether politicians ceded increasingly to the will of journalists or vice versa, beyond debate is the "growing unity" between "governing structures," on the one hand, and Czechoslovak Radio's foreign journalists, on the other, that one of their number, Jiří Dienstbier, described.[76] Indeed, some—most notably the travel writer and erstwhile radio reporter Jiří Hanzelka (profiled in chapter 3)—crossed over at this moment from the world of journalism into that of politics.

*Songs with a Telephone* came to test its presenters' understandings of the limits to press freedom. On August 1, 1968, the exasperated Soviet leader Leonid Brezhnev issued Alexander Dubček's administration with a number of ultimatums—including the reestablishment of censorship—in the Slovak town of Čierna nad Tisou. No audio of the broadcast remains, but a script shows how the program's presenters, Věra Šťovíčková and Jiří Dienstbier, reported on the event.

A single page of scribbled notes reveals how confident the presenters felt by August 1968 about their abilities to improvise live without a written safety net. It points, too, to the sheer amount of negotiation still to be done with Czechoslovak authorities as the program went to air. Dienstbier called this Čierna reporting the high point of his radio career. He recalled consulting as many officials as possible before broadcasting details of the talks, as "we needed to find the exact boundary between the desire to inform fully and the necessity for secrecy, so that Brezhnev could not use against Dubček

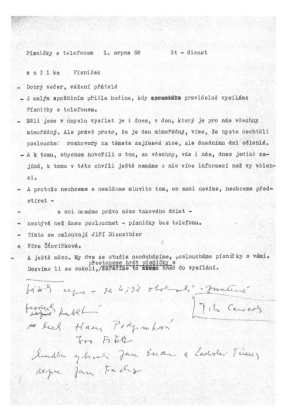

**FIGURE 21.** Script from *Songs with a Telephone*, August 1, 1968. Source: Czech Radio. Reprinted with permission.

218　Chapter 7

the fact that the Czechoslovak administration reveals details that the Soviets insist are secret."[77]

In Dienstbier's recollections, journalists continued earlier practices (outlined in the last chapter) of consulting with political functionaries before making sensitive stories public. Life after censorship was not then, as Lánský may have feared, an information free-for-all in which journalists understood their role to consist primarily of divulging news to the listener. National loyalty and support for the ultimate aims of Alexander Dubček's reform government trumped freedom of information for Dienstbier, leading him and copresenter Šťovíčková to use their discretion.

### Dealing with Censorship's Disappearance

The account that Dienstbier gave of his actions here shows that the effects of censorship's abolition were, in fact, only ever partial. But this then raises the question of why reporters like him were so cautious with their newfound freedoms.

Censorship had affected different Czechoslovak Radio departments—indeed different reporters—differently, as German-language Radio Prague broadcaster František Černý recalls. The Main Press Observation Office (HSTD) had consisted of:

> Two drunks [who] sat in the room they were allocated and [to whom] all programs had to be handed in writing prior to broadcast. Having clarified that nothing in the text was objectionable, they put a stamp underneath it, with which they approved the program . . . Every time I went to these two comrades with a text, an awesome, exhausting dialogue occurred . . . What I had brought them? "It's in German," I'd answer. "What's in it?" they inquired. "Talk of love, life, and so on," I assured them . . . After these words, and without them reading a sentence, they gave me the stamp and the program went to broadcast. They weren't too good at German, and instead of asking for a translation, they preferred to let the text go through . . . They were not so interested in foreign broadcasting. They monitored domestic news reporting like hawks—for example, the texts of Ludvík Vaculík.[78]

Černý's account discredits the censors through humor and exaggeration, bearing traces of the anti-Communism prevalent in the 2010s when it was recorded. But his central insight is important: to press regulators in the 1960s, some reporters were more equal than others. Censors and journalists alike brought to their job assumptions about the significance of different program genres and audiences, and a hierarchy of reporters based on past output and on notions of their influence upon the listener.

The revocation of censorship should have, by this logic, affected certain departments above all. But Černý suggests that radio staff's response to its rollback was collective: "even when censorship was lifted, auto-censorship existed," he recalls, explaining "I sought the advice of my colleagues and comrades . . . whether such and such can go into a broadcast or not. Quite simply we watched ourselves so as to avoid any big trouble."[79] Luboš Dobrovský concurs, practically boasting that "in the team that Milan Weiner led, we were all sufficiently responsible to know, without being warned, how far we could go."[80] Dobrovský voices pride that he and colleagues exercised auto-censorship without needing to be "warned." He terms this self-restraint "responsibility"—but to what or to whom?

The answer is threefold: journalists felt "responsibility" to each other, to professional standards that they themselves had created and codified over the past two decades, and lastly to the ideals of the Prague Spring. Peer pressure exercised a form of social control. Radio reporters wrote with one eye on their colleagues—seeking their advice, in Černý's telling, and judging their team's output accordingly, according to Dobrovský. Habit provided a second reason for their caution. Those in the radio affected by the Prague Spring were often long-term employees who had already established their own sense of journalistic professionalism by 1968. If you had spent the past twenty years performing, and perfecting, certain practices and were then told they no longer applied, it is not clear that you would transform your behavior or your approach to your job overnight either. Finally, belief in the aims of the Prague Spring served to temper reporters' output. While the aims of the Prague Spring were diverse, Pavel Kohout captures its political objectives pithily as "federalization, rehabilitation, democratization and a new economic model."[81] In the focal point of this chapter, Milan Weiner's newsroom, meanwhile, the agenda additionally included advocating for the end of censorship, the upholding of Czech and Slovak workers' rights, the rejection of violence as a state-building technique, and a vocal condemnation of anti-Semitism.

Discussions of press freedom spread beyond the corridors of Czechoslovak Radio in 1968 and were not entirely shaped by journalists. A worker's committee was set up in defense of freedom of speech in April of that year. Press freedom debates, moreover, inflected the "invitation to invade," authored by some high-ranking Politburo members for Soviet leader Leonid Brezhnev's attention. This document drew different conclusions from developments in the Czechoslovak press. Its signatories judged that "the press, radio, and television—which are effectively in the hands of right-wing forces—have influenced popular opinion to such an extent that elements hostile to the Party have begun to take part in the political life of our country, without any opposition from the public."[82] For its signatories, the uncensored press was not "free." Instead, it had been taken over by a rival political faction and was being used to promote their propaganda, excluding those with different views. Those in charge of the country's media fomented "counterrevolution" through neglecting Czechoslovakia's allies and isolating Czechs and Slovaks with endless stories fostering both "nationalist" and "chauvinist" sentiments.[83] Journalists had abandoned their duty to foster overseas solidarity with brotherly states in the current wave of introspection.

It was changes in press legislation in Czechoslovakia in 1968 that led members of the Moscow Politburo to wring their hands and, on the other side of the Iron Curtain, Western media analysts to rub theirs. But journalistic practice did not change in lockstep with press laws in 1968. Just because information was "free" did not mean, in the views of Czechoslovak Radio's journalists, that its dissemination was desirable, nor even that its broadcast formed the ultimate duty of their profession. These reporters were acutely aware of their position as mediators between authorities and audiences. Their concerns were arguably akin to those of their Western peers at public broadcasters, aware of but loathe to report upon, say, the substance abuse problems or marital indiscretions of prominent politicians.

Such a comparison between Czech and Slovak journalists and their peers in the West only works, however, to an extent. As professed "communist journalists," Weiner and his team suggested throughout 1968 that they had responsibilities to minimize inequality and to perfect the running of a communist state that their Western counterparts did not.[84] The lifting of censorship clearly proved a massive, international bone of contention for Czechoslovakia within the Eastern Bloc. It certainly also presented individual Czech and Slovak journalists with new leveraging power. But historical analysis benefits from understanding freedom of the press in Czechoslovakia as a society-specific discursive project, which did not necessarily indicate Czechoslovakia's shifting allegiance from one Cold War ideological bloc to another; nor did it—with its calls, for example, to establish a bureaucracy to defend free speech—necessarily resonate with or preempt preoccupations regarding this topic today.[85]

By exercising caution in what they wrote during the Prague Spring, the reporters profiled here were not hedging their bets. This is demonstrated by the massive ramifications for these journalists' careers following the Soviet-led invasion (when practically all failed to disavow their "responsible" conduct during the Prague Spring). Reporters' timidity can be better explained by their judgment that reforms underway in Czechoslovakia were still at risk and by their conviction that they held the power to derail such reforms. The summer of 1968 was "a moment of hope, albeit hope still threatened," claimed "The Two Thousand Words": underneath the oft-cited sense of hope, then, there remained on the part of some cultural elites a less frequently articulated sense of fear.[86]

These correspondents were not inured to the poor international reception of the Prague Spring on which they reported. The foreign news that they *did* relay, examined here, consisted of East German criticism of Czechoslovakia, emergency talks with the Soviet Union in Čierna nad Tisou, and reflections on the usefulness of the Sino-Soviet split as a model for understanding Prague's current Moscow policy. None of these paints a rosy picture of the state's foreign relations in 1968. Moreover, the lifting of censorship did not just pit Czechs and Slovaks against hostile foreigners: there were vocal constituencies within Czechoslovakia too who challenged the move—and the changes to Czechoslovak Radio's output that it helped inaugurate. Many of these opponents (for example Indra and Biľak) occupied real positions of power and made no secret of their hopes to rein in changes to the media taking place in 1968.

### Radio during and after the Invasion

No matter how cautious they were, journalists' efforts at discretion were not enough to stop Warsaw Pact tanks invading Czechoslovakia on the night of August 20, 1968. First seizing Prague's Ruzyně airport, invading forces from each of the Warsaw Pact countries except Romania then set out to occupy a number of strategic points around the Czechoslovak capital, chief among them Czechoslovak Radio's headquarters on Vinohradská Avenue.

Their attempts to do so gave rise to some of the only fighting that took place during the Soviet-led invasion. Invading troops' efforts to storm the building became audible in real time, alongside reporters' attempts, for as long as possible, to withstand them.

A letter from listener Josef Jarolím stressed how dramatic the resultant programming sounded to audiences. He wrote to Věra Šťovíčková that "I rec-

**FIGURE 22.** Two flag-wielding Czechoslovak citizens outside the Czechoslovak Radio headquarters in Prague, photo by Josef Koudelka, August 1968. Reprinted with permission.

ognized your pleasant voice on the fateful morning [of August 21]," recalling that "you announced to the whole nation that foreign armies had crossed the border into our republic and you asked the whole nation for calm and balance."[87] Almost four months after it had happened, Jarolím used highly emotive language to stress the effect that the broadcasts had left upon him:

> What happened next I can say ranks among the most dreadful moments of my 22 years of life. The sound of shots being fired became more and more audible in the reports being broadcast on the radio and that was perhaps the cruelest thing for everyone gathered around the radio receiver. Everyone asked themselves: is this possible? They soon received the evident answer that it was. And then came the moment that I might never forget to the end of my life: you announced that the occupiers had broken into the radio building and shouted into the microphone "Long Live the Czechoslovak Socialist Republic!" and then our national anthem played. A watery film covered every eye at that moment and no one was ashamed of the tears.[88]

From dread to disbelief to tearfulness, Jarolím described a quick succession of moods. He aimed to convey the clarity of his memories by temporal specificity and recourse to detail—in particular of what he had heard (Šťovíčková's "pleasant voice," ever more audible gunfire, shouting, the national anthem).

Over the days that followed, radio reporters broadcast clandestinely from a range of makeshift studios in the Prague districts of Žižkov, Nusle, and the New Town. The reporters promoted passive resistance to the invasion, encouraging citizens to remove street signs to disorientate invading troops. Radio again assumed an important role connecting Czechs and Slovaks as trains ceased to run and as those who had been away from home found themselves stranded. Reporters also beseeched listeners not to believe what they heard on Radio Vltava, a station urging listeners to accept the invasion, which broadcast in Czech from East Germany (a fact it failed to disclose). According to Paulina Bren, these broadcasters additionally "listed areas with heavy shooting to be avoided, and offered a reassuring presence, particularly through their oft-repeated mantra and station identification: 'Be with us, we are with you!' "[89] Listening to Czechoslovak Radio's reporting from Italy, where he had been on holiday, Pavel Kohout suggested that its output stirred his patriotism to new heights—he dubbed the institution a "national treasure" on account of its broadcasts.[90]

224　Chapter 7

When Dubček and other members of the Politburo flew back from Moscow on August 27, this marked "the end of the dramatic events that had begun [at the institution] on the night of August 20," judge radio historians Zdeněk Bouček and Jiří Hubička.[91] President Ludvík Svoboda gave a speech, the tone of which allegedly dismayed listeners to the extent that an emergency round table with the radio reporters who had come to vocalize the Prague Spring, Jiří Dienstbier, Karel Jezdinský, and Ondřej Neff, was held to counteract it. At 5:30 that afternoon, First Secretary of the Communist Party Alexander Dubček broadcast a radio address calling for citizens to "normalize" the situation in Czechoslovakia. Reporters then seemingly returned to business as usual within the broadcaster's headquarters on Vinohradská Avenue. Censorship returned, but was initially allocated to "popular" members of each news desk who would not slow down the transmission of the news.[92] This system of in-house control provided reform politicians with a fudge, allowing for the simultaneous existence and nonexistence of censorship—in the earlier, Novotný-era, HSTD sense of the word. External censors were reintroduced to Czechoslovak Radio in spring 1969.[93]

More effective when it came to overhauling radio content were changes to staffing.[94] Jiří Dienstbier became, as planned, Czechoslovak Radio's US correspondent in autumn 1968. But the reports he filed soon came to be voiced by somebody else. As admiring listener and subsequent fellow dissident Petr Pithart recalls, "some other speaker was preferred to read his testimony from the launch of Apollo 11 in July 1969. By that time Dienstbier was supposed to disappear from the world for good."[95] The removal from the microphone of Dienstbier and others, such as Věra Šťovíčková, served as a prelude to their quiet removal from the radio altogether over the next year and a half.

Foreign correspondents Sláva Volný, Karel Jezdinský, and Karel Kyncl emigrated, with the first pair coming to rank among the most popular voices on RFE and Kyncl appearing on the BBC, as well as establishing the samizdat video news service *Videožurnal* from London by the 1980s.[96] Milan Weiner was hospitalized with cancer in 1968 and died of the illness in February 1969. As they disappeared from the radio, these foreign correspondents simultaneously destroyed many tapes of themselves, which they deemed to be potentially incriminating if they fell into the wrong hands.[97]

Czechoslovak Radio under its new manager, Karel Hrabal, worked to make these reporters more inaudible still. In a small number of instances archivists rescued tapes of these personalities when they removed the speaker's name from the labeling.[98] In a few cases, the sound archive has been enriched by reporters' donations from their personal collections following the Velvet Revolution in 1989.[99] But if this chapter has drawn largely from written documents to discuss the sound of Czechoslovak Radio in 1968, then this is due to multiple subsequent efforts to make a sonic reconstruction of radio during the Prague Spring and Warsaw Pact invasion as difficult as possible.

"For many, perhaps most Czechs and Slovaks," Jonathan Bolton argues, "the week of the invasion was tragic, but also more exciting, meaningful and memorable than the Prague Spring itself."[100] This week came to be indelibly linked to the voices of a cohort of reporters largely based around Milan Weiner's foreign news desk. Forty-five years later, how Jiří Dienstbier sounded at the time was still recalled by Petr Pithart.[101] Others still remembered how audibly "upset" Alexander Dubček had sounded when he had spoken upon his return from Moscow on August 27, signaling that the tone of his voice had communicated to them then that "the game was up."[102] Closer to the time, workers at the Cultural House in Prostějov sent a Christmas card to Šťovíčková wishing her a future in which "she would never again have to speak about Czechoslovakia with tears in her voice."[103] Reflecting on the sadness she detected in Šťovíčková's voice during one of her final radio appearances in October 1968, Marta Bednaříková wrote that it "reminded me again of August 21."[104] There was a particular tone of Šťovíčková's that served as an aural trigger for Bednaříková, one now permanently linked to the invasion. When Bednaříková heard it, she was taken back to her experiences of August radio listening all over again.

Rather than their names announced at the beginning and end of reports, these reporters' radio signatures were their voices. Fan mail suggests that Šťovíčková and Dienstbier's voices came to evoke more than an image of the speaker; they contained particular timbres that referred listeners back to invasion events. These speakers had already enjoyed trust at the time of the invasion (their voices were "recognizable" and "pleasant," as Jarolím had it, when they resounded from radio receivers on August 21). They had built this level of recognition, in some cases, through a presence on Czechoslovak Radio spanning more than twenty years.

226  Chapter 7

Trust in those voices presumably only grew in the week following the invasion when various new radio stations popped up claiming to represent the stance of the Dubček government saying wildly different things. In an ether full of forgeries, Šťovíčková, Dienstbier, and other foreign correspondents' voices-as-signatures distinguished them and the information they conveyed from pale imitations. Containing within themselves audible reminders of the invasion and its aftermath, such reporters' voices had to vanish in an ensuing political culture characterized, for Milan Kundera, by state-sponsored "forgetting."[105] Written scripts could, however, remain—as they retained little or none of the associative power of their tapes.

### Conclusion

These reporters' "vocal signatures" were not established in 1968 alone. Most of the reporters profiled in this chapter had, in fact, begun their work at the radio in the immediate postwar years and by this moment now more or less constituted the establishment—which they sought to refine and improve, rather than tear down, through their involvement in the Prague Spring that year.[106]

The Prague Spring was, as many contemporaries noted, a time when seemingly everything was up for discussion and there were no more taboos. Certainly, programming such as *Songs with a Telephone* suggests that topics could shift from foreign news to what was on in Prague's theaters to new music reviews to economic reform. But for all of the discussion among those who brought the Prague Spring most forcefully to Czechoslovak Radio's frequencies in 1968, there seems to have been remarkable consensus about what was desirable and how the radio might contribute to that. Indeed, the memoirs of journalists and reformist politicians suggest that the consensus spanned the reformist wing of the Czechoslovak Communist Party.[107] As legislation removed politicians further from the Czechoslovak newsroom, journalists and reformist politicians appeared to enjoy an ever-closer relationship.

If the Prague Spring brought many topics that had been discussed in private to the airwaves for the first time, then Weiner and his news team suggested that it was at the impetus of listeners that they initiated such on-air conversations. Listener letters were routinely styled as the catalyst for reporters' journalistic remit and approach. The inclusion of an ever-wider variety of listeners' voices seemingly "directly" via the telephone also lent radio programming in 1968 an air of being highly responsive to the people. This reflected a change in journalists' understandings of themselves as representing the people in negotiations with authorities.

As Milan Weiner explained, the suggestion of a diversity of opinions was not enough for the engaged socialist journalist to present to listeners. Instead, the reporter should push for particular ideals, such as the eradication of corruption, the upholding of workers' rights, the condemnation of anti-Semitism, and freedom of expression. In order to push for such tenets, however, journalists gatekept and edited the feedback they received from listeners, granting particular opinions more credence than others. The end result was highly exciting journalism, to be sure, but, in its insistence upon inclusivity while in fact prioritizing certain opinions over others, it perhaps alienated some of the constituencies marginalized on account of their "non-reformist" views. It perhaps also created fertile ground for an anti-elitist, anti-expert backlash over the years to come.

1968 ended badly for each and every one of the correspondents discussed in this chapter. But while they were excluded from the radio, the Communist Party and public life, the ways in which they had fused politics and entertainment in 1968 were noted by cultural officials in the nascent political regime following the invasion (which came to be called the "normalization" regime). The particular form of showbiz politics, socialist style, that some of journalists profiled here had pioneered over the course of the 1960s underlay the biggest political spectacles of the television age (such as the Anti-Charter in 1977), outlined by Paulina Bren in *The Greengrocer and His TV*.[108] Bereft of their "vocal signatures," meanwhile, Czechoslovak Radio lost elements of the relationships it had cultivated with listeners over the past two decades, as well as shedding embarrassing or inconvenient reminders of its conduct during recent months. With the silencing of these reporters, radio's second "golden age" was over.

# Conclusion
# From Socialist Media to Social Media

**STUDYING RADIO UNDER SOCIALISM** has shown how socialism was partially created, articulated, and consolidated by those outside of the formal governing structures of the Czechoslovak Communist Party. Reporters were so much more than stooges, and their listeners were so much more than dupes. It was through the work they did beyond merely following orders that the skeleton of socialist lawmaking took on flesh and blood. By understanding how both reporters and listeners became actively, if unevenly, involved in the project of creating media that roused, affected, and entertained, we see how these two constituencies became invested in the project of setting socialism's very terms—terms that came to be used by those in government too. The input of all of the above could sometimes be offered begrudgingly, and if socialist radio could bring its listeners pleasure, then it did not do so unfailingly. The politicians cited here were often berating an aspect of the media, reporters enjoyed their work writing particular genres or in particular postings over others, and listeners suggested that specific broadcasts captivated their imaginations, while others alienated them. Their nuance suggests both the discernment of media actors and audiences in highly restricted media environments, and how the creation and perpetuation of an authoritarian society can be contributed to by those with thoughtful and articulate reservations about certain elements of that society.

As I finish writing this book in Berlin, a trip to the now derelict Cold War radio listening station at Teufelsberg makes clear how much the media landscape has altered since that time. There are, nonetheless, ways in which this study of Cold War radio can help us better understand aspects of today's media environment. The trust and affection audiences can feel for news which flouts liberal journalistic norms can be explained, I have argued, by the personal relationship those audience members have with the person delivering the news.[1] This was the case with censored and propaganda-tinged radio reports from the 1940s to 1960s, penned and read by reporters understood, in turn, by listeners as experts and "friends," and it is the case with social media today—in an albeit reconfigured way.[2]

This argument provides an alternative, and less dismissive, explanation of the current allure of "fake news" which does not reduce its consumers to buffoons, nor cast them pityingly as captive victims of special interests. The observation that media consumption is a fundamentally social activity and builds upon, enhances, and reworks existing social connections holds true and matters, moreover, irrespective of where one sits on the political spectrum.

In the case of Czechoslovak radio during socialism, listeners came to develop relationships with reporters whom they understood as the authors of news articles (irrespective of whether some of those journalists, like Vladimír Kučera, used pseudonyms). Despite the active presence of censors in Czechoslovak Radio over the majority of the years analyzed here, which was publicly understood if never officially trumpeted, the censor never achieved co-authorial status in what was resolutely an auteurist society. These audience-reporter relationships often turned on reporters' voices as a "vocal signatures," vouchsafing the content that they presented, although never completely: this relationship could hinge instead on the familiarity of a reporter's name being repeatedly invoked and credited with authorship in a familiar context—for example, in the nightly *Radio Newsreel*.

In thousands of pieces of fan mail, a small percentage of the medium's listeners sought to establish something approaching mutuality in the relationship between the reporter and themselves, divulging details of their own lives or their opinions on current affairs in response to reporters' views. The letters that reporters received were, of course, far from unanimously rosy: threats, complaints, anti-Semitic diatribes, and other forms of personal abuse are also archived in the collections examined here. Irrespective of content, however, embarking upon writing a letter to the reporters in question marked an investment of time in them and served to intensify the far from negligible listener-reporter relationship.

For all of the thousands of listeners who wrote to radio personalities during these decades, millions did not. That many of these individuals cultivated some form of relationship with the institution of state radio by way of its reporters is evidenced by the complaints or praise they jotted down in their diaries or other writings, the nostalgic or ironic mention they made of aspects of the broadcaster's output in interviews with pollsters or later oral histories, the recordings these individuals made of reporters' work which they then painstakingly preserved, or listeners' behavior towards some of the radio's leading lights encountered on the street—which spanned from heckling to hugging. That the radio's social capital derived, above all, from the people who staffed the medium was suggested by former employee Jana Peterková, whose account of the impostor syndrome she experienced upon her first day at work there in the 1960s opened this book.[3] From that moment until this very page, *Red Tape* has argued that the social significance of a medium can be effectively recovered by examining the interpersonal relationships that this medium fostered, negated, and reworked.

Today on social media, it is not primarily a relationship of friendship between the reporter and the consumer which fosters acceptance of news, liberal or illiberal. Instead, it is the individual recommending the content— whose relationship to the end consumer is also often styled as one of distant affinity or "friendship"—who vouches for that content. Indeed, authorship of a sizeable chunk of news flagged as "fake" remains opaque.[4] While the social profile of the author is not completely irrelevant (to which the prominence of high-profile individuals on both liberal and illiberal news channels attests), it is certainly only one of the relationships, and perhaps not the most important one, fostering acceptance of news—particularly on social media. Authorial intent never translated neatly into what past radio listeners derived from the news, to which this book is testament. It is pushed further down the list of reader's considerations, though, through the process of relaying news via social contacts, which adds layers of agenda each time the story is shared. But original authorial intention should not be relegated entirely to the background; awareness of this remains one of the best tools we have to understand what media actors are setting out to achieve.

Czechoslovak citizens in the 1940s through the 1960s reappropriated mass culture to fit their own ends; they employed Austrian and German radio as study aids, for example, or participated in communities of sound fostered around brass music or Mozart appreciation rather than around Communism/anti-Communism. Similarly today, audiences use news and mass media to pursue their own agendas. People share news stories on social media to show themselves to be erudite, to praise or criticize stories' content and thus to let off steam, and to foster connections with sympathetic fellow readers.

But media platforms now profit from audiences' reappropriation of news. Behind a language of user empowerment, the parasitic business model of social media is fundamentally obscured. As *Red Tape* has shown, news consumers have always used news and do not need a gaggle of tech firms to allow them to do this. Part of news' social value has always resided in the way it was reworked in the retelling or sharing. This value, and the imaginative work producing this value, has been monetized to profit tech entrepreneurs and advertisers.

Does this current media landscape, then, alter the qualitative experience of consuming the news? I have avoided using the term "consumer" to describe the socialist-era radio listeners described here, but have used the term to describe today's audiences. This avoidance reflects a distaste for the connotation of passivity often attached to the term and which overlooks, both historically and currently, the dynamic and idiosyncratic ways in which people employ mass media. But above all, the term "consumer" suggests that, at root, the relationship between media and audience members is an economic one, whereas I have argued that the nature of the socialist era radio-listener relationship in Czechoslovakia, while extremely varied, came to be built upon a notional premise of "friendly exchange" with the reporter as a basis for ideological discussion and, ultimately, listener persuasion. Of course this was disingenuous: while technological changes in some ways facilitated the inclusion of radio listeners into broadcasts, to call what ultimately happened an "exchange" between reporters and listeners (even at a moment when such "exchanges" were prioritized, peaking with the Weiner/Záruba debate) is a stretch. Today, on the other hand, the disingenuousness resides less in the "exchange" and more in the "friendly" part of this equation. It is not false consciousness on the part of those sharing or reading the news on social media to feel that they are involved in an act of friendship or reading among friends. It is disingenuous of platforms fostering such exchanges to trumpet the friendship- rather than income-generating aspects of their work.

Tuning into Czechoslovak Radio overseas in the wake of the Soviet-led invasion, Pavel Kohout caught the familiar voice of a friend on the air. While it is a cliché to characterize radio waves as difficult to pin down, Kohout likened them much less conventionally here to a rope. The reporter was the climber, "hindered by a mist," while the listener helped—or spurred—the speaker to higher heights, rendering him "secure" through the power of concentrated listening.[5] Far from directionless and ethereal, radio was a tie that bound, along which a tension ran. The tension was created by the conjoined but divergent positions of reporter and listener. Reporters could only scale such dizzying heights on account of the help they received from listeners serving as their balance—or perhaps listeners handed reporters the rope with which to hang themselves. In August 1968, these were, after all, far from friendly skies. But, by the end of radio's second and final "golden age" they were filled with, and perhaps navigable on account of, an intricate web of connections between those broadcasting on the radio and their audiences. Socialism's red stars did not twinkle airily in the ether. Millions of threads of reinforcement connected them directly to their listeners.

# Notes

## Introduction

1. Jana Peterková, interview with Rosamund Johnston, October 26, 2016.

2. Muriel Blaive, "The Reform Communist Interpretation of the Stalinist Period in Czechoslovak Historiography and its Legacy," in *East European Politics and Societies* (November 2021): 7.

3. Bradley Abrams, *The Struggle for the Soul of the Nation: Czech Culture and the Rise of Communism* (Lanham, Boulder, New York, Toronto and Oxford: Rowman and Littlefield, 2004), 12

4. Gordon Allport and Hadley Cantril, *The Psychology of Radio* (New York and London: Harper and Brothers, 1935), 22

5. See Andrei Zhdanov "New Aspects of World Conflict: The International Situation," September 22, 1947. https://soviethistory.msu.edu/1947-2/cold-war/cold-war-texts/zhdanov-on-the-international-situation/. Last modified April 29, 2022; and for Dwight D. Eisenhower and John Foster Dulles's reflections upon Eastern Europeans' isolation and "captivity," see Susan Carruthers, *Cold War Captives: Imprisonment, Escape and Brainwashing* (Berkeley, CA: University of California Press, 2009). For literature on socialist internationalism see, for example, James Mark, Paul Betts, Alena Alamgir, Péter Apor, Eric Burton, Bogdan Iacob, Steffi Marung, and Radina Vučetić, *Socialism Goes Global: The Soviet Union and Eastern Europe in the Age of Decolonization* (Oxford: Oxford University Press, 2022); James Mark, Artemy Kalinovsky, and Steffi Marung (eds.), *Alternative Globalizations: Eastern Europe and the Postcolonial World* (Bloomington: Indiana, 2020), and Patryk Babiracki and Austin Jersild (eds.),

234 Notes to the Introduction

*Socialist Internationalism in the Cold War: Exploring the Second World* (London: Palgrave, 2016).

6. See analysis from the period, for example, Curt Beck, "Czechoslovakia's Penetration of Africa, 1955–1962," *World Politics* 15, no. 3 (1963): 403–416. doi:10.2307/2009470.

7. See, for example, Tony Prince and Jan Šesták, *The Royal Ruler and the Radio DJ* (Slough: DMC Publishing, 2017) and "23.10.2019—30.8.2020—Technika v diktaturách," last modified June 12, 2020, http://www.ntm.cz/Technika_v_dik taturach.

8. For sources from the period, see Miloslav Disman, *Československý rozhlas v boji* (Prague: Orbis, 1946); Miloslav Disman, *Hovoří Praha* (Prague: Svoboda, 1975), and E. F. Burian, *Voláno rozhlasem I* (Prague: Svoboda, 1945). For more recent examples, see Eva Ješutová (ed.), *Od mikrofonu k posluchačům. Z osmi desetiletí českého rozhlasu* (Prague: Radioservis, 2003).

9. Mary Heimann, *Czechoslovakia: The State That Failed* (New Haven, CT: Yale University Press, 2011).

10. This term, originally penned by John Ledyard, is revived and explained by Larry Wolff in *Inventing Eastern Europe: The Map of Civilization on the Mind of the Enlightenment* (Stanford, CA: Stanford University Press, 1994), 6.

11. The Archive of the Southeast Moravian Museum (AMJM), box sign. 4031-1 Texty pro Cs. Rozhlas. "Zprávy Československého rozlasu v neděli, 28. listopadu."

12. Jacques Ellul, *Propaganda: The Formation of Men's Attitudes* (New York: Random House, 1973).

13. See Pavlína Kourová, "Kampaň proti 'Americkému brouku' a její politické souvislosti," https://www.moderni-dejiny.cz/clanek/kampan-proti-americke mu-brouku-a-jeji-politicke-souvislosti/. November 19, 2009, *Moderní Dějiny*. Accessed April 28, 2022.

14. Věra Šťovíčková-Heroldová, *Po světě s mikrofonem* (Prague: Radioservis, 2009), 20–21.

15. Natalia Roudakova, *Losing Pravda: Ethics and the Press in Post-Truth Russia* (Cambridge: Cambridge University Press, 2017), 56.

16. AMJM, box 960. Letter from K. Převrátil to Hanzelka and Zikmund (no. 111) in "Korespondence Čs. rozhlasu: dopisy posluchačů (1947–1949)," 16.

17. See Fred Siebert, Theodore Peterson, and Wilbur Schramm. *Four Theories of the Press: The Authoritarian, Libertarian, Social Responsibility, and Soviet Communist Concepts of What the Press Should Be and Do* (Champaign: University of Illinois Press, 1963); for more recent versions of this argument, see Anne Applebaum, *Iron Curtain: The Crushing of Eastern Europe, 1944–1956* (New York:

Anchor Books, 2013), 174–191 and what Agata Zysiak has called "neototalitarian" works of scholarship from the region itself, for example Jaroslav Pažout (ed.), *Informační boj o Československu/ v Československu (1945–1989)* (Prague: Ústav pro studium totalitních režimů & Technická univerzita v Liberci, 2014).

18. Roudakova, *Losing Pravda*; Simon Huxtable, "Making News Soviet: Rethinking Journalistic Professionalism after Stalin, 1953–1970," *Contemporary European History* 27, no. 1 (February 2018): 59–84; Dina Fainberg, "Unmasking the Wolf in Sheep's Clothing: Soviet and American Campaigns against the Enemy's Journalists, 1948–1953," *Cold War History* 15, no. 2 (2015); Sune Bechmann Pedersen and Marie Cronqvist "Foreign Correspondents in the Cold War," *Media History* 26, no. 1 (2020): 75–90.

19. National Archives; Prague, Czech Republic (NA CR). ÚV KSČ Antonín Novotný—zahraničí. Box 4—Afrika. 1261/0/44 A "Záznam o průběhu konzultací skupiny MZV . . . na MIDu SSSR k otazkám Afriky ve dnech 21.–25. listopadu 1961."

20. Paulina Bren, *The Greengrocer and His TV: The Culture of Communism after the 1968 Prague Spring* (Ithaca, NY, and London: Cornell University Press, 2010), 20.

21. See, for example, Wilbur Schramm, "The Soviet Communist Theory of the Press" (which discusses the case of the "satellites" too), in Fred Siebert, Theodore Peterson, and Wilbur Schramm, *Four Theories of the Press* (Urbana: University of Illinois Press, 1984), 105–146, and Ellul, *Propaganda,* kindle position 85.

22. Melissa Feinberg, *Curtain of Lies: The Battle over Truth in Stalinist Eastern Europe* (New York: Oxford University Press, 2017); A. Ross Johnson, *Radio Free Europe and Radio Liberty: The CIA Years and Beyond* (Redwood City, CA: Stanford, 2010); A. Ross Johnson and Eugene Parta (eds.), *Cold War Broadcasting* (Budapest: Central European University Press, 2010); Anna Bischof and Zuzana Jirgens (eds.), *Voices of Freedom—Western Interference? 60 Years of Radio Free Europe* (Göttingen: Vandenhoeck and Ruprecht, 2015); Isvtán Rév, "Just Noise? Impact of Radio Free Europe in Hungary" in *Cold War Broadcasting,* ed. A. Ross Johnson and Eugene Parta (Budapest: Central European University Press, 2010); Paweł Machcewicz, *Poland's War on Radio Free Europe* (Redwood City, CA: Stanford University Press, 2015); Filip Pospíšil, "Inspiration, Subversion and Appropriation: The Effects of Radio Free Europe Music Broadcasting," *Journal of Cold War Studies* 21, no. 4 (Fall 2019): 124–149; Prokop Tomek, *Československá redakce Radio Free Europe* (Prague: Academia, 2015).

23. David Edgerton, *The Shock of the Old* (London: Profile, 2019).

24. See, for example, Rebecca P. Scales, *Radio and the Politics of Sound in*

*Interwar France, 1921–1939* (Cambridge: Cambridge University Press, 2016); Suzanne Lommers, *Europe—On Air: Interwar Projects for Radio Broadcasting* (Amsterdam: Amsterdam University Press, 2012); Carolyn Birdsall, *Nazi Soundscapes: Sound, Technology and Urban Space in Germany 1933–1945* (Amsterdam: Amsterdam University Press, 2012); Elena Razlogova, *The Listener's Voice: Early Radio and the American Public* (Philadelphia: University of Pennsylvania Press, 2011); Ekhard Jirgens, *Der Deutsche Rundfunk der 1. Tschechoslowakischen Republik* (Regensburg: Con Brio, 2017); Peter Richard Pinard, *Broadcast Policy in the Protectorate of Bohemia and Moravia* (Frankfurt: Peter Lang, 2015).

25. Bren, *The Greengrocer and His TV*; see also Christine E. Evans, *Between Truth and Time: A History of Soviet Central Television* (New Haven, CT, and London: Yale, 2016), Kristin Roth-Ey, *Moscow Prime Time: How the Soviet Union Built the Media Empire That Lost the Cultural Cold War* (Ithaca, NY and London: Cornell University Press, 2011), and Anikó Imre, *TV Socialism* (Raleigh, NC: Duke University Press, 2016).

26. See David Vaughan, *Battle for the Airwaves: Radio and the 1938 Munich Crisis* (Prague: Radioservis and Cook Communications, 2008), 20; For the techno-optimism of the young Czechoslovakia, see also Felix Jeschke, *Iron Landscapes: National Space and the Railways in Interwar Czechoslovakia* (New York and Oxford: Berghahn, 2021), 137–163.

27. Rosie Johnston, "The Role of Radio in the Modern Age," Radio Prague, June 5, 2008. https://english.radio.cz/role-radio-modern-age-8596411. Accessed April 11, 2022.

28. See Czech Radio archive, Prague (CRA). Box "Pozůstalost František Kožík, 1934–1993," Ladislav Daneš, "František Kožík a Objevení Ameriky."

29. Vaughan, *Battle for the Airwaves*, 22–23.

30. See Heidi Tworek, *News from Germany: The Competition to Control World Communications, 1900–1945* (Cambridge, MA: Harvard University Press, 2019), 5–13

31. Vaughan, *Battle for the Airwaves*, 27–30.

32. Vaughan, *Battle for the Airwaves*, 41.

33. Pinard, *Broadcast Policy*, 70.

34. See, for example, István Deák, *Europe on Trial: The Story of Collaboration, Resistance and Retribution during World War II* (New York: Routledge, 2015), 33–34.

35. For more on how Czechs and Slovaks listened to foreign radio during the war, see Erica Harrison, "Radio and the Performance of Government: Broadcasting by the Czechoslovaks in Exile in London, 1939–1945" (Unpublished dissertation, University of Bristol, 2015).

36. See Benjamin Frommer, *National Cleansing: Retribution against Nazi Collaborators in Postwar Czechoslovakia* (Cambridge and New York: Cambridge University Press, 2005), 223–226.

37. Miroslav Šmoldas, oral history interview with Karel Sieber, conducted November 7, 2002. https://www.praguecoldwar.cz/smoldas.htm. Accessed April 21, 2022.

38. See Disman, *Hovoří Praha*, 61.

39. Abrams, *The Struggle for the Soul of the Nation*, 10.

40. Rosamund Johnston, "*The Peace Train*: Anticosmopolitanism, Internationalism and Jazz on Czechoslovak Radio during Stalinism," in *Remapping Cold War Media: Institutions, Infrastructures, Translations,* ed. Alice Lovejoy and Mari Pajala (Bloomington: Indiana University Press, 2022), 48. On the case of the Czechoslovak secret police, see Molly Pucci, *Security Empire: The Secret Police in Communist Eastern Europe* (New Haven, CT: Yale University Press, 2020), 78.

41. Stephen Lovell, *Russia in the Microphone Age: A History of Soviet Radio, 1919–1970* (New York and Oxford: Oxford University Press, 2015); see also Roudakova, *Losing Pravda,* and Huxtable, "Making News Soviet."

42. See, for example, Pucci, *Security Empire*; Patryk Babiracki, *Soviet Soft Power in Poland: Culture and the Making of Stalin's New Empire, 1943–1957* (Chapel Hill: University of North Carolina Press, 2015); Rachel Applebaum, *Empire of Friends: Soviet Power and Socialist Internationalism in Cold War Czechoslovakia* (Ithaca and London: Cornell University Press, 2019); John Connelly, *Captive University: The Sovietization of East German, Czech and Polish Higher Education, 1945–1956* (Chapel Hill: University of North Carolina Press, 2000), and Alice Lovejoy, *Army Film and the Avant Garde: Cinema and Experiment in the Czechoslovak Military* (Bloomington: Indiana University Press, 2014).

43. For Kotkin's definition, see Stephen Kotkin, *Magnetic Mountain: Stalinism as Civilization* (Berkeley: University of California Press, 1997), 23; for Czechoslovakia's position as a Stalinist stronghold, see Muriel Blaive, *Une déstalnisation manqué: Tchécoslovaquie 1956* (Paris: Éditions Complexe, 2004), and Kevin McDermott, *Communist Czechoslovakia, 1945–1989: A Political and Social History* (London: Palgrave, 2015), 92.

44. Abrams, *The Struggle for the Soul of the Nation,* 37.

45. Pavel Kohout, "25 let v ekonomice: Čtyři proklatě drahé omyly." *Česká pozice*, November 16, 2014. https://ceskapozice.lidovky.cz/tema/25-let -ekonomickych-omylu.A141112_220527_pozice-tema_kasa. Accessed April 28, 2022.

46. See CIA-ER IM 68–118. "Intelligence Memorandum: Broadcasting in the

Czechoslovak Crisis," last modified November 14, 2018, https://www.cia.gov/library/readingroom/document/cia-rdp85t00875r001600010068-6.

47. See Tony Judt, *Postwar* (New York: Penguin, 2005), 438; Bren, *The Greengrocer and His TV*, 21; Marci Shore also examines the social importance of the Writers' Conference in "Engineering in the Age of Innocence: A Genealogy of Discourse inside the Czechoslovak Writers' Union, 1949–67." *East European Politics and Societies* 12, no. 3 (1998): 397–441. doi:10.1177/0888325498012003002.

48. See "Rozhlasový projev Alexandera Dubčeka po návratu z Moskvy." Czech Radio. https://temata.rozhlas.cz/rozhlasovy-projev-alexandera-dubceka-po-navratu-z-moskvy-7965831. Accessed April 28, 2022.

49. Bren, *The Greengrocer and His TV.*

## Chapter 1

1. "Architecture of the Communist Era," last modified March 18, 2019, https://www.czechtourism.com/a/architecture-of-the-communist-era/.

2. Norman Corwin. "One World Flight—Single Episodes: Czechoslovakia," last modified October 4, 2018, https://archive.org/details/OTRR_One_World_Flight_Singles/One_World_Flight_47-02-18_ep06_Czechoslovakia.mp3.

3. František Gel and Rudolf Krešťan, *Budeš v novinách* (Prague: Albatros, 1976), 67.

4. Eva Ješutová (ed.) *Od mikrofonu k posluchačům. Z osmi desetiletí českého rozhlasu* (Prague: Radioservis, 2003), 216.

5. Miloslav Disman, *Hovoří Praha* (Prague: Svoboda, 1975), 61. In this sense, the history of Czechoslovak Radio is unlike that of Czechoslovak film, which was identified as a key industry and nationalized immediately following the Second World War.

6. For a comparison with the film industry in Czechoslovakia, see Alice Lovejoy, *Army Film and the Avant Garde: Cinema and Experiment in the Czechoslovak Military* (Bloomington: Indiana University Press, 2014), 11

7. Melissa Feinberg, *Elusive Equality: Gender, Citizenship and the Limits of Democracy in Czechoslovakia* (Pittsburgh, PA: University of Pittsburgh, 2006), 194.

8. In one instance, a conflict between Ministry of Information and Ministry of Post employees over who should direct the establishment of a United Nations radio office in Czechoslovakia resulted in no regional subsidiary being created at all (perhaps representing a win for the Ministry of Information, which had long voiced reservations about the project). See Czech Foreign Ministry Archive, Prague, Czech Republic (AMZV). Mezinárodní odbor 1945–1955, Box 58, doc. 63.439/47-IV, "Rozhlasová síť OSN," August 26, 1947, p. 2.

9. See Petr Bednařík, Jan Jirák, and Barbora Köpplová, *Dějiny českých médií* (Prague: Grada, 2019), 234.

10. For the contours of these debates, see Bradley Abrams, *The Struggle for the Soul of the Nation: Czech Culture and the Rise of Communism* (Lanham, Boulder, New York, Toronto, and Oxford: Rowman and Littlefield, 2004).

11. Molly Pucci, *Security Empire: The Secret Police in Communist Eastern Europe* (New Haven, CT : Yale University Press, 2020), 88.

12. Anne Applebaum, *Iron Curtain: The Crushing of Eastern Europe, 1944–1956* (New York: Anchor Books, 2013), 203.

13. David Vaughan, *Battle for the Airwaves: Radio and the 1938 Munich Crisis* (Prague: Radioservis and Cook Communications, 2008), 22–23.

14. Bednařík, Jirák, and Köpplová, *Dějiny českých médií*, 227.

15. See Peter Richard Pinard, *Broadcast Policy in the Protectorate of Bohemia and Moravia* (Frankfurt: Peter Lang, 2015). Bednařík, Jirák, and Köpplová suggest that both the press and the radio rested on "shaky foundations" in the first days of the Third Republic on account of their wartime performance, but the pervasive and resonant myth of the "radio revolution" helped boost the radio's credentials. Bednařík, Jirák, and Köpplová, *Dějiny českých médií*, 231.

16. Ješutová, *Od mikrofonu k posluchačům*, 191.

17. Andrea Orzoff, *Battle for the Castle: The Myth of Czechoslovakia in Europe* (Oxford: Oxford University Press, 2009), 82.

18. Ibid., 71.

19. Pinard, *Broadcasting Policy*, 371. For Beneš and allies losing the war of words in the run-up to Munich, see Vaughan, *Battle for the Airwaves*.

20. This is documented in Erica Harrison, "Radio and the Performance of Government: Broadcasting by the Czechoslovaks in Exile in London, 1939–1945" (Unpublished dissertation, University of Bristol, 2015).

21. Harrison, "Radio and the Performance of Government," 63.

22. Ibid.

23. Jaroslav Seifert, "Tím hořkým chlebem dní . . . ," last modified September 9, 2018, https://poezie.wgz.cz/rubriky/poezie/poezie-ruzni-autori/poezie-ruzni -autori.

24. See, for example, CRA. AF00529_2_AF3936—Projev presidenta Dr. E Beneše v Mělníku, October 14, 1945 and CRA. AF00531_6_AF3944—Projev prezidenta Dr. E. Beneše ve Znojmě, June 13, 1947.

25. Corwin, "One World Flight—Single Episodes: Czechoslovakia."

26. NA CR, Ministerstvo Informací, box 27, doc. 60049, "Porada v presidiu ministerstva informací dne 24. května 1945 dopol."

27. Ibid.

28. Vance Kepley, Jr. " 'Cinefication': Soviet Film Exhibition in the 1920s," *Film History* 6, no. 2 (Summer 1994): 262.

240 Notes to Chapter 1

29. See CRA, AF03145_1_AF10698—První celostátní rozhlasová konference, hovoří A. Zápotocký, January 13, 1949.

30. Karel Kaplan, *Československo v letech 1945–1948, 1. Část* (Prague: SPN, 1991), 60–61.

31. Feinberg, *Elusive Equality*, 194.

32. To hear this, visit " 'Prosíme českou policii, voláme české vojsko, voláme všechny Čechy!' znělo před 70 lety z éteru," last modified March 19, 2019, https://www.rozhlas.cz/bitvaorozhlas/pribehyzvysilani/_zprava/prosime-ceskou-policii-volame-ceske-vojsko-volame-vsechny-cechy-znelo-pred-70-lety-z-eteru--1486363.

33. Mančal's call to "all Czechs" was rendered iconic in texts such as Disman's *Československý rozhlas v boji* and through repeated radio broadcast. It was also monumentalized in a plaque outside of the Czechoslovak Radio building, visible on Prague's Vinohradská Street to this day.

34. Corwin, "One World Flight—Single Episodes: Czechoslovakia."

35. Tony Judt, "The Past Is Another Country: Myth and Memory in Postwar Europe," in *The Politics of Retribution in Europe: World War II and its Aftermath*, ed. István Deák, Jan Gross, and Tony Judt (Princeton, NJ: Princeton University Press, 2000), 307.

36. Heidi Tworek, *News from Germany: The Competition to Control World Communications, 1900–1945* (Cambridge, MA: Harvard University Press, 2019), 46.

37. See Joseph Goebbels, "The Radio as the Eighth Great Power," last modified October 17, 2018, http://research.calvin.edu/german-propaganda-archive/goeb56.htm.

38. Pinard, *Broadcasting Policy*, 70

39. Ibid.

40. Jiří Weil, *Life with a Star* (London: Daunt, 2012), 234.

41. CIA-RDP79R01141A001200120002–2: "Post and Telecommunications Services in Czechoslovakia, 1950–1957," last modified March 5, 2019, https://www.cia.gov/library/readingroom/document/cia-rdp79r01141a001200120002-2.

42. See Petr Szczepanik, *Továrna Barrandov: Svět filmařů a politická moc, 1945–1970* (Prague: NFA, 2016); also Ivan Klimeš, "A Dangerous Neighbourhood: German Cinema in the Czechoslovak Region, 1933–1945," in *Cinema and the Swastika: The International Expansion of Third Reich Cinema*, ed. Roel Vande Winkel and David Welch (New York: Palgrave Macmillan, 2007), 112–129.

43. In an oral history, Karel Ruml recalled that German troops placed dynamite under the bridges of Nymburk as they retreated in 1945. http://www.ncsml.org/Oral-History/Cleveland/20101007/63/Ruml-Karel.aspx, last mod-

ified March 5, 2019. Paul Brunovský suggested that two of Piešťany's bridges were "blown out by the Germans." See https://ncsml.omeka.net/items/show/4174, last modified June 11, 2020.

44. Jan Antonín Baťa, *Budujme stát pro 40 000 000 lidí* (Zlín: Tisk Zlín, 1937), 118.

45. Ibid.

46. Baťa, *Budujme stat,* 117.

47. For a breakdown of which industries were nationalized and when in the Third Republic, see Miloslav Bernasek, "Czechoslovak Planning, 1945–1948," *Soviet Studies* 22, no. 1 (July 1970): 97.

48. See NA CR. Ministerstvo Informací, box 50.

49. CRA, AF00184_15, "Prohlášení hlasatelů Československého rozhlasu (květen 1945)," May 31, 1945.

50. Ibid. The announcers referred indirectly here to reporter Alois Kříž and former Minister of Education Emanuel Moravec. For biographies of both men and details of their wartime radio output, see Pinard, *Broadcasting Policy.*

51. CRA, AF00184_15, "Prohlášení hlasatelů Československého rozhlasu (květen 1945)," May 31, 1945.

52. Disman, *Československý rozhlas v boji,* 7.

53. See "5. květen—den Československého rozhlasu," *Náš Rozhlas* 13, no. 19 (May 5, 1946): 6.

54. See Abrams, *The Struggle for the Soul of the Nation,* 139–155.

55. F. K. Zeman, "K 5. květnu," *Náš Rozhlas* 14, no. 20 (May 18, 1947): 2.

56. Ibid.

57. Ibid.

58. Ibid.

59. Frederick Corney, *Telling October: Memory and the Making of the Bolshevik Revolution* (Ithaca, NY: Cornell University Press, 2004), 10.

60. NA CR, Ministerstvo Informací, box 64, doc. 60218, "Karel Joch, Podbaba 6—žádost o odstranění hlasatelů, kteří byli činní za doby nesvobody" letter from Karel Joch to Václav Kopecký, dated July 5, 1945.

61. Ibid.

62. Ibid.

63. Ibid.

64. Ibid.

65. Ibid.

66. Gabo Repoš, "Prvé slobodné rozhlasové slovo na území Československej republiky," *Náš rozhlas* 13, no. 2 (January 6, 1946): 3.

67. Ibid., 1.

242  Notes to Chapter 1

68. Herbert Jarošek, interview with David Vaughan. Paměť národa. "Herbert Jarošek (1925–2016)," last modified September 13, 2018, http://www.pametnaro da.cz/witness/index/id/2070.

69. Ibid.

70. Laštovička remained in this position until 1948, when he was appointed Czechoslovak ambassador to Moscow.

71. Bednařík, Jirák, and Köpplová, *Dějiny českých médií,* 248–249.

72. I alternate between the terms "Czechoslovak Radio" and "Czech radio" because, during the war, radio in the Protectorate had merely sought to cover the Czech lands and had thus been referred to as Czech radio. Afterwards, the broadcaster returned to its earlier configuration of Czechoslovak Radio.

73. Pinard, *Broadcasting Policy,* 92.

74. Harrison, "Radio and the Performance of Government," 118.

75. Charles Heller, oral history with the National Czech and Slovak Museum and Library, last modified September 17, 2018, https://www.ncsml.org/exhibits /charles-heller/.

76. Doug Hill, *Not So Fast: Thinking Twice about Technology* (Athens: University of Georgia Press, 2013), 103–118.

77. Hill, *Not So Fast,* 91. Kirsten Haring, *Ham Radio's Technical Culture* (Cambridge, MA and London: MIT Press, 2007), 8.

78. CRA, AF00184_15, "Prohlášení hlasatelů Československého rozhlasu (květen 1945)," May 31, 1945.

79. NA CR, Ministerstvo Informací, box 50, doc. 64755, "Vyslání reportažního vozu na slavnost KSČ ve Vokovicích," October 7, 1948.

80. Ibid.

81. The Podbaba Communist Party also asked for a radio to furnish the playground. See NA CR, Ministerstvo Informací, box 50, doc. 64755, "Vyslání reportažního vozu na slavnost KSČ ve Vokovicích," October 7, 1948.

82. Angus Calder, *The Myth of the Blitz* (London: Pimlico, 1991), 14.

83. See oral history with Robert Budway, National Czech and Slovak Museum and Library, last modified October 19, 2018, https://www.ncsml.org/exhibits/ robert-budway/.

84. See NA CR, Ministerstvo Informací, box 29, doc. 62489, April 19, 1946.

85. Feinberg, *Elusive Equality,* 196–197.

86. Josef Jedlička, *Midway upon the Journey of Our Life* (Prague: Karolinum, 2016), 87–88.

87. In an oral history, Zdenka Novak recalls this dancing ban. See https:// www.ncsml.org/exhibits/zdenka-novak/, last modified September 11, 2018. For Nazi policy towards jazz during World War II, see Uta Poiger, *Jazz, Rock and*

*Rebels: Cold War Politics and American Culture in a Divided Germany* (Berkeley, Los Angeles, and London: University of California, 2000). For more on the status of jazz in the Protectorate, see Josef Škvorecký, "Red Music," in *The Bass Saxophone* (Hopewell, NJ: The Ecco Press, 1994), 1–29.

88. Weil, *Life with a Star*, 71.

89. See oral histories with Marcella Tornová Švehlík, (recorded with the National Czech and Slovak Museum and Library. July 28, 2011) and Eva Lutovsky, interviewed April 20, 2010. In *Life with a Star*, furthermore, Jiří Weil's heroine, Ruzena, is shot for listening to foreign radio, despite the only characters one meets in the book engaging in this activity being male. See p. 235.

90. Harrison, "Radio and the Performance of Government," 199.

91. Charles Heller, oral history with the National Czech and Slovak Museum and Library, last modified September 17, 2018, https://www.ncsml.org/exhibits/charles-heller/. And Weil, *Life with a Star*, 88.

92. Judt, "The Past Is Another Country," 295.

93. Bednařík, Jirák, and Köpplová, *Dějiny českých médií*, 232.

94. Ješutová, *Od Mikrofonu k posluchačům*, 193.

95. NA CR Ministerstvo Informací box 64, doc. 65291, "Stížnost na pořady rozhlasu," October 31, 1948.

96. Bednařík, Jirák, and Köpplová, *Dějiny českých médií*, 232.

97. Heda Margolius Kovály, *Under a Cruel Star: A Life in Prague, 1941–1968* (London: Granta, 1986), 48.

98. Ibid., 49.

99. Ibid.

100. Kovály, *Under a Cruel Star*, 50.

101. For more on Zeman and his role in the radio, see Ješutová, *Od Mikrofonu k posluchačům*, 210.

102. Burian, *Voláno rozhlasem I*, 11.

103. Ibid., 11–12.

104. Victor Klemperer, *The Diaries of Victor Klemperer 1945–1959: The Lesser Evil* (London: Phoenix, 2003), 33.

105. Ibid., 72.

106. Ibid., 40.

107. Ibid.

108. Neal Ascherson, foreword to Ryszard Kapuścinski, *The Other* (London: Verso, 2006), 6.

109. Vaughan, *Battle for the Airwaves*, 85.

110. Ješutová, *Od mikrofonu k posluchačům*, 216.

111. Gel and Krešťan, *Budeš v novinách*, 5.

244 Notes to Chapters 1 and 2

112. Ibid.

113. Bednařík, Jirák, and Köpplová, *Dějiny českých médií*, 248.

114. Ješutová, *Od mikrofonu k posluchačům*, 215.

115. Klemperer, *Diaries*, 1.

116. Gel and Krešťan, *Budeš v novinách*, 67.

117. Ješutová, *Od mikrofonu k posluchačům*, 215.

118. Gel and Krešťan, *Budeš v novinách*, 67.

119. Ibid., 66–67.

120. To counter the accusatory tone of these trial broadcasts and another favorite contemporary program, *Černá kronika* [*The Black Chronicle*], Gel also broadcast a program titled *Bílá kronika* [*The White Chronicle*]. Unlike *Černá kronika*, which subjected antisocial behavior to public shame, *Bílá kronika* celebrated good deeds. See Bednařík, Jirák, and Köpplová, *Dějiny českých médií*, 249.

121. See Frommer, *National Cleansing*, 2.

122. For depictions of Nazi radio as a depersonalized medium, see Weil, *Life with a Star.*

## Chapter 2

1. For such accounts from the period, see Josef Josten, *Oh, My Country* (London: Latimer House, 1949); for more contemporary versions see, for example, Eva Ješutová (ed.), *Od mikrofonu k posluchačům. Z osmi desetiletí českého rozhlasu* (Prague: Radioservis, 2003), 257.

2. R. Murray Schafer, *The Soundscape: The Tuning of the World* (Rochester: Destiny Books, 1994), 96.

3. Rostislav Běhal claims, for example, that they "crushed overwhelmed listeners" in "Rozhlas po nástupu totality, 1949–1958," in Eva Ješutová (ed.) *Od mikrofonu k posluchačům,*, 257.

4. See Muriel Blaive, "The Reform Communist Interpretation of the Stalinist Period in Czechoslovak Historiography and its Legacy," in *East European Politics and Societies* (November 2021), 8.

5. Ibid., 9.

6. See Molly Pucci's reflections on this in *Security Empire: The Secret Police in Communist Eastern Europe* (New Haven, CT: Yale University Press, 2020), 10.

7. See Rachel Applebaum, *Empire of Friends: Soviet Power and Socialist Internationalism in Cold War Czechoslovakia* (Ithaca, NY: Cornell University Press, 2019), 45.

8. Stephen Kotkin, *Magnetic Mountain: Stalinism as Civilization* (Berkeley: University of California Press, 1997), 23.

9. Pucci, *Security Empire*, 2.

Notes to Chapter 2  245

10. For other instances of this, see Rosamund Johnston, "*The Peace Train:* Anticosmopolitanism, Internationalism and Jazz on Czechoslovak Radio during Stalinism," in *Remapping Cold War Media: Institutions, Infrastructures, Translations,* ed. Alice Lovejoy and Mari Pajala (Bloomington: Indiana University Press, 2022), 43–60.

11. See, for example, Pucci, *Security Empire*; Patryk Babiracki, *Soviet Soft Power in Poland: Culture and the Making of Stalin's New Empire, 1943–1957* (Chapel Hill: University of North Carolina Press, 2015); Applebaum, *Empire of Friends*; John Connelly, *Captive University: The Sovietization of East German, Czech and Polish Higher Education, 1945–1956* (Chapel Hill: University of North Carolina Press, 2000); and Alice Lovejoy, *Army Film and the Avant Garde: Cinema and Experiment in the Czechoslovak Military* (Bloomington: Indiana University Press, 2014).

12. Pucci, *Security Empire,* 78.

13. Zdeňka Kotalová, "Redakce mezinárodního života Československého rozhlasu v rozmezí let 1966–1969," Unpublished diploma thesis, Charles University Faculty of Social Sciences, 2012, p. 10.

14. See Jan Petránek, *Na co jsem si ještě vzpomněl* (Prague: Radioservis, 2014) and Věra Šťovíčková-Heroldová, *Po světě s mikrofonem* (Prague: Radioservis, 2009).

15. Blaive, "The Reform Communist Interpretation," 8.

16. Karel Kaplan and Marek Janáč, "Poslední slovo obžalovaných v procesu s Miladou Horákovou 'a spol.'" *Soudobé dějiny* 13, nos. 1–2 (2006): 206.

17. Eva Ješutová, interview with Rosamund Johnston, November 7, 2019.

18. See Melissa Feinberg, "Fantastic Truths, Compelling Lies: Radio Free Europe and the Response to the Slánský trial in Czechoslovakia," *Contemporary European History* 22, no. 1 (February 2013).

19. See, for example, Běhal, *Od mikrofonu k posluchačům,* and Kaplan and Janáč, "Poslední slovo obžalovaných."

20. Michael Denning, *Noise Uprising: The Audiopolitics of a World Musical Revolution* (London and New York: Verso, 2015), 69.

21. Ibid., 70.

22. Miro Kern, "Proces a poprava spravili z Jozefa Tisa mučeníka, presne tak, ako si popravený želal," April 12, 2017. https://dennikn.sk/733087/proces-a-poprava-spravili-z-jozefa-tisa-mucenika-presne-tak-ako-si-popraveny-zelal/, last modified April 7, 2021.

23. Petr Blažek, "Rekonstrukce: Prameny k procesu s Miladou Horákovou a jejími druhy," *Sborník Archivu ministerstva vnitra* 4 (2006): 201.

24. Ješutová, *Od mikrofonu k posluchačům,* 191.

246  Notes to Chapter 2

25. See "Prehistorie," last modified Accessed March 26, 2019, https://www.ceskatelevize.cz/vse-o-ct/historie/ceskoslovenska-televize/prehistorie/. See also Martin Štoll, *Television and Totalitarianism in Czechoslovakia: From the First Democratic Republic to the Fall of Communism* (Sydney: Bloomsbury, 2018), 151.

26. See, for example, Josef Jedlička, *Midway upon the Journey of Our Life* (Prague: Karolinum, 2016), 154.

27. Ibid., 79.

28. Ibid., 35.

29. Maggie Andrews, *Domesticating the Airwaves: Broadcasting Domesticity and Femininity* (London and New York: Continuum, 2012), 117.

30. CIA-RDP80–00810A006500180003–1 "Czechoslovakia: Reception of and Reaction to Local and Foreign Broadcasts" dated May 18, 1955: 2. https://www.cia.gov/library/readingroom/docs/CIA-RDP80-00810A006500180003-1.pdf, last modified March 25, 2019.

31. CRA, Proces s Rudolfem Slánským a spol. V., last modified April 27, 2021, https://fileshare.croapp.cz/f.php?h=ow_88rr2.

32. Schafer, *The Soundscape*, 92.

33. Ibid., 92–93.

34. Stephen Lovell, *Russia in the Microphone Age: A History of Soviet Radio, 1919–1970* (New York and Oxford: Oxford University Press, 2015), 179.

35. Petr Bednařík, Jan Jirák, and Barbora Köpplová, *Dějiny českých médií* (Prague: Grada, 2019), 280.

36. Jana Švehlová, interview with Katja David Fox for the National Czech and Slovak Museum and Library, December 7, 2010, http://www.ncsml.org/exhibits/jana-svehlova/. Last modified December 1, 2017.

37. Jedlička, *Midway Upon the Journey of Our Life*, 35–37.

38. RTVS Archive, Bratislava (henceforth RTVS) ID0000013293601001, "Spomienky na Klementa Gottwalda," dated April 1, 1953.

39. See CRA, AF00123_11_AF6053, Interview with Klement Gottwald's mother. November 20, 1948.

40. See Melissa Feinberg, *Curtain of Lies: The Battle over Truth in Stalinist Eastern Europe* (New York: Oxford University Press, 2017), 110.

41. 231/1948: Zákon na ochranu lidově demokratické republiky § 3 (Pobuřování proti republice). October 16, 1948.

42. 86/1950: Trestní zákon § 81 (Pobuřování proti republice). July 18, 1950.

43. An RFE researcher's report from 1965 summarizes this point. The analyst stresses that over the communist period in Czechoslovakia to date, indirect means have been found to punish foreign radio listening. In "VOA Listener Sentenced," September 3, 1965. HU-OSA-300-30-13-1-1354/65; Records of Radio

Free Europe/Radio Liberty Research Institute: Czechoslovak Unit: Information Items: Items [anonymized interviews], 1965–1965 to Items [anonymized interviews] 1968–1968.

44. HU OSA 300-1-2-55908; "Listening Habits and Comments on Operation "Veto" of a CSR Agronomist," March 8, 1955. Records of Radio Free Europe/Radio Liberty Research Institute: General Records: Information Items.

45. *Citizen Brych* (*Občan Brych*, Otakar Vávra, 1958). Circa minute 63.

46. Rosamund Johnston, "Secret Agents: Reassessing the Agency of Radio Listeners in Czechoslovakia, 1945–1953," in *Perceptions of Society in Communist Europe: Regime Archives and Public Opinion*, ed. Muriel Blaive, 15–32 (London: Bloomsbury Academic, 2018).

47. CIA-RDP80–00810A006500180003–1 "Czechoslovakia: Reception of and Reaction to Local and Foreign Broadcasts" dated May 18, 1955: 2. https://www .cia.gov/library/readingroom/docs/CIA-RDP80-00810A006500180003-1.pdf. Last modified March 25, 2019.

48. Ibid.

49. Feinberg, "Fantastic Truths, Compelling Lies."

50. See, for example, Blažek, "Rekonstrukce: Prameny k procesu s Miladou Horákovou," 199, and Běhal, *Od mikrofonu k posluchačům*, 259.

51. Czech National Museum. "Labyrint informací a ráj tisku," last modified July 8, 2022, https://www.nm.cz/virtualne-do-muzea/labyrint-informaci-a-raj -tisku.

52. Petr Šamal, "V zájmu pracujícího lidu," in *V obecném zájmu: Cenzura a sociální regulace literatury v moderní České kultuře 1749–2014, Svazek II*, ed. Michael Wögerbauer et al. (Prague: Academia, 2015), 1101.

53. Ibid., 1103.

54. It is worth noting that Gustav Bareš also did not come out of this clash unscathed. He was stripped of all of his political functions in 1952, when those identified as Jewish by authorities were demoted in conjunction with the Slánský trial. See Jiří Knapík, *Kdo spoutal naši kulturu: portrét stalinisty Gustava Bareše* (Prague: Šárka, 2000).

55. Šamal, "V zájmu pracujícího lidu," 1103–1104.

56. Petránek, *Na co jsem si ještě vzpomněl*, 46.

57. Ibid.

58. Ibid.

59. Běhal, *Od mikrofonu k posluchačům*, 240.

60. Dušan Tomášek, *Pozor, Cenzurováno! Aneb ze života soudružky cenzury* (Prague: Ministertvo Vnitra ČR, 1994), 12.

61. Běhal, *Od mikrofonu k posluchačům*, 257.

248 Notes to Chapter 2

62. Pucci, *Security Empire*, 249.

63. Šamal, *V obecném zájmu*, 1106.

64. Tomášek, *Pozor, Cenzurováno!* 82.

65. Tomášek, *Pozor, Cenzurováno!* 64.

66. Ibid.

67. Věra Homolová, interview with Rosamund Johnston, September 27, 2016.

68. Kaplan and Janáč, "Poslední slovo obžalovaných," 208.

69. Blažek, "Rekonstrukce: Prameny k procesu s Miladou Horákovou," 212–213.

70. CRA, Proces s K. H. Frankem I., last modified April 22, 2021, https://fileshare.croapp.cz/f.php?h=0BfUtDly.

71. Ibid.

72. Eva Ješutová, interview with Rosamund Johnston, November 7, 2019.

73. Jana Peterková, interview with Rosamund Johnston, October 26, 2016.

74. Jaroslav Skalický, "Před 70 lety začal soudní proces s K. H. Frankem. Sledoval ho i rozhlas," dated March 22, 2016. https://www.irozhlas.cz/veda-tech nologie_historie/pred-70-lety-zacal-soudni-proces-s-k-h-frankem-sledoval-ho -i-rozhlas_201603220145_akottova. Last modified March 16, 2021.

75. CRA, Proces s K. H. Frankem I., last modified April 22, 2021, https://fileshare.croapp.cz/f.php?h=0BfUtDly.

76. Helena Čechová, "Československý rozhlas a politické procesy—analyza politických procesů v rozhlasovém vysílání v letech 1949–1952" (unpublished diploma thesis, South Bohemian University in České Budějovice, 2012), 55.

77. CRA, Proces s K. H. Frankem I., last modified April 22, 2021, https://file share.croapp.cz/f.php?h=0BfUtDly.

78. František Kožík, *Rozhlasové umění* (Prague: Kompas, 1940).

79. CRA, Proces s K. H. Frankem III., last modified April 22, 2021, https://file share.croapp.cz/f.php?h=2mbkbF7A.

80. CRA, Proces s K. H. Frankem I., last modified April 22, 2021, https://file share.croapp.cz/f.php?h=0BfUtDly.

81. "Zápis o poradě s filmem, tiskem a rozhlasem . . ." cited in Pavlína Formánková and Petr Koura, *Žádáme trest smrti! Propagandistická kampaň provázející process s Miladou Horákovou a spol.* (Prague: ÚSTR, 2008), 213.

82. For more about Horáková's activist past, see Melissa Feinberg, *Elusive Equality: Gender, Citizenship and the Limits of Democracy in Czechoslovakia* (Pittsburgh, PA: University of Pittsburgh, 2006).

83. Čechová, "Československý rozhlas a politické procesy," 55.

84. CRA, Proces s Miladou Horákovou a spol. I., last modified April 22, 2021, https://fileshare.croapp.cz/f.php?h=3e9X36Nz.

Notes to Chapter 2  249

85. CRA, Proces s Miladou Horákovou a spol. V., last modified April 22, 2021, https://fileshare.croapp.cz/f.php?h=1dZZcCFf.

86. See Kaplan and Janáč, "Poslední slovo obžalovaných" and Formánková and Koura, *Žádáme trest smrti!*

87. CRA, Proces s Miladou Horákovou a spol. I., last modified April 22, 2021, https://fileshare.croapp.cz/f.php?h=3e9X36Nz.

88. Alexej Čepička, cited in Pucci, *Security Empire*, 114.

89. Běhal, *Od mikrofonu k posluchačům*, 259.

90. Čechová, "Československý rozhlas a politické procesy," 54.

91. Lovell, *Russia in the Microphone Age*, 165.

92. Ibid., 166, 169.

93. CRA Box 41. Letter from Karel Zavadil to all heads of regional stations, dated March 3, 1954.

94. Lovell, *Russia in the Microphone Age*, 164.

95. HU OSA 300-1-2-9241; "CSR Radio Lacks Technical Equipment," October 19, 1951. Records of Radio Free Europe/Radio Liberty Research Institute: General Records: Information Items; Open Society Archives at Central European University, Budapest.

96. Ibid.

97. CRA Box 41. "Oběžník fonotéky," dated October 16, 1954.

98. CRA Box 41, "Oběžník," dated December 28, 1953.

99. Lovell, *Russia in the Microphone Age*, 177.

100. Kaplan and Janáč, "Poslední slovo obžalovaných," 208.

101. Kaplan and Janáč, "Poslední slovo obžalovaných," 200. For contemporaries referring to the trial as a "theatre," see Kevin McDermott, " 'A Polyphony of Voices?' Czech Popular Opinion and the Slansky Affair," *Slavic Review* 67, no. 4 (Winter 2008), 857.

102. CRA, AF03145 "Antonín Zápotocký hovoří na první celostátní rozhlasové konferenci," January 13, 1949.

103. NA CR, Ministerstvo Informací, box 63, doc. 61742, "Foitova expedice Bangui /další pokyny/" July 6, 1948.

104. Emily Thompson, *The Soundscape of Modernity: Architectural Acoustics and the Culture of Listening in America, 1900–1933* (Cambridge, MA: MIT Press, 2002).

105. Rosemary Kavanová, *Cena Svobody: Život angličanky v Praze* (Prague: Nakladatelství Brána, 2017), 129.

106. Hans-Ulrich Wagner, "Sounds Like the Fifties: Zur Klangarchäologie der Stimme in westdeutschen Rundfunk der Nachkriegszeit," in *Sound. Zur Technologie und Ästhetik des Akustischen in den Medien*, ed. Harro Segeberg and Frank Schätzlein (Marburg: Schüren, 2005), 277.

250 Notes to Chapter 2

107. Siobhan McHugh, "The Affective Power of Sound: Oral History on Radio," *Oral History Review* 39, no. 2 (2012), 189.

108. Wagner, "Sounds Like the Fifties."

109. CRA, Proces s Miladou Horákovou a spol. IV., last modified April 26, 2021, https://fileshare.croapp.cz/f.php?h=1dZZcCFf.

110. CRA, Proces s Miladou Horákovou a spol. V., last modified April 22, 2021, https://fileshare.croapp.cz/f.php?h=1dZZcCFf.

111. Kaplan and Janáč, "Poslední slovo obžalovaných," 208.

112. Feinberg, *Curtain of Lies*, 23.

113. Čechová, "Československý rozhlas a politické procesy," 56.

114. CRA, Proces s Rudolfem Slánským a spol. I., last modified April 26, 2021, https://fileshare.croapp.cz/f.php?h=2ASt-jgC.

115. Feinberg, *Curtain of Lies*, 4.

116. Ibid., 124–125.

117. Heda Margolius Kovály, *Under a Cruel Star: A Life in Prague, 1941–1968* (London: Granta, 1986), 141.

118. McDermott, "'A Polyphony of Voices?,'" 857.

119. Allen W. Dulles, "Brain Warfare—Russia's Secret Weapon" (excerpts from an address given at Princeton University on April 10, 1953). https://www.cia.gov/readingroom/document/cia-rdp70-00058r000100010023-4.

120. McDermott, "'A Polyphony of Voices?,'" 858.

121. CRA, Proces s Rudolfem Slánským a spol. IV., last modified April 26, 2021, https://fileshare.croapp.cz/f.php?h=2ASt-jgC.

122. CRA, Proces s Miladou Horákovou a spol. II., last modified April 26, 2021, https://fileshare.croapp.cz/f.php?h=1dZZcCFf.

123. CRA, Proces s Miladou Horákovou a spol. II., last modified April 26, 2021, https://fileshare.croapp.cz/f.php?h=1dZZcCFf.

124. CRA, Proces s Rudolfem Slánským a spol. II., last modified April 26, 2021, https://fileshare.croapp.cz/f.php?h=2ASt-jgC.

125. CRA, Proces s K. H. Frankem I., last modified April 22, 2021, https://fileshare.croapp.cz/f.php?h=0BfUtDly.

126. *Proceedings of the Trial of Slansky et al in Prague, Czechoslovakia, November 20–27, 1952 as broadcast by the Czechoslovak Home Service* (date, publisher and publisher location unidentified), 57.

127. Artur London, *The Confession* (London: Murrow, 1970), 248.

128. CRA, Proces s Rudolfem Slánským a spol. II., last modified April 26, 2021, https://fileshare.croapp.cz/f.php?h=1iGkEVrC.

129. Ibid.

130. HU OSA 300-1-2-32350; Records of Radio Free Europe/Radio Liberty

Research Institute: General Records: Information Items; "Reactions to Slansky Trial in Liberec," March 20, 1953, and HU OSA 300-1-2-28416; "Reaction in Prague to Slansky Trial," December 3, 1952.

131. See Feinberg, "Fantastic Truths, Compelling Lies" and McDermott, "'A Polyphony of Voices?'"

132. Paul Barton, *Prague à l'heure de Moscou:Analyse d'une démocratie populaire* (Paris: Édition Pierre Horay, 1954), 100.

133. Michal Frankl, "Prejudiced Asylum: Czechoslovak Refugee Policy, 1918–1960," *Journal of Contemporary History* 49, no. 3 (2014).

134. NA CR Ministerstvo Informací, box 63. Doc. 64562, "Opis: Zpráva," November 7, 1947.

135. CRA, Proces s Rudolfem Slánským a spol. III., last modified April 26, 2021, https://fileshare.croapp.cz/f.php?h=1Fq_2xFI.

136. Feinberg, *Curtain of Lies*, 3.

137. See Barton, *Prague à l'heure de Moscou*, 15–26.

138. Kaplan and Janáč, "Poslední slovo obžalovaných"; Feinberg, *Curtain of Lies*, 5.

139. See Marián Lóži, "A Case Study of Power Practices: The Czechoslovak Stalinist Elite at the Regional Level (1948–1951)" in *Perceptions of Society in Communist Europe*, ed. Muriel Blaive (London: Bloomsbury Academic, 2018), 49–65.

140. See Čechová, "Československý rozhlas a politické procesy," 53, 56.

141. CRA, Proces s Rudolfem Slánským a spol. V., last modified April 26, 2021, https://fileshare.croapp.cz/f.php?h=ow_88rr2.

142. McDermott, "'A Polyphony of Voices?,'" 864.

143. HU OSA 300-1-2-33353; Records of Radio Free Europe/Radio Liberty Research Institute: General Records: Information Items; "People's Reaction at Blovice to Slansky's Execution," April 11, 1953.

144. McDermott, "'A Polyphony of Voices?,'" 850, 863.

145. HU OSA 300-1-2-32350; Records of Radio Free Europe/Radio Liberty Research Institute: General Records: Information Items; "Reactions to Slansky Trial in Liberec," March 20, 1953.

146. McDermott, "'A Polyphony of Voices?,'" 855.

147. HU OSA 300-1-2-29559; Records of Radio Free Europe/Radio Liberty Research Institute: General Records: Information Items; "Rumors about Slansky and Geminder," January 9, 1953.

148. HU OSA 300-1-2-37443; Records of Radio Free Europe/Radio Liberty Research Institute: General Records: Information Items; "Mrs. Slansky Arrested?," August 6, 1953.

149. HU OSA 300-1-2-37880; Records of Radio Free Europe/Radio Liberty

252  Notes to Chapters 2 and 3

Research Institute: General Records: Information Items; "Slansky Trial Victims Set Free," August 18, 1953.

150. McDermott, " 'A Polyphony of Voices?,' " 851.

151. CRA, Zdeněk Nejedlý, *Na okraj dne*, December 14, 1952.

152. Ibid.

153. This is analyzed in depth in Melissa Feinberg, "Fantastic Truths, Compelling Lies."

154. See CRA, Zdeněk Nejedlý, *Na okraj dne*, November 30, December 7, and December 14, 1952. See also Václav Kopecký, *Proti kosmopolitismu jako ideologii amerického imperialismu* (Prague: Orbis, 1952).

155. Allen W. Dulles, "Brain Warfare—Russia's Secret Weapon" (excerpts from an address given at Princeton University on April 10, 1953) https://www.cia.gov/readingroom/document/cia-rdp70-00058r000100010023-4.

156. Tomášek, *Pozor, Cenzurováno!* 64.

157. Blaive, "The Reform Communist Interpretation," 12.

Chapter 3

1. NA CR box 63. Ministerstvo Informací, 1945–1953. Letter from František Foit to Bohuslav Horák, dated July 6, 1948, in doc 63710, "F. V. Foit—vyřízení dopisu z dne 6.VI.1948."

2. NA CR box 63. Ministerstvo Informací, 1945–1953. Letter from Bohuslav Horák to František Foit, dated August 9, 1948 in doc 63710, "F. V. Foit—vyřízení dopisu z dne 6.VI.1948."

3. NA CR box 63. Ministerstvo Informací, 1945–1953. Letter from Bohuslav Horák to František Foit, dated January 1949 in doc 60365, "Foit—odpověď na dopisy z ledna 1949."

4. František Foit made his first trip around Africa in 1932. See Sarah Lemmen, "Globale Selbst- und Fremdverortungen auf Reisen: Tschechische Positionierungsstrategien vor und nach 1918," in *Verflochtene Geschichte: Ostmitteleuropa*, ed. Frank Hadler and Matthias Middell (Leipzig: Leipzigeruniversitätsverlag, 2010), 128.

5. Philip Muehlenbeck, *Czechoslovakia in Africa, 1945–1968* (New York and London: Palgrave Macmillan, 2016), 2–3.

6. Alice Lovejoy, "The World Union of Documentary and the Early Cold War," in "Globalized Media Archaeologies," ed. Daniel Morgan, special issue, *boundary 2* 49, no. 1 (2022); 165–193.

7. Magdalena Preiningerová and Blanka Cekotová, *Archiv H+Z—Muzeum jihovýchodní Moravy ve Zlíně: katalog fondů* (Zlín, Muzeum jihovýchodní Moravy ve Zlíně, 2015): 4.

8. Eva Ješutová (ed.), *Od mikrofonu k posluchačům. Z osmi desetiletí českého rozhlasu* (Prague: Radioservis, 2003), 215.

9. Jiřina Šmejkalová, "Command Celebrities: The Rise and Fall of Hanzelka and Zikmund," *Central Europe* 13, nos. 1–2 (2015), 72–86.

10. See, for example, the collection of essays edited by Jaroslav Pažout (ed.), *Informační boj o Československu/ v Československu (1945–1989)* (Prague: Ústav pro stadium totalitních režimů & Technická univerzita v Liberci, 2014). See also Karel Kaplan, *Československo v letech 1945–1948, 1. Část* (Prague: SPN, 1991), 61.

11. Ješutová, *Od Mikrofonu k posluchačům*, 215.

12. Věra Šťovíčková-Heroldová, *Po světě s mikrofonem* (Prague: Radioservis, 2009), 20–21.

13. AMJM box "Čs. rozhlas, Čs. televize," sign. 965. Letter from Jiří Hanzelka and Miroslav Zikmund to Jiří Hronek, March 10, 1948; AMJM box "Čs. rozhlas, Čs. televize," sign. 965. Letter from Jiří Hanzelka and Miroslav Zikmund to Jiří Hronek, dated June 10, 1948.

14. AMJM box "Čs. rozhlas, Čs. televize," sign. 965. Letter from Jiří Hanzelka and Miroslav Zikmund to Karel Pech, dated July 27, 1948.

15. Jaromír Slomek, Jiří Hanzelka, and Miroslav Zikmund, *Život snů a skutečnosti* (Prague: Primus, 1997), 65.

16. Ibid. 54.

17. See Kevin McDermott, " 'A Polyphony of Voices?' Czech Popular Opinion and the Slansky Affair," *Slavic Review* 67, no. 4 (Winter 2008), Melissa Feinberg, "Fantastic Truths, Compelling Lies: Radio Free Europe and the Response to the Slánský trial in Czechoslovakia," *Contemporary European History* 22, no. 1 (February 2013), and Sylva Sklenářová, "Nizozemská špionážní aféra: Proces s Janem A. Louwersem v březnu 1950," *Soudobé dějiny* 15, no. 1 (2008): 62–84.

18. NA CR box 63. Ministerstvo Informací, 1945–1953. Doc. 69203, "Sochař Foit—Studijní cesta do Afriky," dated July 2, 1947.

19. Sarah Lemmen, "Locating the Nation in a Globalizing World: Debates on the Global Position of Interwar Czechoslovakia," *Bohemia* 56, no. 2 (2016): 469.

20. Slomek, Hanzelka, and Zikmund, *Život snů a skutečnosti*, 49.

21. Muehlenbeck, *Czechoslovakia in Africa*, 3.

22. Ibid., 18.

23. Ibid.

24. Ibid.

25. Ibid., 22.

26. Ibid., 20.

27. Lemmen, "Locating the Nation," 459.

28. Muehlenbeck, *Czechoslovakia in Africa*, 20.

254 Notes to Chapter 3

29. Hanzelka and Zikmund's show, furthermore, sparked a trend. In 1951, the children's travel program *Pohledy do světa (Glimpses of the World)* was launched, described by historians Martin Franc and Jiří Knapík as a particularly interesting example of Czechoslovak Radio output—see *Volný čas v českých zemích 1957–1967* (Prague: Academia, 2013), 49. And radio transcripts from that same year include the chronicles of one Sailor Lesný, who recounted his seafaring adventures to Czechoslovak audiences from distant shores each weekend.

30. See František Foit and Irena Foitová, *Z Telče do Afriky a nikdy zpět: Vzpomínky na druhou africkou cestu* (Telč: Muzejní spolek v Telči, 2006), 183–187.

31. Molly Pucci, "A Revolution in a Revolution: The Secret Police and the Origins of Stalinism in Czechoslovakia," *East European Politics and Societies* 32, no. 1 (February 2018): 3–22.

32. Linda Piknerová, "Czecho(Slovak)—Southern African Relations: From Adventurers to Development Partnership?" in *A History of Czechoslovak Involvement in Africa: Studies from the Colonial through the Soviet Eras*, ed. Jan Dvořáček, Linda Piknerová, and Jan Záhořík (Lewiston, NY, and Lampeter, Wales: Edwin Mellen Press, 2014), 56.

33. NA CR ÚV KSČ Antonín Novotný—zahraničí. Box 4—Afrika. 1261/0/44 A "Záznam o průběhu konzultací skupiny MZV . . . na MIDu SSSR k otazkám Afriky ve dnech 21.—25. listopadu 1961."

34. Sarah Lemmen, *Tschechen auf Reisen: Repräsentationen der außereuropäischen Welt und nationale Identität in Ostmitteleuropa 1890–1938* (Cologne, Weimar, and Vienna: Böhlau, 2018), 184.

35. František Foit, *Autem napříč Afrikou: deník jedinečné cesty z Prahy do Kapského města, díl 1* (Prague: Self-published, 1932).

36. See Slomek, Hanzelka, and Zikmund, *Život snů a skutečnosti*.

37. AMJM Box 960. Letter from "listeners from—illegible—Moravia" to Hanzelka and Zikmund (number 104) in "Korespondence Čs. rozhlasu: dopisy posluchačů (1947–1949)," 16.

38. AMJM Box 960. Letter from L. Stříšková to Hanzelka and Zikmund (number 39) in "Korespondence Čs. rozhlasu: dopisy posluchačů (1947–1949)," 16.

39. Lemmen, "Globale Selbst- und Fremdverortungen auf Reisen," 138.

40. AMJM Sign. 4077–1 (Afrika). Jiří Hanzelka and Miroslav Zikmund, letters 68 to 71.

41. NA CR Ministerstvo Informací, 1945–1953 box 63. "Stříbrná Tatříčka u divokých Babingů," 6, in doc 63710, "F. V. Foit—vyřízení dopisu z dne 6.VI.1948."

42. NA CR Ministerstvo Informací, 1945–1953 box 63. "Stříbrná Tatříčka u divokých Babingů," 6, in doc 63710, "F. V. Foit—vyřízení dopisu z dne 6.VI.1948."

43. NA CR Ministerstvo Informací, 1945–1953 box 63. "Stříbrná Tatříčka u divokých Babingů," 6, in doc 63710, "F. V. Foit—vyřízení dopisu z dne 6.VI.1948."

44. On the racial hierarchies propounded in Foit's interwar writing, see Lemmen, *Tschechen auf Reisen,* 215–218.

45. NA CR Ministerstvo Informací, 1945–1953 box 63. "Stříbrná Tatříčka u divokých Babingů," 6, in doc 63710, "F. V. Foit—vyřízení dopisu z dne 6.VI.1948."

46. CRA CRA09424/7—Čtvrthodinka inženýrů Hanzelky a Zikmunda— závěrečná (dated 1.1.1952).

47. Lovejoy, "The World Union of Documentary and the Early Cold War," 17.

48. Bradley Abrams, *The Struggle for the Soul of the Nation: Czech Culture and the Rise of Communism* (Lanham, Boulder, New York, Toronto, and Oxford: Rowman and Littlefield, 2004), 3.

49. Kaplan, *Československo v letech 1945–1948,* 28. See also Abrams, *The Struggle for the Soul of the Nation,* 34.

50. About one quarter of the postwar Czechoslovak population was between fifteen and thirty years old at the period. Abrams, *The Struggle for the Soul of the Nation,* 33.

51. Mischa Honeck, *Our Frontier Is the World: The Boy Scouts in the Age of American Ascendancy* (Ithaca, NY: Cornell University Press, 2018), 11.

52. Šmejkalová, "Command Celebrities," 76.

53. Pavel Skopal, "Letters to the Heroes: Exhibition and Reception of Hanzelka and Zikmund's Travelogues in Czechoslovakia of the 1950s," *Participations* 11, no. 2 (November 2014), 64.

54. For more on how this star system worked, see the work of Šarka Gmiterková, for example: "Betrayed by Blondness: Jiřina Štěpničková between Authenticity and Excess—1930–1945," *Celebrity Studies* 7, no. 1 (2016): 45–57.

55. Anikó Imre, *TV Socialism* (Raleigh, NC: Duke University Press, 2016), 116.

56. Melissa Feinberg, *Elusive Equality: Gender, Citizenship and the Limits of Democracy in Czechoslovakia* (Pittsburgh, PA: University of Pittsburgh, 2006), 196.

57. NA CR Ministerstvo Informací, 1945–1953. Box 63. "Jak jsme natáčely zvuky na Sahaře" in doc 63710, "F. V. Foit—vyřízení dopisu z dne 6.VI.1948."

58. Šmejkalová, "Command Celebrities," 76.

59. Skopal, "Letters to the Heroes," 63.

60. AMJM "Korespondence čtenáři a posluchači, 1949–1951" (3. část) ev. č. 111. Letter from Věra Luthová to Jiří Hanzelka and Miroslav Zikmund, dated January 4, 1951.

61. AMJM "Korespondence čtenáři a posluchači, 1949–1951" (2. část) ev. č. 111. Letter from the "Karna" vocational school to Jiří Hanzelka and Miroslav Zikmund, dated February 13, 1951.

62. AMJM "Korespondence čtenáři a posluchači, 1949–1951" (2. část) ev. č. 111. Letter from the "Karna" vocational school to Jiří Hanzelka and Miroslav Zikmund, dated February 13, 1951.

63. AMJM "Korespondence čtenáři a posluchači, 1949–1951" (2. část) ev. č. 111. Letter from the "Karna" vocational school to Jiří Hanzelka and Miroslav Zikmund, dated February 13, 1951.

64. Muehlenbeck, *Czechoslovakia in Africa*, 2.

65. AMJM "Korespondence čtenáři a posluchači, 1949–1951" (2. část) ev. č. 111. Letter from the "Karna" vocational school to Jiří Hanzelka and Miroslav Zikmund, dated February 13, 1951.

66. AMJM "Korespondence čtenáři a posluchači, 1949–1951" (2. část) ev. č. 111. Letter from the "Karna" vocational school to Jiří Hanzelka and Miroslav Zikmund, dated February 13, 1951.

67. AMJM "Korespondence čtenáři a posluchači, 1949–1951" (1. část) ev. č. 111. Letter from Eva Pomajzlová to Jan Rolf, dated October 16, 1951.

68. Listeners were aware of this and sometimes praised the presenters of Hanzelka and Zikmund's reports for their reading. See, for example, AMJM box 960. Letter from Captain Bruno Hnilica to Hanzelka and Zikmund (number 51) in "Korespondence Čs. rozhlasu: dopisy posluchačů (1947–1949)," 16.

69. AMJM box "Čs. rozhlas, Čs. televize," sign. 965. Letter from Jiří Hanzelka and Miroslav Zikmund to Lída Humlová, dated February 21, 1949. Box "Čs. rozhlas, Čs. televize."

70. See Skopal, "Letters to the Heroes," 61.

71. AMJM "Čs. rozhlas, Čs. televize," sign. 965. Letter from Jiří Hanzelka and Miroslav Zikmund to Karel Pech, dated October 10, 1951.

72. Ibid.

73. Ibid.

74. Imre, *TV Socialism*, 117.

75. Letter from Jan Číp to Jiří Hanzelka and Miroslav Zikmund, dated July 22, 1948; letter from Josef Hanka to Jiří Hanzelka and Miroslav Zikmund, also July 22, 1948, and letter from Ing. Turek, on "Zoologická zahrada—Praha VIII Troja" letterhead to Jiří Hanzelka and Miroslav Zikmund, dated July 22, 1948—all AMJM "Korespondence čtenáři a posluchači, 1948–1951" (1. část) ev. č. 110. For Foit's work sourcing a chimpanzee, see NA CR. Ministerstvo Informací, 1945–1953. Box 63, doc. 65771, "Foitova expedice—odpověď na zprávy z prosince 1948."

76. AMJM "Korespondence čtenáři a posluchači, 1949–1951" (1. část) ev. č. 111. Letter from Jiří Hanzelka and Miroslav Zikmund to Kamila Kováčová, dated October 26, 1951.

Notes to Chapter 3 257

77. Ibid.

78. AMJM "Korespondence čtenáři a posluchači, 1948–1951" (1. část) ev. č. 110. Letter from Karel Hesek to Jiří Hanzelka and Miroslav Zikmund, dated July 29, 1948.

79. AMJM box "Čs. rozhlas, Čs. televize," sign. 965. Letter from Jiří Hanzelka and Miroslav Zikmund to Lída Humlová, dated January 4, 1950. Box "Čs. rozhlas, Čs. televize."

80. See Franc and Knapík, *Volný čas v českých zemích*, 30–31, 409.

81. NA CR. Ministerstvo Informací, 1945–1953. Box 28, doc. 63865. "Reorganisace odborných rozhlasů," dated August 30, 1946.

82. Šmejkalová, "Command Celebrities," 73.

83. Piknerová, "Czecho(Slovak)—Southern African Relations," 21.

84. Ibid., 55.

85. Jay David Bolter and Richard Grusin, *Remediation: Understanding New Media* (Cambridge, MA: MIT Press, 1999), 28.

86. See AMJM. Box 960. "Korespondence Čs. rozhlasu: dopisy posluchačů (1947–1949)." Letter from Stanislav Forman to Hanzelka and Zikmund (no. 133), 17 and letter from "elektrikaři vozovny Pankrác" to Hanzelka and Zikmund (no. 224), 33.

87. In one report, the pair reflected upon the reasons for Foit's "failure" to scale the mountain. They therefore stressed the scale of the feat they were setting out to achieve and handily discredited their rival. See AMJM Sign. 4077–1 (Afrika). Jiří Hanzelka and Miroslav Zikmund, letter 120, 2.

88. Skopal, "Letters to the Heroes," 70.

89. AMJM Sign. 4077-1 (Afrika). Jiří Hanzelka and Miroslav Zikmund, letter 123, 1.

90. Ibid.

91. Mary Louise Pratt, *Imperial Eyes: Travel Writing and Transculturation* (London and New York: Routledge, 2003), 202.

92. Ibid..

93. Pratt, *Imperial Eyes*, 204.

94. Ibid. 205.

95. AMJM Sign. 4077-1 (Afrika). Jiří Hanzelka and Miroslav Zikmund, letter 120, 1.

96. AMJM Sign. 4077-1 (Afrika). Jiří Hanzelka and Miroslav Zikmund, letter 121, 1.

97. AMJM Sign. 4077-1 (Afrika). Jiří Hanzelka and Miroslav Zikmund, letter 122, 1.

98. Pratt, *Imperial Eyes*, 204.

258  Notes to Chapter 3

99. AMJM Sign. 4077-1 (Afrika). Jiří Hanzelka and Miroslav Zikmund, letter 121, 1.

100. Ibid.

101. For the hermelín reference, see AMJM Sign. 4077-1 (Afrika). Jiří Hanzelka and Miroslav Zikmund, letter 121, 1. For mention of the Alps, see AMJM Sign. 4077-1 (Afrika). Jiří Hanzelka and Miroslav Zikmund, letter 122, 1.

102. AMJM Sign. 4077-1 (Afrika). Jiří Hanzelka and Miroslav Zikmund, letter 119, 3.

103. Pratt, *Imperial Eyes*, 202.

104. AMJM Sign. 4077-1 (Afrika). Jiří Hanzelka and Miroslav Zikmund, letter 123, 3.

105. Bolter and Grusin, *Remediation,* 41–42.

106. Šmejkalová, "Command Celebrities," 74.

107. Bolter and Grusin, *Remediation,* 33–34.

108. NA CR box 63. Ministerstvo Informací, 1945–1953. Letter from Bohuslav Horák to František Foit, dated August 9, 1948 in doc 63710, "F. V. Foit—vyřízení dopisu z dne 6.VI.1948."

109. Felix Jeschke, *Iron Landscapes: Nation Building and the Railways in Czechoslovakia, 1918–1938* (New York and Oxford: Berghahn, 2021), 64–101..

110. AMJM Sign. 4077-1 (Afrika). Jiří Hanzelka and Miroslav Zikmund, Letter no. 37, 1–2.

111. Ibid.

112. Sarah Lemmen, "Noncolonial Orientalism? Czech Travel Writing on Africa and Asia around 1918," in *Verflochtene Geschichte: Ostmitteleuropa,* ed. Frank Hadler and Matthias Middell (Leipzig: Leipzigeruniversitätsverlag, 2010), 209.

113. AMJM Sign. 4077–1 (Afrika). Jiří Hanzelka and Miloslav Zikmund, Letter 39, October 7, 1947, 2.

114. Ibid.

115. Ibid.

116. Ibid.

117. For more details of the latter, see "Osudná Libye Hanzelky a Zikmunda," https://www.rozhlas.cz/archiv/zamikrofonem/_zprava/osudna-libye-hanzelky -a-zikmunda--1729122. Accessed June 13, 2019.

118. AMJM Box 960. Letter from M. Kudrnová to Hanzelka and Zikmund (no. 136) in "Korespondence Čs. rozhlasu: dopisy posluchačů (1947–1949)," 20.

119. Slomek, Hanzelka, and Zikmund, *Život snů a skutečnosti,* 16.

120. Ibid.

121. Honeck, *Our Frontier Is the World,* 5.

Notes to Chapter 3  259

122. AMJM Sign. 4077-1 (Afrika). Jiří Hanzelka and Miroslav Zikmund, letter 176.

123. See Patryk Babiracki and Austin Jersild's introduction to *Socialist Internationalism in the Cold War* (London: Palgrave MacMillan, 2016), 1–16. See also Rosamund Johnston, "*The Peace Train:* Anticosmopolitanism, Internationalism and Jazz on Czechoslovak Radio during Stalinism," in *Remapping Cold War Media: Institutions, Infrastructures, Translations,* ed. Alice Lovejoy and Mari Pajala (Bloomington: Indiana University Press, 2022).

124. AMJM Sign. 4077-1 (Afrika). Jiří Hanzelka and Miroslav Zikmund, letter 141.

125. Chad Bryant, *Prague in Black: Nazi Rule and Czech Nationalism* (Cambridge, MA: Harvard University Press, 2009), 6.

126. Lemmen, *Tschechen auf Reisen,* 192.

127. AMJM Box "Čs. rozhlas, Čs. televize," sign. 965. Letter from Jiří Hanzelka and Miroslav Zikmund to Karel Pech, dated August 22, 1948.

128. Report 189 for example presents Vítězslav Tomeš as a fine representative of Czechoslovakia in South Africa, while the Czechoslovak members of the French Legion discussed in letter 9 are referred to as "the first expatriates that we cannot feel sorry for being abroad." See AMJM sign. 4077-1 (Afrika). Jiří Hanzelka and Miroslav Zikmund, letters 9 and 189.

129. See, for example, AMJM box 960. "Korespondence Čs. rozhlasu: dopisy posluchačů (1947–1949)," letter from Jan Honsa to Hanzelka and Zikmund (no. 67), or letter from M. Kousal to Hanzelka and Zikmund (no. 103).

130. See AMJM "Korespondence čtenáři a posluchači, 1949–1951" (1. část) ev. č. 111. Letter from Jiří Hanzelka and Miroslav Zikmund to Antonín Šafář, July 17, 1951.

131. Slomek, Hanzelka, and Zikmund, *Život snů a skutečnosti,* 69.

132. CRA AF00315_7_AF5671—Ministr V. Kopecký proti reakci a zahraniční emigraci (September 18, 1948).

133. See Václav Kopecký, *Proti kosmopolitismu jako ideologii amerického imperialismu* (Prague: Orbis, 1952), 6.

134. Slomek, Hanzelka, and Zikmund, *Život snů a skutečnosti,* 52.

135. Dušan Segeš, "Remigration tschechoslowakischer Staatsbürger aus der Bundesrepublik Deutschland in die ČSR in den 1950er-Jahren," in *Flüchtlinge und Asyl im Nachbarland. Die Tschechoslowakei und Deutschland 1933 bis 1989,* ed. Detlef Brandes, Edita Ivančiková, and Jiří Pešek (Munich: Klartext, 2018), 233.

136. For more on these programs, see Tomek, *Československá redakce Radio Free Europe,* 128.

260  Notes to Chapters 3 and 4

137. Segeš, "Remigration tschechoslowakischer Staatsbürger," 231.

138. Tara Zahra, *The Great Departure: Emigration from Eastern Europe and the Making of the Free World* (New York: Norton, 2016), 223.

139. CRA Box 41. "Směrnice k cestám zaměstnanců čs. rozhlasu do ciziny" (undated).

140. For more details, see http://www.ntm.cz/Hanzelka_a_Zikmund_70. Accessed April 22, 2017.

141. Lovejoy, "The World Union of Documentary and the Early Cold War," 17.


**Chapter 4**

1. Stephen Kotkin, *Magnetic Mountain: Stalinism as Civilization* (Berkeley: University of California Press, 1997), 23.

2. For Stalinism's persistence in Czechoslovakia, see, for example, Jacques Rupnik, *Histoire du parti communiste tchécoslovaque: Des origines à la prise du pouvoir* (Paris: Les presses de Sciences Po, 1981) and Muriel Blaive, "Perceptions of Society in Czechoslovak Secret Police Archives: How a 'Czechoslovak 1956' was Thwarted," in *Perceptions of Society*, 101–123 (London: Bloomsbury Academic, 2018); for de-Stalinization beginning in the mid-1950s, see Molly Pucci, *Security Empire: The Secret Police in Communist Eastern Europe* (New Haven, CT: Yale University Press, 2020), 2.

3. Kevin McDermott, *Communist Czechoslovakia, 1945–1989: A Political and Social History* (London: Palgrave, 2015), 92.

4. Ibid.

5. Jane Curry, *Poland's Journalists: Professionalism and Politics* (Cambridge: Cambridge, 1990), 45.

6. Ibid.

7. Jana Suková, "Svaz českých novinářů v období Pražského jara," Bachelor's thesis, Charles University, 2013, 12–13.

8. Marci Shore, "Engineering in the Age of Innocence: A Genealogy of Discourse in the Czechoslovak Writers' Union, 1949–1967," *East European Politics and Societies* 12, no. 3 (1998): 422.

9. Ibid., 413.

10. Pavel Kolář, "The Party as a New Utopia: Reshaping Communist Identity after Stalinism," *Social History* 37, no. 4 (November 2012): 410.

11. Kolář, "The Party as a New Utopia," 404–405.

12. See Václav Kopecký and Klement Gottwald's comments in CRA Box 65. "Poznámky z celostátní ředitelské schůze, 8–9.1.1952," p. 1.

13. See David Vaughan, " 'My First Love Was a Drill': Building the Socialist State," last modified June 2, 2021, https://english.radio.cz/my-first-love-was-a-drill-building-socialist-state-8559042.

Notes to Chapter 4   261

14. CRA DF06401_DF2672, "Okénko lidových autorů a vypravěčů," dated 1955.

15. Daniela Stavělová et al., *Tíha a beztíže folkoru: Folklorní hnutí druhé poloviny 20: století v českých zemích* (Prague: Academia, 2022), 315.

16. HU OSA 300-1-2-70375: "Slovak Radio Answers Listeners' Questions," April 26, 1956. Records of Radio Free Europe/Radio Liberty Research Institute: General Records: Information Items; Open Society Archives at Central European University, Budapest.

17. Ibid.

18. Stavělová et al., *Tíha a beztíže folkoru,* 284.

19. CRA Box 65, "Zápis z programovej rady . . ." dated November 2, 1956.

20. Ibid.

21. For more on limited communication between the blocs, see Anders Stephanson, "Fourteen Notes on the Very Concept of the Cold War," last modified December 3, 2020, https://issforum.org/essays/PDF/stephanson-14notes.pdf.

22. See, for example, Vojtech Mihálik, cited in Shore, "Engineering in the Age of Innocence," 424.

23. Matěj Kratochvíl, " 'Our Song!' Nationalism in Folk Music Research and Revival in Socialist Czechoslovakia," *Studia Musicologica* 56, no. 4 (2015): 401.

24. See HU OSA 300-1-2-59753; Records of Radio Free Europe/Radio Liberty Research Institute: General Records: Information Items; "Comments of "Valka" Refugees on the Redefectors Kucera and Schneider," July 5, 1955.

25. "Beseda s navrátilcem Vladimírem Kučerou ve Švermově," last modified July 8, 2019, Národní muzeum eSbírky: https://tinyurl.com/yzsuebfh. Henceforth referred to as "Meeting with Vladimír Kučera in Švermov: Národní muzeum eSbírky."

26. Meeting with Vladimír Kučera in Švermov: Národní muzeum eSbírky."

27. Prokop Tomek, *Československé bezpečnostní složky proti Rádiu Svobodná Evropa: Objekt Alfa* (Prague: Úřad dokumentace a vyšetřování zločinů komunismu, 2006), 41.

28. Dušan Segeš, "Remigration tschechoslowakischer Staatsbürger aus der Bundesrepublik Deutschland in die ČSR in den 1950er-Jahren," in *Flüchtlinge und Asyl im Nachbarland. Die Tschechoslowakei und Deutschland 1933 bis 1989,* ed. Detlef Brandes, Edita Ivančiková, and Jiří Pešek (Munich: Klartext, 2018), 230.

29. Paulina Bren, " 'Mirror, Mirror, on the Wall . . . Is the West the Fairest of Them All:' Czechoslovak Normalization and its (Dis)Contents" in *Kritika: Explorations in Russian and Eurasian History* 9, no. 4 (Fall 2008): 841.

30. Ibid., 842.

262  Notes to Chapter 4

31. Susan Carruthers, *Cold War Captives: Imprisonment, Escape, and Brainwashing* (Berkeley, Los Angeles, and London: University of California Press, 2009), 96.

32. Ibid., 81.

33. Marie Cronqvist, "From Socialist Hero to Capitalist Icon: The Cultural Transfer of the East German Children's Television Programme Unser Sandmännchen to Sweden in the Early 1970s," *Historical Journal of Film, Radio, and Television* 41, no. 2 (2021): 378–393.

34. Tara Zahra, *The Great Departure: Emigration from Eastern Europe and the Making of the Free World* (New York: Norton, 2016), 242.

35. Ibid., 243.

36. To compare Kravchenko's and, for example, Bruno Folta's press conferences, see British Pathe "Interview with Victor Kravchenko (1949)," last modified June 25, 2021, https://www.youtube.com/watch?v=OG8b7u_rlrE. and "Československý filmový tydeník," last modified June 25, 2021, https://www.ceskatelevize.cz/porady/1130615451-ceskoslovensky-filmovy-tydenik/204562262700041/.

37. Zahra, *The Great Departure*, 236–237.

38. Ibid., 223.

39. See, for example, Jiří Hronek, *V širošírém světě* (Prague: Státní nakladatelství dětské knihy, 1954) and Čestmír Suchý, Jiří Hochman, and Jiřina Brejchová, *Emigranti proti národu* (Prague: Mladá fronta, 1953).

40. Petr Vidomus, " 'Američan—a musí emigrovat do Československa!'—Škvoreckého jazzman Herbert Ward optikou zpráv FBI," *Soudobé dějiny* nos. 1–2 (2017): 186.

41. Ibid., 187.

42. Pavel Horák, *Bohumil Laušman—politický životopis: Riskantní hry sociálnědemokratického vůdce* (Prague: Mladá fronta, 2012).

43. Pavel Tigrid, *Politická emigrace v atomovém věku* (Prague: Prostor, 1990), 72.

44. For the last radio trials, see CRA "Proces proti protistátní luďácké organizaci B-156." For more on the shift in messaging, see "The Sound and the Fury," *News from Behind the Iron Curtain* 3, no. 2 (February 1954): 10.

45. Bren, " 'Mirror, Mirror," 833.

46. Czech literary bibliography research infrastructure. Institute of Czech Literature, Czech Academy of Sciences—https://clb.ucl.cas.cz/ (ORJ identifier: 90136) (henceforth CLBRI): digital periodical archive. *Rudé právo* July 8, 1955, p. 3.

47. CLBRI: digital periodical archive. *Rudé právo,* July 8, 1955, p. 3 and "Neš-

vary kapitalismu," last modified January 30, 2018, http://www.pribehrozhlasu
.cz/tenkrat-v-rozhlase/1954/1954_5.

48. CLBRI: digital periodical archive. *Rudé právo,* June 20, 1955, p. 3.

49. CLBRI: digital periodical archive. *Rudé právo,* June 20, 1955, p. 3; *Rudé právo* June 16, 1955, p. 3.

50. CLBRI: digital periodical archive. *Rudé právo,* July 9, 1955, p. 3.

51. CLBRI: digital periodical archive. *Rudé právo,* June 20, 1955, p. 3.

52. Bren, " 'Mirror, Mirror," 846.

53. CLBRI: digital periodical archive. *Rudé právo,* June 24, 1955, p. 4.

54. Pavel Kolář, *Der Poststalinismus: Ideologie und Utopie einer Epoche* (Vienna, Cologne, and Weimar: Böhlau, 2016), 10–11.

55. Kolář, "The Party as a New Utopia," 405.

56. For reference to Stalin's "mistakes," see "Speech to 20th Congress of the C.P.S.U.," last modified February 8, 2019, https://www.marxists.org/archive/khrushchev/1956/02/24.htm. For the way that history was reconceptualized in a post-Stalinist environment, see Kolář, "The Party as a New Utopia," 410.

57. Kolář, "The Party as a New Utopia," 404.

58. Ibid., 412.

59. Laušman had been a prominent Social Democrat who fled Czechoslovakia in 1949. His "heretical" left-wing views were no longer part of the rap sheet against him upon his return in 1954. For more, see Horák, *Bohumil Laušman,* 278.

60. "Press Conference with Vladimír Kučera: Národní muzeum eSbírky."

61. "Nešvary kapitalismu," last modified January 30, 2018, http://www .pribehrozhlasu.cz/tenkrat-v-rozhlase/1954/1954_5.

62. https://tinyurl.com/28rv6mkj, last modified February 12, 2018. Henceforth referred to as "Press Conference with Bruno Folta: Národní muzeum eSbírky."

63. "Press Conference with Bruno Folta: Národní muzeum eSbírky."

64. Ibid.

65. This is something Dina Fainberg finds in other examples of Cold War–era journalism, East and West, in "Unmasking the Wolf in Sheep's Clothing: Soviet and American Campaigns against the Enemy's Journalists, 1948–1953," *Cold War History* 15, no. 2 (2015): 157.

66. https://tinyurl.com/msv5j8z9. April 10, 2018. Henceforth referred to as "Interview with Bušová-Kasalová: Národní muzeum eSbírky."

67. https://tinyurl.com/54atbmm5. "Press Conference with Vladimír Kučera: Národní muzeum eSbírky."

68. Ibid.

264  Notes to Chapter 4

69. Ibid.

70. Suchý, Hochman, and Brejchová, *Emigranti proti národu*, 16.

71. See, for example, Ferdinand Peroutka, "Projev při zahájení vysílání Rádia Svobodná Evropa," *Ferdinand Peroutka pro Svobodnou Evropu* (Prague: Radioservis, 2013) or RFE broadcasts such as 2473 RFE—"16th Anniversary of T. G. Masaryk's Death" (September 14, 1953). Libri Prohibiti, Prague.

72. See "Press Conference with Bruno Folta: Národní muzeum eSbírky" and "Interview with Bušová-Kasalová: Národní muzeum eSbírky."

73. Fainberg, "Unmasking the Wolf in Sheep's Clothing," 157.

74. CRA Box 41. "Směrnice k cestám zaměstnanců čs. rozhlasu do ciziny" (undated).

75. In this turn of phrase and in much of the framing of this chapter, I am indebted to Paulina Bren's article " 'Mirror, Mirror."

76. Shore, "Engineering in the Age of Innocence," 424.

77. HU OSA 300-1-2-68887; Records of Radio Free Europe/Radio Liberty Research Institute: General Records: Information Items; "Interview with Czech Surgeon," March 16, 1956.

78. HU OSA 300-1-2-51913; Records of Radio Free Europe/Radio Liberty Research Institute: General Records: Information Items; "Right or Wrong . . . It's Lausman's Headache," November 4, 1954.

79. Ibid.

80. Ibid.

81. Melissa Feinberg, *Curtain of Lies: The Battle over Truth in Stalinist Eastern Europe* (New York: Oxford University Press, 2017), xx–xxii.

82. Muriel Blaive, *Promárněná příležitost: Československo a rok 1956* (Prague: Prostor, 2001), 78.

83. Jan Rychlík, *Deník 1955* (Prague: Revolver, 2006), 63–64.

84. Bohumil Hrabal, *Mr. Kafka: And Other Tales from the Time of the Cult* (New York: New Directions, 2015), 59. "Ingots" was first published in 1965 but written at an earlier period.

85. Feinberg, *Curtain of Lies*, 139.

86. RFE's founders believed one of the station's goals should be to demobilize its ideological enemies by stoking their fears. For more, see Arch Puddington, *Broadcasting Freedom: The Cold War Triumph of Radio Free Europe and Radio Liberty* (Lexington: University of Kentucky, 2000), 18.

87. Paweł Machcewicz, *Poland's War on Radio Free Europe* (Redwood City, CA: Stanford University Press, 2015) and Tomek, *Československá redakce Radio Free Europe*.

88. Heda Margolius Kovály, *Under a Cruel Star: A Life in Prague, 1941–1968* (London: Granta, 1986), 94.

Notes to Chapters 4 and 5  265

89. Frantz Fanon, *A Dying Colonialism* (New York: Grove, 1965), 85–86.

90. HU OSA 300-1-2-64082; "Slovak Listener Compares Linz and Prague Programs," November 17, 1955. Records of Radio Free Europe/Radio Liberty Research Institute: General Records: Information Items; Open Society Archives at Central European University, Budapest.

91. HU OSA 300-1-2-68893; "Brno Woman Listener Complains Czechoslovak Radio Bores Her," March 16, 1956. Records of Radio Free Europe/Radio Liberty Research Institute: General Records: Information Items; Open Society Archives at Central European University, Budapest.

92. See NA CR Ministerstvo Informací, box 29, doc. 65359, "Všeobecné poznámky z týdne od 18. do 24. října 1948" dated November 13, 1948 and doc. 63717, "Rozhlasové noviny v měsíce květnu 1948 . . . ," dated September 14, 1948.

93. See for example AMJM box 960. Letters nos. 111, 203, and 280 in "Korespondence Čs. rozhlasu: dopisy posluchačů (1947–1949)."

94. Mihálik, cited in Shore, "Engineering in the Age of Innocence," 424; see also Václav Havel, *Open Letters: Selected Writings 1965–1990* (New York: Alfred A. Knopf, 1991), 5.

95. Muriel Blaive, "The Reform Communist Interpretation of the Stalinist Period in Czechoslovak Historiography and its Legacy," in *East European Politics and Societies* (November 2021), 3.

## Chapter 5

1. See Mari Pajala, "A Forgotten Spirit of Commercial Television? Co-productions between Finnish Commercial Television Company Mainos-TV and Socialist Television," *Historical Journal of Film, Radio, and Television* 39, no. 2 (2019): 366–383, Frank Bösch and Cristoph Classen, "Bridge over Troubled Water? Mass Media in Divided Germany," in *A History Shared and Divided: East and West Germany since the 1970s*, ed. Frank Bösch (Oxford: Berghahn, 2018), 551–602, and Petr Szczepanik, "Hollywood Going East: State Socialist Studios' Opportunistic Business with American Producers," in *Remapping Cold War Media: Institutions, Infrastructures, Translations*, ed. Alice Lovejoy and Mari Pajala (Bloomington: Indiana University Press, 2022), 227–244.

2. See Prokop Tomek, *Československá redakce Radio Free Europe* (Prague: Academia, 2015), 263.

3. Bösch and Classen, "Bridge over Troubled Water?," 566.

4. Lisa Parks and Nicole Starosielski, *Signal Traffic: Critical Studies of Media Infrastructures* (Champaign: University of Illinois, 2015), 3.

5. Carolyn Birdsall and Joanna Walewska-Choptiany, "Reconstructing Media Culture: Transnational Perspectives on Radio in Silesia, 1924–1948," *Historical Journal of Film, Radio and Television* 39, no. 3 (2019): 440.

266 Notes to Chapter 5

6. See, for example, Leslie Waters, *Borders on the Move: Territorial Change and Forced Migration in the Hungarian-Slovak Borderlands* (Rochester, NY: University of Rochester Press, 2020), David Gerlach, *The Economy of Ethnic Cleansing: The Transformation of the Czech-German Borderlands after World War II* (Cambridge: Cambridge University Press, 2017), and Eagle Glassheim, *Cleansing the Czechoslovak Borderlands: Migration, Environment, and Health in the Former Sudetenland* (Pittsburgh, PA: University of Pittsburgh Press, 2016).

7. Glassheim, *Cleansing the Czechoslovak Borderlands*, 6.

8. For example, Paulina Bren, *The Greengrocer and His TV: The Culture of Communism after the 1968 Prague Spring* (Ithaca, NY, and London: Cornell University Press, 2010), Christine E. Evans, *Between Truth and Time: A History of Soviet Central Television* (New Haven, CT, and London: Yale University Press, 2016), Kristin Roth-Ey, *Moscow Prime Time: How the Soviet Union Built the Media Empire that Lost the Cultural Cold War* (Ithaca, NY, and London: Cornell University Press, 2011), and Anikó Imre, *TV Socialism* (Raleigh, NC: Duke University Press, 2016).

9. Reinhold Wagnleitner, *Coca-Colonization and the Cold War: The Cultural Mission of the United States in Austria* (Chapel Hill: University of North Carolina Press, 1991).

10. Arch Puddington, *Broadcasting Freedom: The Cold War Triumph of Radio Free Europe and Radio Liberty* (Lexington: University of Kentucky, 2000), 131.

11. Ibid.

12. This title varied. Radio Vienna and *Deutschlandfunk* were frequent contenders, although Voice of America often topped listener polls. Tomek, *Československá redakce Radio Free Europe*, 274.

13. Tomek is not alone in this. See also A. Ross Johnson and Eugene Parta (eds.) *Cold War Broadcasting: Impact on the Soviet Union and Eastern Europe* (Budapest: Central European University Press, 2012) and Paweł Machcewicz, *Poland's War on Radio Free Europe* (Redwood City, CA: Stanford University Press, 2015).

14. Tomek, *Československá redakce Radio Free Europe*, 254.

15. See Václav Havel, cited in Johnson and Parta, *Cold War Broadcasting*, 346.

16. This point is made eloquently by Jonathan Bolton in *World of Dissent: The Plastic People of the Universe, Charter 77, and Czech Culture under Communism* (Cambridge, MA: Harvard University Press, 2012), 36–37.

17. Puddington, *Broadcasting Freedom*, 58, 313. See also Johnson and Parta, *Cold War Broadcasting*, 350.

18. See, for example, Filip Pospíšil, "Inspiration, Subversion and Appropriation: The Effects of Radio Free Europe Music Broadcasting," *Journal of Cold*

*War Studies* 21, no. 4 (Fall 2019): 124–149 and Amir Weiner, "Foreign Media, the Soviet Western Frontier, and the Hungarian and Czechoslovak Crises," in Johnson and Parta, *Cold War Broadcasting*, 317. For Šesták's understanding of the political significance of Western radio listening, see Tony Prince and Jan Šesták, *The Royal Ruler and the Radio DJ* (Slough: DMC Publishing, 2017), 72. The link between Western radio and anti-Communism is also explored by Tom Stoppard in *Rock 'n' Roll* (London, Faber, 2006).

19. See "23.10.2019—30.8.2020—Technika v diktaturách," http://www.ntm .cz/Technika_v_diktaturach. Last modified June 12, 2020.

20. Miroslav Vaněk, "Twenty Years in Shades of Grey? Everyday Life during 'Normalization' Based on Oral History Research," in *Czechoslovakia and Eastern Europe in the Era of Normalisation, 1969–1989*, ed. Kevin McDermott and Matthew Stibbe (London: Palgrave Macmillan, 2022).

21. Propaganda films such as *They Shall Not Pass* (*Neprojdou*, Zbyněk Brynych, 1952) cast Czechoslovak Radio listening as a model politically engaged behavior by depicting the state's border guards doing so while conducting their work. Police documents from the same period show, on the other hand, how law enforcement interpreted foreign radio listening as politically suspect. See, for example, the trial documents of Josef Kuldan et al., Archiv bezpečnostní složek, Prague (ABS), V-PL, V-1178 MV (Kuldan Josef a spol.).

22. I follow Melissa Feinberg and Nicholas Schlosser, who both address the difficulties of using such listener interviews in their research, and both conclude that such sources do, nevertheless, provide valuable insight into the Cold War Central European media environment. See Melissa Feinberg, *Curtain of Lies: The Battle over Truth in Stalinist Eastern Europe* (New York: Oxford University Press, 2017), xx and Nicholas Schlosser, *Cold War on the Airwaves: The Radio Propaganda War against East Germany* (Champaign: University of Illinois, 2015), 69.

23. For details of interwar German-language broadcasting on Czechoslovak Radio, see Ekhard Jirgens, *Der Deutsche Rundfunk der 1. Tschechoslowakischen Republik* (Regensburg: Con Brio, 2017) and for the wartime use of German, see Peter Richard Pinard, *Broadcast Policy in the Protectorate of Bohemia and Moravia* (Frankfurt: Peter Lang, 2015).

24. Petr Szczepanik, "Hollywood in Disguise: Practices of Exhibition and Reception of Foreign Films in Czechoslovakia in the 1930s," in *Cinema, Audiences and Modernity*, ed. Daniel Biltereyst, Richard Maltby, and Philippe Meers (London and New York: Routledge, 2011), 182.

25. See NA CR box 43, Ministerstvo Informací, doc. 64731, "Přidělení rozhlasových vln," November 14, 1947.

268 Notes to Chapter 5

26. NA CR box 27, Ministerstvo Informací, doc. 60728, "Zápis o jednání XXV. schůze jednatelského sboru," February 17, 1947.

27. NA CR box 29. Ministerstvo Informací, doc. 67247, "Odpověď na dotaz dobrovolného zpravodaje průzkumu rozhlasového poslechu p. Zdeňka Tušla, č. zpr. 0217," November 23, 1946.

28. See NA CR box 29. Ministerstvo Informací, doc. 65359, "Všeobecné poznámky z týdne od 18. do 24. října 1948," November 13, 1948.

29. See NA CR box 29. Ministerstvo Informací, doc. 60637, "Studium posluchačů rozhlasu," September 29, 1945.

30. Jan Rychlík, "Komunistická propaganda v Československu 1945–1989 z tematického hlediska," in *Informační boj o Československsku/ v Československsku, 1945–1989*, ed. Jaroslav Pažout (Prague: Technická univerzita v Liberci and ÚSTR, 2014), 25.

31. A Ministry of Information source cited in Martin Štoll, *Television and Totalitarianism in Czechoslovakia: From the First Democratic Republic to the Fall of Communism* (Sydney: Bloomsbury, 2018), 110.

32. For detailed analyses of jamming in socialist Czechoslovakia, see Prokop Tomek "Rušení zahraničního rozhlasového vysílání pro Československsko," *Securitas Imperii*, no. 9 (2002) and Milan Barta "Přestaňte okamžitě rušit modré," *Paměť a dějiny*, no. 3 (2012).

33. HU OSA 300-1-2-68887; Records of Radio Free Europe/Radio Liberty Research Institute: General Records: Information Items, "Interview with Czech Surgeon", March 16, 1956.

34. Ibid.

35. HU OSA 300-1-2-75981; Records of Radio Free Europe/Radio Liberty Research Institute: General Records: Information Items, "Interview with Czech Official," November 7, 1956.

36. Ibid.

37. For more on the radio debates between Radio Free Europe and Czechoslovak Radio at this moment, which he likens to a "ping-pong game," see Dušan Segeš, "Remigration tschechoslowakischer Staatsbürger aus der Bundesrepublik Deutschland in die ČSR in den 1950er-Jahren" in *Die Tschechoslowakei und Deutschland 1933 bis 1989*, ed. Detlef Brandes, Edita Ivančiková, and Jiří Pešek (Munich: Klartext, 2018), 230.

38. CIA-RDP80–00810A006500180003–1 "Czechoslovakia: Reception of and Reaction to Local and Foreign Broadcasts" dated May 18, 1955: 2. Last modified March 25, 2019. https://www.cia.gov/library/readingroom/docs/CIA-RDP80 -00810A006500180003-1.pdf.

39. Tomek, *Československá redakce Radio Free Europe*, 305.

40. Ibid., 305.

41. For a tirade by Ideological Commission Chief Vladimír Koucký against West German television in 1964, for example, see NA CZ box KSČ-ÚV-10/5: Ideologická komise ÚV KSČ 1958–1968. Svazek 2, arch. jed. 12. "Zápis 6. Schůze ideologické komise ÚV KSČ, 13.4.1964," p. 27.

42. HU OSA 300-6-2 Box 1—Media and Opinion Research Dept. E Euro (July 1962—December 1965), "The Audience of Western Broadcasts in Czechoslovakia, September 1964."

43. HU OSA 300-6-2 Box 2—Media and Opinion Research Dept. E Euro (January 1966—December 1967), "Listening to Western Stations in Czechoslovakia, III, June 1966."

44. Paulina Bren, *The Greengrocer and His TV*, 120.

45. Tomek, *Československá redakce Radio Free Europe*, 303.

46. Ibid.

47. Ibid.

48. Ibid., 267.

49. Niklas Perzi, Hildegard Schmoller, Ota Konrád, and Václav Šmirkdal (eds.), *Nachbarn: Ein Österreichisch-Tschechisches Geschichtsbuch* (Weitra: Bibliothek der Provinz, 2019), 235.

50. HU OSA 300-1-2-2593; Records of Radio Free Europe/Radio Liberty Research Institute: General Records: Information Items; "German Taught Instead of English," July 18, 1951.

51. "60 Jahre deutschsprachige Publikationen in der Tschechoslowakei: Von 'Aufbau und Frieden' zur 'Prager Zeitung,'" last modified October 29, 2020, https://deutsch.radio.cz/60-jahre-deutschsprachige-publikationen-der -tschechoslowakei-von-aufbau-und-8560071.

52. HU OSA 300-1-2-25872; Records of Radio Free Europe/Radio Liberty Research Institute: General Records: Information Items; "Foreign Press and Books in Czechoslovakia," September 25, 1952.

53. HU OSA 300-1-2-13724; Records of Radio Free Europe/Radio Liberty Research Institute: General Records: Information Items; "Umschwung in Verhaeltnis zu den Deutschen," January 8, 1952.

54. See, for example, HU OSA 300-1-2-13870; Records of Radio Free Europe/ Radio Liberty Research Institute: General Records: Information Items, "Arrival of Skilled German Workers," January 11, 1952, and HU OSA 300-1-2-17942; Records of Radio Free Europe/Radio Liberty Research Institute: General Records: Information Items; "Exchange of Experience between CSR and Eastern Germany," April 5, 1952.

55. Eva Hazdrová-Kopecká, "Jazykové kurzy v rozhlasu," last modified October 19, 2020, https://temata.rozhlas.cz/jazykove-kurzy-v-rozhlasu-8023922.

56. Vojtěch Mastný tuned in to BBC and Voice of America broadcasts in

270  Notes to Chapter 5

English, rather than German, to learn a language he was trying to master in Czechoslovakia in the mid-1950s. Radio in a major European language had the additional benefit, he suggested, of being less provincial than foreign news translated into Czech and Slovak. See Vojtěch Mastný, interview with Katja David Fox. National Czech and Slovak Museum and Library, last modified September 2, 2019, https://ncsml.omeka.net/items/show/4240.

57. Prince and Šesták, *The Royal Ruler*, 94.

58. Karel Gott, cited by Jan Šesták in "Karel Gott—Zwischen zwei Welten: Mein Leben," last modified October 30, 2020, https://sestak.blog.idnes.cz/blog .aspx?c=410568.

59. See HU OSA 300-6-1; Records of Radio Free Europe/Radio Liberty Research Institute: Media and Opinion: Administrative Files, "Analysis Report 3," February 25, 1963.

60. NA CR box 43. Ministerstvo Informací, doc. 64731, "Přidělení rozhlasových vln," November 14, 1947.

61. Glassheim, *Cleansing the Czechoslovak Borderlands*, 6–8.

62. Prince and Šesták, *The Royal Ruler*, 107.

63. See HU OSA 300-1-2-68887; Records of Radio Free Europe/ Radio Liberty Research Institute: General Records: Information Items, "Interview with Czech Surgeon," March 16, 1956. That Western radio listening became a pleasure that some associated with the experience of driving in their own private cars is suggested, furthermore, by HU OSA 300-1-2-75936; Records of Radio Free Europe/ Radio Liberty Research Institute: General Records: Information Items "Interview with a Czech Student," November 5, 1956. See also Tomek, *Československá redakce Radio Free Europe*, 311.

64. HU OSA 300-1-2-33203; Records of Radio Free Europe/Radio Liberty Research Institute: General Records: Information Items; "Faithful Listeners of Rias in the CSR," April 9, 1953.

65. Martin Matiska, in a discussion with the author, June 2020.

66. For elaboration, see "Falco byl miláčkem Čechů. Smrt nejslavnějšího evropského zpěváka je dodnes záhadou." *Eurozpravy.cz*, last modified July 1, 2020, https://eurozpravy.cz/magazin/254917-falco-byl-milackem-cechu-smrt -nejslavnejsiho-evropskeho-zpevaka-je-dodnes-zahadou/.

67. Tomek, *Československá redakce Radio Free Europe*, 305.

68. For a more detailed history of the consolidation of statewide Austrian radio, see Berthold Molden, " 'Die Ost-West Drehscheibe': Österreichs Medien im Kalten Krieg," in *Zwischen den Blöcken. NATO, Warschauer Pakt und Österreich*, ed. Manfried Rachensteiner (Vienna: Böhlau, 2010), 687–774.

69. HU OSA 300-6-2 Box 2—Media and Opinion Research Dept. E Euro (Jan-

uary 1966–December 1967), "Listening to Western Stations in Czechoslovakia, III, June 1966."

70. R. Eugene Parta, head of the Radio Free Europe/ Radio Liberty department analyzing listener data in the 1970s and 1980s, makes this point explicitly. See Johnson and Parta, *Cold War Broadcasting*, 82–84.

71. Molden, " 'Die Ost-West Drehscheibe," 726.

72. Bren, *The Greengrocer and His TV*, 121.

73. See, for example, Molden, " 'Die Ost-West Drehscheibe' " and Jiří Čistecký, "Tschechoslowakei und Österreich um 1968," last modified November 19, 2020, https://www.mzv.cz/file/2923100/Tschechoslowakei_und_Osterreich_um_ 1968__Jiri_Cistecky_.pdf.

74. HU OSA 300-6-2 Box 2—Media and Opinion Research Dept. E Euro (January 1966–December 1967), "Listening to Western Stations in Czechoslovakia, III, June 1966."

75. HU OSA 300-6-2 Box 2—Media and Opinion Research Dept. E Euro (January 1966–December 1967), "Listening to Western Stations in Czechoslovakia, III, June 1966."

76. Bösch and Classen, "Bridge over Troubled Water?," 556.

77. For film details, see https://www.imdb.com/title/tt0129764/. Last modified June 17, 2020.

78. " 'Autofahrer Unterwegs' feiert 90. Geburtstag," last modified October 4, 2019, https://www.nachrichten.at/kultur/Autofahrer-unterwegs-feiert-90 -Geburtstag;art16,2704978.

79. " 'Autofahrer Unterwegs' feiert 90. Geburtstag."

80. See Perzi et al., *Nachbarn*, 337 and Yuliya Komska, *The Icon Curtain: The Cold War's Quiet Border* (Chicago and London: University of Chicago Press, 2015), 140.

81. Perzi et al., *Nachbarn*, 342.

82. HU OSA 300-1-2-3239; Records of Radio Free Europe/Radio Liberty Research Institute: General Records: Information Items; "Warm Welcome to the Guests from East Germany," July 30, 1951 and HU OSA 300-1-2-9922; Records of Radio Free Europe/Radio Liberty Research Institute: General Records: Information Items; "Austrian Athletes Not Allowed to Move Freely While in Slovakia," October 30, 1951.

83. Perzi et al., *Nachbarn*, 342.

84. Vaněk, "Twenty Years in Shades of Grey?"

85. HU OSA 300-6-2 Box 2—Media and Opinion Research Dept. E Euro (January 1966–December 1967), "Listening to Western Stations in Czechoslovakia, III, June 1966."

272 Notes to Chapter 5

86. Suzanne Lommers, *Europe—On Air: Interwar Projects for Radio Broadcasting* (Amsterdam: Amsterdam University Press, 2012), 275.

87. NA CR box 29. Ministerstvo Informací, doc. 65359, "Všeobecné poznámky z týdne od 18. do 24. října 1948," November 13, 1948. On RWR's antipathy toward jazz, see Wagnleitner, *Coca-Colonization*, 120.

88. Wagnleitner, *Coca-Colonization*, 113.

89. Ibid., 117.

90. Ibid., 119.

91. Ibid., 113.

92. HU OSA 300-1-2-20487; Records of Radio Free Europe/Radio Liberty Research Institute: General Records: Information Items; "Criticism of Western Broadcasts," May 30, 1952.

93. HU OSA 300-1-2-31330; Records of Radio Free Europe/Radio Liberty Research Institute: General Records: Information Items; "Entertainment in CSR Today," February 25, 1953.

94. "Criticism of Western Broadcasts." See also HU OSA 300-1-2-19664; Records of Radio Free Europe/Radio Liberty Research Institute: General Records: Information Items; "Listening Habits and Opinion about World Events of a Worker," May 15, 1952, and HU OSA 300-1-2-20027; Records of Radio Free Europe/Radio Liberty Research Institute: General Records: Information Items; "Criticism of Western Broadcasts," May 21, 1952.

95. Wagnleitner, *Coca-Colonization*, 119.

96. Evans, *Between Truth and Time*, Kindle position 242.

97. Ibid., 288.

98. Ibid., 303.

99. The most famous example of this is *Mikrofórum*, which began broadcasting on Czechoslovak Radio to counter RFE music programming in 1965. See Pospíšil, "Inspiration, Subversion and Appropriation" and Tomek, *Československá redakce Radio Free Europe*.

100. Michel de Certeau, *The Practice of Everyday Life* (Berkeley, Los Angeles, and London: University of California Press, 1984), xviii.

101. See Johnson and Parta, *Cold War Broadcasting*, 82–84.

102. News and entertainment are not, of course, incompatible. They were understood by radio professionals at the period, however, as two separate genres with different, if overlapping, conventions. These discrete genres, furthermore, were intended to elicit different forms of audience response.

103. Bacher, cited in Molden, " 'Die Ost-West Drehscheibe,' " 720.

104. Tworek, *News from Germany*, 5.

105. Bösch and Classen, "Bridge over Troubled Water?," 566.

Notes to Chapters 5 and 6    273

106. Komska, it should be noted, also questions just how "quiet" the Czecho-slovak-German border was. For more, see *The Icon Curtain: The Cold War's Quiet Border.*

**Chapter 6**

1. CRA, DF04317, *Velký svět u mikrofonu.* December 25, 1963.

2. Ulf Hannerz highlights that such wildlife stories constitute a staple of re-porting from Africa. See Ulf Hannerz, *Foreign News: Exploring the World of Foreign Correspondents* (Chicago and London: University of Chicago Press, 2004), 130–131.

3. For a more vituperative and less comical example of this, see Jiří Hronek, *V široširém světě* (Prague: Státní nakladatelství dětské knihy, 1954).

4. Zdeňka Kotalová, "Redakce mezinárodního života Československého rozhlasu v rozmezí let 1966–1969," Unpublished diploma thesis, Charles University Faculty of Social Sciences, 2012, 2–3.

5. Milan Rykl, "Renesance rozhlasu 1959–1968," *Od Mikrofonu k posluchačům: z osmi desetiletí českého rozhlasu,* ed. Eva Ješutová (Prague: Radioservis, 2003), 293.

6. Many of them published books. Šťovíčková and Kyncl both made forays into radio drama and, in 1968, Kyncl starred in a film, *Muž na útěku (Man on the Run).*

7. HU OSA, 300-30-13, Information Items (1965–1968), Item 10/68, February 9, 1968, p. 2.

8. Ibid.

9. CRA box Věra Šťovíčková, Korespondence, letter to Věra Šťovíčková from Dr. Jan Pixa, dated November 28, 1968.

10. Kotalová, "Redakce mezinárodního života Československého rozhlasu v 60. Letech," 86.

11. See Tony Judt, *Postwar* (New York: Penguin, 2005), 438.

12. See Jana Suková, "Svaz českých novinářů v období Pražského jara," Bach-elor's thesis, Charles University, 2013, 20.

13. Hannerz, *Foreign News,* 93.

14. Ryszard Kapuściński makes these claims in *The Shadow of the Sun* (New York: Penguin, 1998). They are disputed by his biographer, Artur Domosławski, *Ryszard Kapuściński: A Life* (London: Verso, 2013).

15. Petr Drulák, "Novinář Jiří Dienstbier," in *Jiří Dienstbier: Rozhlasový Zpravodaj, 1958–1969* (Prague: Radioservis, 2013), 11.

16. Věra Šťovíčková, *Afrika rok jedna* (Prague: SPN, 1963), 14.

17. This is how Milan Rykl, for example, narrates it in Ješutová, *Od Mikrofonu k posluchačům,* 291.

274 Notes to Chapter 6

18. Věra Šťovíčková-Heroldová, *Po světě s mikrofonem* (Prague: Radioservis, 2009), 20–21.

19. Ibid., 16.

20. Ibid., 49.

21. She had spent two years previously in Poland as Czechoslovak Radio's foreign correspondent there. Ibid., 43–45.

22. Philip Muehlenbeck, *Czechoslovakia in Africa, 1945–1968* (New York and London: Palgrave Macmillan, 2016), 61.

23. For the goods that Czechoslovakia exported, see Muehlenbeck, *Czechoslovakia in Africa*, 61. For critical analysis of memories of the dearth of tropical fruit, see Miroslav Vaněk and Pavel Mücke, *Velvet Revolutions: An Oral History of Czech Society* (New York: Oxford University Press, 2016), 140.

24. Muehlenbeck notes that Guinea "became the center of Czechoslovakia's massive propaganda efforts on the African continent" in *Czechoslovakia in Africa*, 61. See also Petr Zídek, *Československo a francouzská Afrika, 1948–1968* (Prague: Libri, 2006), 65.

25. See, for example, her interview with Sudanese football team Al Hilal's Czech coach on April 20, 1965, or her journey to the construction site of the Aswan Dam with a team of Egyptologists, in CRA box Věra Šťovíčková, Afrika, 1965, Věra Šťovíčková, "Mají pravdu ti Češi, kteří říkají . . ." and "Země, která už zítra nebude."

26. Šťovíčková, *Afrika rok jedna*, 17.

27. The Czechoslovak economy entered into recession in 1962, and its dire state spurred a host of reform proposals, as well as leading to the abandonment of the third five-year plan. See Tony Judt, *Postwar*, 427. In an oral history, George Knessl remembered what this meant for individual workers, recalling that by the mid-1960s, "our factory was working at something like only 16% capacity. I thought I would have to emigrate for economic reasons." See National Czech and Slovak Museum and Library interview with George Knessl, last modified September 3, 2019, https://ncsml.omeka.net/items/show/4057.

28. Muehlenbeck, *Czechoslovakia in Africa*, 134.

29. CRA DF09837—*Sedmilháři z rozhlasu*, dated May 15, 1968; box Věra Šťovíčková, Afrika, 1968, Věra Šťovíčková, "Celnice je barometr," and box Věra Šťovíčková, Afrika, 1958–1960, "Pobřeží Slonoviny—klín ve společenství svobody."

30. CRA box Věra Šťovíčková, Korespondence, letter from Ksenia Ivanovová to Věra Šťovíčková, dated December 20, 1968.

31. Šťovíčková-Heroldová, *Po světě s mikrofonem*, 53–54.

32. Šťovíčková sent many of these telegrams from the local Czechoslovak

Embassy. See, for example, CRA box Věra Šťovíčková, Afrika, 1965, "Sudanský tisk vycházející jak v jazyce arabském..."

33. Journalist Věra Homolová suggested this in an oral history recorded on September 27, 2016.

34. Věra Šťovíčková, *Bouře nad rovníkem* (Prague: Magnet, 1967), 45.

35. Šťovíčková, *Bouře nad rovníkem*, 49.

36. Lutz Mükke, *Korrespondenten im Kalten Krieg: Zwischen Propaganda und Selbstbehaputung* (Cologne: Herbert von Halem, 2014), 20.

37. Ibid.

38. Ibid., 29.

39. Šťovíčková-Heroldová, *Po světě s mikrofonem*, 76.

40. This clearly continued to rankle Šťovíčková many years later. See Šťovíčková-Heroldová, *Po světě s mikrofonem*, 82.

41. I have looked for materials produced by/about Věra Šťovíčková in the secret police archive in Prague. Debriefings from the 1950s and 1960s did not end up there. Her file dates from the 1970s and follows her movements and meetings with foreigners once she was dismissed from the radio and after she signed Charter 77.

42. Petr Zídek, *Češi v srdci temnoty* (Prague: Universum, 2013). See also the work of Mikuláš Pešta, for example, "L'internationalisme tchécoslovaque en Afrique à travers l'exemple de l'aide à la construction d'infrastructures militaires et de securité en Guinée, 1958–1965," in *Marges impériales en dialogue. Échanges transferts, interactions et influences croisés entre les espaces postcoloniaux francophones et la périphérie soviétique européenne dans la seconde moitié du XXe siècle*, ed. Matthieu Boisdron and Krisztián Bene, 159–170 (Pécs: Université de Pécs, 2022).

43. Jiří Dienstbier, "Fízlové, střezte se žen," in *Jiří Dienstbier*, 209–210.

44. Mükke, *Korrespondenten im Kalten Krieg*, 20.

45. Muehlenbeck, *Czechoslovakia in Africa*, 2. In his excellent overview of Prague's relations with francophone African states (which clearly inspired Muehlenbeck's work), Zídek elaborates that Czechoslovakia had embassies in Guinea, Ghana, and Ethiopia at this time, and consular representation in Congo and South Africa. See Zídek, *Československo a francouzská Afrika*, 30.

46. Ulf Hannerz argues that a media monopoly of information on Africa remains to this day. See *Foreign News*, 136.

47. CRA box Věra Šťovíčková, Afrika, 1968, "Svět u mikrofonu," dated May 20, 1968.

48. CRA box Věra Šťovíčková, Afrika, 1968, Věra Šťovíčková, interview with Sylva Součková for the Anglophone African service of Radio Prague, April 8, 1968.

276  Notes to Chapter 6

49. Šťovíčková, *Afrika rok jedna*, 35.

50. CRA box Věra Šťovíčková, Afrika, 1958–1960, Věra Šťovíčková, "Mikrofon mladých," dated July 24, 1960.

51. James Mark and Péter Apor, "Socialism Goes Global: Decolonization and the Making of a New Culture of Internationalism in Socialist Hungary, 1956–1989," *The Journal of Modern History* 87, no. 4 (December 2015): 866.

52. CRA box Věra Šťovíčková, Afrika, 1968, Věra Šťovíčková, interview with Sylva Součková for the Anglophone African service of Radio Prague, April 8, 1968.

53. Ibid.

54. Ibid.

55. NA CR. Box 4—Afrika. 1261/0/44 A ÚV KSČ Antonín Novotný—zahraničí. "Záznam o průběhu konzultací skupiny MZV . . . na MIDu SSSR k otazkám Afriky ve dnech 21.–25. listopadu 1961," p. 51.

56. Mark and Apor, "Socialism Goes Global," 867.

57. Neal Ascherson, foreword to Ryszard Kapuścinski, *The Other* (London: Verso, 2006), 9.

58. Šťovíčková, *Bouře nad rovníkem*, 55.

59. Ibid., 45.

60. Ibid., 75.

61. Ibid.

62. Zbyněk Kožnar, on the cover of Šťovíčková, *Bouře nad rovníkem*.

63. CRA box Věra Šťovíčková, Afrika, 1965. Věra Šťovíčková, "Myšlení XX. Století" for *Plamen* magazine.

64. Ibid.

65. CRA box Věra Šťovíčková, Afrika, 1968, Věra Šťovíčková, interview with Sylva Součková for the Anglophone African service of Radio Prague, April 8, 1968.

66. Ibid.

67. Ibid.

68. Ibid.

69. She suggested, for example, that she took the words of American journalist John Gunther (that "Africa is lost") into consideration when assembling a fifteen-part series of radio reportage about the African continent that aired between July and August 1959. Au contraire, Šťovíčková found the continent taking its place among equals after centuries of being subject to slavery, colonialism, and oppression. See CRA box Věra Šťovíčková, Afrika, 1958–1960, "RN 19:00, 6.8.59."

70. CRA box Věra Šťovíčková, Afrika, 1968, Věra Šťovíčková, interview with

Sylva Součková for the Anglophone African service of Radio Prague, April 8, 1968. For the lack of direct speech in Šťovíčková's reporting see, for example, CRA box Věra Šťovíčková, Afrika, 1958–1960, "Hodinka s presidentem," in which Šťovíčková meets with Guinean leader Ahmed Sékou Touré and largely describes him and his words in reported speech. For the negative example of the Western journalist, see CRA box Věra Šťovíčková, Afrika, 1958–1960. Věra Šťovíčková, "Kolonialismus do muzea," dated July 12, 1959.

71. Luboš Dobrovský, interviewed in Slava Volný ml. (ed.), *Jsme s Vámi, Buďte s námi* (Prague: Prostor, 2013), 45.

72. Šťovíčková criticized the tourist industry particularly harshly in a radio report about Côte d'Ivoire in 1959. See CRA box Věra Šťovíčková, Afrika, 1958–1960, Věra Šťovíčková, "Pobřeží Slonoviny—klín ve společenství svobody."

73. Šťovíčková, *Bouře nad rovníkem*, 290.

74. Curt Beck, "Czechoslovakia's Penetration of Africa, 1955–1962," *World Politics* 15, no. 3 (1963): 416.

75. CRA box Věra Šťovíčková, Afrika, 1968, Věra Šťovíčková, interview with Sylva Součková for the Anglophone African service of Radio Prague. April 8, 1968.

76. Šťovíčková reiterated this point in an interview with Slava Volný ml. in *Jsme s Vámi, Buďte s námi*, 63.

77. CRA box Věra Šťovíčková, Afrika, 1958–1960, Věra Šťovíčková, "Mikrofon mladých," dated July 24, 1960. On the history of this program, see Rykl, "Renesance rozhlasu," 312.

78. CRA box Věra Šťovíčková, Afrika, 1958–1960, Věra Šťovíčková, "Mikrofon mladých," dated July 24, 1960.

79. See Šťovíčková, *Afrika rok jedna*, 16.

80. CRA box Věra Šťovíčková, Afrika, 1958–1960, Věra Šťovíčková, "Kolonialismus do muzea," dated July 12, 1959.

81. CRA box Věra Šťovíčková, Afrika, 1958–1960, Věra Šťovíčková, "Mikrofon mladých," dated July 24, 1960.

82. Ibid.

83. Šťovíčková, *Afrika rok jedna*, 14.

84. For two examples of this, see the National Czech and Slovak Museum and Library's oral history interviews with Vladimir Pochop, last modified September 3, 2019, https://ncsml.omeka.net/items/show/4236 and Vojtěch Mastný, last modified September 3, 2019, https://ncsml.omeka.net/items/show/4240, interview with Katja David Fox.

85. CRA, DF04318, *Velký svět u mikrofonu*, dated December 12, 1963.

86. Ibid.

278  Notes to Chapter 6

87. In a reflective piece upon his time in France, Čierný again wheeled out an interview with a model as representative of the work of which he was proudest. See Ján Čierny, "Rozhlasový korešpondent pod Eiffelovkou," in *Tu Bratislava: Rozhlas v retrospektíve a perspektíve* (Bratislava: Obzor, 1966), 96–97.

88. CRA, DF04318, *Velký svět u mikrofonu*, dated December 25, 1963.

89. Čierny, "Rozhlasový korešpondent pod Eiffelovkou," 94.

90. CRA, DF04318, *Velký svět u mikrofonu*, dated December 25, 1963.

91. Ibid.

92. The year this audio was produced, 1963, saw the release of *From Russia with Love*—the second in the series of film adaptations of Fleming's books, which the author had been publishing since 1952. Two of Fleming's books were translated and released in Czechoslovakia in 1968 and 1969—*Dr. No* and *Goldfinger.*

93. Čierny, "Rozhlasový korešpondent pod Eiffelovkou," 96.

94. Dienstbier, "Fízlové, střezte se žen" in *Jiří Dienstbier,* 209–210.

95. Ibid., 210.

96. Ibid.

97. Dienstbier, "Dcery americké revoluce," in *Jiří Dienstbier,* 211.

98. Ibid.

99. Ibid.

100. Ibid.

101. Milan Kundera, *The Joke* (New York: Faber and Faber, 1992), 176.

102. Ibid., 254.

103. Ibid., 176.

104. Ibid.

105. Kundera, *The Joke,* 249 Another character, Jaroslav, suggested Helena's interview technique consisted of "disgorging" information from unwilling respondents, 254.

106. Kundera's protagonist Ludvík mused that he disliked radio journalists the most among a profession he despised: "In my view newspapers have one extenuating attribute: they make no noise. Their tediousness is silent; they can be put aside, thrown into the wastebasket. The tediousness of the radio lacks that extenuating attribute; it persecutes us in cafés, restaurants, trains, even during our visits to people who have become incapable of living without nonstop feeding of the ears" (see pp. 175–176). Here, the author repackaged sentiments about the proliferation and ubiquity of radio articulated since the rise to popularity of the transistor radio in Czechoslovakia in the early 1960s.

107. Kundera, *The Joke,* 175–176.

Notes to Chapter 6  279

108. Ješutová, *Od Mikrofonu k posluchačům*, 294.

109. Ibid., 293.

110. The Czechoslovak Union of Writers is often understood to have ushered in the Prague Spring through its criticisms of earlier Communist practices and the contemporary limits to the freedom of speech at its congress in 1967. It is true that the Union of Journalists distanced itself from these criticisms at the time. But the journalistic profession was much more reformist in attitude than the leadership of its union would suggest. There was considerable overlap between both vocations. Ludvík Vaculík, one of the writers penalized for his statements at the 1967 writer's conference was, for example, a prominent Czechoslovak Radio reporter. Šťovíčková, moreover, contributed to the Union of Writers' periodical, *Plamen*. Many writers were members of both unions. See Suková, "Svaz českých novinářů v období Pražského jara," 20.

111. CRA box Věra Šťovíčková, Korespondence, letter from Ksenia Ivanovová to Věra Šťovíčková, dated December 20, 1968.

112. See Article 20.3 of the 1960 Czechoslovak Constitution, https://www.psp .cz/docs/texts/constitution_1960.html. Accessed January 9, 2020.

113. Interview with Šťovíčková in Slava Volný ml. (ed.), *Jsme s Vámi, Buďte s námi*, 64.

114. Šťovíčková-Heroldová, *Po světě s mikrofonem*, 47.

115. CRA box Věra Šťovíčková, Afrika, 1968, Věra Šťovíčková, interview with Sylva Součková for the Anglophone African service of Radio Prague. April 8, 1968.

116. CRA box Věra Šťovíčková, Afrika, 1958–1960, Věra Šťovíčková, "Mikrofon mladých," dated July 24, 1960.

117. Šťovíčková-Heroldová, *Po světě s mikrofonem*, 55–56.

118. See CRA box Věra Šťovíčková, Korespondence, "p.f. 69—Lidé a země."

119. See, for example, CRA box Věra Šťovíčková, Afrika, 1958–1960; "Zahraniční rubrika—Št," dated January 3, 1960, and an interview with Gadagbé, dated April 26, 1960.

120. Šťovíčková, *Afrika rok jedna*, 44.

121. CRA box Věra Šťovíčková, Korespondence, letter from Ksenia Ivanovová to Věra Šťovíčková, dated December 20, 1968.

122. CRA box Věra Šťovíčková, Korespondence, letter from Jitka Novohradská to Věra Šťovíčková, dated September 9, 1968.

123. CRA box Věra Šťovíčková, Korespondence, letter from a Mrs. Němcová to Věra Šťovíčková, dated October 8, 1968.

124. CRA box Věra Šťovíčková, Korespondence, letter from Marta Bednaříková to Věra Šťovíčková, dated October 9, 1968.

280 Notes to Chapters 6 and 7

125. CRA box Věra Šťovíčková, Korespondence, letter from Margareta Kalabová to Věra Šťovíčková, dated November 22, 1968.

126. CRA box Věra Šťovíčková, Korespondence, letter from Věra Vortelová to Věra Šťovíčková, dated November 9, 1968.

127. CRA box Věra Šťovíčková, Korespondence, letter from Milada Přikrylová to Věra Šťovíčková, dated October 9, 1968.

128. See Richard Dyer, *Stars* (London: British Film Institute, 1998), 26, 34.

129. Simon Huxtable, "Making News Soviet: Rethinking Journalistic Professionalism after Stalin, 1953–1970," *Contemporary European History* 27, no. 1 (February 2018): 79.

130. Muehlenbeck, *Czechoslovakia in Africa*, 87–123.

131. Šťovíčková-Heroldová, *Po světě s mikrofonem*, 81.

132. Ibid.

133. Ibid., 82.

134. CRA box Věra Šťovíčková, Afrika, 1968, letter from Věra Šťovíčková to an unnamed comrade, dated March 19, 1968.

135. Muehlenbeck, *Czechoslovakia in Africa*, 119–120.

136. CRA box Věra Šťovíčková, Afrika, 1968, letter from Věra Šťovíčková to an unnamed comrade, dated March 19, 1968.

137. Ibid.

138. CRA box Věra Šťovíčková, Afrika, 1968, letter from Věra Šťovíčková to an unnamed comrade, dated March 19, 1968.

139. The letter was addressed to a Foreign Ministry official, as Šťovíčková writes about "private debates which have taken place in places responsible outside of the Foreign Ministry as well." See CRA box Věra Šťovíčková, Afrika, 1968, letter from Věra Šťovíčková to an unnamed comrade, dated March 19, 1968.

140. Ibid.

141. See, for example, CRA box Věra Šťovíčková, Afrika, 1968, "Československo a nigerijská válka," radio script dated May 7, 1968.

142. CRA box Věra Šťovíčková, Afrika, 1968, Oldřich Pěta, "Čs. Letadla nebombardují," *Svoboda* 77, no. 184, dated April 28, 1968.

143. See Rosamund Johnston, "Southern Hospitality? Czechoslovak Relations with Africa until 1989," *Czech Journal of Contemporary History* 5 (2017): 175–182.

## Chapter 7

1. The example which will be examined in most depth in this chapter is "Letter from Czech Communist Politicians to Brezhnev Requesting Soviet Intervention in the Prague Spring," August 1968, History and Public Policy Pro-

gram Digital Archive, published in Czech in *Hospodářské noviny*, July 17, 1992. Translated for CWIHP by Mark Kramer, last modified January 9, 2019 (henceforth referred to as "Letter . . . to Brezhnev").

2. See for example Ústav pro soudobé dějiny, "Stenografický záznam porady šesti komunistických stran v Drážďanech 23. března 1968," last modified October 3, 2022, http://www.68.usd.cas.cz/files/dokumenty/edice/323.pdf.

3. Melissa Feinberg, *Communism in Eastern Europe* (London: Routledge, 2021), 102.

4. Ibid.

5. Pavel Kohout, *Z deníku kontrarevolucionáře* (Brno: Větrné mlýny, 2013), 30.

6. Teraz.sk. "Československý prezident Antonín Novotný sa narodil pred 110 rokmi," last modified August 3, 2022, https://www.teraz.sk/magazin/ceskoslovensky-prezident-antonin-novotny/109821-clanok.html.

7. CRA_DF07169/2, "Vnitropolitický komentář M. Weinera," dated March 10, 1968.

8. Kevin McDermott, *Communist Czechoslovakia, 1945–1989: A Political and Social History* (London: Palgrave, 2015), 126–127.

9. See Czech Television. "Zrušení cenzury Národním shromážděním," last modified November 20, 2018, https://www.ceskatelevize.cz/vse-o-ct/historie/ceskoslovenska-televize/1968-1969/1968/zruseni- cenzury-narodnim -shromazdenim/.

10. Ludvík Vaculík, "Two Thousand Words That Belongs to Workers, Farmers, Officials, Scientists, Artists, and Everybody," last modified August 4, 2022, https://www.pwf.cz/rubriky/projects/1968/ludvik-vaculik-two-thousand -words_849.html. Henceforth referred to as Vaculík, "Two Thousand Words."

11. For the full minutes of this meeting (in Czech), see Ústav pro soudobé dějiny, "Stenografický záznam porady šesti komunistických stran v Drážďanech 23. března 1968," last modified October 3, 2022, http://www.68.usd.cas.cz/files/dokumenty/edice/323.pdf.

12. Petr Andreas, "Od odpovědnosti ke kontrole—cenzura za rané normalizace (září 1968—srpen 1969)," *Soudobé dějiny* 27, nos. 3–4: 452.

13. "Letter . . . to Brezhnev."

14. Andreas, "Od odpovědnosti ke kontrole," 439.

15. Kieran Williams, *The Prague Spring and Its Aftermath: Czechoslovak Politics, 1968–1970* (Cambridge: Cambridge University Press, 1997), 4.

16. Eva Ješutová (ed.), *Od mikrofonu k posluchačům. Z osmi desetiletí českého rozhlasu* (Prague: Radioservis, 2003), 295.

17. CIA-ER IM 68–118. "Intelligence Memorandum: Broadcasting in the

Czechoslovak Crisis," last modified November 14, 2018, https://www.cia.gov/library/readingroom/document/cia-rdp85t00875r001600010068-6.

18. Slava Volný ml. (ed.), *Jsme s Vámi, Buďte s námi* (Prague: Prostor, 2013), 9.

19. Ješutová, *Od Mikrofonu k posluchačům*, 321.

20. Jiří Černý, "Tranzistorový teror," in *Jiří Černý . . . na bílém* (Prague: Galén, 2014), 25.

21. Kohout, *Z deníku kontrarevolucionáře*, 208.

22. CRA_AF07679/1: "Vnitropolitický komentář red. Milana Weinera" (dated only "1968").

23. Jiří Macoun. "Nejužitečnější vánoční dárek 20. století. Tranzistor slaví 65 let," last modified August 17, 2021, https://www.idnes.cz/technet/technika/tranzistor-65-let.A121220_143704_tec_technika_kuz.

24. HU OSA 300-6-2, Box 3, Media and Opinion Research Department, Eastern Europe (January 1968–December 1969), "Listening to Western Broadcasts in Czechoslovakia before and after the Invasion," January 1969.

25. CIA-ER IM 68–118. "Intelligence Memorandum: Broadcasting in the Czechoslovak Crisis," last modified November 14, 2018, https://www.cia.gov/library/readingroom/document/cia-rdp85t00875r001600010068-6.

26. CRA_AF07679/1: "Vnitropolitický komentář red. Milana Weinera."

27. Ibid.

28. Ibid.

29. Ibid.

30. Paulina Bren, *The Greengrocer and His TV: The Culture of Communism after the 1968 Prague Spring* (Ithaca, NY, and London: Cornell University Press, 2010), 21.

31. David Edgerton, *The Shock of the Old* (London: Profile, 2019), xi.

32. Mark Kurlansky, *1968: The Year That Rocked the World* (New York: Ballantine, 2004), Kindle position 2%.

33. Williams, *The Prague Spring and Its Aftermath*, 4.

34. "Listening to Western Broadcasts in Czechoslovakia before and after the Invasion."

35. See Bren, *The Greengrocer and His TV.*

36. CRA box Věra Šťovíčková, Afrika, 1968, Věra Šťovíčková, interview with Sylva Součková for the Anglophone African service of Radio Prague. April 8, 1968.

37. CRA_AF08585/8, "Vnitropolitický komentář M. Weinera," dated March 26, 1968.

38. CRA_DF07169/1, "Vnitropolitický komentář M. Weinera," dated March 8, 1968.

Notes to Chapter 7 283

39. Jana Suková, "Svaz českých novinářů v období Pražského jara," Bachelor's thesis, Charles University, 2013, 27.

40. Muriel Blaive, "The Reform Communist Interpretation of the Stalinist Period in Czechoslovak Historiography and its Legacy," in *East European Politics and Societies* (November 2021), 6–7.

41. See CRA_DF07715_DF39682—*Padesátá léta 1. pás.* (2.6.1968), CRA_DF 07716_DF39684—*Padesátá léta 2. pás* and CRA_DF07717_DF39685—*Padesata leta 3. Pás,* June 2, 1968.

42. Kyncl only interjected once in an interview with Rudolf Slánský Jr. When the latter suggested that he believed the show trials were a product of the socialist revolution, Kyncl added that all revolutions—not just socialist ones—could result in such excesses. Thus he voiced his defense of socialism as a political system.

43. See CRA_DF07718_DF3688—*Spirála.*

44. For his story, see Martin Groman, *Stanislav Budín: Komunista bez legitimace* (Prague: ÚSTR, 2015).

45. Martin Schulze Wessel, *Pražské jaro: Průlom do nového světa* (Prague: Argo, 2018), 183.

46. "Letter . . . to Brezhnev."

47. "Letter . . . to Brezhnev."

48. CRA box Věra Šťovíčková, Afrika, 1968, Věra Šťovíčková, interview with Sylva Součková for the Anglophone African service of Radio Prague. April 8, 1968.

49. CRA_DF07169/2, "Vnitropolitický komentář M. Weinera," dated March 10, 1968.

50. Ibid.

51. Suková, "Svaz českých novinářů," 31.

52. For a key text on this topic from this year, see Václav Havel, "Na téma opozice" ("On the theme of an opposition"), last modified January 2, 2019, http://www.68.usd.cas.cz/files/dokumenty/edice/404.pdf. On the contrary, in "Two Thousand Words," Vaculík suggested that renewed faith in the Communist Party as the agent of democratization was required.

53. CRA_DF07169/2, "Vnitropolitický komentář M. Weinera," dated March 10, 1968.

54. Ibid.

55. Ibid.

56. Věra Šťovíčková-Heroldová, *Po světě s mikrofonem* (Prague: Radioservis, 2009), 102.

57. Heda Margolius Kovály, *Under a Cruel Star: A Life in Prague, 1941–1968* (London: Granta, 1986), 180.

284 Notes to Chapter 7

58. Schulze Wessel, *Pražské jaro*, 13.

59. Bren, *The Greengrocer and His TV*, 24.

60. "Letter . . . to Brezhnev."

61. CRA box 41. "Záznam o poradě svolané k projednání otázek veřejných estrád . . . ," dated July 23, 1954.

62. CRA box 41. "Jak organisovat v redakci práci s dopisy?" dated April 14, 1955.

63. CRA HA21662_Karel Kyncl, "Rozhlasová romance."

64. Christoph Classen, "Captive Audience? GDR Radio in the Mirror of Listeners' Mail," *Cold War History* 13, no. 2 (2013): 241.

65. Ješutová, *Od Mikrofonu k posluchačům*, 332.

66. Andreas, "Od odpovědnosti ke kontrole," 456.

67. CIA-RDP79–00891A001100050001–6. "Czechoslovakia Handbook," last modified August 31, 2021, https://www.cia.gov/readingroom/docs/CIA-RDP79 -00891A001100050001-6.pdf.

68. See CRA box Věra Šťovíčková, Afrika, 1968. "Písníčky po telefonu," undated (but presumably from March 26 given the nature of the news covered).

69. Suková, "Svaz českých novinářů," 23.

70. Martin Štoll, *Television and Totalitarianism in Czechoslovakia: From the First Democratic Republic to the Fall of Communism* (Sydney: Bloomsbury, 2018), 160.

71. Ibid.

72. Kohout, *Z deníku kontrarevolucionáře*, 36.

73. Volný, *Jsme s Vámi, Buďte s námi*, 90–91.

74. Suková, "Svaz českých novinářů," 23.

75. Andreas, "Od odpovědnosti ke kontrole," 460.

76. Jiří Dienstbier, *Jiří Dienstbier: Rozhlasový Zpravodaj, 1958–1969* (Prague: Radioservis, 2013), 226.

77. Dienstbier, *Jiří Dienstbier: Rozhlasový zpravodaj*, 226.

78. Volný, *Jsme s Vámi, Buďte s námi*, 26.

79. Ibid.

80. Ibid., 39.

81. Kohout, *Z deníku kontrarevolucionáře*, 30.

82. "Letter . . . to Brezhnev."

83. Ibid.

84. CRA_DF07169/2, "Vnitropolitický komentář M. Weinera," dated March 10, 1968.

85. For appeals to establish such a bureaucracy, see Vaculík, "Two Thousand Words"; on what today's preoccupations are, see Andrea Czepek, Melanie Hell-

wig, and Eva Nowak (eds.), *Press Freedom and Pluralism in Europe: Concepts and Conditions* (Bristol: Intellect, 2009), 19.

86. Vaculík, "Two Thousand Words."

87. CRA box Věra Šťovíčková, Korespondence. Letter from Josef Jarolím to Věra Šťovíčková, dated November 4, 1968.

88. Ibid.

89. See Bren, *The Greengrocer and His TV*, 28.

90. Kohout, *Z deníku kontrarevolucionáře*, 86.

91. Ješutová, *Od Mikrofonu k posluchačům*, 345.

92. Andreas, "Od odpovědnosti ke kontrole," 448.

93. Ibid., 475.

94. Ibid.

95. Petr Pithart, "Novinář Jiří Dienstbier," last modified January 17, 2019, https://www.novinky.cz/kultura/salon/303097-petr-pithart-novinar-jiri-dienstbier.html.

96. For more on *Videožurnal*, see Alice Lovejoy, " 'Video Knows no Borders'— Samizdat Television and the Unofficial Public Sphere in 'Normalized' Czechoslovakia," in *Samizdat, Tamizdat and Beyond: Transnational Media during and after Socialism,* ed. Friederike Kind-Kovács and Jessie Labov (New York: Berghahn, 2013) , 206–217.

97. Miloslav Turek, interview with Rosamund Johnston, November 7, 2019.

98. See Týdeník Rozhlas. "Rozhlasová stopa Ludvíka Vaculíka," last modified January 17, 2018, http://www.radioservis-as.cz/archiv15/26_15/26_tema.htm.

99. See Karel Kyncl's unedited Vietnam tapes, now accessible at CRA.

100. Jonathan Bolton, *World of Dissent: The Plastic People of the Universe, Charter 77, and Czech Culture under Communism* (Cambridge, MA: Harvard University Press, 2012), 11.

101. See Pithart, "Novinář Jiří Dienstbier."

102. See, for example, Jan Pokorný, "Zdeněk Svěrák: V nouzi se rychle ukáže, kdo je srab a kdo není," last modified November 3, 2021, https://radiozurnal.rozhlas.cz/zdenek-sverak-v-nouzi-se-rychle-ukaze-kdo-je-srab-a-kdo-neni-7555708.

103. CRA box Věra Šťovíčková, Korespondence. Letter from Hana Jandová and Dana Součková to Věra Šťovíčková, 1968.

104. CRA box Věra Šťovíčková, Korespondence. Letter from Marta Bednaříková to Věra Šťovíčková, dated October 9, 1968.

105. CRA box Věra Šťovíčková, Korespondence. Letter from Josef Jarolím to Věra Šťovíčková, dated November 4, 1968. For Milan Kundera on forgetting

during normalization, see *The Book of Laughter and Forgetting* (New York: Harper, 1999).

106. Williams, *The Prague Spring and Its Aftermath*, 4.

107. See, for example, Kohout, *Z deníku kontrarevolucionáře;* Dienstbier, *Jiří Dienstbier: Rozhlasový zpravodaj,* and Šťovíčková-Heroldová, *Po světě s mikrofonem.*

108. See Bren, *The Greengrocer and His TV,* 104.

## Conclusion

1. For a reflection upon what constitutes "liberal journalistic norms," see Daniel C. Hallin and Paolo Mancini, *Comparing Media Systems: Three Models of Media and Politics* (Cambridge: Cambridge University Press, 2004), 198–248.

2. For the sense of friendship felt towards a voice on the radio, see Pavel Kohout, *Z deníku kontrarevolucionáře* (Brno: Větrné mlýny, 2013), 86–87.

3. Jana Peterková, interview with Rosamund Johnston, October 26, 2016.

4. See, in the Czech case, the weekly magazine *Respekt*'s investigations into the staffing of website *Aeronet*. For example, "Kdo tu píše pro Putina," last modified August 13, 2021, https://www.respekt.cz/tydenik/2016/18/kdo-tu-pise-pro -putina.

5. Kohout, *Z deníku kontrarevolucionáře*, 86–87.

# Bibliography

**Archival Materials**
*Prague, Czech Republic*
Archive of the Czech Ministry of Foreign Affairs (AMZV)
　　Mezinárodní odbor (MO/OMO/OMEO) 1945–1970
Czech Radio archive (CRA)
　　Archivní fond
　　Dokumentační fond
　　Fond ústředního ředitele
　　František Kožík—pozůstalost (1934–1993)
　　*Náš rozhlas*
　　Věra Šťovíčková—pozůstalost
National Archive of the Czech Republic (NA CR)
　　Fond 311: Monitory M, 1945–1956
　　Fond 861: Ministerstvo Informací
　　Fond 1261/0/44: ÚV Novotný—II. část
　　Fond 1261/1/8: Ideologická komise ÚV KSČ 1958–1968
Security Services Archive (ABS)
　　Vyšetřovací spisy (V)
CLBRI—Czech literary bibliography research infrastructure, Institute of Czech
　　Literature
　　Digital Periodical Archive

288 Bibliography

*Zlín, Czech Republic*
The Archive of the Southeast Moravian Museum (AMJM)
    Archiv Inženýrů Hanzelky a Zikmunda

*Bratislava, Slovakia*
Rozhlas a televízia Slovenska (RTVS)
    Zvukový fond
    Písomný fond

*Budapest, Hungary*
Open Society Archive (OSA)
Fond 298: Records of the Free Europe Committee
Fond 300: Records of Radio Free Europe/Radio Liberty Research Institute
*News from Behind the Iron Curtain* (https://catalog.osaarchivum.org/catalog/
    QorEQdeG)

**Interviews**
*Prague, Czech Republic*
Věra Homolová, September 2016
Eva Ješutová, November 2019
Martin Matiska, June 2020
Jana Peterková, October 2016
Miloslav Turek, November 2019

*United States*
Paul Brunovsky, May 2010
Robert Budway, December 2011
Charles Heller, interviewed by Misha Griffith, July 2010
George Knessl, November 2010
Eva Lutovsky, interviewed by Ed Herrmann, April 2010
Vojtěch Mastný, interviewed by Katherine David Fox, October 2010
Zdenka Novak, February 2011
Vladimir Pochop, May 2012
Karel Ruml, May 2010
Jana Švehlová, interviewed by Katherine David Fox, December 2010
Marcella Tornová Švehlík, July 2011

**Websites**
https://archive.org/
https://ceskapozice.lidovky.cz/

https://www.ceskatelevize.cz/
https://www.cia.gov/
https://clb.ucl.cas.cz/
https://www.czechtourism.com
https://dennikn.sk/
https://digitalarchive.wilsoncenter.org/
https://esbirky.cz/
https://eurozpravy.cz/
https://www.idnes.cz
https://www.imdb.com/
https://issforum.org/
https://www.iwm.org.uk/
https://www.marxists.org/
https://www.moderni-dejiny.cz/
https://www.mzv.cz
https://www.nachrichten.at/
https://ncsml.org/
https://www.nm.cz/
https://www.novinky.cz
https://www.ntm.cz/
http://www.pametnaroda.cz
https://poezie.wgz.cz/
https://portal.rozhlas.cz/
https://praguecoldwar.cz/
https://www.psp.cz/
https://www.pwf.cz/
http://research.calvin.edu
https://www.respekt.cz
https://soviethistory.msu.edu/
https://www.telegraph.co.uk/
https://www.teraz.sk/
http://www.usd.cas.cz/
https://www.youtube.com/

**Published Works**

Abrams, Bradley. *The Struggle for the Soul of the Nation: Czech Culture and the Rise of Communism.* Lanham, MD: Rowman and Littlefield, 2005.

Allport, Gordon, and Hadley Cantril. *The Psychology of Radio.* New York and London: Harper and Brothers, 1935.

## 290 Bibliography

Andrews, Maggie. *Domesticating the Airwaves: Broadcasting Domesticity and Femininity.* London and New York: Continuum, 2012.

Andreas, Petr. "Od odpovědnosti ke kontrole—cenzura za rané normalizace (září 1968—srpen 1969)." *Soudobé dějiny* 27, nos. 3–4 (2020).

Applebaum, Anne. *Iron Curtain: The Crushing of Eastern Europe.* New York: Anchor, 2013.

Applebaum, Rachel. *Empire of Friends: Soviet Power and Socialist Internationalism in Cold War Czechoslovakia.* Ithaca, NY, and London: Cornell University Press, 2019.

Arendt, Hannah. *The Origins of Totalitarianism.* New York: Meridian Books, 1958.

Babiracki, Patryk, and Austin Jersild (eds.). *Socialist Internationalism in the Cold War.* London: Palgrave MacMillan, 2016.

Balbi, Gabriele, and Andreas Fickers (eds.), *History of the International Telecommunication Union: Transnational Techno-Diplomacy from the Telegraph to the Internet.* Berlin: de Gruyter, 2020.

Barta, Milan. "Přestaňte okamžitě rušit modré." *Paměť a dějiny*, no. 3 (2012).

Barton, Paul. *Prague à l'heure de Moscou: Analyse d'une démocratie Populaire.* Paris: Édition Pierre Horay, 1954.

Baťa, Jan Antonín. *Budujme stát pro 40 000 000 lidí.* Zlín: Tisk Zlín, 1937.

Bechmann Pedersen, Sune, and Marie Cronqvist. "Foreign Correspondents in the Cold War." *Media History* 26, no. 1 (2020): 75–90.

Beck, Curt. "Czechoslovakia's Penetration of Africa, 1955–1962." *World Politics* 15, no. 3 (1963): 403–416.

Bednařík, Petr, Jan Jirák, and Barbora Köpplová. *Dějiny českých médií.* Prague: Grada, 2019.

Bernasek, Miloslav. "Czechoslovak Planning, 1945–1948." *Soviet Studies* 22, no. 1 (July 1970).

Biltereyst, Daniel, Richard Maltby, and Philippe Meers (eds.). *Cinema, Audiences and Modernity.* London and New York: Routledge, 2011.

Birdsall, Carolyn. *Nazi Soundscapes: Sound, Technology and Urban Space in Germany 1933–1945.* Amsterdam: Amsterdam University Press, 2012.

———, and Joanna Walewska-Choptiany. "Reconstructing Media Culture: Transnational Perspectives on Radio in Silesia, 1924–1948." *Historical Journal of Film, Radio and Television* 39, no. 3 (2019).

Bischof, Anna, and Zuzana Jirgens (eds.). *Voices of Freedom—Western Interference? 60 Years of Radio Free Europe.* Göttingen: Vandenhoeck and Ruprecht, 2015.

Blaive, Muriel. *Promárněná příležitost: Československo a rok 1956.* Prague: Prostor, 2001.

———. *Une déstalnisation manqué: Tchécoslovaquie 1956*. Paris: Éditions Complexe, 2004.

———, ed. *Perceptions of Society in Communist Europe: Regime Archives and Public Opinion*. London: Bloomsbury Academic, 2018.

———. "The Reform Communist Interpretation of the Stalinist Period in Czechoslovak Historiography and its Legacy." *East European Politics and Societies* (November 2021).

Blažek, Petr. "Rekonstrukce: Prameny k procesu s Miladou Horákovou a jejími druhy." *Sborník Archivu ministerstva vnitra* 4 (2006).

Bolter, Jay David, and Richard Grusin. *Remediation: Understanding New Media*. Cambridge, MA: MIT Press, 1999.

Bolton, Jonathan. *World of Dissent: The Plastic People of the Universe, Charter 77, and Czech Culture under Communism*. Cambridge, MA: Harvard University Press, 2012.

Bösch, Frank, ed. *A History Shared and Divided: East and West Germany Since the 1970s*. Oxford: Berghahn, 2018.

Brandes, Detlef, Edita Ivančiková, and Jiří Pešek. *Flüchtlinge und Asyl im Nachbarland. Die Tschechoslowakei und Deutschland 1933 bis 1989*. Munich: Klartext, 2018.

Bren, Paulina. " 'Mirror, Mirror, on the Wall . . . Is the West the Fairest of them All:' Czechoslovak Normalization and its (Dis)Contents." *Kritika: Explorations in Russian and Eurasian History* 9, no. 4 (Fall 2008).

———. *The Greengrocer and His TV: The Culture of Communism after the 1968 Prague Spring*. Ithaca, NY, and London: Cornell University Press, 2010.

Brenner, Christiane. *Mezi Východem a Západem*. Prague: Argo, 2015.

Bryant, Chad. *Prague in Black: Nazi Rule and Czech Nationalism*. Cambridge, MA: Harvard University Press, 2009.

Burian, Emil F. *Voláno rozhlasem I*. Prague: Svoboda, 1945.

Calder, Angus. *The Myth of the Blitz*. London: Pimlico, 1991.

Carruthers, Susan. *Cold War Captives: Imprisonment, Escape, and Brainwashing*. Berkeley, Los Angeles, and London: University of California Press, 2009.

Čechová, Helena. "Československý rozhlas a politické procesy—analyza politických procesů v rozhlasovém vysílání v letéch 1949–1952." Unpublished diploma thesis, South Bohemian University in České Budějovice, 2012.

Černý, Jiří. *Jiří Černý . . . na bílém*. Prague: Galén, 2014.

De Certeau, Michel. *The Practice of Everyday Life*. Berkeley, Los Angeles, and London: University of California Press, 1984.

Classen, Christoph. "Captive Audience? GDR radio in the Mirror of Listeners' Mail." *Cold War History* 13, no. 2 (2013).

Connelly, John. *Captive University: The Sovietization of East German, Czech and*

*Polish Higher Education, 1945–1956.* Chapel Hill: University of North Carolina Press, 2000.

Corney, Frederick. *Telling October: Memory and the Making of the Bolshevik Revolution.* Ithaca, NY: Cornell University Press, 2004.

Cronqvist, Marie. "From Socialist Hero to Capitalist Icon: The Cultural Transfer of the East German Children's Television Programme *Unser Sandmännchen* to Sweden in the Early 1970s." *Historical Journal of Film, Radio, and Television* 41, no. 2 (2021): 378–393.

Curry, Jane. *Poland's Journalists: Professionalism and Politics.* Cambridge: Cambridge, 1990.

Czepek, Andrea, Melanie Hellwig, and Eva Nowak (eds.). *Press Freedom and Pluralism in Europe: Concepts and Conditions.* Bristol: Intellect, 2009.

Deák, István. *Europe on Trial: The Story of Collaboration, Resistance and Retribution during World War II.* New York: Routledge, 2015.

———, Gross, Jan, and Tony Judt (eds.). *The Politics of Retribution in Europe: World War II and its Aftermath.* Princeton, NJ: Princeton University Press, 2000.

Denning, Michael. *Noise Uprising: The Audiopolitics of a World Musical Revolution.* London and New York: Verso, 2015.

Dienstbier, Jiří. *Jiří Dienstbier: Rozhlasový zpravodaj, 1958–1969.* Prague: Radioservis, 2013.

Disman, Miloslav. *Československý rozhlas v boji.* Prague: Orbis, 1946.

———. *Hovoří Praha.* Prague: Svoboda, 1975.

Domosławski, Artur. *Ryszard Kapuściński: A Life.* London: Verso, 2013.

Dvořáček, Jan, Linda Piknerová, and Jan Záhořík. *A History of Czechoslovak Involvement in Africa: Studies from the Colonial through the Soviet Eras.* Lewiston, NY, and Lampeter, Wales: Edwin Mellen Press, 2014.

Dyer, Richard. *Stars.* London: British Film Institute, 1998.

Edgerton, David. *The Shock of the Old: Technology and Global History.* London: Profile, 2019.

Ellul, Jacques. *Propaganda: The Formation of Men's Attitudes.* New York: Random House, 1973.

Evans, Christine E. *Between Truth and Time: A History of Soviet Central Television.* New Haven, CT, and London: Yale, 2016.

Fainberg, Dina. "Unmasking the Wolf in Sheep's Clothing: Soviet and American Campaigns against the Enemy's Journalists, 1948–1953." *Cold War History* 15, no. 2 (2015).

Fanon, Frantz. *A Dying Colonialism.* New York: Grove, 1965.

Feinberg, Melissa. *Elusive Equality: Gender, Citizenship and the Limits of Democracy in Czechoslovakia.* Pittsburgh, PA: University of Pittsburgh, 2006.

———. "Fantastic Truths, Compelling Lies: Radio Free Europe and the Response to the Slánský Trial in Czechoslovakia." *Contemporary European History* 22, no. 1 (February 2013).

———. *Curtain of Lies: The Battle over Truth in Stalinist Eastern Europe.* New York: Oxford University Press, 2017.

———. *Communism in Eastern Europe.* London: Routledge, 2021.

Fickers, Andreas, and Pascal Griset. *Communicating Europe: Technologies, Information, Events.* London: Palgrave Macmillan, 2019.

Foit, František. *Autem napříč Afrikou: deník jedinečné cesty z Prahy do Kapského města, díl 1.* Prague: Self-published, 1932.

———. and Irena Foitová. *Z Telče do Afriky a nikdy zpět: Vzpomínky na druhou africkou cestu.* Telč: Muzejní spolek v Telči, 2006.

Formánková, Pavlína, and Petr Koura. *Žádáme trest smrti! Propagandistická kampaň provázející process s Miladou Horákovou a spol.* Prague: ÚSTR, 2008.

Franc, Martin, and Jiří Knapík. *Volný čas v českých zemích 1957–1967.* Prague: Academia, 2013.

Friedrich, Carl J., and Zbigniew K. Brzezinski. *Totalitarian Dictatorship and Autocracy.* Cambridge, MA: Harvard University Press, 1956.

Frommer, Benjamin. *National Cleansing: Retribution against Nazi Collaborators in Postwar Czechoslovakia.* Cambridge: Cambridge University Press, 2004.

Gel, František, and Rudolf Krešťan. *Budeš v novinách.* Prague: Albatros, 1976.

Gerlach, David. *The Economy of Ethnic Cleansing: The Transformation of the Czech-German Borderlands after World War II.* Cambridge: Cambridge University Press, 2017.

Gibson, Corey. *The Voice of the People: Hamish Henderson and Scottish Cultural Politics.* Edinburgh: Edinburgh University Press, 2015.

Glassheim, Eagle. *Cleansing the Czechoslovak Borderlands: Migration, Environment and Health in the Former Sudetenland.* Pittsburgh, PA: University of Pittsburgh Press, 2016.

Gmiterková, Šarka. "Betrayed by Blondness: Jiřina Štěpničková between Authenticity and Excess—1930–1945" *Celebrity Studies* 7, no. 1 (2016): 45–57.

Groman, Martin. *Stanislav Budín: Komunista bez legitimace.* Prague: ÚSTR, 2015.

Hadler, Frank, and Matthias Middell, eds. *Verflochtene Geschichte: Ostmitteleuropa.* Leipzig: Leipzigeruniversitätsverlag, 2010.

Hallin, Daniel C., and Paolo Mancini. *Comparing Media Systems: Three Models of Media and Politics.* Cambridge: Cambridge University Press, 2004.

Hannerz, Ulf. *Foreign News: Exploring the World of Foreign Correspondents.* Chicago and London: University of Chicago Press, 2004.

Haring, Kirsten. *Ham Radio's Technical Culture.* Cambridge, MA, and London: MIT Press, 2007.

Harrison, Erica. "Radio and the Performance of Government: Broadcasting by the Czechoslovaks in Exile in London, 1939–1945." Unpublished dissertation, University of Bristol, 2015.

Havel, Václav. *Open Letters: Selected Writings 1965–1990*. New York: Alfred A. Knopf, 1991.

Heimann, Mary. *Czechoslovakia: The State That Failed*. New Haven, CT: Yale University Press, 2011.

Hill, Doug. *Not So Fast: Thinking Twice about Technology*. Athens: University of Georgia Press, 2013.

Honeck, Mischa. *Our Frontier Is the World: The Boy Scouts in the Age of American Ascendancy*. Ithaca, NY: Cornell University Press, 2018.

Horák, Pavel. *Bohumil Laušman—politický životopis: Riskantní hry sociálnědemokratického vůdce*. Prague: Mladá fronta, 2012.

Hrabal, Bohumil. *Mr. Kafka: And Other Tales from the Time of the Cult*. New York: New Directions, 2015.

Hronek, Jiří. *V široširém světě*. Prague: Státní nakladatelství dětské knihy, 1954.

Huxtable, Simon. "Making News Soviet: Rethinking Journalistic Professionalism after Stalin, 1953–1970." *Contemporary European History* 27, no. 1 (February 2018): 59–84.

Imre, Anikó. *TV Socialism*. Raleigh, NC: Duke University Press, 2016.

Jedlička, Josef. *Midway upon the Journey of Our Life*. Prague: Karolinum, 2016.

Jeschke, Felix. *Iron Landscapes: National Space and the Railways in Interwar Czechoslovakia*. New York: Berghahn, 2021.

Ješutová, Eva, ed. *Od Mikrofonu k posluchačům: z osmi desetiletí českého rozhlasu*. Prague: Radioservis, 2003.

Jirgens, Ekhard. *Der Deutsche Rundfunk der 1. Tschechoslowakischen Republik*. Regensburg: Con Brio, 2017.

Johnson, A. Ross. *Radio Free Europe and Radio Liberty: The CIA Years and Beyond*. Stanford, CA: Stanford, 2010.

Johnson, A. Ross, and Eugene Parta, eds. *Cold War Broadcasting*. Budapest: Central European University Press, 2010.

Johnston, Rosamund. "Southern Hospitality? Czechoslovak Relations with Africa until 1989." *Czech Journal of Contemporary History* 5 (2017).

———. "Secret Agents: Reassessing the Agency of Radio Listeners in Czechoslovakia, 1945–1953." In *Perceptions of Society in Communist Europe: Regime Archives and Public Opinion*, edited by Muriel Blaive, 15–32 (London: Bloomsbury Academic, 2018).

———. "*The Peace Train:* Anticosmopolitanism, Internationalism and Jazz on Czechoslovak Radio during Stalinism." In *Remapping Cold War Media: In-*

*stitutions, Infrastructures, Translations,* edited by Alice Lovejoy and Mari Pajala (Bloomington: Indiana University Press, 2022).

Josten, Josef. *Oh, My Country.* London: Latimer House, 1949.

Judt, Tony. *Postwar.* New York: Penguin, 2005.

Kaplan, Karel. *Československo v letech 1945–1948, 1. Část.* Prague: SPN, 1991.

———, and Marek Janáč."Poslední slovo obžalovaných v procesu s Miladou Horákovou 'a spol.' " *Soudobé dějiny* 13, nos. 1–2 (2006).

Kapuścinski, Ryszard. *The Shadow of the Sun.* New York: Penguin, 1998.

———. *The Other.* London: Verso, 2006.

Kavanová, Rosemary. *Cena Svobody: Život angličanky v Praze.* Prague: Nakladatelství Brána, 2017.

Kepley, Vance Jr. " 'Cinefication': Soviet Film Exhibition in the 1920s." *Film History* 6, no. 2 (Summer 1994).

Kind-Kovács, Friederike, and Jessie Labov. *Samizdat, Tamizdat and Beyond: Transnational Media during and after Socialism.* New York: Berghahn, 2013.

Klemperer, Victor. *The Diaries of Victor Klemperer 1945–1959: The Lesser Evil.* London: Phoenix, 2003.

Knapík, Jiří. *Kdo spoutal naši kulturu: portrét stalinisty Gustava Bareše.* Prague: Šárka, 2000.

Kohout, Pavel. *Z deníku kontrarevolucionáře.* Prague: Větrné mlýny, 2014.

Kolář, Pavel. "The Party as a New Utopia: Reshaping Communist Identity after Stalinism." *Social History* 37, no. 4 (November 2012).

———. *Der Poststalinismus: Ideologie und Utopie einer Epoche.* Vienna, Cologne, and Weimar: Böhlau, 2016.

Komska, Yuliya. *The Icon Curtain: The Cold War's Quiet Border.* Chicago and London: University of Chicago Press, 2015.

Kopecký, Václav. *Proti kosmopolitismu jako ideologii amerického imperialism.* Prague: Orbis, 1952.

Kotalová, Zdeňka. "Redakce mezinárodního života Československého rozhlasu v rozmezí let 1966–1969." Unpublished diploma thesis, Charles University, Faculty of Social Sciences, 2012.

Kotkin, Stephen. *Magnetic Mountain: Stalinism as Civilization.* Berkeley: University of California Press, 1997.

Kovály, Heda Margolius. *Under a Cruel Star: A Life in Prague, 1941–1968.* London: Granta, 1986.

Kožík, František. *Rozhlasové umění.* Prague: Kompas, 1940.

Kratochvíl, Matěj. " 'Our Song!' Nationalism in Folk Music Research and Revival in Socialist Czechoslovakia." *Studia Musicologica* 56, no. 4 (2015).

Kundera, Milan. *The Joke.* New York: Faber and Faber, 1992.

——. *The Book of Laughter and Forgetting*. New York: Harper, 1999.

Kurlansky, Mark. *1968: The Year That Rocked the World*. New York: Ballantine, 2004.

Larkin, Brian. *Signal and Noise: Media, Infrastructure, and Urban Culture in Nigeria*. Durham, NC: Duke University Press, 2008.

Lemmen, Sarah. "Noncolonial Orientalism? Czech Travel Writing on Africa and Asia around 1918." In *Verflochtene Geschichte: Ostmitteleuropa*, edited by Frank Hadler and Matthias Middell, 209–227. Leipzig: Leipzigeruniversitätsverlag, 2010.

——. "Locating the Nation in a Globalizing World: Debates on the Global Position of Interwar Czechoslovakia." *Bohemia* 56, no. 2 (2016).

——. *Tschechen auf Reisen: Repräsentationen der außereuropäischen Welt und nationale Identität in Ostmitteleuropa 1890–1938*. Cologne, Weimar, and Vienna: Böhlau, 2018.

Lommers, Suzanne. *Europe—On Air: Interwar Projects for Radio Broadcasting*. Amsterdam: Amsterdam University Press, 2012.

London, Artur. *The Confession*. London: Murrow, 1970.

Lovejoy, Alice. *Army Film and the Avant Garde: Cinema and Experiment in the Czechoslovak Military*. Bloomington and Indianapolis: Indiana University Press, 2015.

——. "The World Union of Documentary and the Early Cold War." In "Globalized Media Archaeologies," edited by Daniel Morgan, special issue, *boundary 2* 49, no. 1 (2022); 165–193.

—— and Mari Pajala (eds.). *Remapping Cold War Media: Institutions, Infrastructures, Translations*. Bloomington: Indiana University Press, 2022.

Lovell, Stephen. *Russia in the Microphone Age: A History of Soviet Radio, 1919–1970*. New York and Oxford: Oxford University Press, 2015.

Machcewicz, Paweł. *Poland's War on Radio Free Europe*. Redwood City, CA: Stanford University Press, 2015.

Mark, James, and Péter Apor. "Socialism Goes Global: Decolonization and the Making of a New Culture of Internationalism in Socialist Hungary, 1956–1989." *Journal of Modern History* 87, no. 4 (December 2015).

Mark, James, Paul Betts, Alena Alamgir, Péter Apor, Eric Burton, Bogdan Iacob, Steffi Marung, and Radina Vučetić. *Socialism Goes Global: The Soviet Union and Eastern Europe in the Age of Decolonization*. Oxford: Oxford University Press, 2022.

Mark, James, Artemy Kalinovsky, and Steffi Marung (eds.). *Alternative Globalizations: Eastern Europe and the Postcolonial World*. Bloomington: Indiana, 2020.

McDermott, Kevin. "'A Polyphony of Voices?' Czech Popular Opinion and the Slansky Affair." *Slavic Review* 67, no. 4 (Winter 2008).

———. *Communist Czechoslovakia, 1945–1989: A Political and Social History.* London: Palgrave, 2015.

McHugh, Siobhan. "The Affective Power of Sound: Oral History on Radio." *Oral History Review* 39, no. 2 (2012).

Muehlenbeck, Philip. *Czechoslovakia in Africa, 1945–1968.* New York and London: Palgrave Macmillan, 2016.

Mükke, Lutz. *Korrespondenten im Kalten Krieg: Zwischen Propaganda und Selbstbehaputung.* Cologne: Herbert von Halem, 2014.

Novák, Jan. *Striptease Chicago.* Prague: Mladá fronta, 1992.

Orzoff, Andrea. *Battle for the Castle: The Myth of Czechoslovakia in Europe.* Oxford: Oxford University Press, 2009.

Pajala, Mari. "A Forgotten Spirit of Commercial Television? Co-productions between Finnish Commercial Television Company Mainos-TV and Socialist Television." *Historical Journal of Film, Radio, and Television* 39, no. 2 (2019): 366–383.

Parks, Lisa, and Nicole Starosielski (eds.). *Signal Traffic: Critical Studies of Media Infrastructures.* Champaign: University of Illinois Press, 2015.

Pažout, Jaroslav. *Informační boj o Československu/ v Československu, 1945–1989.* Prague and Liberec: Technická univerzita v Liberci & ÚSTR, 2014.

Peroutka, Ferdinand. *Ferdinand Peroutka pro Svobodnou Evropu.* Prague: Radioservis, 2013.

Perzi, Niklas, Hildegard Schmoller, Ota Konrád, and Václav Šmirkdal (eds.). *Nachbarn: Ein Österreichisch-Tschechisches Geschichtsbuch.* Weitra: Biibliothek der Provinz, 2019.

Pešta, Mikuláš. "L'internationalisme tchécoslovaque en Afrique à travers l'exemple de l'aide à la construction d'infrastructures militarires et de securité en Guinée, 1958–1965." In *Marges impériales en dialogue. Échanges transferts, interactions et influences croisés entre les espaces postcoloniaux francophones et la périphérie soviétique européenne dans la seconde moitié du XXe siècle,* edited by Matthieu Boisdron and Krisztián Bene, 159–170. Pécs: Université de Pécs, 2022.

Petránek, Jan. *Na co jsem si ještě vzpomněl.* Prague: Radioservis, 2014.

Pinard, Peter Richard. *Broadcast Policy in the Protectorate of Bohemia and Moravia.* Frankfurt: Peter Lang, 2015.

Poiger, Uta. *Jazz, Rock, and Rebels: Cold War Politics and American Culture in a Divided Germany.* Berkeley, Los Angeles, and London: University of California Press, 2000.

Pospíšil, Filip. "Inspiration, Subversion and Appropriation: The Effects of Radio Free Europe Music Broadcasting." *Journal of Cold War Studies* 21, no. 4 (Fall 2019): 124–149.

Pratt, Mary Louise. *Imperial Eyes: Travel Writing and Transculturation.* London and New York, Routledge, 2003.

Preiningerová, Magdalena, and Blanka Cekotová. *Archiv H+Z—Muzeum jihovýchodní Moravy ve Zlíně: katalog fondů.* Zlín: Muzeum jihovýchodní Moravy ve Zlíně, 2015.

Prince, Tony, and Jan Šesták. *The Royal Ruler and the Radio DJ.* Slough: DMC Publishing, 2017.

Pucci, Molly. "A Revolution in a Revolution: The Secret Police and the Origins of Stalinism in Czechoslovakia." *East European Politics and Societies* 32, no. 1 (February 2018): 3–22.

———. *Security Empire: The Secret Police in Communist Eastern Europe.* New Haven, CT: Yale University Press, 2020.

Puddington, Arch. *Broadcasting Freedom: The Cold War Triumph of Radio Free Europe and Radio Liberty.* Lexington: University of Kentucky, 2000.

Rachensteiner, Manfried, ed. *Zwischen den Blöcken. NATO, Warschauer Pakt und Österreich.* Vienna: Böhlau, 2010.

Razlogova, Elena. *The Listener's Voice: Early Radio and the American Public.* Philadelphia: University of Pennsylvania Press, 2011.

Roth-Ey, Kristin. *Moscow Prime Time: How the Soviet Union Built the Media Empire That Lost the Cultural Cold War.* Ithaca, NY, and London: Cornell University Press, 2011.

Roudakova, Natalia. *Losing Pravda: Ethics and the Press in Post-Truth Russia.* Cambridge: Cambridge University Press, 2017.

Rupnik, Jacques. *Histoire du parti communiste tchéchoslovaque: Des origines à la prise du pouvoir.* Paris: Les presses de Sciences Po, 1981.

Rychlík, Jan. *Deník 1955.* Prague: Revolver, 2006.

Rykl, Milan. "Renesance rozhlasu 1959–1968." In *Od Mikrofonu k posluchačům: z osmi desetiletí českého rozhlasu*, edited by Eva Ješutová, 289–335. Prague: Radioservis, 2003.

Scales, Rebecca P. *Radio and the Politics of Sound in Interwar France, 1921–1939.* Cambridge: Cambridge University Press, 2016.

Schafer, R. Murray. *The Soundscape: The Tuning of the World.* Rochester, VT: Destiny Books, 1994.

Schlosser, Nicholas. *Cold War on the Airwaves: The Radio Propaganda War against East Germany.* Champaign: University of Illinois, 2015.

Schulze Wessel, Martin. *Pražské jaro: Průlom do nového světa.* Prague: Argo, 2018.

Segeberg, Harro, and Frank Schätzlein (eds.). *Sound: Zur Technologie und Ästhetik des Akustischen in den Medien*. Marburg: Schüren, 2005.

Shore, Marci. "Engineering in the Age of Innocence: A Genealogy of Discourse in the Czechoslovak Writers' Union, 1949–1967." *East European Politics and Societies* 12, no. 3 (1998).

Siebert, Fred, Theodore Peterson, and Wilbur Schramm. *Four Theories of the Press: The Authoritarian, Libertarian, Social Responsibility, and Soviet Communist Concepts of What the Press Should Be and Do*. Champaign: University of Illinois Press, 1963.

Sklenářová, Sylva. "Nizozemská špionážní aféra: Proces s Janem A. Louwersem v březnu 1950." *Soudobé dějiny* 15, no. 1 (2008): 62–84.

Skopal, Pavel. "Letters to the Heroes: Exhibition and Reception of Hanzelka and Zikmund's Travelogues in Czechoslovakia of the 1950s." *Participations* 11, no. 2 (November 2014).

Škvorecký, Josef. *The Bass Saxophone*. Hopewell, NJ: Ecco Press, 1994.

Slomek, Jaromír, Jiří Hanzelka, and Miroslav Zikmund. *Život snů a skutečnosti*. Prague: Primus, 1997.

Šmejkalová, Jiřina. "Command Celebrities: The Rise and Fall of Hanzelka and Zikmund." *Central Europe* 13, nos. 1–2 (2015).

Solovič, Ján, et al. *Tu Bratislava: Rozhlas v retrospektíve a perspective*. Bratislava: Obzor, 1966.

Stavělová, Daniela, et al. *Tíha a beztíže folkoru: Folklorní hnutí druhé poloviny dvacátého století v českých zemích*. Prague: Academia, 2022.

Štoll, Martin. *Television and Totalitarianism in Czechoslovakia: From the First Democratic Republic to the Fall of Communism*. Sydney: Bloomsbury, 2018.

Stoppard, Tom. *Rock 'n' Roll*. London, Faber, 2006.

Šťovíčková-Heroldová, Věra. *Afrika rok jedna*. Prague: SPN, 1963.

———. *Bouře nad rovníkem*. Prague: Magnet, 1967.

———. *Po světě s mikrofonem*. Prague: Radioservis, 2009.

Suchý, Čestmír, Jiří Hochman, and Jiřina Brejchová. *Emigranti proti národu*. Prague: Mladá fronta, 1953.

Suková, Jana. "Svaz českých novinářů v období Pražského jara." Bachelor's thesis, Charles University, 2013.

Szczepanik, Petr. *Továrna Barrandov: Svět filmařů a politická moc, 1945–1970*. Prague: NFA, 2016.

Thompson, Emily. *The Soundscape of Modernity: Architectural Acoustics and the Culture of Listening in America, 1900–1933*. Cambridge, MA: MIT Press, 2002.

Tigrid, Pavel. *Politická emigrace v atomovém věku*. Prague: Prostor, 1990.

Tomášek, Dušan. *Pozor, Cenzurováno! Aneb ze života soudružky cenzury*. Prague: Ministertvo Vnitra ČR, 1994.

Tomek, Prokop. "Rušení zahraničního rozhlasového vysílání pro Československo." *Securitas Imperii*, no. 9 (2002).

———. *Československé bezpečnostní složky proti Rádiu Svobodná Evropa: Objekt Alfa*. Prague: Úřad dokumentace a vyšetřování zločinů komunismu, 2006.

———. *Československá redakce Radio Free Europe*. Prague: Academia, 2015.

Tworek, Heidi. *News from Germany: The Competition to Control World Communications, 1900–1945*. Cambridge, MA: Harvard University Press, 2019.

Vande Winkel, Roel, and David Welch (eds.). *Cinema and the Swastika: The International Expansion of Third Reich Cinema*. New York: Palgrave Macmillan, 2007.

Vaněk, Miroslav. "Twenty Years in Shades of Grey? Everyday Life during 'Normalization' Based on Oral History Research." In *Czechoslovakia and Eastern Europe in the Era of Normalisation, 1969–1989*, edited by Kevin McDermott and Matthew Stibbe (London: Palgrave Macmillan, 2022).

———, and Pavel Mücke. *Velvet Revolutions: An Oral History of Czech Society*. New York: Oxford University Press, 2016.

Vaughan, David. *Battle for the Airwaves: Radio and the 1938 Munich Crisis*. Prague: Radioservis, 2008.

Vidomus, Petr. "'Američan—a musí emigrovat do Československa!'— Škvoreckého jazzman Herbert Ward optikou zpráv FBI." *Soudobé dějiny*, nos. 1–2 (2017).

Volný, Jr., Slava, ed. *Jsme s Vámi, Buďte s námi*. Prague: Prostor, 2013.

Wagnleitner, Reinhold. *Coca-Colonization and the Cold War: The Cultural Mission of the United States in Austria*. Chapel Hill: University of North Carolina Press, 1991.

Waters, Leslie. *Borders on the Move: Territorial Change and Forced Migration in the Hungarian-Slovak Borderlands*. Rochester, NY: University of Rochester Press, 2020.

Weil, Jiří. *Life with a Star*. London: Daunt, 2012.

Williams, Kieran. *The Prague Spring and Its Aftermath: Czechoslovak Politics, 1968–1970*. Cambridge: Cambridge University Press, 1997.

Wögerbauer, Michael, et al., eds. *V obecném zájmu: Cenzura a sociální regulace literatury v moderní České kultuře 1749–2014, Svazek II*. Prague: Academia, 2015.

Wolff, Larry. *Inventing Eastern Europe: The Map of Civilization on the Mind of the Enlightenment*. Stanford, CA: Stanford University Press, 1994.

Zahra, Tara. *The Great Departure: Emigration from Eastern Europe and the Making of the Free World*. New York: Norton, 2016.

Zídek, Petr. *Československo a francouzská Afrika, 1948–1968*. Prague: Libri, 2006.

———. *Češi v srdci temnoty*. Prague: Universum, 2013.

# Index

Pages followed by "n" refer to notes.

advertising, 31, 91, 115, 162, 164, 169
Africa, 9–10, 87–115, 168–186, 273n2, 275n46
*Africa, Part I* (*Afrika I. Část*, Jaroslav Novotný, 1952), 96, 102
Africa Policy, Czechoslovakia's, 168–196, 275n45
African women, 180, 191
Algeria, 88, 141–142,175, 181–182
*Alle Neune* (radio game show), 145–146, 148–149, 159–160, 165–167
Allport, Gordon, 4
anti-communism, 150, 218, 231
anti-German sentiment, 6, 79
anti-Nazi resistance, 14, 34, 40–41
anti-Semitism, 19, 79–83, 199
Aškenazy, Ludvík, 65
Austria, 5, 17, 107, 142–167. *See also* German-language radio
*Autofahrer Unterwegs* (Austrian driving show), 147, 161–163

Bacher, Gerd, 166
Bardot, Brigitte, 186
Bareš, Gustav, 64, 247n54
Baťa, Jan Antonín, 30–31
Baťa (shoemaking firm), 31, 110
Bělík, Eduard. *See* Slánský Trial
Ben Bella, Ahmed, 181–182
Beneš, Eduard, 6, 14–15, 26–33, 51, 81
Biafran War, the, 193–195
Biľak, Vasiľ, 200, 211
Birdsall, Carolyn, 148
Blaive, Muriel, xii, 4, 53, 85, 144, 206
Bond, James, 177, 187–188
borderlands, 148, 157–158
bourgeois nationalism, 199
brainwashing, 44, 84, 233n5 (Introduction)
Bratislava, 6, 57, 61, 122, 123, 144, 163, 246, 278, 288, 299
Bren, Paulina, 19, 127, 132, 155, 161, 203–204, 211, 223, 227, 264n75

302 Index

Brezhnev, Leonid, 216
British Broadcasting Company, the (BBC), 14, 26, 34–42, 45, 59, 63, 141, 154, 224
Brno, 158
Brožová-Polednová, Ludmila, 76
Budín, Stanislav, 207
Burian, Emil, 43–44
Bušová-Kasalová, Helena, 128, 131, 134–136

Cantril, Hadley, 4
celebrity, 89–90, 99–10, 103, 105, 193
censorship, 3, 63–68, 73, 90, 175–176, 181, 193–195, 216, 224; revocation of, 18, 199–201, 218–221
Central African Republic, 181
Central Europe, 5, 54, 147; radio listeners in, 154, 167, 179
Central Intelligence Agency (CIA), 17, 30, 59, 63, 77, 84, 154, 201–202, 215
Černý, František, 218
Černý, Jiří, 201–203
České Budějovice, 30, 81, 145–148, 158–159, 166
China, 205
Čierna nad Tisou, 217, 221
Čierny, Ján, 186, 278n87
Cincibus, Josef, 32, 71, 81
Citizen Brych (Občan Brych, Otakar Vávra, 1958), 62–63
class, 40, 88, 134, 155, 182, 208
Cold War, the, 4–5, 7, 9–11, 19, 77, 91, 93, 111, 124, 127, 128, 137, 143, 146–151, 157, 161, 164, 166–167, 176, 195, 221, 229
Communist functionaries, 7, 16, 65, 80, 83, 86, 103, 104, 113, 150, 156, 160, 176, 199, 200, 218

Communist journalists, 18, 25, 190, 199, 220. See also socialist journalists
Communist Party, 2, 4, 15–18, 25–28, 64, 67, 82, 93, 119–120, 146, 149, 155, 171, 198–200, 207–209, 216; Ideological Commission, 2, 269n41; support base, 4, 125; Twentieth Congress of the Soviet Communist Party, 17, 120
Communist sympathizers, 51
Communist takeover of Czechoslovakia, 16, 19, 23–25, 28, 54–55, 61, 90, 92, 93, 115
Conakry, 172, 175; Czechoslovak-sponsored school of journalism in, 172–173
Corwin, Norman, 21, 27
cross-border contacts: between radio listeners, 147
Czech Radio archive, 10, 55, 57, 83, 86, 169, 171, 196
Czechoslovak history, 13–19, 144, 180, 204–205; of the postwar period, 25
Czechoslovak politicians, 2, 17–19, 54, 64, 81, 92, 166, 215–216, 224, 228; mindset, 26; in exile, 14, 25–26. See also Communist functionaries
Czechoslovak Press Agency (ČTK), 130, 189, 205, 207
Czechoslovak Radio, 1, 6, 8–10, 15–20, 23–26, 28, 31, 33–50, 54, 63–69, 74, 80–81, 90, 114, 121–124, 151–152, 165, 169, 199, 204–207, 212, 224
Czechoslovak Radio Day, 32–33
Czechoslovak Radio's Anglophone Africa service, 179–180, 184
Czechoslovak Radio's foreign corre-

spondents, 45–46, 175–176, 177, 187, 191, 205, 213, 219–221
Czechoslovak Radio staff, 1, 23–25, 34, 55, 65, 73, 121, 123–124, 199, 206
Czechoslovakia, 23–30; state radio in, 1, 1, 117
Czechoslovakia's shifting allegiance: Cold War, 93, 221
Czechoslovakism, 6

Dacko, David, 181
decision-making (of reporters), 12, 68
democracy, 15, 134; social democracy, 165
de-Stalinization, 17, 62, 118–121, 124, 189
diaries, 44, 94, 139–140, 215
Dienstbier, Jiří, 20, 169–170, 187–188, 214, 216–218, 224–225
Disman, Miloslav, 23, 32, 240n33
dissident, 150, 224
Dobrovský, Luboš, 219
"Doctor's Plot", 80
Dresden, 44, 46, 200
Dubček, Alexander, 18–19, 199, 224–225

East Germany. See Germany
economy, 17, 74, 88, 173, 198–199, 274n27
Egypt, 92, 109–110, 194
emigrants, 113, 128
émigré press conference, 120–121, 125–130, 135
Ethiopia, 92, 177, 275
expertise, 35, 47, 56, 182–186, 193
experts, 11, 67, 69, 82, 123, 137, 157, 171, 173, 179, 185, 191, 194, 229
exports, Czechoslovak, 92, 173

factory, 31, 40, 95, 121–122; factory radio, 58–59, 63
"fake news," 20, 229
Faix, Květoslav, 126
Falco (Austrian singer), 159
Fanon, Frantz, 141–142, 182
fascism, 209
federalization, 198, 219
Feinberg, Melissa, xi, 24, 28, 63, 77, 80, 140, 198, 267n22
Fight for Peace (boj za mír), 104
film, 38, 61–62, 95–96, 106, 113, 129–130, 151, 187–188, 273n6; industry, 15, 30, 238n5; material specificities of, 66
Fitzgerald, Ella, 169
FM receivers, 6. See also technology
Foglar, Jaroslav, 111
Foit, František, 87–89, 91–98, 116
Foit, Morris, 116
folk music, 122. See also music
Folta, Bruno, 133–136
foreign correspondents, 45. See also Czechoslovak Radio's foreign correspondents
foreign currency reserves, 74, 173
foreign trade, 31, 88, 91–94, 101, 115, 123, 172–173
France, 13, 172, 186
Frank, Karl Hermann, 48, 55–56, 68–72
freedom: of the press, 219–221
Frommer, Benjamin, 48

game shows, 145–146, 165
Gel, František, 22, 45–47, 50, 71, 244n120
Geminder, Bedřich, 79–80, 83
generations, 154, 156, 166, 184, 200

304 Index

German-language radio, 146–149, 151–155, 166, 167
German speakers, 78, 147
Germany, 13–14, 46, 60, 74–76, 124, 128, 131, 135–136, 147, 151, 203, 223
Ghana, 177, 181
global socialism, 5. *See also* socialist internationalism
Gott, Karel, 157
Gottwald, Klement, 6, 60–61
Gottwaldov (Zlín), 7, 100
Graf, Otto, 126
governance, 12
Guinea, 168, 171–173, 175, 185

Hajdů, Vavro, 80, 119. *See also* Slánský Trial.
Hanzelka, Jiří 7–10, 87, 89, 91–98, 105–116, 184–185, 216
Hejda, Jiří. *See* Horáková Trial
Heller, Charles, 35–36
Hilger, Ernst, 145
Homolová, Věra, 67–68
Horák, Bohuslav, 87, 104, 108
Horáková, Milada, 16, 87. *See also* Horáková trial
Horáková trial, the, 56–58, 65, 68, 72–74, 76–78, 81
*Hlavní správa tiskového dohledu* (HSTD), 66, 218
Hrabal, Bohumil, 140
Hrabal, Karel, 224
Hronek, Jiří, 34, 273n3
Hungary, 25, 123, 205
hypermediacy, 108

Indra, Alois, 200, 211, 221
infrastructure, 14, 17, 21–22, 29–30, 41, 46, 50, 84, 145, 148, 152, 158, 165–166, 175

interviews (conducted by radio reporters), 27, 67, 134, 169, 180, 183, 186, 191, 203, 206, 210, 278n87, 283n42; with radio listeners, 149, 154, 155, 164–165, 267n22, 270n63. *See also* oral histories
interwar period, 13, 25–26, 79, 88, 91–92, 109–110, 127, 134, 164
"Invitation to Invade," 200, 211, 220
Iron Curtain, 57, 75, 85, 117–118, 124, 128, 137, 163, 220
Isopp, Rosemarie, 161
Italy, 13, 223

jamming, 5, 153–155, 158–159
Jarolím, Josef, 222. *See also* radio listeners
jazz, 40, 164, 242n87. *See also* music
Jedlička, Josef, 38, 40
Ješutová, Eva, xii, 26, 46, 69, 201
"Jewish background" (Communist Party functionaries judged to have), 16, 113, 78, 247n54; journalists persecuted on account of, 46, 65, 207, 209. *See also* anti-Semitism
Jirotka, Zdeněk, 213
journalistic ranking systems, 9
journalists 2–4, 7–9, 11, 16, 18–20, 34, 59, 65, 119–121, 129–130, 137, 169–171, 176–177, 182–184, 198–201, 207–208, 212–213, 216, 218, 221, 227; autonomy of, 4, 25, 137, 171; Czechoslovak, 2, 16, 128, 200, 208. *See also* Communist journalists and socialist journalists

*kádrování* (political reliability checking), 2, 175
Kapuściński, Ryszard, 170, 180, 273n14

Kavan, Rosemary, 75
Kenya, 116
Khrushchev, Nikita, 5, 17, 93, 117, 132–133
Kilimanjaro reports (of Hanzelka and Zikmund), 106–108, 110–111, 115
Kisch, Egon Erwin, 45
Klemperer, Victor, 44–46
Kohout, Pavel, 198, 202, 215, 219, 223, 232
Kopecký, Václav, 24, 55, 62, 66, 87, 89, 91, 105, 113, 116, 241, 252, 259, 260
Košice government, 23, 31
Kotkin, Stephen, 16, 54
Kovály, Heda Margolius, 42–44, 49, 77, 141, 210
Kučera, Vladimír, 125–127, 133–134, 137, 229
Kundera, Milan, 188–190, 226, 278n106
*Kurzwellenaktion* (Nazi foreign radio listening ban), 35
Kyncl, Karel, 169, 200, 206–207, 212–213, 224

language barriers: between media users, 147
Laštovička, Bohuslav, 34, 242n70
Latin America, 19, 93, 113
Laušman, Bohumil, 128, 130, 133, 138
legal system, 48, 61–62, 73, 80; reporting on, 54–55; reform of, 17, 118–120
Lemmen, Sarah, 88, 92, 94–95, 109
letters (from radio listeners), 3, 100, 111, 123, 143, 169, 174, 192, 194, 212–213, 226, 229
liberalization, 119
liberal journalistic norms, 229, 286n1
*Lidové noviny* (interwar newspaper), 45

limits to press freedom, 216. *See also* freedom: of the press
Linz (Austria), 142, 145, 146, 148, 160
Listeners' opinions. *See* radio listeners
listening habits 62, 147, 152, 155, 159, 166; wartime, 38; in the Eastern Bloc, 146; in the provinces, 160
literary depictions of radio listening, 40, 58, 118
London (United Kingdom), 14, 26, 35, 38–39, 224. *See also* British Broadcasting Company
London, Artur, 79, 119
Louwers, Johannes, 90
Lovejoy, Alice, xi–xii, 89
Lovell, Stephen, 60, 73

management of sound, 12
Masaryk, Jan, 51, 207
Masaryk, Tomáš Garrigue, 26, 42, 51
masculinity, 40, 99
Matějová, Veronika, 186–187
memoirs, 8, 44, 54, 167, 171, 173, 176, 193, 226
memory, 40, 169–170, 173, 196, 206
Mihálik, Vojtech 138
Ministry of Foreign Affairs, 26, 151, 180, 195
Ministry of Information, 24, 28, 37, 64, 87–89, 92
Ministry of the Interior, 2, 159
Ministry of Post, 24, 238n8
misogyny, 188, 192
*Mladý svět* (magazine), 201
Moravec, Emanuel, 241n50
Moscow, 7, 14, 19, 186, 196, 200, 242n70
Munich, 125, 136; crisis, 13, 26, 37, 45, 99,

306 Index

music, 30, 40–41, 56, 122, 142, 152, 157–158, 160, 164–165, 203, 206, 231, 242n87, 272n99

National Front, the, 23–24
nationalist activists, 6, 152
nationalization (of Czechoslovak Radio), 23, 28; of industry, 15, 31, 95, 238n5
Nejedlý, Zdeněk, 28, 83, 86, 90
newspapers, 22, 25–27, 45, 48, 66, 99–100, 130, 162, 163, 203, 278n106; as a source base, 26; in the German language, 156
Niesner, Walter, 161
normalization, 19, 204, 216; regime, 227
Novotný, Antonín, 17–18, 119, 195–196, 198–199, 215
Nuremberg, 46–47, 125
Nuremberg Trials, 22, 45, 71

One World Flight. See Corwin, Norman
Optikotechna (in Přerov), 74
oral histories, 30, 37, 40, 60, 150, 240n43, 274n27
Österreichischer Rundfunk (ORF), 145, 148, 160, 164–166
Ostrava, 122

Peroutka, Ferdinand, 153
Peroutková, Slavka, 140
Peterková, Jana, 1–2, 69, 230
Petránek, Jan, 65, 186
Pithart, Petr, 224–225
Plamen (magazine), 182, 259n110
Poland, 98, 119–120, 274n21
popular culture, 160, 162
potato beetle, 8

post-Stalinism, 120
professionalization, 122–124, 133–137
propaganda, 7–9, 35–36, 131, 138–139, 142, 153, 169, 171, 220, 229,
Protectorate of Bohemia and Moravia, 14, 26, 29–30, 34, 40, 45, 242n72, 243n87
Pragocentrism, 6, 34
Prague Spring, the, 3, 4, 18–20, 161, 170–171, 182, 187, 189, 195, 197–201, 226
Prague Uprising, the, 29, 34
press conference, 125–133, 136, 138
Pucci, Molly, 24, 54, 66, 93

race, 83, 111–112, 115
radio aesthetics, 56
radiofication, 27
Radio Free Europe (RFE), 5, 63, 83, 113, 116, 126, 137, 139–141, 169; staff, 161
Radiojournal, 13
radio listeners, 26, 157–158; Czecho-slovak, 30, 107, 117, 144; female, 37, 63; socialist-era, 231
radio management, 1, 201
Radio Moscow, 26, 34, 54, 202
Radio Newsreel, The, 34, 57, 76
radio revolution, 29–34, 239n15; myth of the, 34
radio's second "golden age", 2, 10, 146, 227, 232
radio transmitters, 14, 21–22, 30. See also infrastructure
radio trials, 52, 56–57, 69–73, 77, 79. See also show trials
Radio Vienna, 5, 142, 144
Radio Vltava, 223
Reception data, 117, 138
Red-White-Red (RWR), 164,

reform, 118, 120; professional, 121; legal, 144

reporters, 170, 176, 182–183, 187–189, 198–200, 205, 211, 213, 218–231; female, 188; German, 177

resistance (defeminization of), 40. *See also* women's cultural consumption

resistance to communism, 5, 167

rock 'n' roll, 150, 157. *See also* music

Romania, 221

Rozhlas a televízia Slovenska (RTVS), 6

*Rudé Právo (Red Right)*, 132, 153

Rundfunk im amerikanischen Sektor (RIAS), 154, 158, 160

Rychlík, Jan, 139–140

Schafer, R. Murray, 59–60

Scouting (movement), 111

secret police (StB), 29, 11, 66, 67, 76, 79, 93, 119, 128, 130, 177, 237, 275

*Sedmilháři* (radio program), 174

Seifert, Jaroslav, 27, 49

Selassie, Haile, 92

"shock of the old," 11, 204

show trials, 73–81

signal jamming, 154

Simone, André (Otto Katz), 209

*Školský rozhlas (School Radio)*, 157,

Slánská, Josefa, 205

Slánský, Rudolf, 55–56, 74, 76, 83, 90, 113

Slánský Trial, the, 81–85, 207

Šling, Otto, 81

Slovakia, 6, 53, 199

Slovak National Uprising, 34

Slovak State (during WWII), 14, 23, 26, 34, 57

Šťovíčková, Věra, 5, 8, 89, 168–195, 210, 214, 217, 222

social media, 229; business model of, 231

social profile: reporters, 230

socialist celebrity, 105. *See also* celebrity

socialist globalization, 5

socialist internationalism, 111, 170, 195

socialist journalists, 3, 12, 18, 182, 183, 198

*Songs with a Telephone* (Písničky s telefonem), 213–214, 216, 226

sound studies, 59

Soviet-led invasion of Czechoslovakia, 198, 200, 221–223

Soviet Union, 5, 16, 25, 27, 67, 73, 80, 131, 171, 176, 177, 193–196, 206, 211, 221, 233, 236, 266, 296, 29

spoken word, 28, 164

*Springman and the SS (Pérák a SS,* Jiří Brdečka and Jiří Trnka, 1946), 38

Stalin, 54, 60, 61, 80, 117, 119

Stalinism, 8, 16–17, 52–54, 60, 84–86, 89, 91, 115

Stalinist radio, 51

"Stalin's bagpipes." *See* jamming

state media, 17, 82, 117, 137, 139, 204

state secrecy, 64

state socialism: media during, 1, 9, 11

Štoll, Martin, 215

Sub-Carpathian Ruthenia, 109

Švehlová, Jana, 61, 246, 288

Švermov meeting, 126

Švermová, Marie, 78, 119, 205. *See also* Slánský Trial

tape, 53, 56, 57, 67, 73, 74, 197–198

"tape age," the, 73–74, 84

tape recorders, 74

Tatra (cars), 87, 89, 91, 94–98, 208

308 Index

technology, 11, 29, 35, 46, 52, 74, 84, 98, 106, 145; faith in, 22, 50, 94, 153
telephone, 214, 215, 227
television, 12, 19, 139, 147, 148, 154, 156, 157, 161, 201, 203, 204, 211, 220, 227, 269
*They Shall Not Pass (Neprojdou, Zbyněk Brynych*, 1952), 60–61, 267n21
Third Czechoslovak Republic, 15, 19, 22–23, 29–30, 48–49, 55, 58, 64, 105
Tigrid, Pavel, 130, 134–135
tinkering, 35
Tiso, Jozef, 57
Tito, Josip Broz, 54
Tomek, Prokop, 126, 149–150, 156,
Touré, Ahmed Sekou, 172, 277n70
tracing shows (following WWII), 43–44, 49
trade on the African continent. *See* foreign trade
transistor radios, 201–202
transnational, 4, 7, 148
travelogues, 90, 108–109
TV tower in Žižkov, 21
Twitter (now X), 20

underground broadcasts, 30
Union of Journalists, the, 24, 119, 170, 279n110
United States of America, 15, 49, 75, 89, 128, 149, 164, 169, 187–188
Urválek, Josef. *See* Slánský Trial

Vaculík, Ludvík, 200
vernacularization drive (at Czechoslovak Radio), 123–125

vocal signatures, 198, 226–227
voice: of reporters, 11, 14, 18, 32–33, 43, 71, 75–76, 101, 125, 137–138, 196, 198, 209, 223–226, 229, 232; of politicians, 27, 60–61, 77, 215; of show trial defendants, 58, 80, 206; "of the people," 124, 127

Ward family (American defectors to Czechoslovakia), 130
Warsaw Pact, the, 18, 20, 197, 198, 221
Washington, D.C., 187
Weil, Jiří, 41
Weiner, Milan (foreign news chief), 202, 205, 207–208, 212, 219, 224
Wolff, Larry, xi, 7
women's cultural consumption, 41
workers' interests, 64, 208, 219
World War, First, 92, 109
World War, Second, 1, 4, 5, 8, 21, 27, 30, 31, 34, 37, 41, 45, 48, 92, 98, 114, 147, 151, 184
Writers' Union, 120, 182, 195, 279n110; Conference (in 1967), 199. *See also Plamen* (magazine)

xenophobia, 86, 90

youth, 40, 99, 132, 202; cult of, 89; enfranchisement, 99

Zahra, Tara, 114, 128
Zápotocký, Antonín, 28, 119–124, 139, 144
Záruba, Josef, 208–211
Zeman, F. K., 33, 43, 243n101
Zilk, Helmut, 160

Printed in the USA
CPSIA information can be obtained
at www.ICGtesting.com
JSHW021538280124
56149JS00002B/2

9 781503 638693